COTTAGES ORNÉS

The charms of the simple life

COTTAGES ORNÉS

The charms of the simple life

ROGER WHITE

Yale University Press
New Haven and London

For Charles Hind and John Boodle

CONTENTS

INTRODUCTION

In Jane Austen's novel *Sense and Sensibility*, published in 1811, the impoverished widow Mrs Dashwood and her three daughters take up residence in Barton Cottage, on a country estate in Devon. 'As a cottage', says the narrative, 'it was defective, for the building was regular, the roof was tiled, the window shutters were not painted green, nor were the walls covered with honeysuckles.'[1] In short, it was a cottage, but not a cottage orné of the type then at the height of fashionability, for that would have been picturesquely irregular, would have had a thatched roof, green shutters and plenty of honeysuckle and other flowering climbers. In a later chapter of the novel the fashionable fop Robert Ferrars declares,

I am excessively fond of a cottage; there is always so much comfort, so much elegance about them. And I protest, if I had any money to spare, I should buy a little land and build one myself, within a short distance of London, where I might drive myself down at any time, and collect a few friends about me, and be happy. I advise every body who is going to build, to build a cottage. . . . Some people imagine that there can be no accommodations, no space in a cottage; but this is all a mistake . . . if people do but know how to set about it, every comfort may be as well enjoyed in a cottage as in the most spacious dwelling.[2]

Ferrars is here referring to the cottage of Lady Elliott, whose dining room was capable of accommodating eighteen couples![3]

One of the great advantages of a cottage over the more standard Georgian classical box, Ferrars believed, was that its rooms lent themselves to easy rearrangement for supper parties and card tables and, by extension, to the social informality that had gradually suffused the lives of the Regency middle and upper classes. It was in these first decades of the nineteenth century that an architectural genre whose vocabulary ultimately derived from vernacular buildings intended for people at the bottom of the social scale was finally adopted by those of the most exalted rank. As such it inevitably attracted the barbed shafts of satirists, not all as mild as Miss Austen. Thomas Love Peacock, in his 1817 novel *Melincourt*, has an old countryman dismiss the fashion in these words:

Ah zur! . . . every now and then came a queer zort o' chap dropped out o' the sky like – a vundholder he called un – and bought a bit of ground vor a handvul o' peaper, and built a cottage horny, as they call it – there be one there on the hillside – and had nothing to do wi' the country people, nor the country people wi' he: nothing in the world to do, as we could zee, but to eat and drink, and make little bits o' shrubberies . . . the Squire could never abide the zight o' one o' they gimcrack boxes.[4]

Robert Southey incorporated the cottage orné into his poem, 'The Devil's Walk' (1799), focusing on the patent absurdity of the rich and very rich playing at being peasants:

He [the Devil] saw a Cottage with a double coach-house,
A Cottage of gentility!
And he own'd with a grin
That his favourite sin
Is the pride that apes humility.[5]

The phenomenon of the cottage orné has been alluded to by authors often enough, but always *en passant* – as a minor episode in British cultural history, and particularly as a symptom of the Picturesque; as a chapter in biographies of such late Georgian architects as John Nash; or as a slightly condescending sub-heading in accounts of the genuine vernacular cottage. Architectural historians generally prefer to be taken seriously, which means that a genre whose essence is non-serious, ornamental, indeed frivolous, is apt to be regarded as somewhat peripheral, even as an embarrassment. The quotations above are enough to indicate that in the period when the genre was at its most popular and fashionable, there were plenty of people who mocked it and thought it unworthy of attention, so it was hardly to be expected that the ensuing generations of serious-minded Victorians would take it to their hearts when they despised many more weighty manifestations of Georgian taste.

OPPOSITE Blackbrook Cottage, Fareham, Hampshire

There is no point in pretending that the cottage orné is a weighty manifestation of anything, but closer inspection reveals not only that at its best it offers a great deal of light-weight charm but also that it was a surprisingly numerous phenomenon. It is arguably the only architectural genre that spans the entire social spectrum, and as a consequence it constitutes a broad-based pyramid, with the very select handful of royal and imperial cottages at the apex, shading down through the more ample ranks of those built for the aristocracy and middle classes, into the cottages and lodges of the working classes (primarily though not exclusively rural), which still dot the English countryside in considerable numbers. For this sociological reason alone the genre would merit study, even if strong arguments could not be made for its aesthetic interest. In fact some of the leading architects of late Georgian England – Robert Adam, Henry Holland, John Soane, John Nash – tried their hands at cottage design at one social level or another. Others attempted to garner commissions by publishing books of cottage designs. Paradoxically this may perhaps have robbed them of commissions, since the pattern books not only helped popularize the idiom but also made it accessible to local builders. At the working-class level it is very difficult to identify specific architects, even though these may have been employed by the owners of the estates to which the cottages provided an embellishment. However, the basic quality that sets the cottage orné apart from the vernacular cottage is that it has not just been run up by a builder, carpenter or indeed the owner/occupier to meet basic utilitarian needs, but has been designed with aesthetic intention. A true vernacular cottage may very well be charming and picturesque, especially if it comes with a thatched roof and roses round the door, but it was not constructed with charm and picturesqueness as conscious priorities. Artists like Gainsborough were to make the undesigned cottage (usually authentically decrepit) part of their stock-in-trade, but the influential pattern-book architect P. F. Robinson was to sum up the view of many that vernacular buildings lacked artistic interest, and that the creativity and imagination of the trained architect were required; merely to copy was not enough.[6]

In some senses the cottage orné represents an intensification of qualities found in the vernacular vocabulary. Thus thatched roofs are frequently, though not invariably, a feature of both categories – indeed it is easy to forget that thatch is, or was, the predominant roofing material for cottages in large parts of the British Isles. The curvaceous profile of vernacular thatch was taken up and exaggerated for orné purposes, often ending up in billowing undulations that can only be the result of conscious intention rather than accident. Similarly, the rough wooden posts that a peasant might deploy for a porch, or to support an overhang, become in the hands of cottage orné architects verandahs of the knobbliest tree trunks, often with the bark left on and with bossy cankers as tokens of maximum rusticity. Such verandahs might be floored with pavements of animal knucklebones – something, obviously, with an authentic rural origin and yet very rarely found on genuine vernacular cottages. Eaves boards, a necessary functional feature, were taken up and embellished with frills and cusps.

Of course, however fanciful the external result, if the cottage was intended for working-class occupation no attempt would be made to make the interior correspond; the ornamental effort was made for the sole benefit of the owner of the estate, whose views it would improve. It is only as the social scale is climbed that interiors start to rise above the most basic, and even then relative simplicity would probably be the watchword, since enjoying the supposed charms of the simple life was part of the object of the exercise. By the time the upper echelons of the aristocracy and royalty are reached, needless to say, simplicity is a relative quality – relative, that is, to the opulent and heavily gilded salons that might be the client's normal habitat.

A common misconception is that, because of the French-sounding name, the cottage orné is a concept of French origin, and the Petit Hameau at Versailles is often cited as the prime, indeed the earliest, example. In fact 'cottage orné' might claim to be the earliest example of Franglais, seemingly first deployed in an English pattern book of 1805.[7] 'Orné' is certainly a French word, but 'cottage' is definitely English, the corresponding French word being 'chaumière'.[8] As it happens, the cottages included in Marie Antoinette's Hameau are externally straightforward copies of genuine vernacular examples, yet were never intended for even the shortest occupation by peasants, let alone royalty. Moreover, the Versailles Hameau was not begun until 1783 and was preceded by the Hameau at Chantilly, begun in 1774 (and undoubtedly France's first), which in turn was preceded by Queen Charlotte's cottage at Kew of 1771. By that date, indeed, buildings which can realistically be called ornamental cottages had been going up in England for at least a decade and maybe longer. In any case, there is no evidence of the French *hameaux* being mentioned, still less illustrated, in any English publication of the period, so they could not have exercised any influence except via the very few outside French royal or aristocratic circles permitted to visit them.

So the ornamental cottage as a genre was an English invention that spread quickly to Ireland (and less quickly to Scotland and Wales), and was exported first to the Continent and then much further afield – to the outposts of the British Empire and to the former colonies of North America. Examples began to appear in South Africa in the early years of the nineteenth century, after the British had ousted the Dutch. In the United States the pioneer was Alexander Jackson Davis, perhaps as early as 1836, but it was in the following decade that examples proliferated with the help of the pattern books published by his friend Alexander Jackson Downing. Even if at first sight the frivolity of the genre might seem alien to the New World, the inventory of known examples is surprisingly long and covers not just New England, where it might perhaps have been expected to catch on, but the southern states as well.[9]

If one reason why the cottage orné is less well known and less appreciated than it arguably deserves to be is that it has been written off as aesthetically lightweight, another must be that it is a peculiarly vulnerable building type from a purely physical point of view. Though the basic structure might be of durable brick or stone, the embellishments that raise it to an art form are liable to have been made of materials such as thatch and timber, along with appliqué bark and twigs, trellis or delicately leaded window tracery: all susceptible to decay, neglect and vandalism, especially once fashions changed. At the very top end of the social scale, George IV's Royal Lodge in Windsor Great Park – surely the largest example of all – survived just months after his death in 1830 before being demolished and cannibalized by his successor William IV for re-use elsewhere on the royal estate. Further down the scale it is all too easy and too common for the detail of a cottage to be progressively eroded – knobbly tree-trunk verandahs being replaced when they decay by posts as plain as telegraph poles, and Gothick windows with plastic. In the most numerous category of all, the gate lodge to country estates, the cramped quarters for which Georgian peasants were expected to be grateful, have long since ceased to be acceptable, hence the likelihood of sizeable extensions that are anything but sympathetic. As used to be the case with the enormous category of Georgian garden buildings and 'follies', planners and conservation officers have been slow to recognize that, once the fragile detail is whittled away, the whole point of the cottage orné is lost. When that stage is reached, it is almost kinder to allow the building to be demolished.

Finally, there is the knotty question of where the cottage orné ends and where another category begins. It will be argued in Chapter One that the genre is likely to have evolved gradually out of the ornamental rustic buildings that begin to appear in English gardens in the mid-eighteenth century, following the example of Queen Caroline's Merlin's Cave at Richmond of 1735. These continue throughout the Georgian period and into the Victorian, and their vocabulary seems gradually to have been adopted and applied to the cottages that were constructed as the playthings of the wealthy and the adornment of their estates from perhaps the 1750s. Already at this stage there is a distinction to be drawn between the ornamental cottage and the Gothic cottage pure and simple, but it is one that is not always easy to define. This becomes ever more the case as the Georgian era shades into the Victorian, when features such as frilly eaves boards and Tudoresque windows and chimneys are applied to buildings that are imperceptibly losing their whimsicality and becoming indefinably but unmistakably earnest.

1 Jane Austen, *Sense and Sensibility* [1811] (Harmondsworth, 1969), p. 61.

2 Ibid., p. 255.

3 Austen's last, unfinished novel *Sanditon*, of 1817, also contains an explicit reference: 'He is running up a tasteful little cottage *ornee*, on a strip of waste ground Lady Denham has granted him . . .' (Everyman edition, 1996, p. 19). In fact, the original manuscript, held at King's College, Cambridge, has the word 'ornèe' with a grave rather than acute accent. I am grateful to Stephen Alexander for pointing this out.

4 Thomas Love Peacock, *Melincourt* [1817] (London, 1896), p. 247.

5 Robert Southey, 'The Devil's Walk', *The Morning Post* (6 September 1799).

6 P. F. Robinson, *Designs for Farm Buildings* (London, 1830), p. 2. See below, Chapter Four.

7 Robert Lugar's *Architectural Sketches for Cottages* (London, 1805), p. 10, refers to 'The Cottage Ornée [*sic*], or Gentleman's Cot'.

8 As in the Chaumière au Coquillages at Rambouillet. See below, Chapter Eight.

9 See below, Chapter Nine.

CHAPTER ONE

RUSTIC ROOTS

The popularity of the ornamental cottage – the newly built, architect-designed house that made the original rural model more visually pleasing by adding decorative embellishments – may have reached its apogee under the Prince Regent, but it was a genre that had its roots much earlier and that persisted well into the Victorian era, gradually developing and metamorphosing until it ended up as a staple of the Arts & Crafts movement. The cottage orné may not be high art, but it is a particularly fascinating genre. Its origins go back at least to the middle of the eighteenth century, to the rustic garden pavilions and estate cottages designed for smart clients by architects such as William Kent and Thomas Wright. The thatched garden pavilion Kent designed in 1735 for Queen Caroline's garden at Richmond, known as Merlin's Cave [fig 1/1], may have been the first such. Despite its name this was entirely above ground, and externally constituted a cluster of steeply pitched thatched roofs that as much as anything resembled a collection of native huts, referred to in the *Gentleman's Magazine* for September 1735 as 'something like an old Haystack, thatch'd over . . .' Two years earlier Mrs Mary Delany[1] had already noted, in a letter to Jonathan Swift, that in his forest park at Cirencester, Lord Bathurst had 'greatly improved the wood house, which you may remember but a cottage, not a bit better than an Irish cabin'. However, this was probably the transformation of a genuine vernacular building, which in any case became Alfred's Hall – what Delany refers to as 'a venerable castle', complete with tower, battlements and stained glass.[2]

The earliest dateable example of a freshly built, architect-designed cottage as opposed to a garden pavilion seems to be Egge Cottage [fig 1/2] on Edgehill in Warwickshire, designed by the local squire and gentleman-architect Sanderson Miller on his Radway estate and built in 1743–4. It was the first Gothic essay of a man who was rapidly to become a guru of the early Gothic Revival (the celebrated mock-castle on Edgehill followed in

1747–50). In a letter to Miller in 1745, Deane Swift (cousin of Jonathan Swift) wrote, 'How I long to see your Thatched House, but how much more the architect.'[3] The thatched roof and simple Gothic windows gave a cosy air to rough stonework whose rounded corner bastions evoked the remains of an ancient fortress, colonized for domestic use. The interior, unlike a genuine vernacular cottage, was stone-vaulted, and intended for scholarly contemplation, picnics and other entertainments. Miller kept part of his large library in the cottage, and he encouraged George Ballard, an impoverished Oxford-based scholar of Anglo-Saxon, to stay and study there, while his diary for 7 October 1749 refers to 'Concert in the Thatched House'.[4]

For contemporaries, the cottage exuded a genuine air of venerable antiquity, and was evidence of Miller's antiquarian learning – something that helped to burnish his credentials as an authority on medieval Gothic. The Rev. James Merrill, fellow of Trinity College, Oxford and also a poet, penned a poem that was actually displayed in the cottage for visitors to read:

> Within this solitary cell
> Calm thoughts, and sweet contentment dwell,
> Parents of bliss sincere; Peace spreads around
>   her balmy wings,
> And, banished from the courts of Kings,
> Has fixed her mansion here.[5]

OPPOSITE 1/1 Merlin's Cave, Richmond Gardens, designed by William Kent in 1735. Detail from John Rocque's *An exact plan of the royal palace gardens and park at Richmond with Sion House and on the opposite side of the Thames*, 1754

ABOVE 1/2 Egge Cottage, Edgehill, Warwickshire, designed for himself by Sanderson Miller in 1743–4

The geographical focus of Miller's work was the English Midlands, and he is known to have designed a Gothic pavilion for the Enville Hall estate on the Staffordshire–Worcestershire border in 1750.[6] It is therefore quite possible that Miller contributed the design for a small cottage [fig 1/3] (sometimes known as the Hermitage, though not used as such) that formerly stood in a clearing in a wood on the circuit of Enville's celebrated grounds. First referred to in 1756 by Dr Richard Pococke, the peripatetic bishop of two Irish dioceses, when it was described as a 'pheasantry and hermitage for the keeper of the fowl',[7] the building is recorded both by an image on a tureen in the 'Frog Service' produced by Wedgwood for Catherine the Great, and by an undated early photograph. The latter shows it with undulating roof (in the photograph lead sheeting has replaced the original heather thatch) and rather crude Gothic door and window embrasures, certainly architect-designed rather than vernacular, and in view of Miller's earlier performance at Egge Cottage his name seems plausible.[8] The cottage appears to have been permanently inhabited by a female keeper of the fowl, who may well have found the coloured glass in the windows inconvenient. Very interesting light is indeed shed on the whole concept of cottage dwelling by a letter about the Enville specimen from Joseph Heely, published in 1777:

> Whether it be the name, or the simplicity that commonly surrounds the dwellings of indigence . . . or rather, whether it be from the insinuating effusions of the muse, that true happiness is only to be found in a sequestered rural life, is of little consequence . . . a cottage, properly situated within the precincts of a riding, or in such extensive grounds as these, is an object that always excites pleasure, and impresses on the mind extreme soothing; and no one, in my opinion, has a juster claim from situation, to be admired, than this, so delightfully environed by the loveliest of woody hills, and twining valleys: nothing can be more retired, nothing more cheerful, though solitude itself. . . . Believe me, this humble cot, its little circular sloping lawn in front, and the graceful clustering trees, that verge the area, and form a perfect canopy over the buildings, have greater powers to charm the eye of taste, than the most

magnificent temple, loaded with all the finery art can give.[9]

A not dissimilar bogus pedigree to that of Egge Cottage is suggested by a William Kent drawing [fig 1/4] that shows a thatched cottage tacked onto the side of what appears to be a church steeple that has lost its church.[10] Father Time, sickle over his shoulder, hovers alongside the tower, altering the time on the clock. In the foreground stand a woman in an Elizabethan farthingale and a gesticulating man in cleric's robes. Kent's illustrations for Spenser's epic poem *The Faerie Queene*, possibly made shortly before Kent's death in 1748, feature more such 'designed' rustic structures. A thatched cottage with 'primitive' rustic classical porch features in 'Una leaves the Old Woman's House', while the illustration for 'The Witches Son loves fair Florimell' includes a thatched cottage with rough timber bracing on the exterior walls.[11] The edition in which the illustrations appear was not published until 1751, and it is not known when Kent drew them. It has been suggested that they could date from very early in his career, perhaps even predating his work at Hampton Court and Esher (i.e. early 1730s). On the one hand it is perhaps improbable that Kent would have done the illustrations speculatively, maybe twenty years before they achieved publication. On the other, it is likely that it was in about 1730 that he painted three 'medieval' canvases of scenes from the life of Henry V. These survive in the Royal Collection and could well have been commissioned by Queen Caroline, whose interest in matters medieval is attested by the busts she commissioned of English monarchs from William the Conqueror, and by Merlin's Cave.[12]

No cottages designed by Kent are known to have been built, but the immediate lineal descendants of what he sketched for other purposes in the *Faerie Queene* are those

1/4 William Kent, capriccio with cottage

1/5 Badminton, Gloucestershire: Frog and Toad Hall, designed by Thomas Wright, probably in the 1750s

designed by the architect-cum-mathematician-cum-astronomer Thomas Wright (1711–86). He has been described by his biographer as being 'on the whole a minor architect whose principal contribution was in the design of rustic buildings where he seems to have been in the forefront of fashion'.[13] His architectural idiom was clearly indebted in general terms to that of Kent, and on the latter's death in 1748 Wright succeeded him as the preferred architect on the Badminton estate of the 4th Duke of Beaufort, to whose daughters he also acted as tutor. The cottages he designed on the Badminton estate, although they cannot be precisely dated, are likely to be among the earliest surviving examples of the cottage orné in its proper sense – that is, a building in vernacular idiom but designed by an architect with additional ornamental features that mark it out as having a conscious aesthetic effect. At Badminton he seems to have been responsible for titivating existing humdrum vernacular cottages of estate workers with the addition of thatched roofs and frilly eaves, so that they contributed more positively to the appearance of Badminton village and the wider estate. A good example in the village is Thatch Cottage, clearly an existing single-storey cottage with rooms in the roof, to which a full two-storey addition has been made at one end, with pretty leaded glazing and

exaggerated cusping to the eaves.[14] The Deerkeeper's House in the park is likewise a standard Cotswold cottage where the stone-tiled roof was submerged in thatch (recently removed), given a decorative edging and a rustic porch added supported on gnarled tree trunks. Most striking is Frog and Toad Hall, [fig 1/5] a cottage at the crossroads in the centre of the village, which appears to have been entirely new-built. Its rustic verandah seems almost to be subsiding beneath the weight of the enormously deep thatch, from which tiny Gothic windows struggle to emerge. Already in these Badminton cottages most of the key ingredients of the orné formula are present.[15]

The Badminton prettifications probably date from the 1750s (possibly though not certainly before the death of the 4th duke in 1756), but there are no drawings, bills or land surveys to provide more precise dating. The same campaign must have produced the Root House [fig 1/6] or Hermit's Cell, which seems to be the earliest such garden structure surviving in the British Isles. Placed among ancient oak trees in the park, it shares the rustic idiom of some of the Badminton cottages, but was built from scratch and, as its name suggests, is constructed entirely of wood – compacted roots for walls, door and window shutters covered in patterns of bark and moss, an inverted

1/6 Badminton, Gloucestershire: the Root House or Hermit's Cell, designed by Thomas Wright

tree-fork for the door arch, and a crowning thatched roof. The interior, now in parlous condition,[16] has a simplified version of a fan vault, again executed in timber, bark and moss, with a central knobbly boss intended to attach the vault to the invisible roof structure above. For favoured visitors to Badminton a footman would be dispatched to sit inside at a table cut from a tree trunk, dressed as a hermit and quite possibly contemplating a skull. The building's more general use is indicated by the seat set into a recess on the exterior, whose rustic back rail has lettered in nails the inscription 'Here loungers loiter, here the weary rest'.[17] Wright's responsibility for the Badminton Root House is proved by a sketch of it amongst a collection of his designs in the Avery Library, New York, and his interest in the general field of rustic garden buildings is reflected in the collection of designs published as *Arbours* and *Grottos* in 1755 and 1758 respectively.[18]

Other rustic structures in England attributable to him include the root house known as Dr Jenner's Hut, in the grounds of Berkeley Castle, Gloucestershire, a smaller version of the Badminton Root House;[19] a root house at Spetchley Park, Worcestershire;[20] and a now-vanished root house at Wrest Park, Bedfordshire, built in 1749 and intended as 'a habitation of the priest of Mithras'.[21] Wright travelled a good deal in Ireland, and may also have been responsible for 'a thatch'd open house supported by the bodies of fir trees etc' at Lord Limerick's garden at Dundalk, noted by Bishop Pococke in 1752.[22] At Limerick's Tullymore Park, Co. Down, Pococke saw 'a thatch'd open

place to dine in which is very Romantick', on the north side of which Limerick had 'begun to build a pretty lodge, two rooms of which are finished, designing to spend the summer months here'.[23] A thatched hermitage at Belle Isle on the edge of Lough Erne, Co. Fermanagh, was recorded by Jonathan Fisher in his *Scenes of Ireland* (1795), where it is described as 'a handsome cottage with a kitchen and other conveniences in a sweet retired place'.[24] These three Irish structures have disappeared, but at Florence Court near Enniskillen, where Wright is known to have dined with the owner John Cole in 1746, there survives a rustic thatched pavilion (recreated by the National Trust in 1993 on the site of the original) similar to Badminton and also probably to the ones at Dundalk and Tullymore.[25] Plates C [fig 1/7], D and E of Wright's *Arbours* each represent designs for rustic pavilions. Of C, a thatched rustic octagon supported on tree-trunk columns and open on five sides, his text comments, 'The Frame of this Building will be best made of the old rugged Trunks of Maple.' The interior, he said, was to be finished with ivy, honeysuckle and moss, there were to be windows of painted glass, and the floor was to be of horse's teeth or pebbles – all materials that were to enter the general vocabulary of British rustic buildings.[26]

If Wright produced a design drawing (as opposed to the sketch referred to) for the Badminton Root House, it does not survive, but a perfect example of how an architect might present such a building to a potential client is provided by Thomas Sandby's design [fig 1/8] for a

ABOVE 1/7 Thomas Wright, *Arbours*, 1755, Plate C
BELOW 1/8 Thomas Sandby, design for a hermitage or root house in Windsor Great Park

hermitage or root house for Windsor Great Park.[27] Probably produced in the 1760s or 1770s, and probably intended for the Duke of Cumberland's park at Virginia Water, this shares with Badminton the combination of inverted-V entrance, thatched roof and a circular aperture as a kind of surrogate rose window – here supplied by a disused cart wheel. In such cases, no doubt, the builder and craftsmen would be left to work out how to interpret the elevational design and the construction. Further rustic designs by Sandby survive in the Sir John Soane Museum, including an extraordinary one that is halfway between root house and pagoda [fig 1/9].[28] The ground floor resembles the Windsor hermitage, but there are in addition two diminishing upper storeys, with an external gallery encircling the middle one. In the same collection is a design for a circular two-storeyed pavilion with a conical thatched roof supported on a peripteral tree-trunk verandah, and another for an octagonal single-storey root house, looking rather like a thatched rustic chapter house.[29] Additional designs in a rustic idiom show Sandby considering the application of the vocabulary to buildings that were clearly intended for occupation, and form a transition from garden pavilion to residential

cottage orné. At one end of the social scale is a drawing with elevation and plans for a pair of extremely small and basic thatched cottages, with simple Gothic windows and both entrance doors placed within a single central recess.[30] At the other end of the scale are a plan and elevation for what must be accounted a proper cottage orné.[31]

The furnishings required for a hermitage were described as early as 1748 by Mrs Mary Delany after her visit to that on Lord Orrery's estate at Caledon, Co. Tyrone – an indication that the stereotype was apparently already established by the mid-eighteenth century.

> Nothing is completed yet but an hermitage, which is about an acre of ground – an island, planted with all the variety of trees, shrubs and flowers that will grow in this country, abundance of little winding walks, differently embellished with little seats and banks; in the midst is placed an hermit's cell, made of the roots of trees, the floor is paved with pebbles, there is a couch made of matting, and little wooden stools, a table with a manuscript on it, a pair of spectacles, a leathern bottle; and hung up in different parts, an hourglass, a weatherglass and several mathematical instruments, a shelf of books, another of wooden platters and bowls, another of earthen ones, in short everything that you might imagine necessary for a hermit.[32]

One of the finest recorded examples of a rustic hermitage in Britain was the 'Sanctuary of the Hermit Finch' in the grounds of the vast baroque mansion at Burley-on-the-Hill in Rutland, very much in the Sandby manner. It was burnt down by schoolchildren in 1965, but not before it had been drawn and described by Barbara Jones, who called it 'a mixture of gnome's house and horror'.[33] Although dated 1807 in its floor of pebbles and animal knuckle bones, it was in a direct line of descent from the Badminton Root House, which conceivably its unknown designer might have visited. Hidden in woods near the house, it was slightly larger than Badminton (Jones calculated the diameter as being 20 feet) and more elaborate, with a projecting porch under the thatch overhang, and a rustic rib vault within. Since it was provided with a chimneypiece and massive stone chimney, and subdivided

internally into main room and bedroom, it was evidently intended for at least intermittent residence, though perhaps only in summer since it seems the windows were never glazed. The surprisingly full complement of furniture included four built-in rustic armchairs, three triangular stools and a table fashioned from half an enormous elm boss, its top scattered with bones. In the tiny, ill-lit bedroom were the hermit's austere bed, with old sacks for covering, and a bedside table and stool.

Possibly finer still, and certainly larger, was the hermitage built in the spacious garden of the vicarage at Louth in Lincolnshire.[34] It was the creation of the eccentric Wolley Jolland, vicar from 1780 until his death in 1831, and was already considered a visitor attraction by 1791 when the Hon. John Byng left one of the earliest descriptions. Byng noted that it was

> finish'd with curious taste, and trouble: therein
> are several rooms, recesses and chapels, all lighted
> by old stain'd glass (once in Tattershall Church);
> the ornamental parts are of fir cones, the tables
> of polish'd horse bones; with many inscriptions
> around, and upon the ground, from the Scriptures.
> It is throughout the work of infinite labour, and
> highly curious; and so must the framer be, who
> was not at home.[35]

Byng's travelling companion Colonel Bertie suggested that the vicar should have his gardener 'properly attired as an hermit, and to be found in some of the recesses, at his studies'. The hermitage was created during the 1780s, and indeed Byng was preceded in 1790 by Humphry Repton, who recalled his visit in some detail when compiling his memoirs in 1814.[36] From this and other descriptions it is apparent that the porch led into the hermit's cell, which gave in turn into his bedroom, his library (furnished with bamboo furniture and trinkets sent from India by Jolland's brother), and finally the chapel. The latter, according to Repton, had a floor of polished horse's teeth, walls hung with glittering Indian fabrics, and the whole was dappled with coloured light from a stained-glass window. Contemporary views show the exterior to have had a somewhat amorphous form, with a deep thatched roof and Gothic windows. By the time of Jolland's death the building was already showing

signs of decay, and the new-broom vicar who succeeded him swept it away.

Perhaps even earlier than Wright's precocious essays in the genre of rustic garden building is the Thatched House [fig 1/10] in Richmond Park. It is impossible to date the present structure precisely, but it is said to have been built by Sir Robert Walpole in his capacity as Ranger of the park, supposedly in 1727 and certainly prior to his death in 1745.[37] Here, supposedly, he entertained George II after hunting expeditions. The building is of two storeys, perched on a steep slope commanding a wide prospect over Kingston, and the simple whitewashed exterior has an equally simple verandah, encircling the upper floor and supporting a thatched roof. This simplicity belies the interior, where the main room now has charming and sophisticated neoclassical painted decoration, variously attributed to Angelica Kauffman, Biagio Rebecca and Antonio Zucchi. However, Edward Croft-Murray attributed the basic wall decoration (which is oil on plaster) to Pietro Maria Borgnis and the missing roundels (oil on canvas) to Zucchi.[38] He suggested that a possible date would be around 1775–8, when Borgnis and Zucchi were working together on the Etruscan Room

at Osterley Park, and certainly on stylistic grounds the Thatched House decoration is likely to have been carried out during the tenancy of General Sir William Meadows (1769–85), though probably supervised by his wife as he was away on active service a good deal. The themes of the missing roundels were the Birth of Venus and the story of Cupid and Psyche.[39]

One of the earliest rustic cottages (as opposed to rustic summerhouses or hermitages) built for leisure use must have been that known as 'Straw Hall' [fig 1/11] in the woods above Hardwick Court, overlooking the Thames near

Whitchurch in Oxfordshire. Hardwick was the home of Mrs Philip Lybbe Powys (born Caroline Girle in 1739), who kept a diary from 1756 till her death in 1808. She married Philip Lybbe Powys in August 1762, and first referred to Straw Hall shortly afterwards in a letter to a friend:

> Hardwick Woods you may perhaps have heard of, as parties come so frequently to walk in them, and request to drink tea in a cottage erected for that purpose in a delightful spot commanding a noble view of the Thames.[40]

It is tempting to assume that it was a kind of wedding gift from husband to new wife, but in fact it must have existed at least since 1756, since in that year Philip's brother Thomas Powys, later Dean of Canterbury, wrote a poem which was placed over the door:

Within this cot no polished marble shines,
Nor the rich product of Arabian mines;
The glare of splendour and the toys of state,
Resigned, unenvied, to the proud and great;
Whilst here reclined, those nobler scenes you view
Which Nature's bold, unguided pencil drew.[41]

Remarkably, Straw Hall still exists, secreted on a wooded hillside yet commanding views over the Thames. With its deep thatch, Gothick windows and rustic verandah it is pure Hansel and Gretel, and already of classic cottage orné form. The composition is asymmetrical, the higher section containing a room with the simplest of Gothic alcoves at the inner end, clearly the place for taking tea. The lower section contains the kitchen where the refreshments would have been prepared, and a narrow staircase leading to a room in the roof perhaps provided the option of a resident caretaker. Even more remarkably, Thomas Powys's poem, painted on board, is still in place on the entrance porch.

There is a direct link between Straw Hall and another early ornamental cottage, that at Park Place near Henley-on-Thames. Mrs Lybbe Powys described her first visit to Park Place in September 1762, just a month after her marriage, when she mentions General Conway's 'pretty cottage' and says that he got the idea from Straw Hall.[42] General (later Field Marshal) Henry Seymour Conway bought the estate in 1752, and he and his wife subsequently laid out the grounds in the prevailing taste, including the so-called Happy Valley running down to the Thames. Mrs Lybbe Powys was there again in August 1766, and her journal describes the cottage in slightly more detail:

a Gothic root-house which hangs pendant over
the river is exceedingly pretty; the building is
like 'Straw Hall' in our woods, only the inside is
Gothic paper resembling stucco; the upper part
of the windows being painted glass gives a
pleasing gloom.[43]

An undated photo in a book on Park Place privately printed in 1905[44] refers to it as the Chinese Cottage and shows a small two-storeyed structure on a slope, almost enveloped in ivy and with no discernible Chinese features. The author says it stood on the site of Bottom House Farm, so presumably it must have disappeared fairly soon after the photo was taken. The possibility, however, is that the Gothic root house 'pendant over the river' referred to in 1766 had already disappeared and was a different, more transient, structure altogether.[45]

The so-called Convent in the Woods [fig 1/12] at Stourhead hovers midway between a hermitage and a cottage orné. An asymmetrical composition built of brick with a facing of rocky tufa and flint, under a thatched roof framed by fantastical chimneys, it was probably built around 1765 for Henry Hoare and was originally called 'the Abbey'. The identity of the designer is mysterious, but the prominence of rocky wall surfaces, and the grotto-like vault of the porch, perhaps suggest the involvement of Joseph Lane of Tisbury, who in 1776 added a vestibule to the 1748 grotto by Stourhead's lake. The Convent was certainly not intended for permanent occupation but rather as a romantic pavilion for the Hoare family and their guests to visit on carriage and riding excursions. It is not mentioned by Horace Walpole in his description of the Stourhead estate in 1762, nor indeed in the Stourhead guide book of 1800; but in 1776 Mrs Lybbe Powys called it

an elegant building, painted glass in the upper part
of the window in miniature [a feature similar to the
one she had admired at Park Place]. Nuns in their
different habits in panels round the room, very pretty
Gothic elbow chairs painted in mosaic brown and
white. Two very ancient pictures found in the ruins
of Glastonbury Abbey – the Wise Men's Offerings –
well painted.[46]

The other relevant building at Stourhead, this time on the main visitor circuit, is the Gothic Cottage. Although seemingly not mentioned by eighteenth-century visitors, and not shown in Bampfylde's sketches of around 1770, it does seem to be marked on the plan made by the Swede F. M. Piper in 1779, just east of the grotto, and is also marked on a 1785 estate map. It therefore probably originated as a modest vernacular cottage already in existence

before the creation of the park. In 1806 it was made a deliberate feature of the circuit by Colt Hoare, for whom it was Gothicized by the architect-antiquary John Carter.[47]

Another early example of a simple cottage built for aristocratic leisure rather than working-class occupation was the Lady's Cottage on the Blickling estate in Norfolk. Built for the Countess of Buckinghamshire soon after her marriage to the 2nd earl in 1761, it is shown in a Humphry Repton watercolour of about 1780 to have been a very simple one-room box with Gothic windows and thatch. A 1793 inventory indicates that it was furnished with a dining table and chairs, along with an impressive array of cutlery, crockery and cooking equipment. It was abandoned in the late nineteenth century and has disappeared completely.[48]

Although the first mention of the term 'cottage orné' came in Robert Lugar's *Architectural Sketches for Cottages* in 1805, the earliest publication to offer designs for what could be described as cottages ornés seems to have been Plaw's *Rural Architecture* of 1785. In the preceding decades, when such templates were simply not available, it is often difficult to identify an architect for buildings such as the Stourhead Convent or the Blickling Lady's Cottage. Sanderson Miller and Thomas Wright are exceptions. Robert Adam, unexpectedly, is another. The collection of his drawings in the Sir John Soane Museum contains a

veritable cornucopia of rustic designs and reveals an unsuspected and hitherto largely unconsidered interest on the part of an outstanding architect otherwise known primarily for his exquisite neoclassical projects.[49]

Adam's picturesque landscape drawings initially owe a good deal to the artist Paul Sandby, with whom he worked for the Board of Ordnance in the Scottish Highlands in the late 1740s, just before he set off for Rome. In Rome he was subjected to the additional influence of Charles-Louis Clérisseau, who introduced him to the existing school there of romantic ruin drawing.[50] After his return to England in 1758, always alert to coming fashions, Adam produced a considerable number of designs in the rustic vein, most if not all of which sadly appear to have remained unexecuted; certainly none is known to have survived, though allowances have to be made for the transience of rustic materials. Nonetheless, they illustrate yet another facet of his protean imagination, and in some respects may be seen as prefiguring the late Georgian preoccupation with the rustic and the picturesque. Some are inscribed to specific clients: for instance, the actor David Garrick, the Hon. Miss Curzon at Kedleston in Derbyshire, the dukes of Bolton and Roxburgh, and the earls of Harborough and Wemyss. A few are dated, the earliest being the plans and elevation for a substantial house for an unidentified client, inscribed '12th March

'1772'. By the 1780s, as commissions in England progressively dried up, Adam's practice was increasingly for clients north of the border, which is reflected in the number of designs for identifiably Scottish clients. Unfortunately he was trying to interest his compatriots in an idiom and a genre for which they showed little enthusiasm and, compared to England, Scotland remains rather barren ground in this respect, perhaps because of an inherent puritanical distaste for what was perceived to be frivolous.

The Adam drawings in the Soane Museum are surprisingly varied in both presentation and architectural vocabulary. They range from very precisely drawn elevations evidently intended for scrutiny by the client, to rough pencil sketches clearly dashed off in a matter of minutes. Another, less common, approach is to show the building rapidly sketched in perspective and in its rural setting. Feeding into such designs are two main strands. One, fortifying his tuition under Clérisseau, is Adam's recollection of the almost styleless buildings he saw on his rambles in the Campagna during his stay in Rome in 1755–7. In late March 1756 he wrote to his family back in Edinburgh about a long walk he had had in the countryside around Rome: 'This is the most intoxicating country in the world for a picturesque hero.'[51] The other strand is a nod towards the theories of a French priest on the primitive origins of classical architecture, published in 1753 in Abbé Marc-Antoine Laugier's *Essai sur l'Architecture*, the frontispiece [fig 1/13] to the 1755 edition of which showed a primitive hut created out of the trimmed trunks and branches of living trees and given a thatched roof.[52] Probably the first published English design to pick up on Laugier's lead was one for a primitive hut with tree-trunk portico illustrated in William Wrighte's *Grotesque Architecture* of 1767, but Adam seems to have been the first British architect to develop the theme for practical use.[53]

Adam's exploration of the rustic genre ranges in size from small ornamental structures intended for the park or garden right through to substantial houses that are unequivocally proper cottages ornés, meant for occupation by the owners of the estates rather than their employees. An example of the former is a sketch with the character of a hermitage [fig 1/14] (perhaps intended for the park at Kedleston Hall), and of the latter, his 'Cottage for Mr Dalzell' [fig 1/15].[54] Perhaps most prescient, however, is a pen and ink perspective of a design for a Gothick house [fig 1/16].[55]

ABOVE **1/14** Robert Adam, sketch for a hermitage, possibly for Kedleston Hall, Derbyshire
BELOW **1/15** Robert Adam, 'Cottage for Mr Dalzell'
OPPOSITE **1/16** Robert Adam, design for a Gothick house

Cottage for Mr Dalzell

A. W. Deleu.
Albemarle Street. Sept.r 1786.

Front of a Cottage for The Honorable Horace Walpole.

Gothic is not a style usually associated with Adam, but in fact he had an early interest in it. Visiting England in the winter of 1749–50 he made a number of sketches of medieval buildings, which seem to have prompted various Rococo Gothick fantasies in the immediately ensuing years. In October 1754, en route for Dover and the Continent, he and his brother James had an excursion to Windsor with Thomas Sandby, who may have showed them not just the castle and St George's Chapel but also his recently completed landscaping at Virginia Water. Study in Italy was hardly conducive to encouraging an interest in Gothic, but Adam returned to the style once he

had established himself in London, with a major scheme to transform Alnwick Castle and associated buildings.[56] The Soane Museum design, dated September 1786, is an extraordinary confection of motifs, with a central section of three bays under cusped gables, book-ended by taller end bays with just the kind of steep cusped gables that were to become part of the standard cottage orné currency in the nineteenth century. The windows are mainly latticed, under Tudor dripmoulds, and each gable has a crowning crucifix. It is a mongrel design that presents more questions than answers, but the really striking feature is the presence of so many motifs that became part of the

1/17 Robert Adam, rustic pavilion design for Horace Walpole
at Strawberry Hill, Twickenham, 1768
1/18 Robert Adam, plan of design for Horace Walpole, 1768

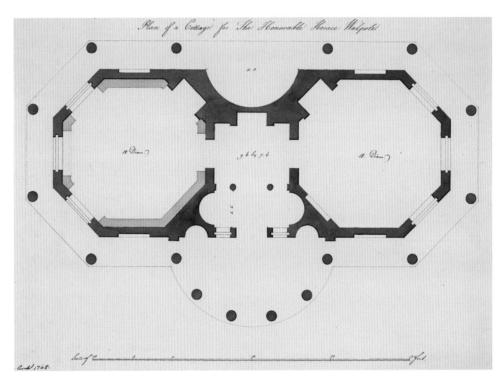

vocabulary of cottage orné architects in the first decades of the next century.

Adam's rustic and cottage designs were clearly all intended for a well-heeled, often aristocratic, clientele. Additional designs survive that were prepared for one of the great taste-formers of the age, Horace Walpole. Adam produced designs, subsequently put into effect, for a Gothick ceiling and chimneypiece for the Round Room at Strawberry Hill, Walpole's pasteboard castle on the Thames at Twickenham. This was in 1766–7, and in the same period he was apparently trying to tempt Walpole with sophisticated cottage schemes, one dated 1766 and the other two years later [figs 1/17, 18].[57] Both exhibit Adam's characteristic spatial ingenuity in their plans, with rooms of different geometric shapes and the use of columned screens. In the 1768 design, which is the more attractive, these are wrapped around by a verandah of rough tree trunks, linked one to the other by leafy garlands. Neither design was taken up and it is uncertain where they might have been intended for at Strawberry Hill. The great American Walpole enthusiast and collector, W. S. Lewis implied the flower garden laid out in 1765, where in 1769 Walpole was to build a smaller and much simpler thatched cottage after a design by his friend John Chute,[58] but the

ABOVE 1/19 Woburn Abbey, Bedfordshire: The Thornery, designed by Humphry Repton in 1808

RIGHT 1/20 Blaise Castle, Bristol: dairy designed by John Nash, c.1805

BELOW 1/21 Swiss Garden, Old Warden, Bedfordshire: the rustic pavilion

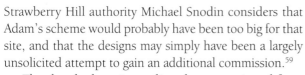

Strawberry Hill authority Michael Snodin considers that Adam's scheme would probably have been too big for that site, and that the designs may simply have been a largely unsolicited attempt to gain an additional commission.[59]

The thatched rustic pavilion theme continued from what might be called the Rococo phase, as exemplified by Thomas Wright, and seamlessly into the era of the Picturesque. In 1808 Humphry Repton designed the Thornery [fig 1/19] for the park at Woburn Abbey – a summerhouse in the hermitage manner. Stone walls sit within a ring of tree trunks and support a steeply pitched thatch with high pointed gables. The interior is lit by rose windows, with stained glass that casts a dim religious light[60] slightly at odds with the pretty treillages and flowers painted on the walls and umbrella vault. Set into the hillside below is a separate tile-lined kitchen with intricate glazing and bark-patterned doors, once with its complement of customized Wedgwood biscuit-ware. John Nash, who was to be one of the key figures in the flowering of the cottage orné, captured the essence of the style in miniature in the exquisite thatched dairy he designed for Blaise Castle [fig 1/20] near Bristol in about 1805.[61] Some twenty years later, another leading proponent of the genre, John Buonarotti Papworth, is likely to have been the designer of the delightful two-storeyed pavilion that provides the focus for Lord Ongley's Swiss Garden at Old Warden in Bedfordshire.[62] Not much is known about Ongley, except that he was born into a military family in 1803 and died a bachelor in 1877. Local legend has it that he laid out his Swiss Garden around a chalet in which he lodged his Swiss mistress. Certainly he created out of nine acres of mature woodland a delicious, inward-looking private world whose hub is a two-storeyed thatched pavilion [fig 1/21]; however, despite the prettiness of its decoration, one room up and one down is unlikely to have satisfied even the most undemanding mistress, so this 'Swiss cottage' – which in fact has nothing very obviously Swiss about it – is probably just an especially attractive specimen of rustic summerhouse. Lord Ongley's efforts to prettify the village cottages at Old Warden will be dealt with in the next chapter.

1 At that point still the widowed Mrs Pendarves.

2 Barbara Jones, *Follies and Grottoes*, 2nd edn (London,1974), pp. 31–3. Lady Llanover, *Autobiography and Correspondence of Mrs Delany*, 6 vols (London, 1861–2), vol. I, p. 421. It is not clear whether 'wood house' refers to a house made of wood or a house in a wood; given the local Cotswold vernacular, invariably stone-built, the latter is more likely. The building is set among trees, though not far from one of the rides through Lord Bathurst's forest park.

3 Arthur Oswald, 'Radway Grange, Warwickshire', *Country Life* (13 September 1946).

4 William Hawkes, ed., *The Diaries of Sanderson Miller of Radway* (Stratford-upon-Avon, 2005). The cottage has been extended and, on the side facing the road, has lost most of its original character.

5 British Library, Add MS 6230, f 40v, quoted Hawkes, *Diaries of Sanderson Miller*, pp. 26–7.

6 Michael Cousins, 'The Garden Buildings at Enville', *The Follies Journal*, 2 (2002), pp. 71–7. The work would have been for the 4th Earl of Stamford.

7 *The Travels through England of Dr Richard Pococke* (Camden Society, 1888), vol. 42.

8 Michael Symes and Sandy Haynes, *Enville, Hagley and the Leasowes* (Bristol, 2010), pp. 97–9. I am grateful to Dr Jane Bradney, the Enville estate archivist, for her help with the Cottage.

9 Joseph Heely, *Letters on the Beauties of Hagley, Enville and The Leasowes* (London, 1777), II, pp. 71–5, quoted in Symes and Haynes, *Enville, Hagley and the Leasowes*.

10 V&A E.898-1928, described in the catalogue as 'a design for a Gothic folly'.

11 V&A E.874-1928; V&A E.888-1928.

12 See Roger White, 'Kent and the Gothic Revival', in *William Kent: Designing Georgian Britain*, ed. Susan Weber (New Haven and London, 2013), p. 249. See also Nicholas Savage, 'Kent as Book Illustrator', in Weber, ed. *William Kent*, pp. 437–41.

13 Eileen Harris, introduction to the facsimile edition of Wright's *Arbours & Grottoes* (London, 1979), no pagination.

14 On the rear elevation of the original cottage it is possible to see stone roof tiles under the thatch – as formerly at the Deerkeeper's House.

15 Two other cottages likely to be from this phase are Pump Cottage, in the village opposite the park gates, with cusped eaves and 'primitive'

stone porches; and Burdon's Lodge, Little Badminton, whose pretty elevation to the park has cusped eaves and Gothick bay windows. The tree-trunk porch on the side elevation has lost its original lead dome (removed in the 1970s).

16 The exterior was carefully restored in 2012 for the 11th duke.

17 Eileen Harris, 'Architect of Rococo Landscapes', *Country Life* (9 September 1971). See also Gordon Campbell, *The Hermit in the Garden* (Oxford, 2013), pp. 109–13.

18 Avery Library, Drawing 34b; Harris, 'Architect of Rococo Landscapes'; see also Michael McCarthy, 'Thomas Wright's "Designs for Temples" and Related Drawings for Garden Buildings', *Journal of Garden History*, I/1 (1981), pp. 55–66, I/3 (1981), pp. 239–52.

19 For the 4th Earl of Berkeley (died 1755), a subscriber to *Arbours*.

20 From the engraved design on the title page of *Arbours*. However, Campbell, *Hermit in the Garden*, p. 125, suggests that this in fact dates from the period 1804–11 when a new mansion was being built at Spetchley.

21 Harris, 'Architect of Rococo Landscapes'.

22 Bishop Pococke, *Tours in Ireland* in 1752, ed. G. T. Stokes (1891), pp. 3–4.

23 Ibid. Wright spent eight days at Tullymore in 1746.

24 Harris ascribes this to Wright on the basis of his two visits to Belle Isle in August 1746, and also on the strength of its similarity to the Avery sketch and to the root house at Berkeley Castle.

25 It does not appear on a map of 1768 but it is suggested that it could nevertheless have been designed by Wright at the time of his visit. Harris, 'Architect of Rococo Landscapes'. A more substantial rustic cottage at Florence Court is discussed in Chapter Six.

26 It is not clear what he means by the windows, as the three back walls on the engraving appear to have blind panels.

27 Royal Library; reproduced in John Harris, *A Garden Alphabet* (London, 1979), n.p., under 'H is for Hermitage'; Jane Roberts, *Royal Landscape: The Gardens and Parks of Windsor* (New Haven and London, 1997), p. 59.

28 Sir John Soane's Museum, vol. 35/200.

29 Soane vols 35/228, 35/227.

30 Soane vol. 36/38

31 Soane vol. 35/63. See Chapter Seven.

32 *The Life and Correspondence of Mrs Delany*, quoted in Valerie Pakenham, *The Big House in Ireland* (London, 2000), p. 37. The Caledon hermitage has not survived, nor do there seem to be any visual records of it.

33 Jones, *Follies and Grottoes*, pp. 182–4.

34 Christopher Sturman, 'A Lincolnshire Hermit: Wolley Jolland (1745–1831)', in *The Georgian Group Report & Journal* (1987), pp. 62–76.

35 C. Bruyn Andrews, ed., *The Torrington Diaries*, 2 (London, 1935), pp. 380–85, quoted in Sturman, 'A Lincolnshire Hermit'.

36 George Carter, Patrick Moore and Kedrun Laurie, *Humphry Repton Landscape Gardener 1752–1818* (Norwich, 1982), cited in Sturman, 'A Lincolnshire Hermit'.

37 An MS note by Horatio Walpole in the British Museum's copy of Robertson's *Topographical Survey* (14) says that Sir Robert built 'the thatched room' in or shortly after 1727.

38 Edward Croft-Murray, *Decorative Painting in England 1537–1837*, vol. 2 (London, 1970), pp. 175, 300. I am grateful to Alastair Laing for confirming Croft-Murray's attribution.

39 On Rocque's 1762 map of Surrey the main house is shown as Burches Lodge; previously it was Aldridge's Lodge till at least 1754. The name Thatched House first appears on Richardson's plan of 1771.

40 Letter of October 24th 1762 to an old friend, quoted in Emily J. Climenson, *Passages from the Diaries of Mrs Philip Lybbe Powys* (London, 1899), p. 98.

41 Ibid., p. 108; W. Fletcher, *A Tour Round Reading* (Reading, 1843), p. 24, notes: 'On the summit of the hill is a small building denominated "Straw Hall", in which parties visiting this spot have been accustomed to rest themselves. The wide command of prospect which it affords, is a feature imparting a double interest to a visit.'

42 Howard Colvin, *A Biographical Dictionary of British Architects 1600–1840* (Colvin B.D.), 4th edn (New Haven and London, 2008), p. 807, says that the amateur architect, Thomas Pitt, Lord Camelford, designed the cottage and other features at Park Place in 1763; the date at least must be incorrect.

43 Climenson, *Passages from the Diaries of Mrs Philip Lybbe Powys*, p. 115.

44 Percy Noble, ed., *Park Place, Berkshire* (1905).

45 Information from Henley Archaeological and Historical Society.

46 Climenson, *Passages from the Diaries of Mrs Philip Lybbe Powys*, p. 171. The building fell into disrepair after World War II, when the painted glass and other fittings were lost, but in 1982 it was repaired by the National Trust. Kenneth Woodbridge, *The Stourhead Landscape* (London, 1974).

47 Letter from Colt Hoare to Carter, Wiltshire Record Office 383.907.

48 Gervase Jackson-Stops, *An English Arcadia 1600–1990*, exh. cat. (Washington DC, 1991), pp. 107–8.

49 The drawings are touched on in John Martin Robinson's *Georgian Model Farms* (Oxford, 1983), pp. 41–4. For a fuller discussion see Roger White, 'Robert Adam's Rustic Designs', *Georgian Group Journal*, vol. XXXIII (2015), pp. 167–78.

50 For Adam's time in Rome see John Fleming, *Robert Adam and his Circle* (London, 1962).

51 Quoted in Fleming, *Robert Adam and his Circle*, p. 200.

52 Abbé Marc-Antoine Laugier, *Essai sur l'Architecture*, 2nd edn (Paris, 1755). See below, Chapter Two, Cordbatt Cottage and Belline lodge.

53 J. M. Robinson, *Georgian Model Farms*, (Oxford, 1983), p. 44.

54 Soane 1/241; Soane 46/152.

55 Soane 2/62.

56 For instance, out in the park, the summerhouse at Hulne Priory (1778–9) and the Brizlee Tower (1777–83).

57 Lewis Walpole Library, Yale University, Farmington, CT. The drawings are discussed in John Wilton-Ely, 'Style and serendipity: Adam, Walpole and Strawberry Hill', *British Art Journal*, XI/3, pp. 7–8.

58 Horace Walpole, Correspondence, Yale edn (New Haven, 1937–83), vol. 4, p. 147, note 6.

59 Personal communication with the author.

60 The phrase first appears in John Milton's *Il Penseroso*.

61 G. S. Repton's drawings of the plans, elevation and section of the Blaise dairy are in his sketchbook, RIBADC 246/4, fols 54 verso and 55.

62 Mavis Batey, 'An English View of Switzerland', *Country Life* (17 February 1977), pp. 364–6. Papworth lived at Little Paxton, not far from Old Warden, and in the 1820s was employed at several houses in the vicinity.

CHAPTER TWO

HOUSING
THE PEASANTS

Although the origins of the cottage orné vocabulary arguably lie in the rustic garden buildings erected in the gardens of the rich from the middle years of the eighteenth century, and although some of the earliest cottages deliberately designed in rustic idiom were the playthings of aristocratic ladies, part of the unique fascination of the cottage orné is the fact that it ran the full gamut of the social scale. At the other end of the scale from the occasional playthings of the aristocratic rich were the cottages intended for full-time occupation by the working-class poor. These were people, characteristically workers or tenants on country estates, for whom residence in a simple cottage was not a lifestyle choice but an unavoidable necessity. The genuine vernacular cottages in which they lived may have looked eminently picturesque from the exterior, but internally the accommodation was likely to be cramped, basic and often squalid and insanitary. Once the cottage orné fashion started to take hold, estate owners saw the desirability of having purpose-designed cottages, primarily for aesthetic reasons of course but also, in some cases, for sociological ones. The provision of creature comforts was never lavish and the rooms were generally small by modern standards, but at least there were likely to be proper foundations rather than earth floors, and possibly even the luxury of a privy.

Many estate owners continued to see the proper housing of the tenantry as an incidental bonus to the ornamentation of their prospect, but for some the equation of a well-housed peasant being a happy peasant was a genuine consideration. This was a moral largely lost on Anglo-Irish landlords,[1] but the alarming events across the Channel from 1789 onwards sharpened the sense of a need for self-preservation, as well as a feeling that a paternalistic aristocracy was called for as a prophylactic against revolution. Such implicit sentiments underlie the texts of many of the architectural pattern books of the late eighteenth and early nineteenth centuries.[2] The peasant accommodation they proposed might still be cramped and basic, but there was nevertheless a clear awareness that, as P. F. Robinson noted in his *Village Architecture* (1830), 'the comforts and well-being of our labouring poor are so intimately connected with every proposal for rendering their dwellings more attractive'.[3] Charles Waistell, in his *Designs for Agricultural Buildings* of 1827, proclaimed that

> The great object . . . with a humane proprietor of landed property, in erecting labourers' cottages (the smallest buildings required for the dwellings of men) is to make the cottagers more comfortable, and by that means render them healthy, stout, and active, and capable of that hard and continued labour which their pursuits require.[4]

Waistell, whose own designs for labourers' cottages were plain in the extreme, and not remotely orné, appealed to the self-interest of the landowner in order to achieve a socially humane objective, while other pattern-book authors hastened to assure their potential clients that such buildings could be made attractive for a very trifling additional expense. P. F. Robinson summed up the argument:

> As a primary step towards improving the condition of the labourer, it is necessary to give him some interest in the land upon which he dwells, or in the cottage which affords him shelter; and where this can be done at a small expense, and the building rendered pleasing, two important objects will certainly be accomplished, of infinite interest, in a national point of view.[5]

The cottages ornés of the working class fall into two basic categories: individual cottages, usually lodges at the gates of an estate or else buildings intended for a particular estate worker; and whole villages or hamlets built anew or else prettified by ornamental touches. Lodges are in fact the most numerous of all the sub-sections of the genre, supplied as they were not just to large country estates but even to much smaller suburban middle-class properties. It is in the nature of things that, with the exception of later lodges derived from pattern book plates, the identity of architects can rarely be established, and their dates likewise. However, the earliest dateable design for a lodge of the genre does indeed have an architect. As part of his work for the Duke of Bolton at Hackwood Park [fig 2/1] in Hampshire, William Kent's protégé John Vardy supplied a

OPPOSITE **2/1** John Vardy, design for a lodge at Hackwood Park, Hampshire, 1761; the earliest dateable design for a cottage lodge

design dated 1761.[6] This was apparently unexecuted, but it would have combined the local vernacular materials of flint and brick with Kent-inspired rustication and various kinds of Gothic window. The unusual feature of Vardy's drawing is that it has a flap that allows the client to judge the effect with and without a thatched roof. With the flap up the building has the scalloped eaves and trefoil finial of the porch at Kent's Esher Place, Surrey, while with it down it indisputably becomes a little cottage orné.

John Plaw was to be one of the more influential designers in the genre, through his pattern books *Rural Architecture* and *Ferme Ornée, or Rural Improvements*, both first published in 1785, and *Sketches for Country Houses, Villas and Rural Dwellings*, of 1800. The latter two publications include the so-called New York [fig 2/2], which had already been built for Colonel John Montresor on his estate at Belmont in Kent.[7] Intended as a pair of dwellings for estate workers, New York is described by Plaw as being 'after the manner of American Cottages', not something he would have seen for himself at that stage of his career[8] and therefore reflecting the fact that Montresor (1736–1799), a British military engineer, had seen two decades of service in North America prior to his retirement in 1779. The cottages have a big cat-slide roof brought down onto an arched verandah that surrounds the timber-framed core on three sides. They are not at all orné, nor are they related to Kentish vernacular, having instead a simple colonial character that also appears on single-storey bungalows in other British colonies. It seems unlikely that Plaw had any involvement in their design or construction, since in *Ferme Ornée* he refers to 'their extreme singularity' and says 'I saw them soon after they were completed', but they certainly impressed him enough to include a very similar design in *Sketches for Country Houses*.[9] In any case, as Geoffrey Tyack observes, New York is 'almost certainly the first English building to be inspired by an American model'.[10]

Another intriguing building, which might in some sense be regarded more as a version of the American log cabin than as a straightforward English cottage orné, is Cordbatt Cottage [fig 2/3] at Rye Foreign in East Sussex. It has, it is true, the classic combination of overhanging thatch supported on tree trunks, but there are no ornamental trimmings and the unusual feature is the wall construction, which consists of sections of log set, cut end out, into what appears to be a pisé, or compacted earth, surround. The underlying influence here is that of contemporary discussions of construction methods using natural raw materials, and by extension, the late Georgian interest in the primitive. Pisé, made by ramming fine loam into a wooden frame, was popularized by François Cointereaux, who founded a School for Rural Architecture in Paris in 1790 and proceeded to issue four booklets on the subject. The technique was quickly picked up by John Plaw; he referred to Cointereaux in the 1795 edition of *Ferme Ornée*, which illustrated a pisé lodge 'originally designed for a great personage'. Like unsawn timber and thatch – materials also deployed in Cordbatt Cottage – pisé was one of the few building materials not taxed during the Napoleonic

wars, and after 1815 its appeal diminished, so this may give a hint as to the possible period of the cottage. It is not large, and is evidently for working-class accommodation, but it is not clear what it could have been a lodge to, as the lane alongside leads to a farm rather than to a country house.

Although the origins of the cottage orné genre as a whole might plausibly be linked to the earlier eighteenth-century interest in rustic garden structures, as discussed in Chapter One, and although leading architects of British neoclassicism such as William Chambers, Robert Adam and John Soane had evidently read and taken note of the Abbé Laugier's writings on the supposed primitive origins of classical architecture,[11] examples of this kind of literal primitivism are rare in the cottage orné field – as they are in late eighteenth-century British architecture more generally. If Cordbatt Cottage is perhaps one such, another might be Smoothway Lodge on the Ugbrooke estate in Devon, which has walls of upright logs. However, as the leading chroniclers of the country house lodge point out, even this has Gothic windows and so it would be mistaken to press the building as an illustration of Laugier's theories.[12] The best – in fact probably the only – surviving example in the British Isles of Laugier-inspired primitivism is (or was, until it was disgracefully allowed to collapse in 2014) the lodge at Belline, Co. Kilkenny [fig 2/4], a simple temple form in which the peripteral columns, composed of de-barked tree trunks, support capitals formed of a

square slab of stone with a twist of rope for the necking. The frieze is made of a split tree trunk, placed with the curved surface outwards – a perfect illustration of the origin of the pulvinated frieze.[13] Old photographs confirm that, like Laugier's primitive hut, the lodge originally had a thatched roof, later replaced in slate. Belline is a miniature Tuscan temple rather than a cottage, but there are also examples of lodges where the verandah columns aspire to the primitive classical rather than to the twiggy Gothic, as at Glevering Hall in Suffolk, probably designed by Humphry Repton who produced a Red Book for the estate layout in 1793.[14] Another such is at Harleston House, Northamptonshire, where, although the main house has been demolished, a little rustic lodge with apsidal end and tree-trunk columns survives at the Lower Harleston end of the drive, a remnant of Repton's landscaping work of *c*. 1808–11.[15]

At its simplest the cottage orné lodge was little more than a single-storey building with a couple of rooms, sometimes with an additional room squeezed into the deep thatched roof. Such a structure could hardly hold more than one or at most two people. As Thomas Dearn put it in his pattern book, *Designs for Lodges and Entrances* of 1823,

an Entrance Lodge is usually intended, either for an old man, and old woman, or both, or for a mother and daughter; in short, for anything but a family. A group of small children, though occasionally picturesque in a situation like this, is not, on the whole, desirable. That neatness and air of comfort, which should mark the approach to a gentleman's residence, would, by such an assemblage, be too frequently destroyed.[16]

P. F. Robinson, by contrast, while noting the advantages experienced by a cottager who possessed 'a scenic dwelling', clearly believed that there were also advantages from the point of view of the owner in having a well-behaved and well-turned out family in residence:

a morning is frequently dedicated to visit the thriving family. The attention of the landlord is met by the assiduity of the tenant, and neatness and even elegance is the result. The woodbine is trained with care round the window, every unseemly object is kept out of sight, and the good wife, anxious to please her benefactress and grateful for the attention paid to her, is ever on the watch for the morning visit, and consequently always in order. The rosy cheeked smiling children, proudly showing the little presents made to them for good behaviour, exhibit a marked contrast to the neighbouring poor.[17]

J. B. Papworth, a leading Regency proponent of the cottage orné, pointed out that the lodge, in whatever architectural style, formed in the visitor's mind an idea of the park owner's character, so a scruffy specimen could hardly create a favourable impression.[18] The lodge in general might herald the architectural idiom of the main house, in which case it would be classical, Gothic, or in the castle style, but when the lodge was a cottage it was very unlikely that progress up the drive would reveal a larger version.

Since classical architects were and are prone to symmetry, those designing lodges in the classical idiom frequently proposed a matching pair, each component usually being very small. Humphry Repton, in his *Observations* of 1803, criticized this practice from the point of view of the occupant, 'who inhabits a dirty room of a few feet square'.[19] Cottage lodges were less prone to such pairings, though the drive to the manor house at Little Milton near Oxford is framed by a matching pair like two Gothick tea caddies. Even so small a lodge as one intended for single occupancy could be invested with considerable charm. A classic example is that to Barton House [fig 2/5] at Morchard Bishop in Devon, single-storeyed with overhanging thatch supported on extremely

gnarled tree trunks, and with prettily leaded Gothic windows.[20] The lodge to Stockton House in Wiltshire is a crisp version of this formula in flint with stone dressings.[21] Similar, though probably capable of taking two people since there is an ill-lit room in the roof, is the lodge to the back drive of Lees Court in Kent. Still single-storeyed, but with a rather more spacious footprint, the Goathill Lodge to a back drive of the Sherborne Castle estate in Dorset has its enormous thatched roof unsupported by posts but flared out like a crinoline above a deep bracketed eaves.[22] The many variants of this particular type of thatched, single-storeyed lodge – and very few are exactly the same – include those to The Grove, at Great Glemham in Suffolk, and three in Norfolk: to Intwood Hall (this one with walls of flint cobbles and a prominent semicircular bow), to Brooke Hall, and in Gas House Hill, Aylsham.

Where the lodge was a single building with a tight footprint, the answer to finding extra space was invariably to squeeze an extra room into the roof – a room that must inevitably have been claustrophobic and ill-lit, since the dormer windows are usually small and sunk deeply into the thatch. Nevertheless this generally added greatly to the visual attraction of the building, as can be seen at Marino Lodge [fig 2/6] (formerly Pauntley Cottage) in Sidmouth. Seemingly built in about 1816 as a lodge for a classical house called Marino,[23] it has very deep overhanging thatch, supported not on tree trunks but on iron posts, with Gothic arches formed between them by curved pieces of iron. The crisply shaped thatch is brought down like a helmet around the solitary dormer, whose sill must be literally at floor level. The lodge at Langton by Spilsby [fig 2/7], Lincolnshire is similarly very simple, a single-storeyed whitewashed octagon with Gothic windows. The tall, conical, thatched roof rises to a chimney at the apex, the overhang supported on iron posts; there is a room in the roof lit by Gothic dormers with delicate glazing of hexagons and diamonds.[24] At the lodge to New Park in the New Forest the roof is really the whole

BELOW **2/7** Langton by Spilsby, Lincolnshire: detail

LEFT **2/8** Lodge at Roudham, Norfolk

point of the design, overshadowing the ground floor to an exceptional degree and shaped, trimmed and scalloped like a piece of sculpture.[25] The architect here might conceivably have been John Nash,[26] to whom has also been attributed the hexagonal lodge with lofty conical thatch at Charborough Park in Dorset.[27] Possibly the most diminutive specimen in this category is the toll house in cottage orné style at Islington, now part of Trowbridge, Wiltshire, where the windows have the 'marginal lights' typical of the Regency and the toll charges are displayed on a board beneath the thatch overhang.

Part of the characteristic vocabulary of the cottage orné is that if it has a thatched roof it is generally made to overhang, and the precise manner in which the overhang is supported can be varied. Knobbly tree trunks have been mentioned, as have metal posts with or without intervening arches. Straightforward wooden posts are common (for instance at Charborough), if rather dull. In some cases, the effect of a lacy arcade is produced by using a combination of tree trunks and branches. A particularly charming example is the lodge at Roudham, Norfolk [fig 2/8], which has the added attraction of a miniature version of the main lodge sitting alongside, like 'mother and daughter'.[28] Another instance is the lodge to Coombe Lodge, Blagdon, Somerset, a building of square plan and pyramidal roof (the latter now tiled though probably originally thatched).

By no means all the cottages built for working-class occupation are gate lodges, some certainly being intended for estate employees with a particular function other than opening and closing gates. One such is the cottage hidden away on the edge of Staverton Thicks, an area of ancient woodland near the village of Butley in Suffolk, and therefore probably intended for a woodman or gamekeeper.

Single-storeyed, and built of pebbles from a nearby shingle beach, it is just three bays wide, with simple Gothic windows to either side of a Gothic door. The thatch bows out above the door and is supported on simple posts.[29] Further north in the same county, Hex Cottage [fig 2/9] on the estate of Cockfield Hall, Yoxford, was a gamekeeper's cottage of exceptional charm. It has simple Gothic windows (except on the rear where they are normal rectangular), thatch and knobbly tree-trunk columns on the south façade supporting an overhang with a Gothic window, framed by appliqué rustic woodwork. Interestingly the window is a dummy and the upper floor seems never to

have been used.[30] Inside the ground floor consists of four rectangular rooms arranged round a central chimney, all very simple. The rooms to the left of the chimney are of equal size, but to the right the sitting room is larger with a narrow kitchen behind, the latter retaining its bread oven. The cottage overlooks water meadows and was probably designed to be seen across these from the gardens of the Hall (no longer possible, due to later plantings), which would help to explain the effort expended in the design of the main elevation. A date of 1835 is suggested, and there are similarities of detail with two other Cockfield estate buildings, the cottage orné east lodge on the main road (which shares the tree-trunk verandah), and the Tudoresque lodge in Yoxford village. As usual, no architect is definitely known, but it may be relevant that Henry Roberts, who is best known as the architect of the Greek Revival Fishmongers Hall in London but who also worked in Gothic and Tudor, designed the Gothic north aisle of Yoxford Church in 1837.[31]

The aptly named Gingerbread House [fig 2/10] on the Jordans estate at Horton in Somerset is another cottage built for a gamekeeper, and it again emphasizes the attention and indeed invention that might go into the design of a building for a mere estate worker, especially if it was going to have a visual impact on the setting of the main house. At Jordans the latter has disappeared, but the cottage stands a few hundred yards from both the site of the

mansion and the surviving shell house, a superb specimen of the genre, with the date 1828 incorporated into its knucklebone floor.[32] It was originally just one room deep, with (probably) parlour and kitchen on the ground floor plus a room in the roof reached by a steep stair. On the main façade, which is canted forward in the centre, three very steep gables are supported on tree-trunk posts, the thatch being drawn up into sharp points – a West Country vernacular feature picked up by the cottage orné designers of the region. The underside of the thatch is lined with strips of bark. The construction is rubblestone, but enough traces remain to show that originally the walls were covered in limewash, which in turn was lined out to give the impression of regular blocks of ashlar. The ground-floor windows and door have triangular heads (their pitch

exactly reflecting that of the gables),[33] another motif popular in the West Country, as can immediately be seen at one of the masterpieces of cottage lodge design, that to Gaunt's House [fig 2/11] at Hinton Martell in Dorset. Here the distinctive leitmotif of the whole design is the triangle – triangular-headed windows, triangular points to the thatch, both on the mushroom-like main roof and on the two lower porches at the angles (the latter supported on tree trunks). This gives an overall impression rather like a tent missing its guy ropes, the downward-facing points of the thatch counterpoised against the upward-facing points of the windows, and with the bosomy curves of the porches syncopated with those of the dormers rising into the roof. The whole design is integrated, inventive and thoughtful in a way not often found in mere lodges, even if the number of component motifs is strictly limited. There appears to be no documentation but it seems probable that the lodge is by the local architect William Evans of Wimborne Minster, who certainly designed the Greek Revival main house for Sir Richard Carr Glyn in about 1809.[34]

The environs of Conock Manor, near Chirton in Wiltshire, offer a fascinating insight into the variety of responses to the challenge of cottage orné design of which a little-known provincial architect might be capable. The manor house itself seems to be seventeenth century in origin but extended and remodelled around 1817 by Richard Ingleman (1777–1838) of Southwell in Nottinghamshire.[35] Most of Ingleman's work was in or around Southwell (he was Surveyor of the Fabric to the Minster there in 1801–8), but in 1810 he also designed the county gaol in Devizes, the nearest town to Conock. His client at Conock was Gifford Warriner, who died in 1820,[36] and it seems quite probable that the three associated cottage lodges are of the same period, created to sit beside the three obviously late Georgian sets of gates. However, whether Ingleman was also the architect is more open to question. Conock Lodge, alongside the gates to the main house, looks like a genuine vernacular thatched cottage titivated by the addition of little Gothick windows and a treillage porch, and as such might have been the work of a builder rather than an architect. It was occupied by a succession of head gardeners.[37] By contrast Flint Cottage [fig 2/12], across the lane but with its own set of neoclassical gate piers, was clearly an architect-designed

new-build, not a reworked vernacular cottage. It is also quite smart, so might perhaps be thought to have been intended as a dower house of some kind, but for the fact that it seems originally to have functioned as two units. The roof is stone-tiled instead of the ubiquitous local vernacular thatch, and the building is symmetrical, with big framing gables, between which runs the verandah – which, very unusually, has a projecting central porch with Gothic arch of grotto-like flint nodules. The gables have frilly eaves, and the gables themselves are weatherboarded with inset quatrefoils. There are crowning cross finials, with another cross, upside-down, within each gable. Two frilly-eaved dormers provide a syncopated rhythm with the two massive chimneystacks.[38] The comparison to be made here is with George Stanley Repton's carefully drawn elevation of John Nash's design for the Double Cottage at Blaise Hamlet, Bristol.[39] The Blaise design is asymmetrical, with a big gable at the right-hand end separated by a recessed alcove from a Gothic porch at the left. If this drawing is duplicated to the other side of the porch we get a symmetrical elevation decidedly reminiscent of Flint Cottage, complete with dormers in the tiled roof and prominent chimneys. The weatherboarded gables of Flint Cottage are ornamented with inset quatrefoils as opposed to being punctured by holes for doves, and the plain Gothic porch of Double Cottage has been made rocky. As for the cross finials, they are a feature found on Repton's drawings for the Blaise Castle House dairy,[40] but omitted on the dairy as built to Nash's design. Altogether, Repton seems a plausible suggestion for Flint Cottage, even if no documentary evidence survives.

The Manor Farm Lodge, sitting alongside a further set of neoclassical gate piers on the main road, seems at first sight an unrelated design. Compact rather than spreading, it is built of brick with a deep thatched roof, the underside of which has a cusped edging and pendants. The windows are given Tudor dripmoulds. The plan is cruciform, with two tree-trunk porches in the roadside angles, so it may originally have been a pair of rather minute cottages for estate worker occupation. The doors within the porches have cut-out Gothic quatrefoils exactly like those on the gables of Flint Cottage, leading to the conclusion that the two buildings, even though in all other respects quite different, are related and contemporary.

The chroniclers of the lodge genre were severe in their judgement of lodges that adopted a cottage idiom.

Because its essence is a *faux naïf* rustic simplicity, a thatched cottage orné can gain nothing in intensity when it is set up at a park gate. . . . One function of a lodge was always to be a cottage. When a lodge is deliberately built to look like a cottage the valuable tension of design is lost because its other function, that of proclaiming the state of the park and house within, has been abandoned. . . . The popularity of the thatched cottage may have been heightened because it provided a relief from the rigid angularity of neoclassical architecture. . . . When a small house was being built which was essentially nothing but a roof, and that roof a flexible blanket of thatch, rounded forms could be indulged in, like a sweet syrup.[41]

It might be thought, however, that lodges need not axiomatically be miniaturized essays in the style of the main house. Architects, and indeed clients, might well have welcomed the opportunity to build in a style ostensibly more relaxed than strict classicism, and in any case a plurality of styles was very much a feature of the late Georgian period when the cottage orné was in its heyday. Moreover, to dismiss such lodges as being 'nothing but a roof' and to liken them to 'sweet syrup' is to overlook not only the very real charm that characterizes many examples, but also their sheer variety and ingenuity of design. Let this section end with four further examples of those qualities, one English, two Scottish and one Welsh.

Unpromisingly embedded in the suburban sprawl that typifies the Hertfordshire side of the M25 motorway is the sole lodge remaining from Cheshunt Park [fig 2/13] (a mansion demolished after its acquisition by Cheshunt Council in 1968).[42] Cheshunt Park was built in 1795 by Oliver Cromwell, London solicitor and descendant of *the* Oliver Cromwell, which might conceivably suggest a rough date for its lodges, but as so often there is no documentation to confirm either this or the designer. What was originally known as Second Lodge is in fact one of the most unusual of its genre, and indeed may well be unique. Its originality lies partly in the fact that the projecting upper floor undulates above the supporting pillars, and partly that the entire wall surface is covered with what at first sight look like little chips of dark stone – actually pebbles and glass[43] – which are lined out into rectangular panels. The thatched roof also undulates with

thatched rustic summerhouse with a brick and tile extension at the rear.

Scotland, as will be explained in a later chapter, is not in general a fruitful hunting ground for the cottage orné, but a major exception is the estate of Taymouth Castle in Stirlingshire. The castle itself represents an earlier building, part sixteenth-century castle and part eighteenth-century house, transformed between 1804 and 1842 into arguably the most spectacular surviving Georgian Gothic mansion in the British Isles.[44] The main entrance into the park surrounding the Castle is appropriately a castellated arch, but elsewhere on the estate are two extraordinary cottage lodges. Rustic Lodge [fig 2/14], at Keltneybridge across the River Tay to the north of the castle, is a single-storey rectangular building with self-consciously aggressive rubble walls and simple rectangular latticed windows. What gives it its particular, indeed sensational, character is the portico across the front, made up of six pairs of the most Laugier-like tree-trunk columns, stripped of their bark though by no means of all their branches, painted fierce pillar-box red, and supporting wildly undulating eaves reminiscent of a Far Eastern temple.[45] The undersides of the eaves have chevron patterns of twigs, the doors are faced with what Barbara Jones[46] calls 'a sunburst of branches', radiating out from a cross shape, and the pavement within the portico is of pebbles, again incorporating a cross shape. As usual there is neither date nor architect, though Jones suggested late 1830s; the architect for the contemporary final phase of the castle was James Gillespie Graham.[47] Fort Lodge [fig 2/15], on the main road that runs along the hillside to the south of the castle, deploys the same vocabulary with even more eccentric abandon. Its eaves undulate both upwards and outwards above a tree-trunk loggia, within which is a concave wall of three sunbursts each originally centred on a stag's head. Although, like Rustic Lodge, the roof is now slated, it seems quite possible that the covering may once have been thatch or indeed heather. Once again the colouring is red, and again much care has been given to the detailed barky embellishments. Barbara Jones comments, 'Here, of course, lies the whole craft of rustic work; to spare no pains in selection. The art lies like all others in seeing its limitations and going beyond them'; and she concludes by dubbing the buildings 'Chinoiserie, Baronial, and Black Forest in one, the Barchinome style'.[48]

unusual freedom, indeed meriting the description of 'a flexible blanket'; and, yet another unusual feature, the coved eaves are lined with curved twigs. Although rather spoiled by later extensions and a very suburban garden, in its materials and form the lodge almost seems to prefigure the work of two famously sculptural architects, Antoni Gaudí and Frank Gehry. First Lodge, demolished at the same time as the mansion, was similar but not identical, and there was also a Gamekeeper's Lodge, which judging from a photo of about 1935 looked like a

Like Scotland, Wales is not particularly rich in cottages ornés of any shape or size,[49] but Pontypool Park [fig 2/16] in Monmouthshire has one of the most extravagantly Brobdingnagian of all lodges, with violently rocky walls recalling one of William Kent's rustic fantasies, or indeed designs by Vanbrugh. The masculine brutality of the stonework – a triumph of the mason's art – contrasts with the feminine, filigree curvaceousness of the eaves. Deep in a wood and looking irresistibly like the witch's gingerbread house, it is dated 1841. It must therefore have gone up in the time of Capel Hanbury Leigh (1776–1861), whose wife Molly Ann had been responsible a few decades earlier for creating a shell grotto elsewhere in the park, so perhaps the lodge was a joint effort embodying their respective personalities, a kind of architectural yin and yang.

REHOUSING THE TENANTRY

One by-product of the Georgian fashion for the landscape park was that owners of estates increasingly found that existing villages – which, characteristically, in earlier centuries had clustered around the manor house and church – compromised their views, especially if the component houses were run-down. In consequence they began to relocate the villages out of sight. The earlier exercises are plain and emphatically non-picturesque, either individually or collectively, as can be seen at Houghton [fig 2/17] in Norfolk, where Sir Robert Walpole began to remove the village (though not the church) in 1729.[50] The new village consists of pairs of houses, of whitewashed brick and pantiles, lined up as regular as soldiers on guard duty to either side of the main approach to the gates of the park. The new houses were very probably better built, almost certainly more sanitary and quite possibly more roomy than those they replaced, but no attempt was made to make them architecturally interesting. Perhaps if William Kent, Sir Robert's interior designer up at the Hall, had been asked to design the village the results might have been different – something like his *Faerie Queene* cottage designs.[51] In the 1760s the landscaping of the grounds of

Nuneham Courtenay in Oxfordshire under the direction of 'Capability' Brown led to the recreation of the village along the main Oxford road, a process that inspired Oliver Goldsmith's poem *The Deserted Village*. Commenting after a visit in 1772, William Gilpin wrote that Nuneham had been built 'with that regularity, which perhaps gives the most convenience to the dwellings of men. For this we readily relinquish the picturesque idea. Indeed I question, whether it were possible for a single hand to build a picturesque village.'[52] Half a century after Houghton, Sir William Chambers expended no more mental effort than Walpole's builder on the relocation of Milton Abbas [fig 2/18] in Dorset, when he was instructed by Lord Milton to remove the ancient market town that clustered around the abbey church and adjoining mansion. Chambers made designs for the houses, seemingly carried out around 1780, and these too are obstinately regular, uninventive and unpicturesque in the way they line up like peas in a pod along the new village street, albeit the street gently curves and is backed by trees.[53]

This attitude persisted even after the advent of the Picturesque. Uvedale Price, one of the chief gurus of the movement, dismissed the approach out of hand: 'Such a methodical arrangement saves all further thought and

2/18 Milton Abbas, Dorset: the village as rebuilt for
Lord Milton, *c.*1780

invention; but it is hardly necessary to say that nothing can be more formal and insipid.'[54] At Hulcote in Northamptonshire, the estate village for the great Hawksmoor house of Easton Neston, new Gothic houses were arranged round a green in about 1817–20, probably to designs by John Raffield, but certainly not picturesquely, as they are all very regular, symmetrical and devoid of ornamental features. The beginnings of a shift in approach can be detected at Ampthill, Bedfordshire. Here pairs of half-timbered and thatched houses, individually more charming and cottagey but still identical, are stationed along roads (Woburn Street, Woburn Road, Almeida Road) on the south-east edge of the Ampthill Park estate, with the dates 1812, 1815 and 1816. The idiom was based on the local vernacular, as were the cottages designed a few years earlier by George Dance junior at East Stratton near Winchester (1806), still individually un-picturesque in the by then fashionable sense of the word and still lined up along the road.[55]

By this stage, however, one of the leading lights in the Picturesque movement had already been applying his mind to the creation of picturesque village groupings. In his Red Book for George John Legh in 1791, Humphry Repton recommended developing an approach to the estate at High Legh in Cheshire via the existing village: 'the whole village may be so picturesquely ornamented as to mark that it belongs to the person whose name it bears'.[56] At Laxton in Northamptonshire, estate cottages of a more architecturally progressive kind than those of Milton Abbas or indeed Ampthill were built for George Evans-Freke, who in 1806 employed Humphry and his son John Adey Repton to supply designs; indeed, one pair of cottages (Nos 9 and 10) has a datestone of 1804. *The Beauties of England and Wales* (1810) confirms that 'several new and comfortable cottages' had already been built. They were originally roofed in thatch, and its replacement with tiles in the early twentieth century makes them look later than they are (say *c.*1840–50), as do the bargeboards, which the county historian Bruce Bailey thinks were added later.[57] The houses are mostly arranged in pairs around a green, but Woodland Cottage, just within the park, still has its thatch, and a rounded end with wooden columns – a reflection, no doubt, of Laugier's 'primitive hut' theories.[58]

BELOW **2/19** Blaise Hamlet, Bristol: Double Cottage and Rose Cottage

BOTTOM LEFT **2/20** Blaise Hamlet, Bristol: Dial Cottage, the pump and Circular Cottage

BOTTOM RIGHT **2/21** Blaise Hamlet, Bristol: the green, with Double Cottage (far left) and Circular Cottage (far right)

The *locus classicus* of the designed Picturesque village is of course Blaise Hamlet [figs 2/19–21] at Henbury on the outskirts of Bristol. In 1795 the Quaker banker John Scandrett Harford commissioned a new classical house from the local architect William Paty, on an attractive hilly estate four miles to the north-west of the city centre and therefore well away from its industrial pollution. Simultaneously with building the house Harford commissioned a Red Book from Humphry Repton (delivered early in 1796), and its recommendations were for once implemented almost in their entirety, with a long drive-way incorporating hairpin bends, caves, rocks and hanging woods (rather than the previous short approach from Henbury village). This was in a period when Repton was in partnership with Nash, to whom he mostly delegated any architectural embellishments of his landscapes. In this case Nash in due course supplied the designs for a delightful thatched ornamental dairy [59] and a gently curving arcaded conservatory. Repton's son George Stanley is said to have designed the castellated entrance lodge, which is very much in Nash's style. Down the drive and well away from the house is the (now vandalized) Timber Lodge, originally thatched and made of bark-covered logs like an eighteenth-century root house, though it is said to be of the 1840s.[60] Nothing precise seems to be known about the building, which sits immediately alongside Repton's drive and was clearly intended as an incident on the long approach to the main house. It was perhaps intended for a gamekeeper, since, further along, the drive passes a small building specifically designated Woodman's Cottage.

Nash's most celebrated contribution to the estate was the Hamlet, which he designed for Harford in 1810; by this stage Nash and Repton senior had fallen out, but Nash was still employing his two sons as office assistants. Intriguingly Nash had already been applying his mind to the challenge of the picturesque village, because in 1803 Richard Elsam noted in his *Essay on Rural Architecture* that

> a most admirable design for a village was publicly
> exhibited in the Royal Academy, a few years since,
> by that ingenious architect Mr. Nash, who by the
> most happy combination of ideas, proves himself a
> perfect master in this branch of the picturesque.[61]

It has sometimes been suggested[62] that Nash must have got the general idea from Marie Antoinette's Petit Hameau at Versailles, begun in 1783, but this private royal domain seems not to have been mentioned in English publications of the period, and Nash himself did not pay his first visit to France until 1814.[63] In any event, comprising nine little cottages (eight of them single, one double) arranged around a green, Blaise Hamlet is a compendium of Nash's previous cottage designs and was described by Nikolaus Pevsner as 'the nec plus ultra' of the Picturesque movement.[64] Nash was the first architect/planner to take to heart Uvedale Price's view that newly created villages should cluster around a green, rather than being lined up along a road, although local circumstances at Blaise precluded the winding stream and the grouping with the church tower that he recommended. The progress of the project can be traced in correspondence in the summer of 1810 between Harford and George Stanley Repton, through whom Nash, absent in Ireland, passed the drawings. Nash himself seems to have paid just two site visits, the first in 1810 to peg out the site and the other (probably in October 1811) to inspect work as it neared completion.

The process of designing and building the Hamlet is, by normal cottage orné standards, exceptionally well documented. The designs of each component cottage are recorded in Repton's 'Pavilion Notebook', and the progress of the commission can be followed in the Harford Papers.[65] Comparison between the drawings and the finished cottages proves that there was a good deal of last-minute adjustment of details for visual effect. This particularly applied to chimneys, lean-tos and outhouses, and indeed Repton emphasized to Harford that it was important to avoid uniformity in these elements, since much of the overall picturesque effect depended on them.[66] Although the houses were intended by Harford for retired employees and therefore had no interior features of decorative note, Nash put much thought and ingenuity into ensuring that externally each was different from the next – some thatched, some tiled, all with a variety of prominent Tudorish chimneys. Nash, via Repton, emphasized the visual importance of the chimneys, which he recommended should be constructed from custom-made moulded bricks. 'These kind of Chimney stacks', wrote Repton to Harford, 'are frequently seen in old Cottages – and generally in old Manor houses and buildings of the reign of Queen Elizabeth and invariably

produce a picturesque effect – their character requires they should be very high.'[67] Each cottage was given its own little verandah or external alcove with fitted seat, where the occupants could sit and enjoy a pint of ale of an evening.

The precise placing of each cottage in relation to the others was very carefully considered, and at Nash's suggestion the hamlet was sited away from the house in a wooded clearing.[68] The architect C. R. Cockerell later confirmed that it had been Nash's idea, not Harford's, to set the cottages apart, rather than arrange them at the entrance to the estate in a display of the landowner's liberality. The latter's benevolence, Nash apparently believed, should not be tarnished 'with the blazon of a coat of arms', since this would offend the self-respect of the elderly occupants by rubbing it in that they were recipients of charity.[69] If the aim was also to ensure peace and privacy to the residents, the Hamlet on the contrary achieved instant celebrity and has been a visitor attraction ever since. This latter fact certainly helped to spread its fame, for it became a popular outing for smart visitors to the spa facilities of Clifton and Bath.[70] Harford's son, conscious of the disruption to residents, introduced restrictions on visiting hours. Entrance to the site was through a gate guarded by a porter, who was under strict instructions to enforce the limited hours, outside which only residents and tradesmen were admitted. At the upper end of the social scale came Prince Hermann Pückler-Muskau in December 1828, who praised it highly in his travel journals. 'No more delightful or well-chosen spot could be found as a refuge for misfortune; its perfect seclusion and snugness breathe only peace and forgetfulness of the world.'[71] He noted that the cottages were 'enwreathed with various sorts of clematis, rose, honeysuckle and vine. . . . The gardens, divided by neat hedges, form a pretty garland of flowers and herbs around the whole village.' The Hamlet's social apogee was reached in 1845 with a visit from the Dowager Queen Adelaide, accompanied by a bevy of foreign royalty. A wider audience was secured by the publication of numerous engraved and painted views,[72] not to mention the production of china models of individual cottages. Such fame for what were basically working-class almshouses was unprecedented.

The Hamlet is an exceptional reflection of Harford's Quaker beneficence, especially since it was intended for

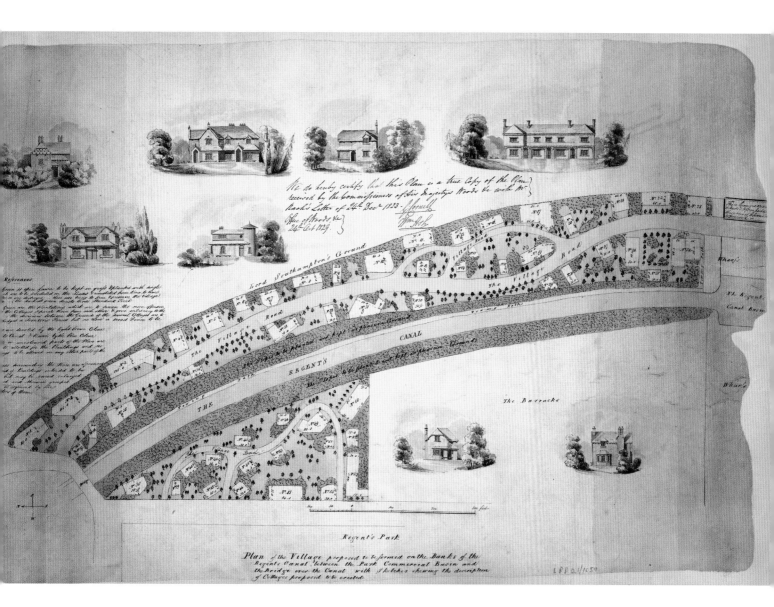

estate workers who had, strictly speaking, outlived their productive usefulness. From an architectural point of view, if not always a sociological one, it was to prove very influential. Nash himself considered following it up with a development on the edge of Regent's Park [fig 2/22], in 1823 submitting a plan with winding roads and little vignettes of Blaise-type cottages.[73] In the event this was not proceeded with. However, a direct link with Blaise can be found in Sir Thomas Dyke Acland's decision to create a hamlet on his Holnicote estate in north Somerset. Acland (10th baronet, 1787–1871), whose main seat was at

Killerton in Devon, had already in 1809[74] started tree-planting around the little village of Selworthy [fig 2/23], which at that stage comprised a church and seven farms. In 1828–9, inspired by a visit to Blaise, he removed some existing farm buildings, paddocks and yards to create a village green and added four new cottages, along with amenities such as lean-to extensions and outside toilets. The cottages were also enhanced with latticed windows (in some cases with ogee-headed lights), with one being given a projecting porch supported on posts plus an oriel, so that they became modestly orné. The project seems to have

been an in-house effort, with Acland acting as his own designer assisted by his estate staff. Like Blaise, the cottages are arranged around a communal lawn and were intended for estate pensioners, with a one-storey cottage for a girl to look after them – what would now be known as sheltered housing with onsite warden. Interestingly, Holnicote House was itself a substantial late eighteenth-century thatched 'cottage', probably begun soon after the early eighteenth-century mansion burned in 1779. It may not have had enough bedrooms to sleep forty for the hunting, as was traditionally said of it, but an early nineteenth-century watercolour shows it long and low, with a thatched roof, Gothick windows and a verandah entwined with creepers. After it burned in 1851 it was replaced in 1859–61 by another thatched, cottage-like house (itself burnt in 1941), designed by the Holnicote agent Robert Birmingham. His drawings for it survive, showing it more modest than its predecessor, with drawing room, library and dining room on the ground floor and six bedrooms above, but still firmly in the Georgian cottage orné tradition.[75] Acland was clearly a convinced admirer of

the cottage idiom, since elsewhere on the estate Buddle Hill is a collection of cottages with Acland additions, and the lodge here is picturesque and thatched, with Gothic glazing and bark nailed to the eaves. Not far from Selworthy, Sir John Trevelyan moved the village on his Nettlecombe estate in the 1790s, and at Woodford (north-east of the main house) there survives a grouping of cottages and houses apparently designed by James Babbage, the agent, from the 1820s onward.[76]

One of the earlier examples of what might be called a village orné occurs at Marford [fig 2/24] in Flintshire, which has been described as 'one of the most imaginatively designed Picturesque villages in Britain'.[77] As so often, dates are hard to come by, but it was seemingly rebuilt between 1805 and 1820 at the instigation of George Boscawen, a descendant of the Trevor family, who came into possession of the Trevors' Trevalyn Hall estate in 1805 at the age of sixty-five, although he never lived there. Different local traditions suggest that Boscawen's wife was the architect; that the inspiration was buildings in France; and that the incorporation of blind cross-shaped recesses on some was to ward off the ghost of the wife of an early eighteenth-century steward. The name of John Nash has also, inevitably, been bandied about. In fact the idiom is an idiosyncratic late development of that of William Kent, combining open-based dentilled classical pediments with Gothic windows (some with fanciful iron glazing referred to in contemporary estate papers),[78] floating Tudor hood-moulds, and an evident love of shallow curved bows, characteristic of the Regency. Unlike Blaise or Selworthy, the houses are mainly haphazardly arranged along the main road that runs through the village, so they do not

cohere visually in anything like the convincingly pictur-esque manner of those exemplars.

Old Warden village [figs 2/25, 26] in Bedfordshire was rebuilt from the mid-1820s for Lord Ongley (1803−77), who settled there after leaving Oxford. He had apparently been much taken with Switzerland on his Grand Tour travels and wished to reflect this on his estate, though whether most visitors would now recognize his Swiss intentions is very doubtful, since the idiom used to dress up the village – thatched roofs, simple Gothic windows, verandahs of trellis, tree trunks or simple posts

2/25 Old Warden, Bedfordshire, a village rebuilt
from the mid-1820s
2/26 Old Warden, Bedfordshire

– is not noticeably different from the stock-in-trade of the cottage orné popular since the late eighteenth century. Furthermore, it is deployed in one of England's flattest landscapes. More specifically Swiss, perhaps, is the skilful way in which cottages are grouped on grassy banks, with fir trees providing a dark backdrop. In Lord Ongley's day the effect was heightened by his insistence that the ladies of the village wear red cloaks and tall hats.[79] The village very successfully deploys a variety of designs, with no two cottages being exactly the same although motifs recur. The effect, overall and individually, is generally one of artful simplicity, with the exception of one cottage that has elaborately sinuous eaves, a massive spiral-fluted chimney and semicircular dormers with pretty radial

glazing, like half-rose windows. If Ongley employed a designer, it may have been J. B. Papworth, who had local connections (and indeed spent the last months of his life not far away at Little Paxton, near St Neots). A number of the designs in his *Rural Residences* (1818) feature the semi-circular eyebrows of thatch over windows that appear on most of the cottages in Old Warden and in the neighbouring village of Northill.[80]

The impulse to prettify estate villages seems to have gathered momentum in the 1820s and 1830s. At Horringer in Suffolk, the estate cottages for the great neoclassical mansion of Ickworth acquired modest embellishments in the time of the 5th Earl (later 1st Marquess) of Bristol (inherited 1803, died 1859). There

is nothing fancy, but some variety, as presumably they were existing cottages titivated. Some of the village houses at Great Tew in Oxfordshire were made more picturesque in the 1820s during the tenure of Matthew Robinson Boulton, probably using as architect Thomas Rickman, best known as a designer of Gothic churches and inventor of the nomenclature of English medieval architecture.[81] A particularly attractive example of the phenomenon is Easton in Suffolk [figs 2/27, 28], where the estate was acquired by the 10th Duke of Hamilton (1767–1852, also 7th Duke of Brandon, a Suffolk title) in 1830.[82] Hamilton was an interesting character, a leading dandy in

his younger days and described as 'the proudest man in England', who instructed that on his death he was to be mummified and buried in an ancient Egyptian sarcophagus. Given his apparent obsession with his status and lineage, Hamilton must certainly have been responsible for building four circular cottages at Easton, adorned with the ducal coronet. With their steep conical thatched roofs rising to a central chimney, these conform to a type of lodge that appears in a number of early nineteenth-century pattern books – for instance the Circular Cottage in John Plaw's *Sketches for Country Houses* of 1800 [fig 4/7],[83] and J. B. Papworth's design for a lodge in *Ornamental*

Gardening of 1823 – but both in the detail of the fenestration and the rather hard red brick used they have a later, perhaps mid-nineteenth-century, feel. Other cottages in Easton are clearly existing buildings that have been made gently orné by the addition of simple Gothic glazing or a twiggy porch (for instance an attractive group fronting the green that includes the White Horse pub), but these retain the light-hearted, rather papery charm of Georgian Gothick, which begs the question of whether the alterations were done very early in the duke's reign or indeed under his predecessor.

Other villages where some effort appears to have been made by the local landowner to improve the general appearance include Erlestoke in Wiltshire; Ockley in Surrey (where the cottages are well spaced out on the edge of an enormous green); and Little Bredy in Dorset. At Sulham in Berkshire one cottage orné is a very superior thatched lodge, sporting lofty and ornate chimneys and a bowed verandah smart enough to lift it out of the working-class category, while another, also thatched, has bogus half-timbering liberally applied to its walls. One of the later examples of the Blaise effect is at Somerleyton [fig 2/29] in north Suffolk. Here Sir Morton Peto, entrepreneur and railway builder, created a new model village some time between 1844, when he began rebuilding Somerleyton Hall, and 1862 when financial difficulties forced him to put the estate on the market (he went bankrupt in 1866); the primary school is dated 1845. The designer is likely to have been John Thomas, architect of the main mansion. A number of houses, mostly twin units but in one case made up of no fewer than five, are placed around the perimeter of a green, though slightly too spread out to cohere in the Blaise manner. Thomas achieved considerable variety, some of the cottages being prosaically of brick and tile but others having sham half-timbering in different patterns, clustered chimneys and undulating thatch. The most attractive component, the school, combines half-timbering (painted the estate colour of maroon), tea-cosy thatch, latticed windows and elaborately patterned chimneys. When the estate was sold they were described as 'twenty-eight cottage residences, of a most Substantial and a highly Ornamental character – showing, in the Domestic Arrangement and in the Sleeping Apartments, a singular and rare attention to the comfort and morality of Peasant Families'.[84]

1 See Chapter Six.

2 See Chapter Four.

3 P. F. Robinson, *Village Architecture* (London,1830), 'Address'.

4 Charles Waistell, *Designs for Agricultural Buildings* (London, 1827), p. 1.

5 Robinson, *Village Architecture*.

6 The date is inscribed on the panel on the projecting centre. See Roger White, 'John Vardy, 1718–65', in Roderick Brown, ed., *The Architectural Outsiders* (London, 1984), pp. 75–6. The drawing is at Hackwood Park.

7 See J. Poesch, 'An American Cottage in Kent', *Country Life* (27 April 1978).

8 Although in 1807, disappointed of finding sufficient British commissions, he was to emigrate to Canada.

9 John Plaw, *Ferme Ornée* (London, 1795), pl. 17; *Sketches for Country Houses*, pl. XIV.

10 Geoffrey Tyack, 'From Practice to Printed Page',*Country Life* (4 February 2008). Plaw's influence on post-1800 cottage orné design will be discussed in Chapter Four.

11 Abbé Marc-Antoine Laugier, *Essai sur l'Architecture*, 2nd edn (Paris, 1755).

12 Timothy Mowl and Brian Earnshaw, *Trumpet at a Distant Gate: The Lodge as Prelude to the Country House* (London, 1985), p. 142.

13 I owe this observation to Dr Edward McParland.

14 For Chaloner Arcedeckne. See George Carter, Patrick Goode and Kedrun Laurie, *Humphry Repton, Landscape Gardener* (Norwich, 1982), p. 162.

15 Ibid., p. 160.

16 Thomas Dearn, *Designs for Lodges and Entrances*, (London, 1823 edn), description to pl. VI.

17 P. F. Robinson, *Rural Architecture*, 2nd edition (London, 1823), p. ii.

18 J. B. Papworth, *Rural Residences* (London, 1818), p. 77.

19 Humphry Repton, *Observations on the Theory and Practice on Landscape Gardening* (London, 1803), p. 142.

20 Another good example is the tiny lodge to Horsecroft Hall, just south of Bury St Edmunds in Suffolk.

21 The lodge, in the village of Codford, is now severed from the Stockton estate by a bypass.

22 Stylistically the lodge is difficult to date, and there are no records for its construction, but it has the same latticed windows as on Sherborne Castle (and other of its estate buildings), which were installed in 1788/9. However, Mrs Ann Smith, Sherborne Castle archivist, believes that it is one of a series of lodges and keeper's cottages built by George Wingfield Digby after he inherited in 1856, noting the existence of another thatched cottage in the castle park built in 1857. If that is the approximate date, Mrs Smith feels the architect might be Philip Hardwick, then working on the restoration of the castle, who also designed other buildings on the estate. Personal communication.

23 Demolished after World War II.

24 The lodge was probably originally an adjunct to the Old Hall at Langton. In 1829 the squire, John Langton, is recorded as having built a barn to his own design and using bricks made on the estate. *British Farmers' Magazine*, III (August 1829), p. 259, cited by John Martin Robinson in *Georgian Model Farms* (Oxford, 1983), p. 60. Nearby at Scremby (once associated with the demolished Scremby Hall) is a close relative, though this time on a rectangular plan with rounded end towards the road, the overhang supported on rustic posts.

25 The lodge is currently sadly neglected.

26 Possibly in association with Humphry Repton's proposals for J. Sutton's estate. See Michael Mansbridge, *John Nash* (London, 1991), p. 60.

27 Nash enlarged the mansion house for Richard Erle-Drax-Grosvenor in 1810. Mansbridge, *John Nash*, p. 163.

28 Mowl and Earnshaw, *Trumpet at a Distant Gate*, p. 142.

29 A second, less interesting, Gothic cottage exists on the opposite, northern, edge of Staverton Thicks, where it was intended for the estate shepherd. There is some doubt as to the actual owner of the woodland in the late Georgian period, but by 1800 it may have become part of the neighbouring Rendlesham estate, then owned by Peter Isaac Thellusson, 1st Baron Rendlesham (d. 1808). For him, apparently, Repton landscaped the grounds pre-1803, and at about the same time J. B. Papworth produced unexecuted designs for alterations to the main house. Peter Reid, *Burke's & Savills Guide to Country Houses: East Anglia* (London, 1981), p. 258, and information from Dr James Bettley.

30 I am indebted for information on Hex Cottage to Argus Gathorne-Hardy, who superintended the recent immaculate restoration.

31 I owe this suggestion to Dr James Bettley.

32 I am grateful to Peter Speke for showing me the cottage and the shell house.

33 This combination of steep-pitched gables and triangular-headed windows also occurs at Four Gables, Clayhanger, Wadeford, Somerset (Jackson-Stops sale particulars).

34 About a mile down the road towards Wimborne is another house obviously by the same architect, with triangle-headed windows, though in this case combined with a tiled roof, frilly eaves and red brick. In the locality Evans also designed Sturminster Newton Church in 1825–7, in correct Perpendicular Gothic; Hurst Bridges at Affpuddle (1839) in his capacity as county surveyor, and Walford Bridge in Wimborne (1802). *The Buildings of England* volume for Dorset (John Newman and Nikolaus Pevsner (Harmondsworth, 1972), p. 74) notes that Alderholt Church of 1849 also has windows with triangular tops – and indeed quotes the twentieth-century architect and writer H. S. Goodhart-Rendel as commenting that it looked like 'the latest thing' by the Arts & Crafts architect E. S. Prior.

35 Colvin, B.D., p. 554.

36 Ibid., p. 554 cites Wiltshire Record Office 451/74 (ix), and *Country Life* (29 June 1951), pp. 2040–44.

37 *Country Life*, loc. cit.

38 According to Nigel Temple ('In Search of the Cottage Picturesque', *Georgian Group Report & Journal* (1988) p. 77), the present chimneys are 'recent replacements of incredibly complex quasi-classical ones'.

39 G. S. Repton, Pavilion Notebook, Brighton Art Gallery & Museums. This connection was first proposed by Nigel Temple in his article 'In Search of the Cottage Picturesque', although Temple also suggested non-specific comparisons with the work of P. F. Robinson. For Blaise Hamlet. see below, pp. 46–8.

40 RIBA Drawings Collection SKB246/4.

41 Mowl and Earnshaw, *Trumpet at a Distant Gate*, p. 137.

42 Much of the agricultural land was sold off during the course of the twentieth century, and after the death of the last private owner in 1968 the council bought what was left as public open space and golf course. Peter Rooke, *Cheshunt's Past in Pictures* (Ware, 1994).

43 According to Rooke, *Cheshunt's Past in Pictures*; and not shells as the *Buildings of England* volume for Hertfordshire (Nikolaus Pevsner, 2nd edn, rev. Bridget Cherry (Harmondsworth, 1977), p. 127) says. The English Heritage list description refers to industrial clinker and glass.

44 Roger White, 'Gothic Wonders; Taymouth Castle, Perthshire', *Country Life* (9 January 2013), pp. 42–7.

45 Jones, *Follies and Grottoes*, p. 190, describes the tree-trunk columns continuing along the sides, but if this were ever so they have completely disappeared.

46 Ibid.

47 Sale particulars of 2012 maintain that the building was probably designed as the focal point of a terrace on the castle side of the Tay that stretched for over 450 yards from Maxwell's Temple to the river bank opposite the lodge. Savills, Perth, January 2012.

48 Jones, *Follies and Grottoes*. The word 'Barchinome' remains a mystery.

49 But see Chapter Six.

50 An earlier example was the village of Chippenham, Cambridgeshire, rebuilt in about 1702 as a series of identical linked cottages.

51 See Chapter One, p. 12.

52 William Gilpin, *Observations, Relative Chiefly to Picturesque Beauty, made in the year 1772* (1786), i. p. 22.

53 Uvedale Price was especially keen on the visual conjunction of cottages and trees. 'Trees, whether singly or in groups . . . are obviously of the greatest use in accompanying buildings of every kind, but there seems to be a much closer union between them and low buildings. Cottages appear to repose under their shade, to be protected, sometimes supported by them; and they on the other hand, hang over and embrace the cottages with their branches.' *Essays on the Picturesque* (1810), ii, p. 351.

54 Ibid., ii, p. 346.

55 J. C. Loudon was to comment in 1836 that 'There is not a greater error in forming artificial villages . . . than always having one side of the buildings parallel with the road', *Encyclopaedia of Cottage, Farm and Villa Architecture* (1836).

56 Quoted in Nigel Temple, *John Nash and the Village Picturesque* (Gloucester, 1979), Appendix V, p. 144.

57 Bruce Bailey, Nikolaus Pevsner and Bridget Cherry, *The Buildings of England: Northamptonshire* (New Haven and London, 2013) p. 387.

58 The Laxton cottage is very similar to that in the grounds of Glevering Hall, Suffolk, where Repton also worked.

59 See Chapter One, p. 26.

60 The timber is in fact applied as a decorative facing to stone walls, which is one reason why the building has survived recent vicissitudes.

61 Richard Elsam, *Essay on Rural Architecture* (London, 1803), note to p. 3.

62 For instance, John Morley, *Regency Design* (London, 1993), p. 83.

63 Colvin, B.D., p. 729.

64 Andrew Foyle and Nikolaus Pevsner, *The Buildings of England: Somerset: North and Bristol* (New Haven and London, 2011), p. 400.

65 Brighton Pavilion Art Gallery and Museum, FA10369. The designs, and specific examples of their influence, are examined in detail in Nigel Temple, *George Repton's Pavilion Notebook* (Aldershot, 1993); Bristol Record Office.

66 Repton to Harford, 23 August 1810.

67 Temple, *John Nash and the Village Picturesque*, Appendix IV, pp. 132, 135.

68 The wooded backdrop of the houses is now much reduced.

69 David Watkin, *The Life and Work of C. R. Cockerell* (London, 1974), pp. 80–81.

70 In Jane Austen's *Northanger Abbey* (originally written 1798–9 and posthumously published in 1817) the heroine expresses a keen desire to visit Blaise to see the Castle, although in the event the expedition from Bath does not take place. Cockerell, not always an admirer of Nash, enthused that the cottages were 'so beautiful that [the Hamlet] is a sight visited from Clifton'. Watkin, *The Life and Work of C. R. Cockerell*.

71 Hermann Pückler-Muskau, *Tour in England, Ireland and France, in the years 1828 & 1829* (1832), ii, pp. 204–5.

72 For instance, George Davey's lithographs of 1826, which illustrated all the Blaise cottages on one sheet, thereby publicizing the full variety of Nash's designs. The introduction noted that 'a visit to them has long formed a favourite Excursion from the village of Clifton and the city of Bristol'.

73 PRO, MPE 911, cited in Temple, *John Nash and the Village Picturesque*, p. 106 and pl. 72. For the evolution of the Regent's Park project as a whole, see J. Mordaunt Crook, 'John Nash and the Genesis of Regent's Park', in Geoffrey Tyack ed., *John Nash, Architect of the Picturesque* (Swindon, 2013), pp. 75–100.

74 The year after he inherited the estate and married Lydia Hoare of Stourhead.

75 Cheryl and Charles Carson, 'A Brief History of Holnicote House', research carried out for the National Trust, 2006, kindly supplied by Ann Lund.

76 Julian Orbach and Nikolaus Pevsner, *Buildings of England: South and West Somerset* (New Haven and London, 2014), p. 484.

77 Brian Earnshaw and Timothy Mowl, 'Mysterious and Unlucky', *Country Life* (22 February 1979), pp. 454–6.

78 The Trevalyn Estate records (Flintshire Record Office, D/TR/34) include the 1815 account of Thomas Jones, ironmonger of Wrexham, with George Boscawen, which lists such component items as 'iron windows with two lights and Gothic tops', 'circular windows' and 'pinnacle ornaments'.

79 *Murray's Guide to Hertfordshire, Bedfordshire and Buckinghamshire* (1895) commented on this, noting that the red matched the paintwork on the cottages.

80 Mavis Batey, 'An English View of Switzerland', *Country Life* (17 February 1977), pp. 364–6.

81 Mavis Batey, 'Pioneer in Preservation: Great Tew, Oxfordshire', *Country Life* (8 March 1979), p. 660.

82 The estate was sold up in 1919 and the main house demolished in 1923.

83 John Plaw, *Sketches for Country Houses* (London, 1800), pl. XII.

84 Sale particulars at Somerleyton Hall, quoted by Gillian Darley, *Villages of Vision* (London, 1978), p. 70, and reproduced in Mark Girouard, *The Victorian Country House* (London, 1979), endpapers. In the gardens of the mansion itself stands another thatched cottage, its walls divided into panels of brick nogging by a timber frame, while Park Cottage, built as a thatched gamekeeper's cottage with detached game larder, has a timber-framed upper floor and roughcast walls.

CHAPTER THREE

AN ABSTRACT OF EDEN

The Middle-Class Cottage

In 1766 Mrs Mary Delany – nowadays known as a peerless creator of *papiers decoupés* – drew a vignette [fig 3/1] of an imaginary rustic cottage, with latticed windows, creepers growing up the walls and French windows opening directly into an informal garden. Underneath she added a poem of her own composing, entitled 'The Cottage', which catches very well the growing sympathy of at least some sections of the educated middle classes – what in the eighteenth century might have been referred to as 'the middling sort', both rural gentry and urban professional – for Nature and simplicity.

A sweeter spot of Earth was never found.
I look & look, & still with new delight;
Such joy my soul, such pleasure fills my sight:
Here the fresh Eglantine, exhales a breath;
Whose odours are of power to raise from Death:
And Nature seems to vary the delight,
To satisfy at once the swell, and sight.
Nor sullen discontent, nor anxious care,
Ev'n tho' brought hither, can inhabit here:
But hence they flee, as from their mortal Foe;
For this sweet place can only pleasure know.

Mrs Delany, although an Englishwoman of intellectual interests and borderline aristocratic background, was in 1766 married to an Irish clergyman and living on the outskirts of Dublin, so her circumstances might certainly at that stage be called 'middling'.[1] She has been described as 'an enthusiast for the Picturesque *avant la lettre*',[2] and already in 1746 had remarked, on an outing to Leixlip on the River Liffey upstream of Dublin, that 'every step shews you some new wild beauty of wood, rocks and cascades'.[3] Her cottage is not architecturally orné in the sense of, say, Mrs Lybbe Powys's Straw Hall, but her poem unconsciously echoes the Reverend James Merrill's poetic tribute to Egge Cottage at Edgehill[4] and prefigures by nearly half a century the similar sentiments of Jane Austen's characters.[5]

The classically educated eighteenth-century Englishman grew up with a familiarity with Roman authors such as Virgil, Horace and Pliny who praised the virtues of rural life, and in very general terms living in the country away from urban vices came to be considered an admirable thing.[6] Such rural retreat was not at this stage a reaction to industrialization, of course, but fitted into a much older polarity between London and elsewhere. Edmund Bartell, writing in 1804, claimed that 'perhaps, of all situations, the romantic retirement of a rural cottage is likely to produce the highest and most refined relish for social happiness',[7] while J. C. Loudon in 1838 considered that

such is the superiority of all rural occupations and pleasures, that commerce, large societies or crowded cities, may be justly reckoned unnatural. . . . Indeed, the very purpose for which we engage in commerce is that we may one day be enabled to retire to the country, where alone we picture ourselves days of solid satisfaction and undisturbed happiness.[8]

Political power was in any case property-based; landowners might exercise their power in London, but they spent a good deal of time on their estates, even if this was primarily to enjoy the country pursuits of hunting and shooting. It was not however necessary to own a country estate to develop a sentimental attachment to the countryside and to rural life. By the middle decades of the eighteenth century, well before the promulgation of theories of the Picturesque by such pundits as Richard Payne Knight and Uvedale Price, the rapid popularization of the English landscape park was leading to a reassessment of what was scenically attractive.[9] Heightened awareness of natural beauty tempted the middle classes to visit 'picturesque' areas, and to build themselves rural retreats. As will be discussed in the next chapter, many of the numerous pattern books published between the 1780s and 1830s were aimed at this sector of society. The earliest was John Plaw's *Rural Architecture* of 1785 – so successful that it ran into at least eight editions – and it was quickly followed by others aimed at a similar audience: what Robert Lugar, in the title of his *Architectural Sketches for Cottages, Rural Dwellings and Villas* (1805) referred to as 'persons of genteel life and moderate fortune'.[10]

Such a term could be applied to a much wider social spectrum than the cottage or lodge intended for peasants and other bottom-end employees. J. B. Papworth, in his

3/1 Mrs Mary Delany, vignette, 1766

pattern book *Rural Residences* of 1818, contended that the term 'cottage orné' was not in fact applicable to the latter at all.

> The cottage orné is a new species of building in the economy of domestic architecture, and subject to its own laws of fitness and propriety. It is not the habitation of the laborious, but of the affluent, of the man of study, of science or of leisure.[11]

An early and unusually well-documented example of a 'gentry' cottage is Sealwood Cottage at Linton in Derbyshire, designed about 1774 by the hack writer and satirist William Combe (1742–1823, author of *The Tour of Dr Syntax in Search of the Picturesque*). His client was the Reverend Thomas Gresley of Netherseal (1734–1785), to whom Combe described his proposals in a letter in October 1773. The cottage was intended for occasional use, as Gresley, a squarson (that is, a squire who was also the local parson), lived at Netherseal Hall, about one and a half miles away, to which it was connected by a drive through a wood. It stood on the edge of the wood, commanding pleasant rural views. The upper room had a canted bay window, plastered walls with dado and cornice, a slate chimneypiece, and a pull-out bed in case Gresley (a widower) wanted to stay overnight. The structure was timber-framed with brick infill, simple Gothic windows and a thatched roof.[12]

Combe's letter is very interesting both in the specific justification advanced for a person of Gresley's class building a cottage as opposed to any other type of house, and for the suggestions regarding planting, which was clearly considered an integral part of the conception.

> On the wood front [i.e. facing the wood] there cannot be too much Ivy; if it is entirely covered with it the better. This ornament is highly natural, and by increasing the gloom of the Entrance will heighten the pleasure of the surprise which is to succeed from the opposite windows. – If a Passion flower also were suffered to creep up the wall on the side of the Door, the Variety would increase, without violating the character of the building.[13]

His preference was for the ferme ornée:

> It possesses a simplicity & variety of character superior to both [the park or garden]. It has more to do with nature than either – I am now considering a Farm merely as it produces a great Variety of Embellishments natural to the rural scene – Among these a Cottage has always been a favourite, & where it is built & dispos'd in character, is more pleasing, because it is more natural, [than] the most costly Temples of Greece, where they are erected to grace the Verdure of an English Lawn.

Sealwood Cottage was to function as a rustic building to which a well-heeled clergyman might retreat for a few hours of relaxation. Within a relatively short time, and certainly by the end of the century, members of the 'middling' social ranks were coming to regard the cottage as somewhere in which they might take up temporary or even permanent residence. This seems to have been particularly true of prosperous merchants and the like in the environs of provincial cities and towns. Ham Hill, at Powick near Worcester [fig 3/2], was built for an unknown client some time after 1800, at which stage it was a small thatched cottage orientated to look northwards over the Teme valley towards the tower of Worcester Cathedral. In this original form it was symmetrical, with elaborate chimneys and a thatched roof and verandah; since there were service rooms in the basement but no first floor to contain bedrooms, it was presumably used for day trips from the city. Thomas France, a rich Worcester cordwainer (maker of shoes and other leather goods), acquired it at some point before 1837,[14] by which date a taller addition on the south side was in place,[15] and this now towers over the earlier building.[16] Orientated in the opposite direction, towards the sun, it made the cottage into a full-time residence. Except at the upper social levels cottages ornés rarely seem to have had elaborate interiors, but the original section of Ham Hill is a happy exception. A panelled Gothic door with octagonal leading in its ogee tracery opens into a rib-vaulted entrance hall, a theme continued in the umbrella-like vault of the dining room [fig 3/3]. Panels of painted glass showing the house from two different angles, copied from the 1837 lithographs, are incorporated into the glazing of one window [fig 3/4]. Most welcome is the survival of a complete window (in the china closet opening off the dining room) glazed in

the typical late Georgian colours of amber and orange [fig 3/5].

Successful local bankers – or perhaps their wives – were another profession for whom a cottage residence on the outskirts of their local urban centre had an appeal. A mile and a half south out of Bury St Edmunds, the county town of West Suffolk, stood Nowton Cottage, built from 1801 onwards for O. R. Oakes, the son of the Bury banker James Oakes. A local publication, *Frost's New Town and Country Ladies Memorandum Book and Fashionable Repository* for 1835,[17] has on its title page a vignette entitled 'Cottage at Nowton', which shows the house to have been quite large and irregular, partly Tudor Gothic and partly thatched and cottagey. A lengthy encomium of its extensive grounds avers that

> to the lovers of nature, this Arcadian little spot offers a variety of attractions. The taste, neatness, elegance and simplicity of the building, whether seen from the grounds or witnessed from within, supply as full an idea of polished contentment, rustic enjoyment, suburban ease, and wealthy independence, as anything to be met with within the limits of the habitable globe. The grounds are a positive abstract

of Eden – an abridgement of Hesperides. . . . From whatever point these grounds and the Cottage are viewed, the eye is presented with a cluster of the most beautiful pictures, placed in a light such as a skilful artists would desire to have a finished painting put in, on which depends the immortality of his fame. Art and nature are so interwoven, that the whole prospect appears like the creation of a fairy dream . . . . The view of Bury from one part of these grounds is exceedingly picturesque.

Unfortunately the cottage so described was replaced after Oakes's death in 1837 with the present, less attractive building.[18] One banker's cottage that does survive is Harford Hills House on the southern outskirts of Norwich, which was built some time between 1807 and 1824 for Joseph Gurney, a partner in the local Quaker banking firm. The house has been much expanded sideways over the years, but the original square thatched nucleus still dominates, a very striking design framed on its main elevation around three deep arches, within which are trefoiled oculi. It seems likely that as originally built this nucleus contained just four spacious rooms – entrance hall, staircase hall, drawing room and dining room – on the ground floor, with bedrooms above. A service wing projects at the rear. No architect is known, but a possible source for the façade design might be found in John Plaw's *Sketches for Country Houses* of 1800.[19] Another substantial cottage with Quaker banking connections in the Norwich hinterland is Bergh Apton

House, originally part of the Brooke House estate and known as The Cottage. This seems to have been built by George Samuel Kett, the only son of Thomas Kett and his Quaker wife Hannah Gurney, who succeeded to the property in 1820; the house is clearly marked on Bryant's map of 1826,[20] and the tithe map of Norfolk drawn up in 1839 confirms Kett's ownership of a sizeable acreage in the parish. The cottage comprises a taller main section and lower range at right angles, all thatched and with Gothic windows and lofty chimneys.[21]

A good example of a cottage orné built for a prosperous provincial tradesman is Selwood Lodge [fig 3/6], which at the time of its erection stood in an area of farmland and orchards a mile or so from the centre of the wool town of Frome in Somerset. It seems originally to have been known as Selwood Cottage, and is said to have been built in 1825 by Charles Willoughby, a local grocer.[22] Within a few years it had been bought by Thomas Sheppard, the eldest son of George Sheppard, Frome's leading cloth manufacturer; the 1851 census lists him living there with five children and five servants.[23] The distinctive features of the exterior are the use of two prominent rounded bows, each with a tripartite Gothic window on the first floor, and the verandah that wraps around them, supported not on rustic posts but on curved brackets. As usual, nothing is known of the architect – and it is clearly architect-designed; but if the tiled roofs are mentally replaced with the thatch they must surely once have had, then a strong kinship becomes apparent with Nash's Circular Cottage at Blaise Hamlet,

which has the same rounded end and precisely the same verandah arrangement. The Gothic porch that punctuates the verandah can be paralleled at Blaise's Sweet Briar Cottage, and there are also strong similarities to a design for the Keeper's House at Sarsgrove in Oxfordshire, which is generally attributed to G. S. Repton.[24]

Selwood Lodge is illustrative of the simpler, even austere end of the cottage orné spectrum. Austerity is perhaps a surprising quality to find in a genre generally associated with ornamental embellishments, but it is certainly present in the gamut of designs put forward by the numerous architectural pattern books of the period.[25] It is there in some though not all of Nash's cottage designs, and most of those by G. S. Repton. Repton's preference for simplicity is confirmed by Sarsgrove Cottage [fig 3/7] on the Oxfordshire–Gloucestershire border, a house that he remodelled circa 1829–30 for the two unmarried daughters of John Haughton Langston, a London merchant banker who had bought the Sarsden estate in 1792.[26] Langston developed a passion for building and maintaining his country estate, but on paper at least he conformed to the type of incomer described by Love Peacock's old man in *Melincourt* as a 'vundholder'.[27] The cottage, buried deep in a wood well away from the main house (on which Repton also worked, as had his father and possibly his brother John Adey), was intended for rather isolated full-time occupation rather than as an occasional retreat. The exterior combines Cotswold ashlar walls with Cotswold stone-tiled roofs, all arranged with studied asymmetry. There is very little to relieve the general simplicity, except for a single-storey bow to the drawing room, which has a ring of tree-trunk columns in the Laugier manner; further such tree-trunk columns form a loggia containing the front door. The slight frilling of the eaves hardly begins to relieve the general sobriety. Restraint is also the hallmark of the interiors, with the exception of the drawing room, which has a cross-vaulted ceiling rather in the manner of Wyatville or Soane. As seems to have been the case with most cottages of this category, the ground floor was given over to the drawing room, dining room, entrance hall and staircase, with a generous service wing partially screened by planting.[28]

The same basic elements found at Selwood Lodge and Blaise Hamlet were found shuffled into a slightly different arrangement at Rose Hill Cottage [figs 3/8, 9] near

Henley-on-Thames: the rounded bow with verandah wrapped round it, the Gothic porch, the clustered chimneys, the main difference being that here the verandah supports were slender tree trunks with their branches left on. This, the traceried French windows within, and the slightly more elaborate porch, produced a less austere overall effect. Here the design was not by Repton but by Robert Lugar, the client being James Franklin Nicholas. The published plan shows the porch opening into an octagonal vaulted hall, with the living room to the right, the dining room ahead and the staircase to the left, so overall quite a modest amount of accommodation. No precise date is known except that it predates 1811 when Lugar illustrated it in his *Plans and Views*.[29]

Another possible Reptonian exercise in restraint is Angeston Grange [fig 3/10], near Uley in Gloucestershire, built soon after 1811 for the Nonconformist clothier Nathaniel Lloyd, whose fortune had been made by the surge in demand for heavy-cloth uniforms created by the Napoleonic wars. The asymmetrical grouping of the gables and the deployment of tall, ornamented chimneys seems to reflect newly completed Blaise Hamlet, not so far away;[30] but in the way the plan cranks around to follow the contours of the wooded hillside against which it is set, Angeston irresistibly seems to recall the Duke of Bedford's much more substantial cottage at Endsleigh in Devon,[31] designed by Jeffry Wyatt and likewise newly completed. In fact the similarity to Endsleigh would originally have been less marked because Angeston was much smaller, its present spreading extent being the result of considerable and unusually sympathetic extension in 1874. The original house, as confirmed by a sale inventory of 1826 (when

3/8 Rose Hill Cottage, near Henley-on-Thames,
Oxfordshire: Robert Lugar's perspective

3/9 Rose Hill Cottage, near Henley-on-Thames, plan

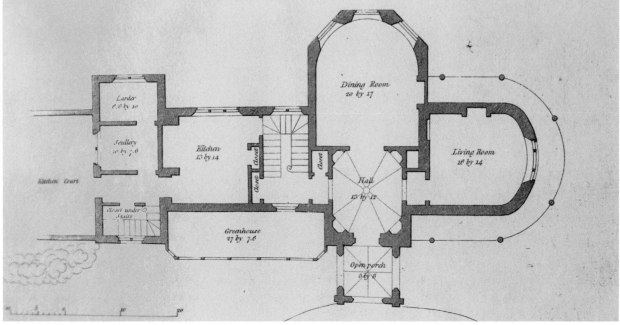

AN ABSTRACT OF EDEN   65

Lloyd became bankrupt), was just one room deep, with three reception rooms – dining room, billiard room and library – each accessed from the octagonal stairhall, with its elegant cantilevered staircase. Although the approach to the house is now by a winding drive from the bottom of the valley, in Lloyd's time it was from the top of the hill via his cloth mill, suggesting that ultimately his priority was commerce over aesthetics.[32] It is worth noting here, however, that while the idea of a cottage orné might appeal to a cloth manufacturer in the otherwise bucolic Cotswolds, in the grittier north of England such people – along with professionals such as lawyers and doctors – invariably built themselves classical boxes in the environs of the growing industrial centres of Manchester, Sheffield or Leeds.[33]

A recurrent feature of those who commissioned cottages for themselves seems to have been their adherence to religious nonconformity in general and Quakerism in particular. Jabez Gibson (1794–1838) was a Quaker banker and brewer of Saffron Walden in Essex,[34] who acquired a half-timbered vernacular cottage belonging to one of the many farms surrounding the town, probably some time in the 1820s or early 1830s. Either he or his son transformed the cottage into Reed Lodge [fig 3/11], extending and encasing it in buff-coloured 'Suffolk' bricks, with an enormous thatched roof with steeply pitched gables and dormers, and clustered chimney stacks. The gable at the centre of the street front, probably representing the late medieval cottage, projects and incorporates the entrance porch, within which is a panelled door in Jacobean style. The simple Tudor mullioned windows are glazed in octagon patterns, and at the rear French windows give access to the once extensive grounds. The main rear gable has exaggeratedly large cusped eaves, though the others are plain.[35] It is not perhaps too far fetched to suggest that it was the theoretical unpretentiousness of the cottage style, with its implications of living a simple life, that made it more attractive to financially successful but pious Nonconformists like Gibson than the prospect of commissioning a smart classical villa.[36] The cottage idiom was also chosen by Mrs Hannah More, writer, philanthropist and social reformer, when she built Barley Wood near Wrington in Somerset in about 1801–2. An early engraving shows a thatched house with full-height bow and encircling creeper-covered verandah, beautifully set on a hillside to command views to the sea.[37]

The Nonconformist place of worship was characteristically a simple brick box, but in one case at least it was a cottage orné chapel. Charles Metcalf and his wife Elizabeth, though landowners in rural Bedfordshire rather than involved in commerce, were resolute non-attenders at their local Anglican parish church in Roxton. This meant that they were obliged each Sunday to make the journey to the meeting house in St Neots, and it was to avoid this that the Metcalfs initiated the conversion of a barn that lay on the perimeter of the small park around their house. This took place in 1808, the first service being on 8 May that year. The Roxton Congregational Chapel [fig 3/12] that resulted was a single-storey room, with bowed end, ogee-headed windows and a thatched roof that at the east, or entrance, end descends onto a portico of branching tree trunks. The effect is charming, and highly reminiscent of a cottage orné or rustic garden pavilion. As the congregation flourished, space became short, and at some time after 1825 the chapel was tripled in size with the addition of bow-ended lateral wings or transepts, all continuing the style of the original. These contained ancillary spaces such as a room in which the children of the local labouring poor could be taught to read, and, in the southern bow, a tiny study for the minister equipped with simple rustic furniture. The chapel remains miraculously well preserved, and still used for its original purpose.[38]

Many Anglican clergy of the period lived in the kind of neat Georgian boxes that are now considered so desirable and consequently rarely still occupied by men of the cloth. The Gothic style was also thought suitable for clerics, and no doubt more lived in houses that were Gothick (or Gothicked) cottages rather than cottages ornés. Nevertheless, the Reverend Thomas Gresley at Sealwood Cottage was an early example of an Anglican clergyman feeling the attractions of a simple – though not too simple – rustic cottage. Rather in the same vein, though more than thirty years later, the Reverend George Glasse built himself the simplest of cottages ornés at Hanwell [fig 3/13] on the western outskirts of London. Single-storeyed under a big thatch roof supported on simple posts, the building has charm out of all proportion to its size, with its ogee-headed front door framed by quatrefoil windows. Glasse, who constructed the house in 1809 on glebe land that belonged to the rectors of Hanwell, may or may not have given it its current name of The Hermitage; but in any case he barely lived to enjoy its rustic attractions, as he committed suicide later the same year. [39] From approximately the same early nineteenth-century date comes the Old Rectory in the remote

Chiltern parish of Great Hamden, again single-storeyed and this time built of the local vernacular materials of flint and brick. Its thatched roof, undulating above the three regularly spaced windows of the road frontage, is really all that marks it out as orné.

The Old Rectory at Winterborne Came in Dorset is a two-storeyed thatched cottage, possibly built for the Reverend William England who was rector between 1804 and 1836. Though it too is essentially a regular three-bay box, it is made orné by the intricate patterns of its glazing and by the rustic verandah which runs across the frontage and keeps much of the light out of the ground-floor rooms behind. The plan is as rational as that of any normal Georgian house of the size, with four rooms arranged either side of a central hall on the ground floor, and four bedrooms above. The fame of the Old Rectory lies in its association with the poet-clergyman William Barnes, who took up residence in 1862 and died there in 1886. In his time the house accommodated Barnes himself, his daughter and three servants – a not untypical clerical household. [40] What is now called Pomfret Lodge, on the estate of the great baroque mansion of Easton Neston in Northamptonshire, was originally built as the

OPPOSITE 3/12 Roxton Congregational Chapel, Bedfordshire, converted from a barn, 1808

BELOW 3/13 The Hermitage, Hanwell, Middlesex, 1809

RIGHT 3/14 Old Vicarage, Kingsteignton, Devon, designed by John Rendle of Teignmouth, 1815

vicarage for the estate village of Hulcote,[41] and is smart out of proportion to the size of the parish and its population. Despite its present name, which links it to the Countess of Pomfret, widow of the 1st Earl of Pomfret, who built a remarkable Gothick house in London,[42] it is certainly after her time since she died in 1761, and the internal detail – the mouldings round the arches in the central lobby, the panelling of doors and shutters, the segmental arches to the dining room alcoves – suggests somewhere between about 1810 and 1830.[43] Architecturally the house is arguably more Gothic cottage than cottage orné, but it retains a twiggy porch on its garden elevation, which is also said to have once had a rustic verandah. Documentation is entirely lacking, and the only architect whose name might conceivably be linked to the house is John Raffield, who certainly worked on the estate in 1822 and may have designed the estate cottages in about 1817–20.[44]

One of the finest examples of a cottage orné clergy house must have been the Old Vicarage or Vicars Hill at Kingsteignton in Devon [fig 3/14]. This was built in 1815 as a vicarage for Dr Thomas Whipham, and Exeter Diocesan records confirm it to have been designed by John Rendle, a builder and surveyor from nearby Teignmouth.[45] The building is thatched, the thatch overhanging on the garden front and supported on what originally would have been knobbly tree trunks.[46] This symmetrical front has two curved bays and the verandah has a pebble floor. Behind

the bays are oval rooms, lit by tall Gothick windows with elaborate metal glazing (incorporating coloured glass). The building has unfortunately been spoilt by unsympathetic subdivision and by the equally unsympathetic immediate environs, demonstrating all too clearly how vulnerable is the character of the cottage orné.[47]

Another segment of late Georgian society to whom the cottage orné had an appeal was that of sea captains, particularly ones who wished to live at or near the sea, or those who retired after the conclusion of the Napoleonic wars. Jane Austen in *Persuasion* – a novel published in 1818 but set in 1814 – has one of her characters comment, 'This peace will be turning all our rich Navy Officers ashore. They will be all wanting a home.'[48] Blackwood Cottage, a substantial house at Fareham in Hampshire, was supposedly built originally for Captain George Purvis in 1798/9, and named 'Cottage' [fig 3/15] to distinguish it from nearby Blackbrook House

where he had previously lived.[49] In the case of Captain Purvis, who in 1798/9 would presumably have been on active service, the location would have been handy for Portsmouth in the event of being recalled to his ship. The architectural evolution of the building is confusing, since a sketch of 1811 shows a small, single-storeyed cottage just three windows wide. This part of the house has been reconstructed or indeed replaced at some point, since it is now two-storeyed, and there were subsequent extensions in the same idiom in 1908 and again in the 1920s by Walter Cave. As it now stands the original thatched core is two-storeyed, with large Gothic windows lighting the ground-floor rooms on the north, entrance front and smaller, simpler Gothic windows to the upper floor. On the north and east fronts tall, spindly tree trunks support the projecting thatch and form a double-height verandah. The garden front has a projecting bay with Gothic glazing, and a metal verandah (possibly later) wrapped around the ground floor. The room behind the bay here is oval, and seems not to have been central to the façade, which in any case has been completely altered by a large westward extension.[50]

It is known that P. F. Robinson, a major pattern-book proponent of the cottage genre, exhibited a design at the Royal Academy in 1808 for a 'Seaman's Cottage' at Sandgate in Kent for 'Captain Waller RN',[51] although the design does not appear to survive and it is not known if it

was ever built. Perhaps the best surviving example of a 'naval' cottage is the Thatched Cottage at Stonely, near Kimbolton in Huntingdonshire, built in 1815 by Captain Frederick Welstead RN. The location is many miles from the sea, but is explained by the fact that on his retirement from the navy Captain Welstead became manager to the Duke of Manchester's Kimbolton Castle estate. The garden elevation here is symmetrical, with thatched and twiggy verandahs framing a projecting central gable with wavy eavesboards and a diminutive bay window with concave rooflet. The thatched roof forms little eyebrows over the bedroom windows.[52]

Another sub-section of the genre is the cottage-style fishing lodge. A modest if undeniably charming example is Tavy Lodge at Tavistock, on the western fringes of Dartmoor. Its once extensive grounds ran down to the fast-flowing River Tavy, a mile upstream from the town. The windows are Gothick, including traceried dormers in what must originally have been a thatched roof, and a central bay whose cusped windows are separated by what look like stylized palm trees. The interiors are simple, but some windows retain typically Regency coloured glass in their heads. As so often, neither an architect nor a precise date are known.

Different in every respect was the fishing lodge at Cadland [fig 3/17], on the banks of the Solent in Hampshire, which was designed by a very smart architect

OPPOSITE **3/15** Blackbrook Cottage, Fareham, Hampshire:
the original cottage on the right, later additions on the left

BELOW **3/16** Cadland, Hampshire: Capability Brown's
landscaping plan

3/17 Cadland, Hampshire: Henry Holland's elevation
and plan for the fishing lodge, *c*.1775

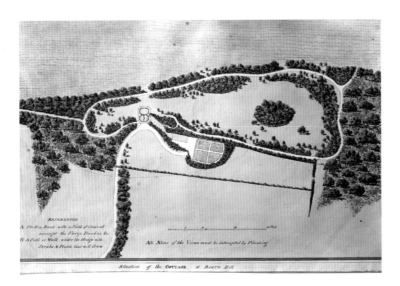

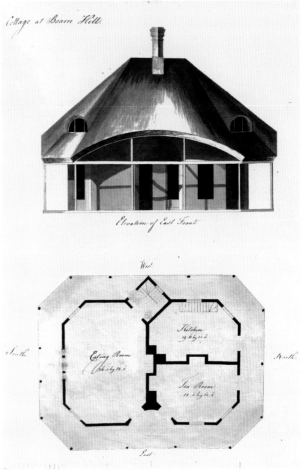

in a sophisticated idiom that is certainly not Gothic and is indeed hard to categorize. The architect was Henry Holland, the client Robert Drummond and the date about 1775. The lodge went up at the same time as Holland and his father-in-law Lancelot 'Capability' Brown were building the main house on the estate, some two miles away. From the beginning the family seems to have regarded this little thatched 'cottage' with particular affection, and it was later to form the nucleus of the present principal residence. Holland's original plan and elevation survive in the family archives and show it to have been a remarkable building, quite without the cosy, faux-vernacular quaintness associated with the cottage orné. There are indeed no period references at all, and there is something strikingly modern about the skeletal verandah that surrounded the ground floor, which was just a cage of uprights and horizontals. Within, the plan was made up of two squashed octagons, one forming a spacious 'eating room' and the other subdivided to provide tea room and kitchen. A staircase, placed diamond-wise at the rear, led up to bedrooms (indicated on the elevation by small semicircular windows in the thatch), though it seems unlikely that family members would have spent the night there. The roof itself must have dominated the exterior, like a woolly hat pulled well down over a face.

Brown's plan for landscaping the setting also survives [fig 3/16]. The site was on the edge of the sea, long rather than deep, with occasional gaps in the shelter belts (including one in front of the cottage) that allowed views of the Solent. On the bottom of his plan Brown wrote 'NB None of the views must be interrupted by Planting.' The cottage was ostensibly a place in which to keep fishing tackle and refresh oneself after a day with rod and line. It was also somewhere that Drummond could entertain friends, and during such a dinner in July 1785 disaster struck, when a spark from the kitchen fire ignited the thatch. Drummond promptly disappeared into the wine cellar to rescue his best vintages.[53]

After the fire the cottage was promptly rebuilt with a slate roof, and as such it appears in a watercolour by Thomas Rowlandson [fig 3/18], probably painted in around 1786

when he was touring the New Forest area with his friend Henry Wickstead.[54] The spot was so pleasant that Drummond had Holland return to add wings in 1803 (these were classical, masking the cottage character of the original centre), a year before he died. His son Andrew Robert Drummond rebuilt the main house on the estate from 1837, with Wyatville as architect; after his death in 1865, the cottage became a dower house for his widow, who enlarged it and lived in it till her death in 1886. The ill-fated building was burnt again during World War I and stayed a roofless shell till 1935–6, when it was rebuilt once again, retaining the old walls where possible, in a neo-Regency style.[55]

Much the most impressive example of the orné fishing lodge, and indeed arguably England's finest surviving cottage orné of any category, is Houghton Lodge [fig 3/19], which stands on the banks of a famous trout stream, the River Test in Hampshire. It is a building that changed hands frequently in its early years, and a sale advertisement of 17 January 1801 gives a helpful early account of its attractions. It is described as

commanding picturesque views of the River Test . . . The Cottage contains six bed-chambers and dressing rooms, a lofty elegant dining room . . . finished in the highest style of Gothic architecture, with windows to the floor, variegated glass, beautiful landscape tablets and sky ceiling. The whole of the buildings . . . completely adapted for the reception of a family of distinction.[56]

A later advertisement, which appeared in the *New Statesman* of 15 May 1815, called it (in estate-agent language not so different from what might be used today) 'Unique Cottage Residence in the Gothic style'. 'The cottage', it continues,

has been erected within a few years, at very great expense, and finished with a very superior and chaste style of Gothic embellishments, affording accommodation for a family of the first respectability. . . . The river Test bounds the premises for a considerable distance, which is celebrated for capital trout fishing.[57]

The Lodge was first advertised for sale in 1799, which used to be thought to place the likely date of building some time in the late 1790s. However, research by Michael Readhead indicates that Sun Assurance policies establish that it was begun by mid-1792 and probably completed by 1795. It was built of brick, timber and thatch for Mrs Bernard, widow of Maurice Bernard, who had inherited the 500-acre estate and died in 1791; she still owned the property in 1800, according to land tax returns for that year, although she was then letting it to a certain Caleb Smith.[58] The name of John Nash has often been suggested as architect, but it seems unlikely that Mrs Bernard would have employed him, as her husband had lent him £1,000 for the speculative development in Bloomsbury over which Nash went bankrupt in 1783, and he did not return to London from Wales until 1796, by which time Houghton was finished. A more plausible architect is perhaps John Plaw, who moved from the capital to Southampton in about 1795; some of the designs in his pattern book *Ferme Ornée* (1795) were for patrons in Hampshire, most relevantly a 'Villa in the Cottage Style . . . in the style of

3/20 Houghton Lodge, Stockbridge: Music Room dome
3/21 Houghton Lodge, Stockbridge: Music Room, the Blue John chimneypiece
OPPOSITE 3/22 Houghton Lodge, Stockbridge: the arch between entrance hall and staircase

Mr Drummond's fishing lodge on the River Avon near Ringwood'. This has a thatched roof, Gothic windows, and an oval 'best parlour' embedded in its main façade.[59] One of the most intriguing aspects of Houghton, nevertheless, is the fact that as originally built, with thatched roof, clustered Tudoresque chimneys, and quite probably a thatched verandah, it irresistibly calls to mind Nash-Repton designs such as the Circular Cottage at Blaise Hamlet, not designed until 1810. Since Houghton – whoever its architect – predates Blaise by some eighteen years, the strong possibility must be that it somehow exercised an influence on Nash.

Externally, like so many later cottages ornés, Houghton is dominated by its enormous roof and tall clustered chimneys, the latter particularly elaborate in their cut-brick patterns and almost worthy of Hampton Court Palace and other Tudor exemplars. The chimneys stand on substantial plinths of plain brick, which would have been concealed by the thick layer of thatch that originally covered the roof. It takes some effort of imagination to reinstate the thatch, but it would certainly have transformed the appearance of the building. The most striking feature of the exterior is the great semi-conical roof of the projecting bow on the river front, which reflects a lofty domed rotunda, or Music Room, within (a 'Superb Rotunda', as it is referred to in the 1799 advertisement). Internally this is perhaps the most impressive single interior of any British cottage orné, with its dome painted to evoke a sky with clouds and fluttering birds [fig 3/20]. Below the cornice is a ring of cusped oculi, and below those tall pointed Gothic apertures, containing variously the three French windows to the lawn, the door from the hall, and mirrored recesses divided into panels by strips of deep blue glass fixed in place by glass rosettes. One of the recesses contains the unique chimneypiece, a striking simplification of one of Batty Langley's boldest designs (adapted from *Gothic Architecture Improved*, plate XLII, first published in 1742), here executed in bands of precious Blue John spar [fig 3/21].

In 1802 Houghton was 'the seat of the Hon. G. Pitt',[60] who in that year succeeded his father as Lord Rivers and moved to Stratfield Saye – soon to become the residence of the Duke of Wellington. Then in 1810 it was tenanted by Lord Arundell of Wardour, who had succeeded to the title in 1808 but did not gain possession of the family seat at Wardour Castle until 1813. It seems likely that he was

arches with the sort of reeded mouldings characteristic of the Regency period [fig 3/22]. Somewhat later, perhaps around 1860, a cast-iron verandah with glazed roof was wrapped around the river frontage, very possibly replacing a thatched rustic verandah that had decayed or was thought to cut too much light out of the reception rooms. It seems likely that it was at this stage that the decision was taken to remove the thatch from the roof altogether and replace it with tiles.

Two of the most idiosyncratic – and atypical – of all cottages ornés were created for pairs of spinster ladies. That at Plas Newydd, Llangollen [fig 3/24], became the home of the most celebrated lesbian couple of their age, Lady Eleanor Butler and Sarah Ponsonby.[62] Having failed in their first attempt to elope together, in 1778 they managed to escape from their oppressive Anglo-Irish background and cross to Wales. Their intention was to set up home in England, but after touring much of Wales they arrived in Llangollen and took lodgings.[63] In May 1780 they rented a very ordinary five-room cottage on a hillside above the town and renamed it Plas Newydd. Here they planned to live 'a life of sweet and delicious retirement'. Initially the house was decorated in a fresh and cottagey manner, with whitewashed walls, varnished doors and chocolate-coloured skirting boards.[64] The dining chairs were upholstered with pale blue convolvulus against a white ground, and Miss Ponsonby described gathering rose buds from the garden and throwing them 'in a careless manner over the Library Table, which had a beautiful effect'.[65] But by 1814 the Ladies of Llangollen were (as Miss Ponsonby put it) 'seized with the Oak carving mania'. This led to elaborate embellishments, oriel windows with stained glass (some of the glass being medieval fragments that the pair had unearthed in the nearby ruins of Vale Crucis Abbey) being added to the upper part of the main front and the lower windows being given wooden canopies carved to within an inch of their lives.[66] A guide book of 1824 recorded that the cottage was now 'ornamented with highly finished carvings, which have been collected from ancient houses in different parts of the kingdom, and fitted together with ingenuity and taste. These decorate almost every part of the interior as well as the exterior.'[67] General Yorke, who had known the Ladies as a child, muddied the waters after he bought the house in 1876 by adding yet more

responsible for a number of alterations to the Lodge, including possibly the insertion of the elaborate cast-iron glazing into the dining-room windows [fig 3/23], very much in the style of those in the stables at Brighton Pavilion, which had been built for the Prince of Wales to William Porden's design in 1804–8. A certain amount of internal replanning seems to have gone on at this time, with the function of rooms being changed.[61] The staircase has spiralling balusters related to cabinet work of the Trafalgar years, and both in the stairhall and the room adjoining the dining room, in what was originally part of the servants' wing, there are ferociously cusped Gothic

woodwork, including bogus external half-timbering.[68]

Despite their initial wish to live a life of quiet retirement, both the house and its eccentric inhabitants became a tourist attraction, and many distinguished visitors beat a track to their door[69] (augmented by English tourists en route to admire the scenery of North Wales), often bringing gifts that added still further to the clutter of the interior. A drawing made surreptitiously by a visitor in 1828 shows the Ladies seated in the library at a table groaning with knick-knacks, wearing the identical dark cloth riding habits that they favoured and with their grey hair cut identically in the male style made fashionable by George IV.

Lady Eleanor died the following year at the age of ninety, and Sarah in 1831 aged seventy-six. By this stage they had laid out the grounds informally, with winding walks leading to rustic structures and viewpoints out over the surrounding landscape – all now gone, the present formal gardens being laid out by Yorke.

If Plas Newydd and its inhabitants were very much *sui generis*, so too was A la Ronde at Exmouth in Devon [fig 3/25]. This unique house was begun in 1795 or 1796[70] for two spinsters, Jane Parminter and her younger cousin Mary, who had spent several years travelling around Europe.[71] The inspiration is said to have been the

octagonal Byzantine church of San Vitale in Ravenna (though the similarity is remote), and therefore it is very unlike other cottages ornés, being completely unrelated to English vernacular. The building is sixteen-sided with a full-height central octagon, which inevitably results in awkwardly wedge-shaped rooms around the perimeter. It was originally thatched, and topped out by eight rectangular latticed windows that lit the octagon; above were a cluster of chimneys and a little onion-domed cupola. A weathervane in the form of a hen rather than the usual cock announced a discreet feminist manifesto. The exterior walls were whitewashed, and the perimeter rooms were lit by alternating rectangular and diamond-shaped windows, eccentrically placed across the sixteen angles. Family tradition maintained that Jane Parminter designed the house herself, although a nineteenth-century writer

claimed that it was built 'from plans by a Mr Lowder'.[72] Mary Parminter was related by marriage to John Lowder, a Bath-based banker turned developer, whose son John (1781–1829) became an architect and in 1816 designed a circular school with wedge-shaped classrooms.[73] However, his first-known design dates from 1803 and when work began at A la Ronde in 1795/6 he was only fourteen or fifteen, so any influence must have been the other way round, and the precise authorship therefore remains a mystery.

The idiosyncrasy of the exterior continues on the inside, which is embellished with the kind of delicate handiwork characteristic of Georgian ladies of leisure – shells, feather work, quill work, cut-outs from engravings. This reaches a virtuoso climax in the gallery around the top of the octagon, which is reached by a narrow Gothic

staircase made to resemble a shell grotto. The gallery decoration combines shells, feathers (including feather pictures of birds), cut paper, lichen, glass, mica, pottery, pebbles, bones and paint [fig 3/26]. Down at ground level, the oddity of the plan results in ingenuities such as doors that slide into walls, lots of useful cupboards in left-over spaces, and fold-away seats that pull down across the arches of the octagon. The drawing room retains Parminter decoration such as marbleized woodwork, a feather frieze, and a chimneypiece with a summer infill, removable in winter, made up of shells large and small that frame a painted landscape. The octagon has a painted decorative scheme of green chevrons perhaps intended to evoke a seaweed-covered underwater cave, and there are bizarrely gawky hall chairs designed and painted by Mary Parminter.

The Parminter cousins may or may not have constitut-ed a lesbian couple, but when Mary died in 1849 (outliving Jane by thirty-eight years) her will specified that only unmarried kinswomen should inherit. However, a some-what complicated legal situation eventually made it possible for the little estate to be transferred in 1886 to a man, the Reverend Oswald Reichel. The home the Parminters had devised for themselves was hardly practical for normal living, and Reichel made a number of alterations that, while undoubtedly an improvement in that respect, did nothing to enhance the appearance of the exterior. The white render was scraped from the walls, thatch was replaced with tiles, clunky dormers were inserted to light the rooms in the roof (which previously had received no natural light), and a catwalk was wrapped around the exterior of the lantern, all taking the building further from its original quasi-rustic appearance.[74]

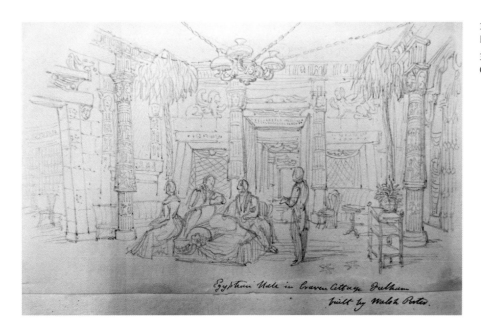

LONDON COTTAGES

The building of villas in the villages around the perimeter of London was well established by the early eighteenth century. Some were smartly up to date in their architecture, Lord Burlington's Palladian villa at Chiswick being an obvious example, and the great majority were at least nominally classical. As the century wore on, however, Gothic began to make an occasional appearance, and it was probably inevitable that in time the growing interest in the idea of the rural idyll would produce architect-designed cottages in the London suburbs, even if the rural fiction was hard to sustain just a few miles from Hyde Park Corner. Possibly the earliest example was the Queen's Cottage in Kew Gardens, built at the behest of Queen Charlotte in 1771, which will be discussed in a later chapter. Though never intended for residential occupation, it must inevitably have set a trend that translated into cottages that were.

Hard on its heels – exactly when is not possible to pinpoint, though about 1778 has been suggested – came Craven Cottage, on the banks of the Thames between Fulham and Hammersmith. This was built in the 1770s for Elizabeth, Baroness Craven (née Lady Elizabeth Berkeley, 1750–1828), using money she had won with a lottery ticket.[75] The building was long and low, with thatch to the roof and porch, though a watercolour of about 1820 suggests that the verandah may have had pantiles or shingles.[76] Leaded casement windows were tucked into the roof. It seems to have been L-shaped in plan, with three interconnecting reception rooms on the garden front and maybe four bedrooms above. The service rooms were in a wing at the back, with separate stables and coach house. As so often, no architect is identified and not enough is known

about the original appearance to hazard a guess on stylistic grounds, but given Lady Craven's social status and fashionability, an architect the house must surely have had. Nor is anything known of the interiors in her time; however, unlike the Queen's Cottage, the reception rooms would have had quite low ceilings. She surrounded the five acres with two rows of willows, which screened the property from its neighbours, though retaining a view of the river with its constant stream of boats between Westminster and the fashionable towns of Richmond and Twickenham upstream. For a few years she seems to have used the cottage as a halfway house between town and country (where her husband and his shooting parties increasingly bored her), entertaining friends such as Horace Walpole and also, very likely, her lover the French ambassador. In 1782 she separated from Lord Craven and went abroad, allowing a friend the use of the cottage, which she said contained 'a pianoforte and a thousand comfortable things'. Eventually widowed and returning to London as the wife of the Margrave of Brandenburg-Anspach, she sold the cottage and bought a fine classical villa on the banks of the Thames at Hammersmith, which was renamed Brandenburg House.

In 1805 Craven Cottage was bought by Walsh Porter, the boon companion and taste guru of the Prince of Wales, who visited him there more than once. In the four years before his death in 1809, Porter made extensive changes with help from Thomas Hopper, whose celebrated maxim, 'it is an architect's business to understand all styles, and to be prejudiced in favour of none', very much sums up the architectural pluralism of the Regency period. The interiors were remodelled as a series of rooms in different styles – a Gothic chapel inspired by Henry VII's Chapel at Westminster Abbey, a mirrored 'Tartar's Tent' lit

by a crescent-shaped window, and above all an Egyptian Hall [fig 3/27]. The latter was an extraordinary fantasy (complete with potted palm trees), drawing on the illustrations in Vivant Denon's *Voyage dans la Basse et la Haute Egypt*, which had been published in Paris and London in 1802.[77] Humphry Repton, visiting because he had heard that the Prince of Wales admired it, found some aspects done 'with good effect', but others 'whimsical and absurd'.[78] Empty from 1872, the cottage was burned down (possibly by tramps) in 1888, and gives its name to a football ground on the site acquired by Fulham Football Club in 1896.

Perhaps in conscious contradistinction from the bustle and noise of the capital, other cottages in the London environs seem to have favoured the designation 'Hermitage'. The Hermitage at Hanwell to the west has been noted, and another such is the Hermitage at Southgate on the northern fringes. This may be the property listed as 'cottage and garden' in the 1801/2 enclosure award, then belonging to the main local landowner William Tash who also owned Broomfield House; otherwise nothing certain appears to be known about it.[79] Another Hermitage cottage survives to the south of the Thames in Camberwell, originally an ancient village nucleus that began to expand in the late Georgian period. The Hermitage in Camberwell Grove is in fact the sole survivor of a trio of cottages ornés in the Grove, a road that originated as a private avenue behind a mansion in the village centre and was then gradually built up residentially after the sale of the estate in 1776. The

Hermitage retains its tree-trunk columns but is now compromised by its pebbledashed walls and the loss of its original thatch; its former appearance is shown in an old photograph.[80] The other two cottages were the creation of the remarkable Dr John Coakley Lettsom (1744–1815). Born in the British Virgin Islands, he was educated in England and began his medical training at St Thomas's Hospital in London. He returned home after the death of his father, freed his slaves and, as the only qualified doctor on the islands, grew richer. Back once more in England he married an heiress and grew richer still. A close friend of Benjamin Franklin and Dr William Thornton (polymathic architect of the United States Capitol building in Washington DC), he became committed to the abolition of slavery, and put his wealth to many charitable purposes, including the foundation of the Royal Humane Society and the Medical Society of London. At Camberwell he built himself a handsome neoclassical villa on the crest of the hill at the southern end of the Grove, on land purchased in 1779.[81] The extent of his estate is shown on a map of 1792[82] in which the Grove is still very largely without buildings. However, on the east side of the road it marks a pool with central fountain, and on the far side of this a cottage [fig 3/28]. The appearance of the pool and cottage was hymned by the Rev. Thomas Maurice in 'Grove Hill, A Descriptive Poem', published in London in 1799, by which time they were evidently part of a mature and admired garden:

With dazzling brilliance while the sun-beams dance
On the chaste bosom of yon bright expanse,
From the too powerful glare and scorching heat
Yon rural Cottage yields a cool retreat:
What though it want the spacious marble base,
What though its roofs no gilded trophies grace,
On lasting oak its modest front it rears,
And neat in rustic elegance appears,
While thick around with mantling foliage twin'd,
It bids defiance to the sun and wind.

A note to the poem describes how

a continuation of Shakespeare's Walk leads to the Cottage and Fountain. The former is supported by the trunks of eighteen oaks, entwined with climbing evergreens, in the manner of the Sybil's Temple. Within this range of oak columns is the sitting room, which in consequence of its less dimensions, admits of a walk between it and the oaken colonnade [sic]: on each side of the entrance are two griffins, the supporters of the City arms, which were removed hither when the Guildhall of London was new fronted in the year 1790. Over the cottage door is a beautiful sculptured tablet, representing Acis and Galatea, in alto relievo.

The description goes on to explain that the pool in front was actually a reservoir fed by underground pipes from a canal, which, rising through the centre of a Portland stone basin, formed a fountain that 'falling again into this Reservoir, preserves it in continual agitation'. The appearance of the cottage is confirmed by an accompanying engraving, showing what was in effect a peripteral temple rendered into Gothic, with thatched roof and ogee-headed windows. An engraving of 1811[83] shows the cottage now heavily encased in creepers, with the fountain rising out of the pool in front. Clearly at this stage the one-room structure could not function other than as a garden pavilion, but an undated later engraving suggests that in time it was probably enlarged to provide residential accommodation, since the frontage is extended to either side and the roof has a row of Gothic dormers. In the process, of course, it lost its peripteral rustic colonnade.

Such an ensemble was unlikely to survive the pressures of intensifying urbanization, and indeed its site is now occupied by a railway line emerging from a cutting on the east side of Camberwell Grove. A third cottage survived rather longer on the opposite side of the road. An engraving of 1798 records 'Dr Lettsom's Park Cottage Camberwell', a building clearly related architecturally to the Fountain Cottage, with Gothic windows and overhanging thatched roof supported on spindly tree trunks. [84] This appearance is confirmed by the photograph on an undated postcard of about 1900.[85] The cottage was noted in the *Weekly Illustrated* of 15 January 1938, which commented, 'Not many thatched roofs in our village now, though you'd have found plenty thirty years ago. In fact, we shouldn't be surprised if this one, at Camberwell Green [sic], is about the only one we've got left.' Known more recently as Thatched Cottage, 'it contained a curving staircase in a generous hall, and elegant bow-ended rooms to the rear'.[86] Sadly it was bomb-damaged in World War II and demolished shortly afterwards.[87]

Highgate, on the breezy and healthsome eastern edge of Hampstead Heath, might be expected to have appealed to individuals wanting quiet retirement not too far from the metropolis. The 1841 sale particulars for Ivy Cottage [fig 3/29] called it 'unquestionably the most elegant of the admired abodes in this delightful vicinity', and continued that 'it must not be forgotten, it is a remove of only three miles from the smoke of London'.[88] The vendor was James Shoolbred, who had made a fortune out of a furniture store in the Tottenham Court Road and ploughed the very considerable sum of £7,000 into improving the property. The vignette accompanying the sale notice depicts a very attractive thatched cottage orné in spacious and mature gardens. Part of Shoolbred's £7,000 had gone into adding an in-keeping extension to one side of the original cottage, which had been built in 1819 for the comic actor Charles Mathews. An early engraving – an image that Mathews also used on his letterhead[89] – confirms that his cottage was a mere three bays wide, with thatched roof, tall asymmetrical chimneys, Gothic windows, boldly cusped central gable and applied half-timbering. Extending to the left was a single-storey Gothic conservatory. Mathews – who apparently referred to Ivy Cottage as his 'Tusculum' in emulation of Pliny's villa outside Rome – housed his celebrated collection of theatrical portraits here.[90] The mystery is just how these were accommodated in such an apparently modest cottage, since there exists a wall plan of two rooms close hung with 'the Histrionic Portraits', and a perspective of a sizeable top-lit gallery with segmental vault – not a cottagey interior at all.[91] After the 1841 sale the property changed hands a number of times, with the cottage progressively expanding until by 1889 it had no fewer than sixteen bedrooms. Thus transformed it survived until 1934 when it was demolished and replaced by a block of flats.

Ivy Cottage stood in Millfield Lane, which still forms part of the eastern edge of the Heath. Here also was another cottage orné, Fitzroy Farm Cottage, successively rebuilt and enlarged until it was finally demolished in 2010. Much less is known about this, but a photograph of about 1907[92] shows it to have been a charming three-bay building with thatch, Gothic windows, cusped eaves and applied half-timbering. The similarities to Ivy Cottage are enough to suggest that both may have had the same designer.[93]

While the majority of cottages ornés of whatever size and social level were newly built, there are also quite numerous examples created by the titivation of existing vernacular buildings. A literary instance is Uppercross Cottage in Jane Austen's novel *Persuasion*. When the squire's eldest son married, the modest village parsonage had received the improvement elevated into a cottage for his residence, 'and Uppercross Cottage, with its viranda, French windows, and other prettiness, was quite as likely to catch the traveller's eye as the more consistent and considerable aspect and premises of the Great House.'[94]

A classic manifestation is Brockley Cottage [fig 3/30] at Brockley, Somerset. This evidently began life as a long

plain vernacular cottage, probably seventeenth century in date, hugging the old road. When the new turnpike road was opened a few yards to the west in about 1837, the building was given a new orné frontage to face it, with large gable, small gable and two porches, each with different and very elaborate eaves boards – that to the smaller gable, incorporating vine trails, being especially fancy. The alterations were carried out for the Smyth-Pigott estate, which owned both Brockley Court and Brockley House in the same village.[95]

The village of Porlock on the north Somerset coast has two characteristic examples of this kind of treatment. Doverhay House, created out of a cluster of older vernacular cottages, was prettified with cusped Gothick windows and cusped eaves. Across the lane, The Gables is a largeish cottage (said to be seventeenth century) ornéd with Gothick windows, thatched verandah and thatch rising into peaks above the first-floor windows – the latter a feature found on vernacular cottages in the region. The two buildings are obviously part of the same campaign, since the orné detail is identical. At Ringmore in south Devon, a village on the slopes of the Teign estuary, Old Stoke House was created from a row of old cottages, the Gothick first-floor windows projecting

upwards into the thatch and given delicate glazing. Frogham Cottage at Barfrestone, Kent, is a modest vernacular cottage re-fronted and extended. The original clapboarded side elevation is at right angles to the white-rendered road frontage, which has a Gothic bay immediately round the corner with coloured glass incorporated in the glazing. The taller right-hand gable has boldly cusped eaves above two tall sash windows with Tudor hoodmoulds over. The lower of these has panels of older painted glass incorporated in the otherwise standard glazing.

Farmhouses were also subjected to a similar treatment. Cliff Cottage (now Puckpool House), near Ryde on the fashionable Isle of Wight, was a farmhouse remodelled as a holiday retreat for himself by the architect Lewis Wyatt soon after 1822, and he in fact retired there in 1835.[96] Rosemorran [fig 3/31], on a hillside above Penzance, is likely to have originated as a late medieval or Tudor gentry farmhouse. In 1796 it was bought from the Harris family of nearby Kenegie by George John, for many years the leading lawyer in Penzance, who had augmented his considerable fortune by mining speculation. It was almost certainly he who transformed the long vernacular range into a fashionable cottage by giving it traceried

Gothick windows that rise into the thatch, and a projecting Gothick porch crowned by a cross.[97] However, such farmhouse upgrading might be carried out for the benefit of the farmers themselves. The eighteenth century saw the emergence of a new social class, the large tenant farmer or 'gentleman farmer'. Such men were likely to be more socially ambitious than the smaller traditional proprietors, sending their sons away to school and dressing their daughters fashionably, and they might very well want a new or architecturally improved farmhouse.[98] This was most likely to result in a neat Georgian box, for which architectural pattern books provided the models from the mid-century onwards, but by the Regency period socially

aspiring farmers would have been aware (or their wives would have made them so) that the Gothic and cottage idioms were equally *à la mode*, if not more so. Biggin Farm at Fordham in Cambridgeshire and Gothic Farm at Heveningham in Suffolk are both examples of much older (in the case of the latter, probably sixteenth-century) farmhouses given Gothic windows in these decades. Bridge Farm at Sandon in Essex [fig 3/32], an early seventeenth-century timbered and plastered farmhouse, was ornéd with cusped bargeboards, Tudor dripmoulds and a cast-iron verandah between the projecting wings, plus attractive cast-iron Gothic railings to separate it from the road; the date is probably some time in the 1830s or 1840s.[99]

1 She was the grand-daughter of an earl. As a senior Anglo-Irish cleric and recognized scholar her husband was part of the Anglo-Irish elite.

2 By Clarissa Orr, her most recent biographer, in a communication with the author.

3 Lady Lanover, ed., *The Autobiography and Correspondence of Mary Granville, Mrs Delany* (London, 1860–61), vol. 2, p. 470.

4 See Chapter One, p. 11.

5 See Introduction, p. 6.

6 There was also some slight influence from the writings of Jean-Jacques Rousseau, though his English admirers were largely confined to a very small aristocratic group; Viscount Nuneham, for instance, who marked his admiration by including tributes to Rousseau in his garden at Nuneham Courtenay, also held Rose Girl festivals to encourage the virtuous poor. I owe this observation to Clarissa Orr.

7 Edmund Bartell, *Hints for Picturesque Improvements in Ornamented Cottages* (London, 1804), p. ix.

8 J. C. Loudon, *Encyclopaedia* (London, 1838), pp. 5–6, cited in Daniel Maudlin, *The Idea of the Cottage in English Architecture 1760–1860* (London, 2015), p. 40.

9 See Chapter Five.

10 Robert Lugar, *Architectural Sketches for Cottages, Rural Dwellings and Villas* (London, 1805).

11 J. B. Papworth, *Rural Residences* (London, 1818), p. 25. This was in relation to Plate VI, a design for a Gothic house, rather than what would generally be thought of as a cottage.

12 Philip Heath, 'Sealwood Cottage, Derbyshire: An Early Cottage Orné by "Dr Syntax"', *Georgian Group Journal*, XVIII (2010), pp. 105–14. The cottage still exists, extended on three occasions and with the thatch being replaced by slate at some point (probably in the early twentieth century).

13 Combe also makes suggestions regarding planting to either side, which he thought should be naturalistic and irregular, intermingled with honeysuckle and rose.

14 Information from Mr Michael Jackson. The building was at one stage renamed Queensberry House after the Marquess of Queensberry who rented it in the late nineteenth century; Lord Alfred Douglas ('Bosie') is said to have been born there. I am grateful to Jeffery Haworth for alerting me to Ham Hill.

15 The date of two lithographs by W. Wood.

16 Confusingly there is date of 1841 on this end, probably referring to alterations after a fire in the roof thatch, after which the building was reroofed in tiles. The thatched verandah was removed in the 1950s.

17 Published in Bury by W. B. Frost.

18 Oakes, who was given the land by his father in 1801, gradually expanded the grounds between then and 1837, creating a series of gardens and pleasure grounds. I am grateful to Dr James Bettley for drawing my attention to Nowton Cottage.

19 Pl. XV. See below, Chapter Four. The only clues to the dating are the fact that the house does not appear on a map of 1807 but is present on Bryant's Map of Norfolk of 1824. It was substantially but tactfully extended with conservatory and (originally) dining room to either side for Campbell Steward sometime between 1893 and 1905. I am grateful to Professor Richard Wilson for drawing my attention to Harford Hills House and to Geoffrey Kelly for kindly allowing me to see his researches on the building.

20 A. Bryant, *Map of the County of Norfolk* (London, 1826).

21 Information from Robert Jennings and Professor Richard Wilson. Kett was a partner in Kett and Back's Norwich Bank, and high sheriff of the county in 1820. *White's Directory* of 1845 lists him living at nearby Brooke House.

22 It is not in fact mentioned in the 1827 rates for Frome but is marked on the 1837 tithe map.

23 I am grateful to Polly Fry for allowing me to see the house and supplying me with Derek Gill's historical notes on the property.

24 As might be expected from a cottage built for a client in 'trade', the interiors of Selwood Lodge are generally quite simple, although there is a top-lit oak staircase, and the south-east bow-window room has a Gothic chimneypiece.

25 See Chapter Four.

26 'Cottage Ornée: Sarsgrove House, Oxfordshire', *Connoisseur* (December 1956), pp. 224–5. Nigel Temple, 'Sarsden, Oxfordshire', *Journal of Garden History*, VI/2 (1986), pp. 107–10.

27 Thomas Love Peacock, *Melincourt* [1817] (London, 1896). Repton's drawings are in the RIBA Drawings Collection, 29481, 29482, 65418.

28 This is confirmed by Repton's plan.

29 Colvin, *B.D.*, p. 663. Lugar's perspective (pl. 22) is copied from his signed watercolour in the Bodleian Library, MS. Top. Oxon. b.91, f193, no.298. Lugar noted that 'it was the owner's wish to adopt the Gothic windows, rather than the common form of the embellished cottage'. The cottage was replaced in 1888 by a house designed by the firm of George & Peto. Geoffrey Tyack, Simon Bradley and Nikolaus Pevsner, *Buildings of England: Berkshire* (New Haven and London, 2010), p. 334. Rose Hill was to form the basis of the cottage Lugar subsequently designed at Puckaster on the Isle of Wight. See Chapter Five.

30 Repton undoubtedly designed a nearby house called The Ridge for another local cloth manufacturer, Edward Sheppard, in about 1815–17, but this was classical.

31 See Chapter Seven.

32 Malcolm Reynes, 'Angeston Grange, Gloucestershire', *Country Life* (1 March 2001), pp. 62–5.

33 Maudlin, *The Idea of the Cottage in English Architecture 1760–1860*, p. 96. An exception is Gorsley Cottage, on the northern edge of Manchester, a pretty thatched Gothick specimen whose original state is recorded in a pencil sketch by Thomas Sunderland. It survives, heavily altered, as Manchester Golf Club. Information from Andrew Martindale.

34 Also a local benefactor insofar as he co-founded the town museum in 1835.

35 Jean Gumbrell, *Down Your Street in Saffron Walden* (Saffron Walden, 1984), pp. 96–7. Information from Kate Hanlon, Saffron Walden Library.

36 For the religious and moral connotations of the cottage idiom in the United States, see Chapter Nine.

37 Enlarged by Ernest George for H. H. Wills in 1900, and altered again by Chester Jones in 1933, the building is now unrecognizable.

38 Stella Gibbs, *Mr Metcalf's Congregational Chapel at Roxton* (Daventry, 2008). I am very grateful to Mrs Gibbs for information on the chapel.

39 According to Sir Montagu Shire, *Some Account of Bygone Hanwell* (Brentford, 1924), p. 35, Glasse was chaplain to the Duke of Cambridge and a classical scholar, but also, it seems an extravagant man with money worries. The parish map of 1814 (Ealing Local History Library) shows the Hermitage to the east of the then Rectory. It had been built on the site of an old house called The Elms (Kate McEwan, *Ealing Walkabout* (Warrington, 1983), p. 215).

40 Alan Chedzoy, 'Winterborne Came Rectory: The Home of William Barnes', *Dorset Proceedings* 123 (2001), pp. 1–6. I am grateful to the current owner, Mr Warren Davis, who has carefully restored the Old Rectory.

41 See Chapter Two, p. 45.

42 Pomfret Castle, Arlington Street, St James's, built 1758–60 and demolished in 1920.

43 The staircase however is of early eighteenth-century type, presumably imported from elsewhere.

44 Raffield first appears as a joiner working on Ford Castle, Northumberland under James Nisbet in the 1770s; hardly anything by him is definitely known, and the last reference to him was exhibiting the Easton Neston gate and lodges at the Royal Academy in 1825. Colvin, *B.D.*, pp. 840–41. The late Dowager Lady Hesketh kindly allowed me to see Pomfret Lodge.

45 It is indeed Rendle's only known work. Colvin, *B.D.*, p. 849.

46 Now crude 4 × 4 posts.

47 The building is now divided into two houses, two-thirds making up The Chantry and the remaining third being known as Elmfield.

48 Jane Austen, *Persuasion* [1818] (Harmondsworth, 1970), p. 47.

49 In recent years it was know as Bishopswood during its role as the official residence of the Bishop of Portsmouth. It is now known as Blackbrook Grove.

50 I am grateful to Mr and Mrs Mark Sedgeley for showing me the house, and to Judith Patrick for sharing the results of her research on Blackbrook for the Hampshire Gardens Trust.

51 Colvin, *B.D.*, p. 880. Sandgate is on the coast west of Folkestone, and in 1808 a large military barracks had just been built on the hill above, a response to the threat of invasion.

52 Captain Welstead's great great grand-daughter Ann Measures kindly supplied me with copies of photographs taken at the time the property finally left the family in 1968. Another example of the naval cottage is West Cottage at Aldwick, on the Sussex coast near Bognor Regis, a traditional flint-and-brick farmhouse which was bought by a sailor with prize money from the Napoleonic wars and turned into a seaside cottage orné with Gothick windows. Mavis Batey, *Regency Gardens* (Princes Risborough, 1995), p. 19.

53 Clive Aslet, 'Manor of Cadland, Hampshire', *Country Life* (1 October 1987), pp. 140–1.

54 Yale Center for British Art, B1975.3.134, where it is inscribed 'Mr Drummond's Cottage' and wrongly located at East Cowes, across the Solent on the Isle of Wight.

55 Aslet, 'Manor of Cadland, Hampshire'. I am grateful to Mrs Maldwyn Drummond for her assistance with Cadland.

56 Quoted by Christopher Hussey, 'Houghton Lodge, Hampshire', *Country Life* (20/27 April 1951).

57 Ibid.

58 Information kindly provided by Michael Readhead.

59 John Plaw, *Ferme Ornée* (1795), pl. 20. Plaw says that the design 'is intended to be built by a Gentleman in Wales', though whether that ever happened is not known. Interestingly, the design was plagiarized within two years of publication, appearing verbatim (with German labels) in Grohmann's *Gartenmagazin für Liebhaber englischer Garten*, vol. 1, pl.10, published in Leipzig in 1797. It was then used as the basis for the Gardener's House at Wörlitz, near Dessau, in 1799. See below, Chapter Eight. Plaw also designed a domed bath-house and fishing lodge at Brockenhurst House, Hampshire, for John Morant (*Ferme Ornée*, pls 1, 14–15), and a cottage orné near Lymington (*Sketches for Country Houses, Villas and Rural Dwellings*, 1800, pls 16, 17).

60 *Cary's Itineraries*, cited in Hussey, 'Houghton Lodge, Hampshire'.

61 A fragment of painted ceiling ornamented with intertwined As was recently discovered.

62 Lady Eleanor (1739–1829) was the youngest daughter of Walter Butler, *de jure* 16th Earl of Ormonde. Sarah Ponsonby (1755–1831) was a member of a junior branch of the Bessborough family, so both had aristocratic backgrounds. Sarah was a thirteen-year-old orphan, at boarding school in Kilkenny, when she first met Lady Eleanor. Elizabeth Mavor, *The Ladies of Llangollen* (London, 1971).

63 Oswestry, just over the border in Shropshire, was as far as they penetrated into England before settling on Llangollen.

64 Letter of Sarah Ponsonby to Sarah Tighe, 11 April 1785, quoted in Mavor, *The Ladies of Llangollen*, p. 69.

65 Journal of Eleanor Butler, quoted in ibid., p. 66.

66 A gift from the Duchess of St Albans.

67 S. and G. Nicholson, *Plas Newydd and Vale Crucis Abbey* (Liverpool, 1824), p. 11.

68 Although the contents had been dispersed at a seven-day auction after Sarah's death, the general turned the house into a shrine to the memory of the Ladies, using such original items as he could recover. Both he and his successor, a Liverpool cotton broker called Robertson, extended the cottage, but their additions were subsequently removed. In 1933 the property was acquired by the local town council.

69 The Ladies' innumerable visitors and admirers included William Wordsworth, Sir Walter Scott, Prince Pückler-Muskau (who called them 'the most celebrated Virgins in Europe') and the future Duke of Wellington. George III's daughter Princess Amelia sent them copies of the etchings made by her sister Princess Elizabeth (Mavor, *The Ladies of Llangollen*, p. 137). The Ladies also became a sought-after feature of local aristocratic society.

70 The lease on the land was acquired in November 1796. Information on A la Ronde kindly supplied by Trevor Adams and the property's research team.

71 The Parminters were a long-established Devon mercantile family, mainly based in Exeter.

72 This is stated in the A la Ronde guidebook without further detail.

73 Colvin, *B.D.*, p. 661.

74 The subsequent history of A la Ronde is that when Reichel's widow put the property up for sale in 1929 it was bought by a niece, Margaret Tudor, from whom it once again passed through female owners until it was acquired by the National Trust in 1991, thereby averting the threat of housing development on its surroundings.

75 Caroline Knight, 'An Early Cottage Orné: Craven Cottage and Lady Craven', *Georgian Group Journal*, XIX (2011), pp. 134–44.

76 London Metropolitan Archives, SC/GL/WAK/F2/q8053504, described as 'Sir Robert Barclay's cottage (known as Craven Cottage) at Fulham'. Knight, 'An Early Cottage Orné', fig. 6.

77 The room is recorded in a pencil sketch by Frederick Fairholt, pasted into an extra-illustrated copy of Thomas Crofton Croker, *A Walk from London to Fulham* (London, 1860), pp. 190–1 (Guildhall Library, London).

78 BL Add MS 62112 1058A, p. 216, quoted by John Morley, *Regency Design* (London, 1993), p. 345. In his pattern book *Designs for Lodges and Entrances* (first edition 1811) Thomas Dearn noted approvingly a particular feature of Craven Cottage: 'An ingenious

kind of paving is to be seen at a whimsical box of the late Walsh Porter Esq., at Fulham, called the Hamlet. Within an oak kirb [*sic*], small pieces of poles are driven into the ground level with the kirb; these are wedged close together, and thus form a cheap and durable pavement.'

79 Information from Kate Godfrey, Enfield Local Studies Centre.

80 Southwark Local Studies Library.

81 The house was demolished in the 1890s.

82 Entitled 'A Plan of Grove Hill, Camberwell, Surrey 1792', engraved in 1793 for Edwards's *Companion from London to Brighthelmston*, and subsequently included in *Grove Hill: An Horticultural Sketch* of 1794.

83 Published in *The Beauties of England and Wales* (1811) and reproduced in William Harnett Blanch, *Ye Parish of Camberwell* (London, 1875), facing p. 304.

84 The building is not shown on the 1792 map.

85 Reproduced for the Camberwell Society in 1972 as no. 12 of *Views of Old Camberwell*.

86 Notes to *Views of Old Camberwell*.

87 Ibid. The site is now occupied by flats at 94 Camberwell Grove.

88 Camden Local Studies Library, Heal Collection A IV 23.

89 Reproduced on a letter of April 1830 in John Richardson, *Highgate, Its History since the Fifteenth Century* (New Barnet, 1983), p. 80.

90 At his death in 1835 these went to the Garrick Club, which still has them.

91 Heal Collection, A IV 25 & 25b.

92 Michael Hammerson, *Highgate from Old Photographs* (Stroud, 2013), pp. 13, 14.

93 Hammerson, *Highgate from Old Photographs*, p. 8, shows a photograph of about 1910 of Hampstead Lane, Highgate, with a thatched cottage orné lodge – 'long gone' – adjoining the gates to Caen Wood Towers. In Highgate West Hill, Hermitage Villas occupy the site of cottages built shortly before 1800. The largest was called The Hermitage, one of whose early tenants is said to have been Walsh Porter (q.v.), who supposedly came to drink and gamble. An illustration of 1886 shows leaded windows, but otherwise the building is so overwhelmed with creepers that it is impossible to tell what it was like. *Streets of Highgate* (Camden History Society, 2007), p. 80.

94 Austen, *Persuasion*, p. 64.

95 According to Andrew Foyle and Nikolaus Pevsner, *The Buildings of*

England, Somerset: North and Bristol (New Haven and London, 2011, p. 429), J. H. Smyth-Pigott made alterations to Brockley House in about 1825.

96 Colvin, *B.D.*, p. 1192, citing G. Brannon, *Vectis Scenery* (1824). The earliest section, facing north, has the remains of a two-tier tree-trunk verandah. The house as it stands is a decidedly incoherent composition, and very far from being one of Wyatt's masterpieces. For the Isle of Wight in general, see below, Chapter Five.

97 George John died in 1847 at the age of eighty-eight. William Wood, *The Parish of Gulval Past and Present* (Penzance, 1956), p. 77. A room to the left of the entrance hall with a significantly higher ceiling is likely to have been remodelled from the medieval/Tudor hall. Such internal detail as survives – notably doors with reeded architraves – appears to be of Regency date. A World War II bomb blew the Gothick glazing from the windows. It also destroyed a nearby thatched cottage with hexagonal Gothick porch topped by a cross finial.

98 See J. M. Robinson, *Georgian Model Farms* (Oxford, 1983), p. 73.

99 Thatched Cottage at Hengrave in Suffolk was given windows with Tudor dripmoulds and cast-iron glazing in lacy octagons, as well as applied trellis and of course a thatched roof. According to James Bettley (*Buildings of England, Suffolk: West* (New Haven and London, 2015), p. 306), the transformation was carried out for Sir Thomas Rokewood Gage of Hengrave Hall 'in the mid-19th century'.

CHAPTER FOUR

COTTAGES TO ORDER

The Role of the Pattern Book

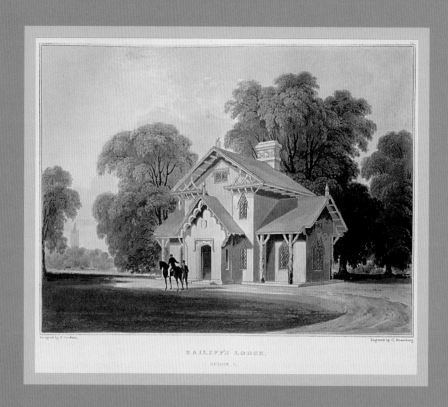

BAILIFF'S LODGE.

For the aspiring young late Georgian architect yet to make his way – and indeed for the established architect keen to capitalize on the market for an increasingly fashionable genre – two potentially fruitful ways of advertising his skills and attracting clients were to exhibit at the Royal Academy in London,[1] and to publish books of his designs. Richard Elsam, in his pattern book *Essay on Rural Architecture* (1803), observed that 'The variety which the pleasing and delightful study of Rural Scenery affords, hath given birth to more productions of the nature of the present undertaking than perhaps to any other.'[2]

Some authors optimistically focused on mansions for the aristocracy and the wealthy. Others thought, perhaps more realistically, that designs for more modest cottages for tenants might be a sprat to catch a mackerel. Thomas Dearne, who first exhibited at the Academy in 1798, seems to have been singularly unsuccessful in attracting clients in either way. Nevertheless he explicitly stated in the introduction to his first book, *Sketches in Architecture* (1806) that

> about to embark on a profession which of all others must stand in need of the powerful agency of interest [patronage], I have adopted the present means of notoriety . . . if this book shall be allowed to possess any degree of merit, I entertain but little doubt of meeting a proportionate reward.[3]

Peter Frederick Robinson, arguably the most successful in practical terms of the many such authors, was well aware of the benefits that accrued from a best-selling pattern book. In the preface to the 1828 third edition of *Rural Architecture* (first published in instalments in 1822/3) he noted smugly that the sales of the book had exceeded all his expectations, and 'the success attending my exertions to restore a species of Architecture, till now sadly neglected and almost forgotten, has been of a most gratifying nature'.[4]

Between forty and fifty cottage-related pattern books were published between the 1780s and the 1840s, almost all in London and a good many of them under the auspices of the Holborn publisher and bookseller J. Taylor.[5]

Some of these books were printed in plain monochrome with severe line engravings, but others were illustrated with aquatints, a softer, subtler technique introduced to England by Paul Sandby in the 1770s. A number appear to have been reissued later, seductively hand-tinted in watercolour, perhaps when the original monochrome plates were becoming worn.[6] Another innovation increasingly followed was to show the building in a beguiling landscape setting, with a preference for hilly and indeed mountainous scenery of a kind rarely if ever found in lowland Britain. A printed catalogue of the books available for sale at J. Taylor's Architectural Library, which can be dated to about 1812, shows that such publications mostly sold for prices between about one and two guineas, the most expensive being John Soane's *Sketches for Cottages, Villas &c* at £2 12s 6d.[7] They were bought not just by potential clients but also by other architects, obviously on the lookout for ideas in a genre they hoped to be able to exploit. John Nash owned cottage books by Joseph Gandy, Robert Lugar, James Malton and John Plaw, and Soane, though not himself a cottage designer, also bought several.[8] A number of surviving volumes bear the names of obscure provincial architects on their fly-leaves – for instance, a copy of P. F. Robinson's *Rural Architecture* is inscribed by David Vaughan, active in the Vale of Glamorgan in the mid-nineteenth century.[9] In the European context such pattern books are peculiar to England, and are not found in the architectural literature of other countries, with the exception of the United States of America, where both English pattern books and their home-grown imitators were profoundly influential.[10]

THE LOWER ORDERS

It is clear from the pattern book texts that a lot of thought was given to matters of social hierarchy – what was appropriate, in terms of accommodation and architectural elaboration, to the different grades of rural society. Some (with the horrors of contemporary Continental social unrest always at the back of their minds) expressed concern for the conditions in which peasants had to live, and urged the desirability of housing them well, so as to encourage good behaviour and high productivity. William Atkinson (circa 1774–1839), a prolific though not especially talented pupil of James Wyatt who specialized in asymmetrical Gothic houses, took a high moral tone in the introduction to his *Picturesque Views of Cottages* of 1805:

> The building of Cottages for the labouring classes of society, and the keeping of them in good repair, are objects of the first national importance; as it is from the active exertions of the industrious labourers, that the other classes derive the greater part of those benefits which they enjoy. Justice requires that everything should be done to encourage cleanliness among them, and to add to their comfort and convenience, which will not fail to have a salutary effect on their conduct and character, and tend, in an essential manner, to render them much more useful in their respective stations. . . . Those gentlemen who expend so many thousands in improving the landscape of their parks, ought never to overlook the adjoining cottage, or to neglect the neighbouring village; for by introducing improvement on these objects, they may add to their pleasure, by producing the most picturesque scenery; and at the same time, add to the comfort and happiness of their fellow creatures.[11]

Two years later William Fuller Pocock claimed that rustic cottages, 'or Habitations of Labourers', constituted a peculiarly interesting category of building, 'whether that interest arises from a heart, wishing to serve the cause of humanity in providing comfortable dwellings for a numerous part of our fellow creatures, or from ideas of improvement in the mind of a great landed proprietor'. Pursuing the line that happy peasants were a matter of national self-interest, he argued that

> the strength and consequent importance of every country depends upon its possessing bold, and numerous peasantry. . . . What is so likely to render them numerous as the possession of comfortable habitations where, after the labours of the day they may enjoy domestic comforts in the midst of their families?

Moreover, he said, if a small garden were attached to the cottages it would help keep the menfolk from the pub, 'whereby their habits of industry are relaxed and their morals corrupted'.[12]

Others clearly thought that the lower orders must be kept firmly in their place and not allowed or encouraged to get above their proper station in life; a number of authors remark on the tendency of labourers to get drunk, and Thomas Dearn went rather further in referring to 'the depravity of this class of men . . . liberally endowed with low cunning'.[13] John Buonarotti Papworth, while feeling that 'the symbols of ease and luxury are incongruous with the labourer's busy life and frugal means, and ought therefore to be omitted',[14] nevertheless conceded that there were embellishments that were appropriate: for instance, 'the porch in which he rests after the fatigues of the day, ornamented by some flowering creeper, at once affords him shade and repose; neatness and cleanliness connected with these and other means of external cheerfulness, bespeak that elasticity of mind, and spring of action, which produce industry and cheerfulness, and demonstrate that peace and content at least dwell with its inhabitants'.[15] He too believed that cottages should be provided with a garden, whose cultivation would remove the temptation to slope off to the village alehouse. 'The morals of the man are preserved, the example of a sober and industrious father is before his children, the wife is happy in the presence of her husband, and society rejoices that another of its members is an honour to his humble state.'[16]

Much of this preoccupation with the morals of the working class is found in pattern books published after the appearance of the Board of Agriculture's Report of 1804 concerning minimum building standards, which was of great importance. Joseph Gandy discussed it in his two works of 1805, *Designs for Cottages, Cottage Farms and Other Rural Buildings* and *The Rural Architect*,[17] and both Edward Gyfford (*Designs for Elegant Cottages and Small Villas*, 1806, and *Designs for Small Picturesque Cottages and Hunting Boxes*, 1806–7) and Robert Lugar advocated the building of cottages for gentlemen's labourers. Lugar in 1815 emphasized the point by comparing the dilapidated cottage so attractive to contemporary artists (such as Thomas Gainsborough, and as published by J. T. Smith in his *Remarks on Rural Scenery*)[18] with the well-built cottage, in good order, with strong thatch and a neat garden: 'These are the true characteristics of the habitation of civilized man, and of the peasant's cot.'[19]

SOCIAL CLIMBING

Of course, the pattern books were not just concerned with designs for the lower orders of society, which offered little prospect of fame and fortune, and the majority offer a socially ascending sequence that starts with modest cottages for the peasantry and works its way up to the middle class and sometimes beyond. One of the earlier publications, Charles Middleton's *Picturesque and Architectural Views for Cottages, Farm Houses and Country Villas* of 1793, states at the outset that 'Cottages are inhabited by the poorer sort of country people, and are chiefly built of slight materials, and frequently by their own skill and labour: they are the work of necessity, for which no rules can be given.'[20] This is in effect a definition of what constitutes the true vernacular, and Middleton's first eleven designs are for cottages to be built as entrance lodges or in different parts of parks or pleasure grounds, which he suggests would be occupied by estate employees and 'may serve the two-fold purpose of use and ornament'. Even the smartest of these, which though thatched and modest without nevertheless concealed a circular domed neoclassical dining room within, was not for permanent occupation by anyone above peasant status, since the ill-lit bedrooms shoe-horned into the roof were for the keeper, not the owner of the estate.[21] When Middleton moved up the social scale, to farmhouses and then to villas, the style abruptly changed to the classical, since in 1793 he clearly could not conceive of anyone above peasant status wanting to live in anything resembling a cottage.

The combination of smart interiors for the exclusive use of the proprietor and his guests with basic accommodation for employees charged with looking after the building was common. As Middleton put it,

> cottages in a more distant situation, are frequently fitted up for the reception of parties engaged in rural amusements; in which, one room must be particularly appropriated to that purpose, finished on a more expensive plan, and of such dimensions as will be capable of containing a large company; with necessary adjoining apartments and lodging rooms for the person who has the care of the building. The Bailiff, Gardener, Park and Gamekeepers, &c, are commonly lodged in such habitations.[22]

Another early publication, John Plaw's *Ferme Ornée* of 1795, offers a design for a fishing lodge in the New Forest 'intended to have been executed with roots and trunks of trees'. 'The plan in front contains accommodation for Tea-drinking parties, Fishing tackle &c. In the back part are accommodations for a Keeper, who would have the care of the waters and fishery, and his family.'[23] Plate 2 of Dearn's *Sketches in Architecture* of 1807, for an ornamental cottage for a park or grounds, contains sufficient accommodation for a bailiff and his wife, together with a dairy, over which is a cheese store, and a tea room for occasional use by the proprietor in summer, 'which, if furnished with a small library, would be an inviting retreat'. It would have been the business of the bailiff's wife, in addition to the management of the dairy, to attend to the tea-room visitors.

Plaw (c.1745–1820), who started as a Westminster architect and master builder before moving to Southampton in about 1795, was a man on the lookout for opportunities of self-promotion. He exhibited at the Royal Academy from 1775, which is also the date of his first-known building, Belle Isle on Lake Windermere, and his pattern book *Rural Architecture*, of 1785, is sometimes said to include the first published designs for cottages ornés. In fact none of the designs are orné; there is one for little cottages, and one for a cottage-cum-shooting or fishing lodge, both thatched but not orné. The others designs in the book are all for classical houses of varying sizes. Its popularity is illustrated by the fact that there were subsequent editions in 1794, 1796, 1800, 1802 and 1804. However, by 1800, when he published *Sketches for Country Houses, Villas and Rural Dwellings*, he had realized that there was a market for middle-class cottages. The book was, he said, 'calculated for persons of moderate income, and for comfortable retirement'. Although the first few designs are unequivocally for peasant occupation, others hedge their bets, being capable of providing two cramped units or one spacious; Plate VI, for example, on the face of it a medium-sized thatched Gothick cottage, could be divided internally into two units, entered from opposite façades. However, as Plaw observes, 'this Double Cottage may be constructed as one, and would be a very comfortable dwelling', with two spacious bow-ended reception rooms. Similarly, Plate VII is two cottages looking externally like one, and capable of being adapted as a single residence, with pyramidal thatched roof, Gothic windows and tree-trunk 'Viranda in the manner of an Indian Bungalow'.[24] Plate XIII, thatched and with an elegant Gothick bow window, is explicitly described as providing 'a comfortable retreat from the bustle of the town, for the man of business or science'. Plaw's one-time pupil J. B. Papworth[25] echoed him when he wrote,

> the cottage orné is a new species of building in the economy of domestic architecture, and subject to its own laws of fitness and propriety. It is not the habitation of the laborious, but of the affluent, of the man of study, of science or of leisure.[26]

There was in fact some confusion about terminology amongst the pattern book writers. Some made do with the simple word 'cottage'. Others used the term 'cottage orné(e)' in the sense that would now be recognizable, while there were those who applied it to buildings with nothing of the cottage about them. Papworth seems to have been especially muddled, using it for Gothic and stripped classical houses as well as ones that were genuinely cottagey; he also used the term 'ornamented cottage', as did Edmund Bartell.[27] W. F. Pocock floated the term 'cabane ornée', which, he said,

> owes its origin to the taste of the present day, and though humble in its appearance affords the necessary conveniences for persons of refined manners and habits, and is, perhaps, more calculated than any other description of buildings for the enjoyment of the true pleasures of domestic life.[28]

It never caught on.

SYMMETRY VERSUS ASYMMETRY

In an age of overriding classicism, it is not surprising that professional architects instinctively turned to symmetry even when designing buildings with a supposedly rustic vernacular inspiration. Some used their pattern books to indulge in the design of buildings with plans and forms that appealed to their interest in geometry while being completely impractical – expecting peasants to live in buildings that were circular, triangular, pyramidal and so on. Joseph Gandy was one of the worst offenders,[29] but

by no means the only one; Plaw, for instance, had a weakness for the circular, supplying a poky cylindrical design for a fisherman or herdsman, another slightly larger for a gamekeeper or cottager,[30] and another larger still for Belle Isle on Lake Windermere.[31]

When it came to publishing designs for cottages most architects again opted for symmetry. Plaw, writing in 1800 in the preface to his *Sketches for Country Houses*, explained that

> the following designs are constructed on the principles of symmetry and correspondence of parts; because I am aware some persons think dwellings on a humble scale, and Cottages, ought rather to be irregular in their forms, and broken in their parts, taking certain structures for examples, which, in my opinion, should rather serve as beacons of danger, warnings of bad taste.[32]

He was certainly referring and responding to James Malton's controversial *Essay on British Cottage Architecture* published two years earlier.[33] Subtitling the book 'an attempt to perpetuate on Principle, that peculiar mode of building, which was originally the effect of Chance', Malton followed Richard Payne Knight (and Humphry Repton) in believing that cottages needed to be asymmetrical if they were to look authentic; Knight had written that the imposition of symmetry on a building was 'the extreme of absurdity and incongruity'. He in turn was reacting to yet earlier pattern books on the cottage theme, in which he said he had found many of the designs grotesque and whimsical, not always practicable in execution, and which 'sported with the eye' rather than satisfying taste and judgement. Some, he complained, were so wretched as to be termed hovels; no better were 'those tasty little dwellings in noblemen's and gentlemen's pleasure grounds, often making [i.e. acting as] the porter's lodge, adorned with handsome Gothic windows and glazed with painted glass'. 'The genuine British Cottage', he declared, 'equally rejects the wretched poverty of the one and the frippery decorations of the other.' Malton thought of a cottage as a small house in the country, of odd, irregular form, with various, harmonious colouring, the effect of weather, time and accident, and the whole environed with smiling verdure.

The designs put forward here and in his subsequent *Designs for Rural Retreats* (1802) were intended

> as hints to Noblemen or Gentlemen of taste, who build retreats for themselves with desire to have them appear as cottages, or erect habitations for their peasantry or other tenants; and to the Farmer as a guide in the construction of his dwelling, that it may agree and correspond with the surrounding scenery.[34]

The campaigning note in his text is unmistakable: 'To gentlemen and persons of cultivated taste, I address this essay, and recommend them to take the Cottage under protection; which, unless speedily done, will be found to exist nowhere but on the canvas of the painter.'[35] In fact, although it has been claimed that the two books established Malton as a pioneer of the cottage orné,[36] none of his designs could actually be called orné [fig 4/1]. They follow the vernacular of the Home Counties, with half-timbering and clapboarding – some indeed could almost be representations of 1920s suburban villas – and it is difficult to identify any instances of their being copied in the decades after publication, although that might be because they so much resemble the authentic item.[37] Malton's main achievement was to stimulate debate and indeed to stir up something of a hornet's nest of indignation amongst the classically trained establishment, which in one sense was an extension of the whole controversy about the Picturesque that had been initiated by his heroes Knight and Price. Richard Elsam (active 1795–1821) was spurred by Malton to publish *An Essay*

on Rural Architecture (London 1803), which he subtitled 'an attempt to refute the principles of Mr James Malton's essay on British cottage architecture'.[38] But in the long run history was arguably with Malton, and others – though not everyone – agreed with him that the cottage was better asymmetrical than symmetrical. Robert Lugar, acknowledging in 1805 that much had been written on this vexed subject, expressed his conclusion that

> the broken line must be considered peculiarly in character for a picturesque Cottage, whether it be the habitation of a gentleman or a peasant. . . . A lean-to closet, a bow-window, a pent-house, chimneys carried high and in masses, or gable ends, are suitable picturesque objects.[39]

PLAIN VERSUS FANCY

There were many aspects of the cottage idiom that generated debate and dissension between its advocates. If the most fundamental was the question of symmetry or asymmetry, another was that of ornament – should, in fact, modern cottages be ornamented at all? Richard Payne Knight set the tone for some by proclaiming that

> rustic lodges to parks, dressed cottages, pastoral seats, gates and gateways made of unhewn branches and stems of trees, have all necessarily a still stronger character of affectation; the rusticity of the first being that of a clown in a pantomime, and the simplicity of the others that of a shepherdess in a French opera.[40]

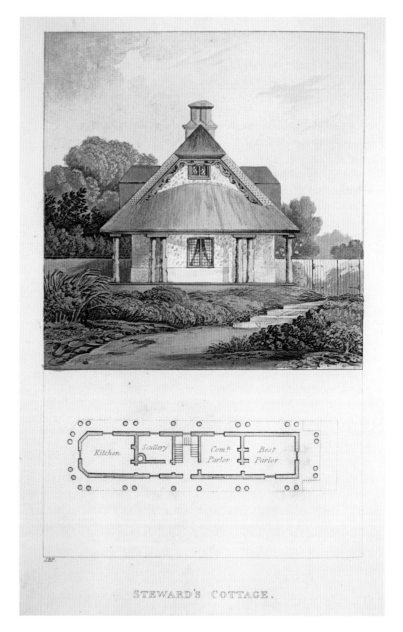

STEWARD'S COTTAGE.

He was in fact dismissive of the whole middle-class cottage orné genre, believing that 'to adapt the genuine style of a herdsman's hut, or a ploughman's cottage, to the dwellings of opulence and luxury, is as utterly impossible as it is to adapt their language, dress and manners to the refined usages of polite society'.[41] Malton claimed never to have found any published designs that he would have called true cottages, and his disciple W. F. Pocock referred disparagingly to other architects' unduly fanciful and impractical designs, whereas he himself had concentrated on economy at the expense of novelty.[42] His designs are indeed very restrained, the cottages all thatched but without fancy eaves. Thomas Dearn, in his *Sketches in Architecture*, referred to 'the avidity with which novelty is sought after by the generality of mankind', having given rise to 'those numberless caprices and absurdities'. 'This insatiable appetite for novelty which characterizes the present times', he commented severely, compelled the artist 'to deviate from the regular path of his profession'. The design to which these strictures were a preamble could be seen as an elegant happy medium, combining Gothic windows, tree-trunk columns and crisp thatch within a neat rectangular footprint.[43] [See fig 10/16]

Edmund Bartell considered that moderation should be the keynote – that 'as a retreat from the hurry of town life, the ornamented cottage is rational and elegant; and it is only to be condemned when carried beyond the bounds of that simplicity which should be its characteristic distinction'.[44] In his view 'frippery, thus employed about the cottage, destroys its simplicity, and gives it a tricked-out appearance of many of the small houses in the suburbs of the metropolis'.[45] John Plaw opted for plainly trimmed thatch but enlivened his designs quite variously with Gothic windows, trellis, tree-trunk columns with the bark left on, even in one case a rocky wall surface.[46] To J. B. Papworth, 'no sort of building is more decorative to rural scenery than that which is designed in the "cottage style"' – provided it wasn't adopted for villas large enough to be termed country mansions, as it had lately been.[47] His own cottage designs are generally restrained, relying on deep thatch, semicircular gables and plain posts for the verandahs. His otherwise simple design for a steward's cottage (plate IV) [fig 4/2], has a playfully curvaceous eaves board to the end gable, as does that for a farm-house (plate X), although the cottage

'adapted to receive trained foliages' (plate VII) [fig 4/3], has trellis arches flanking a central pinnacled Gothic bay window.

As time went on the puritanical resistance to ornament weakened. It was above all P. F. Robinson in the 1820s and 1830s who promoted the deployment of fanciful eaves and picked up on the elaborate chimneys first introduced by Nash and G. S. Repton.[48] The trend was taken even further by architects such as Francis Goodwin in his *Domestic Architecture* (1833–4) and Thomas Ricauti (*Rustic Architecture*, 1840),[49] and for those who wished to incorporate carved decorative details with a reliable medieval or Tudor pedigree, there was also A. C. Pugin's *Ornamental Gables*, published in 1831 and illustrating thirty examples 'selected from ancient examples' in England and France.

COTTAGE ORNEE.

MATERIALS

To the extent that the cottage orné was a derivative of the vernacular cottage, certain of its component materials (notably thatch) already suggested themselves, while other 'rustic' materials like tree-trunk columns and pebble pavements had been popularized in garden buildings of the earlier eighteenth century.[50] Most of the pattern books in fact recommended materials, and some (notably Gandy's *Designs for Cottages* and Plaw's *Sketches*) gave estimates of cost, though Malton sensibly declined to do this since he rightly observed that this must vary according to local conditions, availability of particular materials and so on. Plaw echoed Repton's *Sketches and Hints* ('a work of great taste and ingenuity') in saying that designs for houses needed to be adapted to their particular

situation,[51] but in practice there were only limited regional variations in design and construction – for instance, slate for roofs instead of the otherwise ubiquitous thatch and local stone rather than flimsier walling where the weather was particularly wet, such as the Lake District. As Plaw put it, 'The covering may be of slates, copper, wood painted, or coated, to resist the weather &C; but for cottages, thatch is certainly most characteristic, and may be of straw, reeds, rushes &c.'[52] Bartell called thatch 'warm, and picturesque beyond any other covering', and particularly recommended reed rather than straw;[53] Papworth echoed this preference, saying that reed caught fire less easily and was not so prone to harbour birds, mice and other vermin.[54] Dearn offered a design for a cottage lodge thatched with 'heath' – i.e. heather – which was another material favoured in mountainous areas, especially on the Celtic fringes.[55]

For the main structure of the cottages, a number of authors discussed the pisé or rammed-earth technique.[56] Plaw was perhaps the first English architect to do so, drawing attention to it in the Advertisement to *Ferme Ornée* in 1795, where he referred to it as 'the new method of building walls for cottages &c, as practiced in France'. He alluded to it again in *Sketches for Country Houses*, by which time Henry Holland had translated A. M. Cointereaux's treatise on the subject and the Board of Agriculture had published the method. Papworth likewise referred to it as 'introduced to us by the late Mr Holland, the architect . . . in great repute in Italy and the south of France'.[57] It was of course an authentically rustic method and as such to be restricted to cottages for peasants. More generally, authors recommended brick, but this was never to be exposed, particularly if it was red. Most suggested covering it with roughcast; Robert Lugar[58] felt red brick produced an 'unpleasant fiery tone', though on the other hand whitewash produced 'an inharmonious glare'. Edmund Bartell agreed that it was essential to avoid fierce red brick or the bright, glaring whitewash favoured by the Welsh. 'Where true taste resides, I am persuaded that pure white walls, blue tiles, green shutters, and similar puerilities, will never be found. Frippery, thus employed about the cottage, destroys simplicity.'[59] The answer, it was generally agreed, was to tint the whitewash discreetly so that there was less contrast with the other materials deployed. These might include rubble-stone, flint, brick noggin or weatherboarding.[60]

Whether the cottage was for peasants or clients further up the social ladder, all agreed that rustic tree trunks were admirable for colonnades or to support overhanging thatch: as Bartell put it, 'Trees of a proper size, in their rough state, having only their bark taken off, are the most proper supports; around which the ivy or the woodbine may be properly trained.'[61] In support of this particular feature, Papworth quoted Sir William Chambers on the subject of tree-trunk columns and the structure of the primitive hut.[62] In one of his designs Dearn recommended rustic columns with the bark left on (with stone for the plinth on which they stood),[63] while in another 'the rustic columns are formed of the trunks of the fir in their rough state, with a coat of varnish as a security against the weather'.[64] In his few cottage designs Charles Middleton suggested 'rude trunks of trees, painted green' to support the overhang.[65] Some authors recommended oak as the more durable wood for columns and posts, and both Papworth and Robinson thought that woodwork generally, if not actually of oak, should be grained to imitate it.[66] Opinions were divided as to the desirability of trellis-work; Bartell declared that 'facades of trellis-work, surrounding either doors or windows, never produce a good effect . . . they are also generally painted white or green which, in scenes of this kind, is foreign to every principle of harmony',[67] but most deployed it without demur.

One feature of a cottage that could assume some visual importance was the chimney. Nash and the Repton brothers had demonstrated this at the much admired Blaise Hamlet, and although many of the pattern book designers opted for a very simple approach, the ornamental Tudoresque chimney with clustered groupings and patterned brickwork was increasingly proposed from the 1820s by architects such as P. F. Robinson and Francis Goodwin. This obviously begged the question of cost, so of one such design Robinson wrote:

> An objection may probably be raised to the
> ornamental shafted Chimney, and it is true this
> creates some labour, but a little practice will
> conquer any difficulty which may at first appear, and
> the effect will amply pay for this additional labour.
> Bricks formed in moulds to different patterns are
> easily applied to circular and octangular shafts.[68]

PLANTING

Many authors believed a peasant cottage should have a garden, for the reasons already explained. Middle-class cottages would inevitably have a garden of some kind, and some made suggestions as to its layout and planting. As for the cottage itself, it was generally accepted that it would to a greater or lesser extent support climbers – indeed Papworth's *Rural Residences* includes a design explicitly described as a cottage orné 'adapted to receive trained foliages'.[69] Malton cited Payne Knight's poem *The Landscape*:

> Its roof, with reeds and mosses covered o'er,
> And honey-suckles climbing round the door,
> While mantling vines along its walls are spread,
> And clustering ivy decks the chimney's head.[70]

The importance of climbers, especially flowering ones, to the cottage concept is shown by the names adopted for several of the cottages at Blaise Hamlet: Vine, Sweet Briar, Jessamine, Rose. For Pocock, the architectural ornaments of a cottage could include trellis 'for the support of the shooting tendrils of the vine, or gay luxuriance of the Passion Flower'.[71] For the class-conscious, however, there were distinctions to be drawn even in the kingdom of plants. Lugar decreed that

> Ornamental trellis work may sometimes be used, but
> rather sparingly. . . . If creepers are set to embower
> the trellis work, plant the monthly rose, and clymatis
> or virgin bower, which grow luxuriantly, and when in
> blossom have a beautiful rich appearance, but no
> common creepers or honeysuckles should be seen
> near the Cottage Ornée; their province is to shade
> and enrich the peasant's cot.[72]

INTERIORS

Interior decoration might have been considered to be primarily the province of the owner of a property, but that did not prevent some architects from offering advice. Edmund Bartell's text-heavy *Hints for Picturesque Improvements* noted that it was generally thought that only the exterior of a cottage mattered, and consequently the interior often disappointed. However, in his view 'there

A COTTAGE ORNÉ.

The furniture should correspond with the character of the building; chairs of yew-tree, or elm, and tables of oak or wainscot should take the place of mahogany. The walls white, or, at most, tinged with a wash of some modest, pleasing colour; while the doors, window-frames, floors, skirting, chimney-pieces &c should correspond with the chairs and tables, and be left as from the hands of the carpenter. . . . Paint appears to me to be as unnecessary in the adorned as in the labourer's cottage.[73]

Ricauti went a step further in his *Rustic Architecture* by including designs for rustic furniture, such as a twiggy chair and table.[74] The influential John Claudius Loudon, in his *Encyclopaedia of Cottage, Farm and Villa Architecture and Furniture* of 1836, provided every possible bit of practical information for every aspect of such buildings, outside and in, including furniture from the smart to the humble.

J. B. Papworth in particular felt that clients (and he meant of course the middle class rather than peasants) should consult their architects not just about what he called 'the finishings' but also about the design of the furniture.[75] Given the extreme paucity of contemporary interior views surviving to illustrate what a middle- or upper-class cottage interior looked like, Papworth's lengthy and detailed description of the cottage he designed for two ladies in the Lake District [fig 4/4] is especially valuable, the more so since the implication of his text is that he superintended the interior himself. Whether consciously or not, this vanished and otherwise unrecorded interior evidently had fashionable royal antecedents, since the 1818 description calls to mind both the interiors of the Brighton Pavilion and Princess Elizabeth's decorations at her own cottage at Windsor.[76]

The entrance is by a rustic porch supported by the stems of elm-trees; the little hall and staircase are decorated with trellising, composed of light lath and wicker basket-work, very neatly executed, and painted a dark green: this is placed against the papering of the walls and ceilings, which are of a deep buff colour. Flower-stands and brackets are attached at various parts, from the bottom to the top of the staircase. The railing of the stairs being also of basket-work, the strings &c are painted buff or green, as the occasion

is no necessity for excluding the comforts of life from the ornamented cottage', and he therefore proceeded to give his prescription. For a start, if the exterior detail was Gothic, so should that of the interior be, and in his view it was perfectly permissible to introduce painted or stained glass – though he disliked the 'glaring' colours so characteristic of the period: blues, reds, greens, orange and purples.

required; for every part is so arranged that the green may be relieved by the buff, or the buff by the green. The most elegantly beautiful flowering plants are selected as embellishments, and are tastefully disposed on the several flower-stands; thus the walls are everywhere adorned with them, and some are trained over the trellis of the ceilings, whence they hang in festoons and unite their branches . . .

A small lobby connects the music room, drawing room and parlour, so that they are en suite. . . . [These rooms] are very simply and neatly decorated by compartments coloured in tints resembling an autumnal leaf, the yellow-green of which forms the panels, and its mellower and pinky hues compose a very narrow border and stile that surround them. The draperies are of buff chintz in which sage-green leaves and small pink and blue-and-white flowers prevail; the furniture is cane-coloured. Upright flower stands of basket-work are placed in each angle of the room, and the verandah is constantly dressed with plants of the choicest scents and colours.

The drawing room is fancifully ornamented with paper in imitation of bamboo and basket-work, in the colour of cane upon a sky-blue ground; each side [of the room] is divided into compartments by pilasters, which support a sort of roofing and transverse bamboo rods, to which seem to be suspended the most exquisite works of the Chinese pencil [consisting] of views of their apartments, representations of the costume of the people, and of the natural productions of China. A very able artist has further decorated this room by painting a variety of Oriental plants, as supported by the pilasters &C about which they entwine, and arriving at the ceiling they terminate, after spreading a short distance upon it. The furniture and draperies are the same as in the parlour.

The book-room is coloured a tea-green, which is relieved by blossom colour and brown. The chambers are papered with a small and simple trellis pattern, and the draperies white, with a mixture of lavender colour and buff. In the whole of this cottage there is no portion of gilding; the glasses are let into the walls and covered by the paper decorations; and even the book bindings are unornamented by gold, the lettering being merely stamped upon them.[77]

INFLUENCES

Some index of a pattern book's success was the number of editions it ran to, and certain publications were repeatedly reissued – Plaw's *Rural Architecture* ran to at least eight; Lugar's *Architectural Sketches* ran to three, as did Pocock's *Architectural Designs* and Goodwin's *Domestic Architecture* (also published as *Rural Architecture*). P. F. Robinson was overall probably the most prolific: *Rural Architecture* clocked up five editions, *Designs for Ornamental Villas and Village Architecture* four, and *Designs for Lodges and Park Entrances* three. However, the most basic tests of success were whether the book brought its author any commissions or, failing that, whether anyone else copied the designs. Some authors made a point of noting that individual designs had already been built for such-and-such a client, or had at least been prepared for particular clients. Otherwise it is a question of linking published designs with extant buildings, or trying to detect the influence between the one and the other.

Several of Plaw's published designs found imitators, especially those in *Sketches*.[78] Plate IV/4 [fig 4/5], a circular cottage for a fisherman or herdsman, appears to be the basis for the Round House in the park at Ickworth House, Suffolk, being cylindrical with an inset loggia of tree-trunk columns. The Round House [fig 4/6] is larger and has the addition of a band of half-timbering under the eaves, giving it the appearance of a stunted Victorian water tower; the date is thought to be the 1830s. It now has a conical slate roof but was probably originally thatched, like the other two cottages ornés elsewhere in the same park.[79] Plate XII/12 [fig 4/7] of the same book is another circular cottage, roughcast and thatched, this time with tree-trunk columns spaced out round the perimeter and wreathed in the obligatory climbers. 'It will admit of four bedrooms in the roof and would make a pretty object in a Gentleman's Park, for a Gamekeeper or Cottager', says Plaw. His design is for a keeper's lodge, which he felt would make a convenient dairy, 'for which purpose, some time ago, I gave the drawing to a Gentleman in Yorkshire'. His plate probably supplied the general model for Beehive Lodge at Costessey on the outskirts of Norwich [fig 4/8], and possibly for the four circular lodges on the Duke of Hamilton's estate at Easton, Suffolk [fig 2/28].[80] Another Suffolk Round

LEFT 4/5 John Plaw, *Sketches,* plate IV
ABOVE 4/6 Round House, Ickworth House, Suffolk

BELOW 4/7 John Plaw, *Sketches,* plate XII
BELOW LEFT 4/8 Beehive Lodge, Costessey, Norfolk

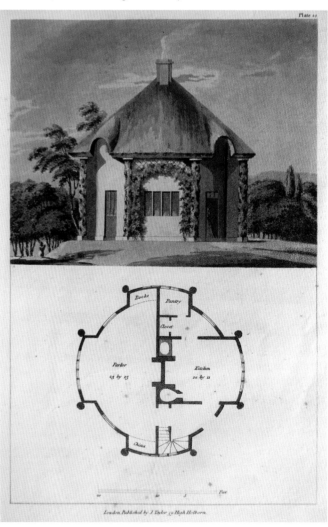

House, that in the grounds of Ixworth Abbey [fig 4/10] to the north of Bury St Edmunds, looks like a circular adaptation of Plaw's rectangular design in Plate VII/7 [fig 4/9], with its encircling tree-trunk verandah, Gothic windows and dormer tucked into the thatch – pyramidal in Plaw's plate, conical in the lodge as built.

Plate XV/15 [fig 4/12], one of Plaw's most striking cottage designs, spawned a number of derivatives. It was, he said, 'of a grotesque Gothic character, with tree trunks in their rude state; and pointed Gothic arches; the roof and arches thatched with straw or reeds'.[81] The key feature is the trio of deep Gothic arches at the centre of the two main elevations, flanked by narrower flat-topped bays that give the impression of an extended Gothic Venetian window. Elm Cottage stood across the lane from the lodge to Nash's East Cowes Castle on the Isle of Wight and was demolished in living memory. It features in George Brannon's engraving of 1820,[82] from which it appears to have been so similar to the published design that it may have been by Plaw himself, who after all lived just across the Solent in Southampton between 1795 and 1807.[83] Another clear derivative, this time with the arches supported on extremely spindly columns, is Thatched House at Wateringbury, Kent. The motif of the three deep arches supported on tree-trunk columns appears on the side elevation at Blackbrook Cottage, Fareham[84] – also within easy range of Southampton [fig 3/15] – and is the dominant motif of the surviving original façade at Harford Hills House, Norwich, built for the Quaker banker Joseph Gurney some time between 1807 and 1824.[85] Umbrella Cottage at Lyme Regis [fig 4/11] could be seen as the most diminutive derivative, with the arches wrapped around the canted road-ward end to produce the eponymous umbrella shape that has caught the eye of visitors arriving in the Dorset resort for the past 200 years or so.[86]

A final Plaw design that can be compared with an extant English building is plate XI/11 in *Ferme Ornée*, for a fishing lodge with a cottage or keeper's house attached. 'Made for the late John Morant Esq., New Forest, Hants, . . . [it] was intended to have been executed with roots and trunks of trees, near the river in his park.' It bears some comparison with Thatched Cottage at Whatlington, East Sussex, which has twin weatherboarded end gables with tall ogee-headed windows, a verandah running between them, and a thatched roof. The much more

London. Published by J.Taylor 59 High Holborn.

elaborate design in plate XX/20 [fig 4/13] of the same volume, that described as a 'Villa in the Cottage Stile', was designed 'in the style of Mr Drummond's fishing cottage, on the river Avon near Ringwood' and was 'intended to be built by a Gentleman in Wales', though whether that ever happened is not known. Interestingly, however, the design was plagiarized within two years of publication, appearing verbatim (with German labels) in Grohmann's *Gartenmagazin für Liebhaber Englischer Garten*, vol. 1, pl.10, published in Leipzig in 1797. It was then used as the basis for the Gardener's House at Wörlitz, near Dessau [fig 4/14], in 1799.[87]

Robert Lugar (*c*.1773–1855) was the son of a Colchester carpenter, and probably had an early association with John Nash (he is noted as being in Carmarthen in 1796, as was Nash); indeed his different idioms – cottage, castle, villa – were very much indebted to Nash and show him to have been an essentially derivative architect. From about 1799 he was practising independently and was soon exhibiting regularly at the Royal Academy – for instance, in 1802 he exhibited a design for a cottage at Eastwood, Co. Tipperary, in 1803 one for 'A Cottage to be built at Dedham, Essex', and in 1804 another for 'Four Cottages'. In 1805 Lugar dedicated his first book, *Architectural Sketches*, to George Ward Esq. Ward had in 1793 bought an estate on the Isle of Wight, becoming a neighbour and close friend of Nash, and perhaps subsequently acting as Lugar's introduction to the Island. In 1814 Lugar designed Puckaster Cottage for James Vine, subsequently illustrated in his *Villa Architecture* (1828) but based (at the request of the client) on the design of Rose Hill Cottage, near Henley, which Lugar had already illustrated in *Plans and Views of Buildings, executed in England and Scotland* (1811).[88] In general terms, it cannot be argued that Lugar was a particularly influential contributor to the genre in the British Isles, but Alexander Jackson Downing was later to recommend *Villa Architecture* to his American readers, along with books by Loudon, Papworth and T. F. Hunt. Hunt's name is hardly known nowadays, but picturesque Irish gate lodges illustrated in his books have been identified as the Drenagh Lodge on the Kenmare estate, Killarney, and the Oldbridge or Lough Dan Lodge on the Glendalough estate, Co. Wicklow.[89] In 1825 he exhibited a design for a cottage in Hertfordshire at the Royal Academy, followed in 1828 by one for a house 'in the old English

domestic style' for a 'principal government officer' in Sydney, New South Wales.[90] Hunt's cottage idiom was so similar (and no doubt indebted) to that of P. F. Robinson that it is often almost impossible to tell their published designs apart.

Peter Frederick Robinson (1776–1858) came from the generation after Plaw, and became its most influential designer of ornamental cottages. First apprenticed to William Porden in 1790, he then became assistant to

Henry Holland, and in 1801– 4 supervised the execution of the latter's works at the Royal Pavilion, Brighton. He was eminently typical of his age in that he could work in a wide variety of styles – Greek Revival, Tudor Gothic, Elizabethan, half-timbered medieval, neo-Norman, Egyptian (the Egyptian Hall in Piccadilly, of 1811–12, was arguably England's first building in the style) and Swiss. The design of the prominently placed Swiss Cottage on the northern edge of Regent's Park (about 1828) was the result of travelling through Switzerland in 1816. However, his books of cottage-style designs were his main claim to fame, much copied throughout the British Isles and further afield. The designs were perfectly set out for use by local builder-architects, many of the simpler ones being very practical and economic to build, enlivened by the carved wooden detail – the latter something easily achieved in the great 'timber' areas of Britain, such as the Severn Valley, which had always had a big supply of very able carpenters.[91] A great advantage from the point of view of the potential client was that Robinson provided a complete picture of what the building would look like, in each case including elevations, one or more accurately drawn floor plans and a seductive perspective.

Robinson's cottage designs were generally picturesquely asymmetrical, and their two particular hallmarks were the very prominent chimneys (usually ornamented) and the exaggerated cusping of the eaves, features picked up by other designers and taken forward into the Victorian era. In *Rural Architecture* (published in instalments in 1822/3, given a second edition in 1826 and a third in 1828) he provided two plates[92] illustrating 'the detail of Ornamental Barge Boards, with the Pendants and Springers', which, he said, 'give a peculiar air of richness to a gable', though he was at pains to point out that such features were not suitable for labourers' cottages [fig 4/15]. A good example of an extant cottage orné with these hallmarks and a definite Robinsonian look about it is Tudor Lodge [fig 4/17], on the Pusey estate on Berkshire, which has close similarities to Designs 1 and 2 in *Rural Architecture* [fig 4/16].[93]

Robinson's other main contribution to the evolution of the cottage genre was to demonstrate how the idiom might be adapted – one might say inflated – to create quite sizeable buildings. This was despite claiming that the term 'cottage' could only really be applied to dwellings on a

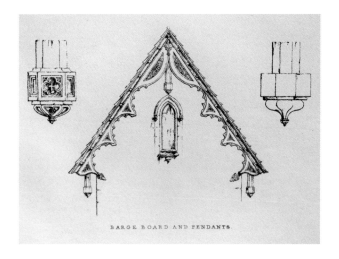

BARGE BOARD AND PENDANTS.

very moderate scale, 'and any endeavour to apply the character to larger edifices has invariably failed, excepting where the architect has produced the appearance of a cluster of cottages'.[94] He was here referring to an unidentified cottage erected to his design a few years previously, 'where an attempt was made to create a Gentleman's residence, upon a scale sufficiently large to acquire the ordinary conveniences without allowing the building to assume too much importance'. The ensuing design, No. XX (plates 89 – 96) [figs 4/18, 4/19], is of a sizeable house

> erected a few years since in Surry [*sic*], and although the Cottage style has been adopted, or rather that perhaps of the Ancient Manor House (for it can hardly from its size be denominated a Cottage), it has internally been arranged with every attention to comfort, and perhaps elegance. . . . The Hall is twenty-one feet by thirteen feet, and twenty-three feet high, being the whole height of the building, it is vaulted, with a gallery across the end. The Drawing Room is thirty-seven feet in length by seventeen feet in width, exclusive of the bay windows.

Robinson's elevations show that everything was to be thatched. The published design composes in a complex and completely irregular way, with numerous projecting bays (some masked by verandahs), overhangs, self-consciously varied gables and different clusterings of chimneys. It is in fact identifiable as Millfield Cottage at Bookham in Surrey [figs 4/20, 4/21], built for Major

RIGHT **4/16** P. F. Robinson,
Rural Architecture, Design 2

BELOW **4/17** Tudor Lodge,
Pusey, Berkshire

DESIGN. Nº 20.

London. Pubᵈ by Carpenter & Son. Old Bond Street. 1829.

General Bayley Willis in 1814, recorded in an 1822 watercolour by John Hassell,[95] and exhibited at the Royal Academy in both 1814 and 1815.[96] The published design forms the basis for what is arguably the finest Welsh cottage orné, Lancych in Pembrokeshire [fig 6/5].[97]

Another extant Robinson building whose design was exhibited at the Royal Academy (though not published) is Cheshunt Cottage at Cheshunt, Hertfordshire, designed for E. Clarke in 1824 and now called the Old Grange.[98] This is said to have been developed out of a seventeenth-century core,[99] which seems possible as the centre block, three storeys high and five windows wide, is entirely regular and not what one would expect if the architect were starting from scratch. This part has three gables with cusped eaves, and sash windows with Tudor dripmoulds. Framing it and creating a slightly more picturesque composition from the road side are projecting lower wings, also with cusped eave; overall, however, it is a very balanced and symmetrical composition.[100] The Hall, at Llanfyllin in Powys, is a sixteenth-century town house transformed in 1830–2 by the addition of identical trim to that at Cheshunt, so very likely by Robinson. Whether employed directly or through his books, Robinson was a pervasive

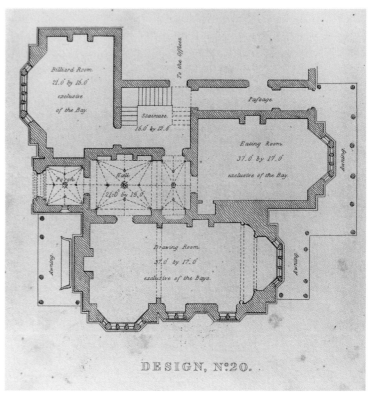

DESIGN, Nº 20.

OPPOSITE 4/18
P. F. Robinson, *Rural Architecture*, Design 20, plate 96

OPPOSITE, BELOW 4/19
P. F. Robinson, *Rural Architecture*, Design 20, plate 93

RIGHT 4/20 Millfield Cottage, Bookham, Surrey: entrance hall

BELOW 4/21 Millfield Cottage, Bookham, Surrey

BAILIFF'S LODGE.
DESIGN 2.

figure in Welsh cottage design. On the Nannau estate, near Dolgellau, Merionethshire, Sir Robert Vaughan, 2nd baronet (d. 1843), built four cottages to designs evidently provided by Robinson and then included in *Rural Architecture*, though omitting so much of the published decorative detail as to be almost unrecognizable. Efail Fach, for instance, is based on Design VI but minus the thatch and bargeboards, and with the half-timbering translated into stone.[101] Elsewhere in Wales, the Vivian family of Singleton Abbey, Swansea employed Robinson not just for their main house but also for smaller buildings, and other of his published designs appear at Singleton and Slebech in Pembrokeshire.[102] Across the Irish Sea, Robinson's influence is found in the lodges of the

Baronscourt estate in Co. Tyrone, theoretically designed by the Irish architect William Vitruvius Morrison but heavily indebted to plates in *Designs for Lodges and Park Entrances*; in the estate cottages of Adare, Co. Limerick, rebuilt in the 1820s and 1830s; and the estate village of Santry, Co. Dublin, based on designs by Lady Helen Domvile that in turn were directly cribbed from Robinson.[103]

Many of the designs offered in late Georgian pattern books are indisputably straightforward to the point of prosaic, no doubt in the expectation that potential clients might feel anything out of the ordinary would either be too expensive or would expose them to comment, or both. However, there were also architects prepared to stick their necks out and publish designs of real originality or eccentricity, even if the chances of finding anyone to translate them into reality were correspondingly fewer. One architect who falls firmly into the second category is Francis Goodwin (1784–1835). The son of a King's Lynn carpenter, he sought to gain commissions by submitting unsolicited designs in a range of idioms and categories – unsuccessfully in the case of his scheme for Magdalen College, Oxford (1822) but more so in the case of church-building committees in the Midlands. He was also an assiduous – though usually unsuccessful – entrant in competitions for more prestigious buildings such as King's College, Cambridge and the House of Commons. His decision to enter the competition for the new Houses of Parliament in 1835 led rapidly to overwork, insomnia and finally fatal apoplexy. His main stylistic veins were neoclassical (including the intimidatingly severe Greek Revival Lisadell Court, Co. Sligo) and Gothic, but in 1833–4 he ventured into what might in his case rather loosely be called the rustic idiom, publishing *Domestic Architecture*, reissued in the year of his death as *Rural Architecture*, with additional designs for cottages and lodges. This two-volume work includes some of the quirkiest cottage designs ever produced – not necessarily attractive, but certainly very singular, to an extent that probably ruled out their ever being realized. Design 2 in the first volume, for instance, for a Bailiff's Lodge, bizarrely manages to combine in a small compass triangular-headed latticed windows, a Tudor porch with strongly cusped eaves, sections of branching tree-trunk verandah and a main gable in the form of an open classical pediment, with rustic branches inserted into the bases [fig 4/22]. Design 4, a Gardener's Lodge, is basically a stripped Tudor cottage with thatched roof, to which have been added porch columns and strange eaves boards of distinctly Indian appearance. Design 5, a Parsonage House, offers a similar combination, in this case with some very strange window shapes. In the second volume, the first design is for a gate lodge, somewhat more conventionally Tudorish, but with what looks like the outline of Windsor Castle optimistically shown in the background. The only one of Goodwin's cottage designs that appears actually to have been built is Design 6, a gate lodge described as 'erected with some variations under the architect's directions, for Henry Hordern Esq. at the approach to Dunstall Hall, from the Stafford Road' [fig 4/23]. Cruciform in plan,

with tall tree-trunk columns spaced out around the perimeter, the building has an extraordinary thatched roof sweeping up to a central cluster of chimney. Although not known to survive, this must have a claim to be one of the most striking cottage orné lodges ever designed, and makes one regret that Goodwin's services in this field were not more widely taken up before his untimely death.[104]

1 John Plaw was one of the earliest architects to exhibit cottage designs at the Academy, starting in 1785, which was presumably connected with the publication of his first pattern book *Rural Architecture* that year. From the inception of the Academy in 1769 people were exhibiting views of English and Welsh scenery, as well as of Italy and the Alps. Algernon Graves, *The Royal Academy of Arts: A Complete Dictionary of Contributors 1769–1904* [1905], 2nd edn (London, 1970).

2 Richard Elsam, *Essay on Rural Architecture* (London, 1803), p. 1.

3 Confusingly Dearn's second book, which came out the following year and contained one or two cottage designs, was also entitled *Sketches in Architecture*.

4 The preface to the 4th edition (1836) stated that 'The very extensive sale of this Work has far exceeded my expectations; and as the demand still continues, or rather increases, a Fourth edition is now called for. As many of the plates were nearly worn out, they have been redrawn at considerable expense.'

5 Most of these publications are listed in Nigel Temple's card index of English pattern books, Temple Papers, RIBADC Box 26. A very few cottage-related books were also published in Edinburgh, such as James Thomson's *Rural Retreats* (1827) and John White's *Rural Architecture* (1856).

6 See P. F. Robinson's comment in note 4.

7 I am grateful to Robin Wyatt for information on this aspect of pattern books.

8 Notably Plaw's *Rural Architecture*, Francis Goodwin's *Domestic Architecture* and Dearn's *Sketches in Architecture*. I am indebted to Helen Dorey, Inspectress of Sir John Soane's Museum, for this information. The Soane Museum has Soane's own copy of the catalogue for the sale of Nash's library in 1835, annotated with prices fetched. A rather half-hearted rustic cottage was built to Soane's design as a lodge to Moggerhanger Park, Bedfordshire in 1806. It had simple Gothic windows and a curious three-legged rustic porch, and was demolished in about 1960. Jane Brown and Jeremy Musson, *Moggerhanger Park* (Moggerhanger House Preservation Trust, 2012), p. 79, fig. 8. There still survives at Moggerhanger a small thatched cottage dated 1800 and with the monogram 'G.T.' over the door, for Godfrey Thornton, Soane's client.

9 Information from Thomas Lloyd.

10 Priscilla Wrightson, Introduction to *Villa and Cottage: The English Picturesque 1780–1840* (London, n.d.). For American pattern books see Chapter Nine.

11 Atkinson's book is subtitled 'selected from a collection of drawings taken in different parts of England and intended as hints for the improvement of village scenery'. It contains designs for twelve cottages, all very simple and vernacular, with no orné features.

12 W. F. Pocock, *Architectural Designs for Rustic Cottages* (London, 1807), p. 5. Pocock (1779–1849), the son of a London carpenter, exhibited at the R.A. from 1799, showing his design for Sir John Eamer's cottage orné at Blackheath in 1811. Much later, in the mid-1830s, he designed Down Cottage at Harting in Sussex for his brother-in-law, Henry Willmer.

13 T.D.W. Dearn, *Sketches in Architecture; consisting of Original Designs for Cottages and Rural Dwellings, suitable to persons of moderate fortune, and for convenient retirement* (London, 1807), p. 4. Dearn (1777–1853) was said to have been the son of the Duke of Cumberland (brother of George III) by Mrs Horton, but because the king refused to recognize their marriage the boy was brought up by surrogate parents, Mr and Mrs Dearn. He moved to Cranbrook in Kent, where he supposedly designed several small houses. His only documented works are a Nonconformist chapel at Cranbrook and a lodge of 1809 at Angley Park, Kent, for Sir Walter James Bt, to whom he dedicated his pattern book *Designs for Lodges*. This is presumably the lodge to Broughton House, Dunton Green, which is an interesting exercise in Soaneian stripped classicism but not at all orné.

14 J. B. Papworth, *Rural Residences* (London, 1818), p. 9.

15 Ibid., p. 10.

16 Ibid., p. 12.

17 The Introduction to *Designs for Cottages* says the book was suggested by hints contained in the Board of Agriculture publication dealing with cottages and farm buildings, and 'originating in the humane desire of increasing the comforts and improving the condition of the Labouring Poor'.

18 J. T. Smith, *Remarks on Rural Scenery* (London, 1797).

19 Quoted by Wrightson, *Villa and Cottage*, n.p.

20 Charles Middleton, *Picturesque and Architectural Views for Cottages, Farm Houses and Country Villas* (London, 1793), p. 1. Middleton (1756–?) was a pupil of the leading mid-eighteenth-century Palladian James Paine and at one point worked in the office of Henry Holland, but despite this he never seems to have struck out successfully on his own.

21 Middleton specifies that the wall panels of the dining room are intended to be painted in *chiaro oscuro* with 'dancing boys &c'.

22 Middleton, *Picturesque and Architectural Views*, p. 1

23 John Plaw, *Ferme Ornée* (London, 1795), p. 6. The design was for John Morant of Brockenhurst House in the New Forest, for whom Plaw also designed a domed classical bath-house (pl. XIV).

24 The exotic link is further suggested by inclusion in the plate of a lady carrying a pot on her head, and cows wallowing in a foreground pool.

25 John Buonarotti Papworth (1775–1847) was born in Marylebone. His father, a leading stuccoist, was much used by Sir William Chambers, on whose advice the son was given an architectural training. He spent two years in John Plaw's office, and exhibited at the R.A. from 1794. A talented draughtsman (he added the name Buonarotti after someone flatteringly compared his drawings to Michelangelo's) and prolific architect, he was widely employed for making additions and alterations to country houses. Between 1813 and 1817 he supplied a succession of coloured plates to *Ackermann's Repository*, which were then republished in 1818 as *Rural Residences* (2nd edn 1832).

26 Papworth, *Rural Residences*, p. 25, text to pl. VI, 'A Cottage Orné' [in fact a Gothic house, not a cottage at all].

27 Edmund Bartell, *Hints for Picturesque Improvements in Ornamented Cottages* (London, 1804). Nothing seems to be known of Bartell, whose book is heavy on text (140 pages) and light on designs (six). His designs, though pleasant enough, are lacking in spark, and it would not be particularly surprising if none actually found imitators in such a competitive field.

28 Pocock, *Architectural Designs for Rustic Cottages*, p. 8.

29 Joseph Gandy, *Designs for Cottages, Cottage Farms and Other Rural Buildings* (London, 1805); *The Rural Architect* (London, 1805). Pl. XLI of the former has a pair of lodges designed as thatched cones, and pl. XXXIX a pair designed as pyramids. Gandy was influenced by the highly idealistic and impractical designs of contemporary French neoclassicists such as Ledoux and Boullée.

30 John Plaw, *Sketches for Country Houses* (London, 1800), pls 4 and 12 respectively.

31 Plaw, *Rural Architecture* (London, 1785), pls 25–30. *Ferme Ornée* has another design (pl. XIII) for a small circular thatched cottage, of which he notes rather bizarrely, 'This cottage, if properly built on wheels, might be moved at pleasure.' Later plates in *Sketches* experimented with quite substantial triangular and octagonal houses in a neoclassical idiom. Not entirely surprisingly, these seem to have found no takers.

32 Plaw, *Sketches for Country Houses*, Preface, p. 3.

33 James Malton, *Essay on British Cottage Architecture* (London, 1798), 2nd edn,1804. Malton (1765–1803) was born in England but accompanied his father Thomas (an architectural draughtsman) to Ireland, finally returning to London in the 1790s, making his living mainly as a topographical artist.

34 Ibid., p. 2.

35 Ibid., p. 11.

36 Colvin, *B.D.*, p. 673.

37 Pl. VII in W. F. Pocock's *Architectural Designs for Rustic Cottages* (1807), 'a double cottage of an irregular and picturesque form', is clearly a crib from Malton.

38 Dedicated to George III's artistic daughter, Princess Elizabeth, who was soon to have her own cottage orné at Old Windsor; see Chapter Seven. Elsam, a quarrelsome character who often fell out with his clients, subsequently published *Hints on improving the Conditions of the Peasantry, with Plans, Elevations and Descriptive Views of Characteristic Designs for Cottages* (1816), dedicated to Thomas Coke of Holkham Hall in Norfolk.

39 Robert Lugar, *Architectural Sketches for Cottages, Rural Dwellings and Villas* (London, 1805), 'Of Cottages', p. 5.

40 Richard Payne Knight, *An Analytical Inquiry into the Principles of Taste* (London, 1805), p. 224.

41 Ibid., pp. 224–5.

42 Pocock, *Architectural Designs for Rustic Cottages*, preface.

43 Dearn, *Sketches in Architecture*, pls XV and XVI.

44 Edmund Bartell, *Hints for Picturesque Improvements*, p. 5.

45 Ibid., p. 11.

46 Plaw, *Sketches for Country Houses*, pl. 3.

47 Papworth, *Rural Residences*, p. 41. He believed his design (pl. X) for a Farm-house or Ornamental Cottage was about as large as could be appropriate for the style.

48 P. F. Robinson, *Rural Architecture* (1823); *Village Architecture* (1830); *A New Series of Designs for Ornamental Cottages and Villas* (1838).

49 For Goodwin, see below, p. 109. For Ricauti, see Chapter Ten.

50 See Chapter One.

51 Plaw, *Sketches for Country Houses*, p. 4.

52 Ibid., Preface, p. 3.

53 Bartell, *Hints for Picturesque Improvements*, p. 17.

54 Papworth, *Rural Residences*, p. 19.

55 Dearn, *Designs for Lodges*, pl. XV.

56 See Chapter Two, p. 31.

57 Papworth, *Rural Residences*, p. 15.

58 Lugar, *Architectural Sketches*, p. 11.

59 Bartell, *Hints for Picturesque Improvements*, pp. 10–12.

60 All mentioned by Pocock, *Architectural Designs for Rustic Cottages*, p. 6.

61 A pamphlet published in 1815, *Fulcher's Hints to Noblemen and Gentlemen of Landed Property, how they may build Farm Houses, Cottages and Offices*, advised 'Let your Columns be Trees just as they grew with a flat Trencher for a Cap, of Stone or Oak Plank', p. 11.

62 Papworth, *Rural Residences*, 1818, p. 17.

63 Dearn, *Sketches in Architecture*, pl. XVI.

64 Dearn, *Designs for Lodges*: pl. III, a lodge for the Hon Colonel Stratford.

65 Middleton, *Picturesque and Architectural Views*, p. 2.

66 Papworth, *Rural Residences* p. 16; Robinson, *Rural Architecture*, Design No. 1, a gate lodge already erected.

67 Bartell, *Hints for Picturesque Improvements*, p. 25.

68 Robinson, *Rural Architecture*, Design No. IV.

69 Papworth, *Rural Residences*, pl. VII.

70 Malton, *Essay on British Cottage Architecture*, p. 6. Uvedale Price in his *Essay on Architecture* (published the same year as Malton's *Essay*, 1798) said that chimneys and climbing plants were important to a picturesque architectural composition.

71 Pocock, *Architectural Designs for Rustic Cottages*, p. 9.

72 Lugar, *Architectural Sketches*, p. 11.

73 Bartell, *Hints for Picturesque Improvements*, p. 47. Elsewhere Bartell alludes to a cottage known to him where mahogany furniture and fashionable wallpaper spoilt the effect of the Gothic studded doors and Gothic windows with their stained glass (p. 54).

74 Thomas Ricauti, *Rustic Architecture* (London, 1840), pl. VII. J. Taylor's *Catalogue of Modern Books on Architecture* (see above, p. 89) includes an anonymous octavo volume entitled *Ideas for Rustic Furniture, proper for Garden Chairs, Summer Houses, Hermitages, Cottages &c.*

75 Papworth, *Rural Residences*, p. 51.

76 See Chapter Seven. For the identity of the Papworth cottage in the Lakes, see Chapter Five, p. 134.

77 Papworth, *Rural Residences*, pp. 49–51.

78 For Plaw's career, see Geoffrey Tyack, 'From Practice to the Printed Page', *Country Life* (4 February 2009), pp. 56–9.

79 It is also related to the circular cottage in *Ferme Ornée*, pl. 13, which has three inset loggias round the perimeter. Another possible source is J. B. Papworth's design for a circular gamekeeper's lodge, published in his *Ornamental Gardening* of 1823, which obviously derives from Plaw's plate in *Sketches*. Of the other two cottages ornés in the Ickworth landscape, Mordaboys appears first on the 1846 Little Saxham tithe map, and the White House, though already shown on the 1815 Chevington tithe map, is thought to have been rebuilt prior to its appearance on the 1839 enclosure map. Both contribute to significant vistas within the park. Information on the Ickworth cottages from Anna Forrest, National Trust, who suggests that they may have been designed by John Field, an obscure London architect and builder recorded in 1827 working on the completion of the great circular mansion for the 5th Earl of Bristol.

80 See Chapter Two, pp. 54–5. They are probably mid-nineteenth century.

81 He provides alternative plans for it as one or two dwellings.

82 George Brannon called it 'a tasty residence' in his *Vectis Scenery* of 1830 (p. 27).

83 He hoped to make his fortune in large-scale building developments there but this didn't materialize, and in 1807 he emigrated to Prince Edward island, Canada, were he died.

84 See Chapter Three, pp. 69–70 .

85 See Chapter Three, p. 63.

86 The cottage started life as an 1820s gardener's cottage to the contemporary Little Cliff, the latter (originally High Cliff Lodge) being built some time between 1825 and 1829 (Richard Bull, *The Listers at High Cliff*, Lyme Regis Museum Research Papers, 2013). The roadside pavilion is octagonal and would have been really small, even if there was a room up in the thatch. It has its supporting pillars enriched with Gothic tabernacles containing little figures. The door looks like reused Continental woodwork, heavily carved, and above is a diamond-shaped window with elaborate tracery. To left and right of the door are oblong windows with pretty Gothic glazing. The building was transformed for himself in the 1920s by the architect Arnold Mitchell (1863–1944), who had retired to Lyme at the beginning of the twentieth century and by 1920 had moved to Little Cliff (now called Upper Cobb House). Mitchell was apparently fond of incorporating ancient statuary and other antique ornaments into his conversions, according to Graham Davis of Lyme Regis Museum. In 2001 a matching octagon was built at the rear.

87 See Chapter Eight, p. 206.

88 Robert Lugar, *Plans and Views of Buildings, executed in England and Scotland* (1811), pl. XXII/22 (plan 21). For Puckaster Cottage, see Chapter Five, pp. 128–9; for Rose Hill, see Chapter Three, pp. 64–5.

89 J.A.K. Dean, *The Gate Lodges of Ulster* (Ulster Architectural Heritage Society, 1994). See below, Chapter Six. Hunt's relevant publications were *Half-a-dozen Hints on Picturesque Domestic Architecture* (1825, 2nd edn 1826, 3rd edn 1833), and *Designs for Parsonage Houses, Alms houses, etc.* (1827).

90 Colvin, *B.D.*, pp. 547–8. Thomas Frederick Hunt (1790–1831) rose by the time of his death to be clerk of works at Kensington Palace. He was well thought of but lived beyond his means and was always being harassed by bailiffs. At one stage he took refuge in the gatehouse of St James's Palace and could only venture out on Sundays for fear of arrest.

91 I owe this observation to Thomas Lloyd. A good example is the former forge at Glanmule, Montgomeryshire, designed by J. W. Poundley for the Brynllywarch estate in about 1840, whose bargeboards could almost be recycled from one of the region's richly carved medieval rood screens. Robert Scourfield and Richard Haslam, *The Buildings of Wales: Powys* (New Haven and London, 2013), p. 128.

92 Robinson, *Rural Architecture*, pls 81, 82.

93 According to Geoffrey Tyack, Simon Bradley and Nikolaus Pevsner, *Buildings of England: Berkshire* (New Haven and London, 2010), p. 433, it was built *c.* 1830–40 for the estate forester, and is 'straight out of the pattern books of P. F. Robinson et al.' Both Designs 1 and 2 are described by Robinson as having been erected as gate lodges. Like Tudor Lodge, Design 2 has a roof of large stone tiles, rather than thatch.

94 Robinson, *Rural Architecture*, text to Design XIX (pls 83–8).

95 Surrey History Centre, Woking.

96 E. W. Brayley, *A Topographical History of Surrey* (1841), p. 473: 'Near Slyfield is Millfield Cottage, the curiously built residence of Robert William Hodges esq.' Daniel Paterson, *Paterson's Roads* (1831), refers to it as Millfield House, the residence of Robert Hodges. The building was considerably enlarged in 1863, with large additions on the south side, and is now the Yehudi Menuhin School. It would seem that the plan published in *Rural Architecture* is the reverse of what exists on the ground. The vaulted double-height hall with gallery is as shown, with the multi-bowed drawing room leading off it. The verandahs have largely gone. The most picturesque elevation is the west, with plenty of cusping to the juxtaposed eaves. In reference to Millfield, Ian Nairn wrote rather unkindly in *The Buildings of England: Surrey*, 2nd edn (Harmondsworth, 1971), p. 367, that 'Robinson could be bad in any style, an unusual attribute for a Regency architect'.

97 See Chapter Six, p. 146.

98 Colvin, *B.D.*, p. 880. The design was exhibited in 1824.

99 Nikolaus Pevsner and Bridget Cherry, *Buildings of England: Hertfordshire*, 2nd edn (Harmondsworth, 1977), p. 126.

100 Along the road, on the same side, is Cheshunt Cottage (actually now two dwellings), which looks like an existing cottage given cusped eaves, Tudor dripmoulds and tall chimneys at the same time. Between this and the Old Grange is now a modern house, but presumably they were originally part of the same property.

101 Richard Haslam, Julian Orbach and Adam Voelcker, *The Buildings of Wales: Gwynedd* (New Haven and London, 2009), pp. 640–41. Robinson states that designs I, II VI and XIII were 'erected for Sir Robert Vaughan Bart near Dolgelly'. Thomas Lloyd comments (personal communication) that 'the very hard and rough local stone made fine detailing impossible, and it is unlikely that any were thatched since the estate is famously on high ground and the buildings must have been very exposed'.

102 Using Design No. I from P. F. Robinson, *Designs for Lodges and Park Entrances, 1833*, described as 'erected in South Wales'. I owe this reference to Thomas Lloyd.

103 See Chapter Six, p. 155.

104 The Dunstall (also known as Demstall) Hall estate lay just to the north of Wolverhampton off the main road towards Stafford, and the lodge is mentioned in Goodwin's obituary. Henry Hordern (1796–1844) expanded the family banking business founded by his father in Wolverhampton. He married in 1828 and settled at Dunstall, becoming a JP and Deputy Lieutenant for Staffordshire.

CHAPTER FIVE

THE REGENCY HEYDAY

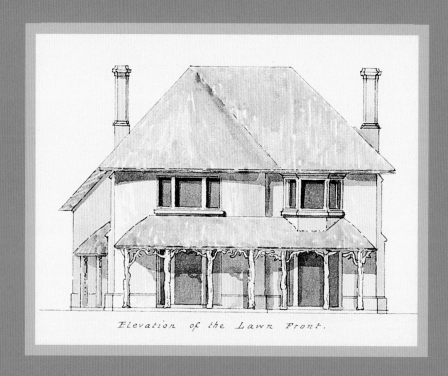

Elevation of the Lawn Front.

For much of the eighteenth century the Grand Tour was the classic way in which the wealthy British engaged in tourism and learned to appreciate the scenic and cultural attractions of the Continent. It was not until rather later in the century that they showed a comparable interest in their own country, and in one respect at least this was born of necessity.

PLACES OF POPULAR RESORT: THE SEASIDE

The outbreak of the French Revolution in 1789 gave tourism in England especially an unexpected boost, since it unsurprisingly made the British nervous of crossing the Channel. The impetus was increased by the declaration of war with France in 1793, after which, apart from two short interludes of peace, it became illegal for British citizens to visit France. Quite apart from those making the Grand Tour (who had tended to pass through France en route for Italy), many English tourists – particularly ones with health problems – had previously headed for southern France in the winter in search of sun, and now could no longer do so. It was at least partly as a reaction to this deprivation that when Sir Richard Hill (1732–1809) developed his extensive and dramatic park at Hawkstone in Shropshire in the 1790s, he equipped it with such travelista vignettes as a Dutch scene *à la* Ruysdael, complete with painted windmill; a 'Scene in Otaheite' (i.e. Tahiti – certainly not on the Georgian tourist circuit, but reliant on prints of Captain Cook's voyages); and a 'Scene in Switzerland', with a rustic bridge spanning a ravine.

The curiosity of the English about their own country was not entirely a new thing, since there had always been plenty of interest in historic sights such as cathedrals and castles, and increasingly this extended to country houses. Visiting the latter became a common activity amongst the leisured classes, as witnessed by the diaries of Mrs Philip Lybbe Powis,[1] the novels of Jane Austen and the publication of official guide books to places such as Stowe.[2] Lady Beauchamp Proctor, returning in 1772 for a second look at the recently completed Holkham Hall in Norfolk, was unpleasantly surprised to find that she had to wait for at least an hour with a crowd of complete strangers while a previous party went round; and by the time the first guide book was published in 1775, the whole business of visiting Holkham had been formalized: 'noblemen and foreigners' on any day of the week except Sunday, and 'by other people' on Tuesdays only.

Developing slowly but progressively in tandem with what might be called heritage and architectural tourism was the appreciation of the natural landscape, actively promoted by the Picturesque taste whereby people were encouraged to see landscapes through the prism of their pictorial potential. Writers such as the Reverend William Gilpin hymned the beauties of British scenery,[3] and a trickle of travel books grew to a flood, boosted by a proliferation of watercolours, aquatints (a process invented in 1773) and lithographs (invented in 1808). For the first time there was a widespread realization that areas such as the Peak and Lake Districts, not to mention Snowdonia, which had previously been shunned as wild and horrid wildernesses,[4] had much to offer the aesthetically aware.

Finally there was the growth of health tourism. This began in the late seventeenth century with inland spas such as Bath, Tunbridge Wells and Epsom, which led the way in a proliferation of places where people went to drink mineral waters. Then in 1750 came Dr Richard Russell's *Dissertation on the Use of Sea Water in the Diseases of the Glands*, which was very successful in awakening an awareness of the supposed health potential of the seaside, and led to the progressive transformation of what had previously been small fishing villages into places of fashionable resort. Doctors began to recommend the relatively mild Devon coast as a possible substitute for those, especially invalids, who had previously headed in winter for southern France, and Torquay received a significant boost in 1829 when the royal physician Dr James Clark specially praised the place in his book on the influence of climate on chronic diseases.[5] The Devon coast gradually became a popular retirement area for invalids, especially, it seems, returning East India Company officials whose health had been ruined by the subcontinent's climate. Inevitably, as in any other health resort, not all those who arrived found the climate as beneficial as they had hoped; Sidmouth parish church, for instance, has a monument to Mary Lisle, of Acton House, Northumberland, who came to the town to recover her health in 1791 and died instead.

OPPOSITE Penzance, Cornwall: design by George Wightwick for Pendrea, executed 1833–4

For resorts to develop there needed to be a clientele able to reach them without too much difficulty, and places for them to stay when they got there. London was far and away the main population centre in England, with a large pool of well-heeled people with the leisure and money to focus on the interests of their health. Until the late eighteenth century Londoners had headed primarily to Bath or Tunbridge Wells if taking the waters, or, if looking for sea breezes and sea bathing, to Brighton or Margate. Then in the last decades of the century came signs of a tourist industry developing along the coast of the West Country, with its centres particularly in the south Devon villages of Exmouth, Teignmouth, Dawlish and Sidmouth, together with Lyme Regis just over the border in Dorset. Exmouth and Teignmouth were the first to blossom, their clientele coming initially from Exeter, which was the region's biggest and wealthiest city and its main social centre.[6] In this period its professional class began to expand rapidly, with many lawyers, doctors, teachers and clergy taking up residence. By the late 1760s such people could take a daily coach down the Exe estuary to Exmouth, or a coach three times a week in season to Teignmouth. Interesting light on the early days of the South Devon resorts is provided by an expatriate American, Samuel Curwen, who visited them all in the years after the American Revolution.[7] At Sidmouth in 1776 he found very few other visitors, whereas two years later he noted that Teignmouth was already 'a bathing town and resorted to by men and company of a much higher rank than Sidmouth can boast . . . the houses [being] of incomparably better appearance'. Dawlish, by contrast, had few visitors and only one bathing machine. In 1779, Curwen spent the whole summer at Exmouth and found it easily the busiest, though there were evidently tensions between the residents and the brash Exeter bourgeoisie who came at weekends and put little into the town's economy (he was particularly outraged by the under-dressed young women who flaunted themselves on the Exmouth promenade). Certainly there was no mixing between the middle-class day-trippers and the more genteel long-stay visitors.

In these early days for West Country tourism most visitors making more than a day trip had to stay in old and very simply appointed houses; Fanny Burney, for instance, visiting Teignmouth in 1773, lodged in a 'small, neat, thatched and whitewashed cottage' owned by a sea captain,

with just two rooms upstairs and two down.[8] Such cottages could be rented for a mere guinea a week. However, there were architectural consequences to the progressive rise in the popularity of the South Devon resorts. Inevitably, as demand increased new houses went up, considerably more spacious and better appointed; more often than not they were conventionally Georgian, of brick with slate roofs, but it was not long before elaborated versions of the local cottage vernacular also began to appear.

Until the end of the century roads both within the region and between it and the rest of the country were terrible, but improvements progressively reduced journey times and made a stay in the West Country more of a realistic proposition even for people previously used to Brighton or Margate. In a period of war when many well-to-do were being affected by rising prices and increased taxation, the provincial resorts seemed cheap to Londoners, and in some cases they had the added attraction of putting a greater distance between them and their creditors. In fact by 1800 visiting seaside resorts, even as far afield as Wales, had become quite the thing for people of the middling ranks of English society generally. Jane Austen, though living well inland in north Hampshire, nevertheless made quite frequent visits with her family to seaside towns – Ramsgate, Lyme Regis, Sidmouth, Dawlish, Teignmouth and possibly as far afield as Tenby and Barmouth in Wales. The summer of 1801 saw them moving between the embryo resorts of the Devon–Dorset coast from their base in Bath.[9] By this stage George III's repeated summer visits to Weymouth, and the evidently beneficial effects on his health, had bestowed a royal blessing on the whole concept of seaside visits, and perhaps as a result an upward shift in social tone can be detected in the arrival lists published by the different resorts: like those for Bath, these began to include many aristocrats – even dukes and duchesses – as well as clergy and high-ranking officers. Indeed, thanks to the war, numerous soldiers and naval men were now stationed along the coast, and naval officers in particular spent their periods ashore at the new resorts with their wives and families.

Such people were unlikely to stay for more than a few weeks, or a couple of months at most, but in addition there was now a growing number of individuals who chose to settle permanently in such resorts.

Such places provided an ideal environment for those with comfortable but limited incomes to lead a leisured and genteel life. In particular, well-off spinsters and widows found urban living, especially in locations where they congregated together in numbers, an opportunity to construct an independent but respectable lifestyle, free from the potentially severe constraints of marriage. The high ratio of women to men found in the spas and seaside resorts, were in part a reflection of this.[10]

It was for this varied cross-section of upper- and middle-class society, from dukes and even royalty down to genteel spinsters, that the resorts had to cater architecturally, and for which cottages ornés of differing sizes sprang up. Sidmouth in particular thereby became arguably the *locus classicus* of the English cottage orné.

SIDMOUTH

At the end of the eighteenth century Sidmouth was still a modest village confined to the angle between the River Sid and the beach, the valley to the west being largely taken up with old strip fields with virtually no houses. Much of this land belonged to the lord of the manor, Captain Thomas Jenkins, who inherited in 1798 at an opportune moment to promote development. Samuel Curwen, in his journal for 1776,[11] noted that in Sidmouth there was 'much genteel company resorting to the town for the benefit of sea-bathing', and in 1794 the Reverend John Swete called it 'the gayest place of resort on the Devon coast'.[12] Even so, in 1801 the population was just 1,252. Half a century later it had virtually tripled.[13] Like most resorts Sidmouth had to indulge in self-promotion, and the town was popularized partly by John Wallis, who arrived from London and set up a Marine Library on the seafront complete with library and shop, which became a focus of fashionable gatherings. Wallis published *Sidmouth Scenery, or Views of the principal Cottages and Residences of the Nobility and Gentry at that Admired Watering Place*,[14] whose engravings recorded many of the elegant residences recently erected and must have helped to make the resort seem irresistible to those contemplating the move there. By 1836 another locally produced guide, Theodore H.

Mogridge's *Descriptive Sketch of Sidmouth*, could record, 'Of late years Sidmouth has been rapidly increasing; numerous detached villas have been erected, sheltered from the colder winds, and rendered suitable in every respect for the residence of families who seek the advantages of a mild and temperate climate.'[15] 'The town is flanked on either side by cliffs of great altitude . . . [the slopes of which] are thickly studded with mansions, villas and cottages ornées [*sic*]',[16] which the author then proceeded to enumerate in great and helpful detail.

Although the same guide described the Sidmouth promenade as a favourite place for fashionable parties, and the town's amenities as including several hotels, a library, billiard room, reading and concert rooms, *The Tourist's and Visitor's Hand-book to Sidmouth* of 1845 seemed to set out to discourage potential visitors and residents by depicting it as largely devoid of things to do. 'There are', it said,

> probably few places in the country to which less historical interest attaches than to the neighbourhood of Sidmouth, which is not remarkable for any event either ancient or modern.

There are further disparaging references in the *Handbook* to the demise of the cricket club, the lack of trout in the River Sid, and of game generally – and to the picnic as the favourite way of killing time.

> . . . The only public amusement which is found for the inhabitants and visitors of the neighbourhood of Sidmouth is the inspection of Knowle Cottage – the marine villa of T L Fish Esq; the liberal owner, who has adorned it with all that can render it tasteful and elegant, permits it to be inspected every Monday from July to October; and none who have visited this celebrated cottage fail to come away interested and amused with the bijouterie that is so lavishly spread forth upon the tables; and the eagerness with which this opportunity of amusement is sought after by the neighbourhood for miles around, shews, almost to demonstration, that if other proprietors were as liberal, or if the inhabitants of Sidmouth generally would make some little erection for the gratification of visitors, they would find their town much more patronized and admired than it is at present.

Mr Fish's Marine Villa [figs 5/1, 5/2], otherwise known as Knowle Cottage, was certainly the most remarkable building that Sidmouth ever boasted, and one of the most spectacular examples of the entire cottage orné genre. It is worth reverting to Mogridge's *Descriptive Sketch* for a full account:

This marine villa was erected by Lord le DeSpencer, AD 1805; it is a thatched building, forming nearly a quadrangle, and which contained about forty rooms; these have been much diminished in number by the present proprietor, who, by his improvements and embellishments, has rendered it a truly picturesque and enchanting residence. . . . The Grounds, about ten acres in extent, have the appearance of a small park. Scattered around are many figures on pedestals, and some foreign animals, whose habits of gentleness admit of their roaming about free and unshackled; among them are Kangaroos, Cape Sheep, two small Buffaloes, Pacas or South American Camels, and several varieties of Deer. Among the Birds are Emews or South American ostriches, Black Swans, Pelicans, Macaws, Crown and Demoiselle Birds, Gold and Silver Pheasants [etc etc] with a great variety of small foreign birds in the aviary or in cages. The suite of Drawing Rooms, nearly one hundred feet long, contain seventy-six tables, arranged in the centre and along the sides, covered with the choicest specimens of the art of the jeweller, and vases, figures &c of splendid Dresden China. The Breakfast room contains rare and valuable assortments of fossils, minerals, shells, corals &c. . . . The liberal proprietor of this elegant place, during his sojourns at Sidmouth (from July to October) throws open his house and gardens for public inspection, every Monday from two o'clock till four . . . this causes a great influx of visitors to Sidmouth on that day.[17]

In the following year, 1837, the Sidmouth bookseller John Harvey published an illustrated guide to Knowle Cottage. The text is comically grovelling and euphoric, larded with phrases such as 'unbounded joy', 'eloquent bursts of admiration', 'the fairy scene', 'the rush of spectators' and

so on, but taken together with the beautiful coloured plates, it nevertheless provides perhaps the fullest account of any significant cottage orné. As reduced in size by Mr Fish, it was an L-shaped building, with a vast thatched roof punctuated by Gothic dormers and coming down low over a verandah. The latter, according to the guide, extended along the south and east fronts to a total length of 315 feet. Twelve feet deep, it was 'entirely supported, at equal distances, by immense oak pollards, completely surrounded by ivy, roses, myrtles and flowering creepers'. There were also flower stands with geraniums and exotics, and thirty-four splendid china vases with flowering balsams. Various compartments of the verandah contained different attractions, such as a Canova bust of Homer, a fountain, a fir palm, specimens of yucca and other rare exotics. The interior was just as crowded with incident. In the entrance hall was a magnificent flower stand around an old oak pollard, with hothouse plants interspersed with goldfish bowls. This led into the 'grand suite of rooms' nearly 100 feet in length referred to by the *Descriptive Sketch*, lighted at each end with bow windows that had stained glass in the upper lights. The centre window of the first room commanded a view of a shell-encrusted fountain on the lawn,

with a jet of more than forty feet, and beyond that a panorama of the sea. The seventy or so tables disposed through the reception rooms were crammed with bijouterie – Dresden china, jewellery, fancy Genevese and Parisian clocks, bronzes. Ten more such tables were somehow shoehorned into Mr Fish's sitting room, which opened into a conservatory at one end of the cottage, and yet more along the 60-foot corridor giving access to the first-floor bedrooms.

As for the gardens, in addition to the extensive menagerie of exotic creatures (which was in fact confined to the outer park), there was on the lawn a domed aviary and a shell-encrusted Gothic summerhouse.

The seats are composed of rustic couches, and a table of the same kind of work is placed in the centre. The back is tastefully lined with green shells, and in niches, on brackets, are placed branches of coral and other marine productions; the shells are very tastefully covered with sea weed and sea moss . . . The view of the church and ocean scenery, together with the rich foliage from this spot, is really quite enchanting.[18]

All in all, it is easy to see why Knowle Cottage should
have proved irresistible to visitors to Sidmouth. Built originally by Lord le Despencer, who let it to the 1st Marquess
of Bute (an indication of the resort's social tone in the
Regency period), by 1821 it belonged to Mr Fish. After
his death in 1861 it passed to the Thornton family. Its
real downward trajectory began in the 1880s when it was
converted into a hotel, the many alterations and additions transforming and effectively ruining it. Conversion
to use as council offices continued the decline, although
the original single-storey cottage with Gothic dormers in
its deep roof, with verandah and cusped edging to the
eaves, can still be discerned within the present building.

Knowle Cottage was built well up the sheltered valley
that runs inland from Sidmouth's somewhat exposed
beach. Between the two is Woodlands [fig 5/3], originally
converted from a cob barn into a cottage by the Rev. Mr
Coplestone and then known as Old Hayes. In 1809 it was
purchased by Lord Gwydir, who renamed it Woodland
Cottage and in 1815 added a parallel range on the west
side, linked to the original cottage by reception rooms.[19]
An engraving published by John Wallis in 1816 shows it
as large, irregular, thatched and still predominantly vernacular rather than orné. Lord Gwydir[20] was a cricket-mad
friend of the Prince Regent, who supposedly visited him
here, although there seems to be no firm record of his
coming to Sidmouth. Gwydir's sister, the 2nd Duchess of
Northumberland, lived next door, which must have
raised the tone of the neighbourhood decidedly. Following
Gwydir's death (in Brighton, as might be expected of one
of the Prince Regent's entourage) in 1820 Woodland
Cottage was bought by Rear Admiral Henry Digby. The
next owner was Shirley Newdick Esq, who expanded the
grounds into a former orchard, with 'fine creepers'
entwining themselves 'in rich profusion' (according to
the *Descriptive Sketch*). Then in 1856 came Mr Johnstone,
who had apparently lived in Italy, and the alterations he
instigated gave Sidmouth its most striking exterior. He
replaced the thatch with slates and gave the dormers a
fantastical edging – supposedly of carved stone imported
from Italy but surely more likely to be terracotta and
English – said to represent seaweed, although it incorporates pierced Gothic roundels. Now painted pale pink,
the effect is like nothing so much as melting strawberry
ice cream – quite appropriate in a seaside town.[21]

Across the road from Woodlands is Powys Cottage
[fig 5/4]. Alternative designs[22] were made by Charles
Augustin Busby (later to become a leading figure in the
development of Brighton and Hove) for Mrs Powys Floyd
in 1815. These show a sizeable thatched orné bungalow,
long and low with the main south-facing rooms arranged
to either side of a glazed conservatory; in the alternative
elevation the flanking rooms are shaded by tent-shaped
verandahs with very seasidey striped canopies. Mrs Powys
Floyd had the latter version built in 1819–26 – and as
such it is shown in Wallis's engraving of 1826, looking
remarkably colonial – but after her death her nephew Sir
John Floyd added an upper floor whose thatched roof
was later replaced in slate. In the 1836 Sketch it is referred
to as

the abode of Miss Ridout; it is a thatched building
of one story; in length, one hundred and twenty feet;
the middle division of which is a conservatory. It is
surrounded with beautiful shrubberies, walks and
gardens, and commands a fine view of the church . . .
with the sea in the distance.

BELOW 5/4 Sidmouth, Devon: C. A. Busby, design for
Powys Cottage, 1815
OPPOSITE 5/5 Sidmouth, Devon: Clifton Place cottages
viewed from the beach

The *Sketch* continues,

> opposite Powis is Audley, formerly the abode of
> the Dowager Lady Audley, now the property and
> residence of the Misses Dawson, by whom it
> has been much enlarged, and converted with a
> considerable share of taste and judgement,
> from a thatched cottage to an elegant mansion.

On the slopes behind, in the suggestively named development called the Elysian Fields, stands Sidholm, built as
Richmond House in 1826 for the Earl of Buckinghamshire
and his new, second, wife. It was originally just three bays
wide with a verandah, but in 1848 the earl, who was also
a clergyman, added a large vaulted room at the rear for
use as his private chapel. As it now stands, the front has
ornamental gables, and windows with Tudor dripmoulds
and marginal lights. The two first-floor oriels have
Chinesey concave hats.[23]

The status of the builders of these Sidmouth cottages
perhaps suggests that the social tone of the resort in the early
decades of the nineteenth century was quite exalted, but by

and large the occupants mentioned in the guides of the
period are evidently middle class, genteel but not aristocratic
– widows, spinsters, clergymen, retired military men. The
Grand Duchess Helene, sister in law of the Tsar, took up
residence in Fortfield Terrace with her entourage for three
months in 1831, but she was very much an exception. So
too were the town's most celebrated visitors the Duke and
Duchess of Kent, who arrived with their infant daughter
Princess Victoria in December 1819 to escape their creditors. They took up residence at Woolbrook Cottage,[24] a few
hundred yards from the west end of the beach, but before
long the duke caught cold on the promenade and he died
the following month. Constructed in about 1810 and now
known as the Royal Glen Hotel, the building is slightly oddly
placed, built into a hillside so that the first-floor drawing
room opens directly into the garden at an upper level. It is
not in fact really a cottage, more a Gothick house, with battlements and fancy glazing, and indeed the latter makes the
building. A few of the drawing-room windows have roundels
of painted glass in the tracery, but otherwise the interiors are
pretty plain – the doors have reeded architraves characteristic of the Regency and that is about all.[25]

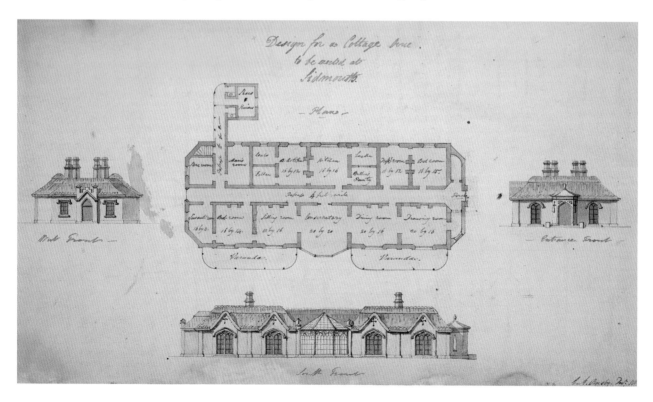

The Duke of Kent's ill-fated walk to the sea would have brought him to Clifton Place [fig 5/5], which climbs the hill at the west end of the beach and is the most picturesque ensemble in the town. Here, former fishermen's cottages were made orné. As the *Sketch* describes it, 'continuing our walk up the hill, and passing Rock and Clifton Cottages, we arrive at Cliff Cottage, the admired residence of Lieut Richard Murray RN, the prospect from which, of ocean, cliff, mountain and valley, is beautiful in the extreme'.[26]

THE WEST COUNTRY

Sidmouth is exceptional in the number of its cottage-style houses, and seems always to have been so. It might be assumed that what appealed to those commissioning houses in one coastal resort might do so at other resorts, but this seems not to have been the case. Lyme Regis, a few miles to the east, developed at much the same time and was indeed the favourite resort of Jane Austen, who included in *Persuasion* an encomium on the charms of the little town and its environs – the Cobb, the seafront animated in season with bathing machines and company, the beautiful cliff scenery to the east, the beach with rocks for watching the ebb and flow of the tides and, above all,

> Pinny, with its green chasms between romantic rocks, where the scattered forest trees and orchards

of luxuriant growth declare that many a generation must have passed away since the first partial falling of the cliff prepared the ground for such a state, where a scene so wonderful and so lovely is exhibited, as may more than equal any of the resembling scenes of the far-famed Isle of Wight.[27]

However, the only cottage orné recorded is the well-known Umbrella Lodge on the main road into town, which was certainly never intended for polite occupation.[28] Further east again along the Dorset coast, Bridport had been a flourishing port in medieval times and remained essentially a country town rather than a resort. In about 1840 it was extended on the southern edge by the small development of Portville, designed and promoted by a minor local architect called Joseph Galpin. This was mainly in a typical late Georgian classical idiom, but it included Belmont Cottage, designed by Galpin for himself and set back behind a sequence of detached villas that could just as well be in Cheltenham.[29] The house still exists, shorn of its grounds. Its gables have fretted eaves boards, with cross finials lending a rather spurious religious air. A contemporary lithograph interestingly appears to show batten-and-board construction of the kind later promoted in the U.S.A. by A. J. Davis,[30] but the walls are now smooth plaster, and one of the two porches shown in the lithograph has gone.

Moving west along the coast from Sidmouth, Budleigh Salterton was a small fishing village that developed slowly

in the early nineteenth century, though the pebble beach meant that it was never as popular as sandy Sidmouth or Exmouth. It retains two cottages ornés that are clearly by the same anonymous designer: Lyndale, which has striking three-sided arches to all its windows and a central mandorla-shaped window, sharply pointed; and Fairlynch [fig 5/6], with the same mandorla but normal Gothick windows, plus a tiny thatched belvedere on its roof.[31] Exmouth, though blessed with a fine sandy beach, and, as has been seen, the first of the South Devon resorts to develop, never seems to have acquired a distinctive architectural ethos; the eccentric A la Ronde (see Chapter Three) stood some distance inland, and was always much too *sui generis* to set a trend.

As was often the case, local landowners tended to take a lead in encouraging development. At Exmouth it was the first Baron Rolle of Bicton House, and at Dawlish and Teignmouth Lord Courtenay of Powderham Castle. The old village of Dawlish was a mile inland, and a new settlement began to develop on the seafront at the end of the eighteenth century. As Samuel Curwen's comment quoted above indicates, in the 1770s it was still a place of no account, but by 1793 the *Gentleman's Magazine* could describe it as 'a bathing village' where 'summer lingers and spring pays her earliest visits'.[32] By this stage buildings were beginning to proliferate, including terraces and individual villas, though none in a coherent way. In the next few years the stream flowing through the valley was straightened so that it ran through a broad lawn. At the head of this is Brookdale, thatched, with Gothic bay windows facing towards the sea. A second cottage, 'Minadab' is well out of the centre, on the coast road south to Teignmouth. In addition to being a port for the export of Dartmouth granite and local ball clay, Teignmouth was in 1803 called 'a fashionable watering place', and it too acquired a sprinkling of cottages ornés, of which Wodeway in Woodway Road is a charming specimen [fig 5/7], with its Gothick bay windows and thatched roof topped by a weathervane. The mid-1820s saw the erection of the classical Den Crescent, with an assembly room at its centre, and this coincided with the construction in 1825–7 of a timber bridge to connect the town with the village of Shaldon across the estuary. Facing the traveller crossing into Shaldon is Hunter's Lodge (the name is justified by the frieze of swags and fox heads running across the façade)

– more a diminutive Gothick cottage than a cottage orné, but its projecting bays with Gothick windows (all with intricate glazing) mark it as the work of the same anonymous designer as Wodeway and Brookdale. Similar glazing appears in the adjoining hamlet of Ringmore, where Old Stoke House is a row of old thatched cottages prettified with Gothick windows.[33]

Torquay also began to develop in the 1790s, and after a slow start was to eclipse the other South Devon resorts, particularly after a railway branch line reached it in 1848, but it seems to have generated classical terraces and Italianate villas rather than cottages ornés. The exception was Woodbine Cottage, built for Miss Anne Johnes and depicted in an engraving of 1823, where the Plymouth-based architect John Foulston is given as the author. The engraving shows a sizeable single-storey building, with verandah entwined with climbers, and Gothic dormers in the thatched roof.[34] A second engraving of 1823 shows the wider setting, complete with a bathing machine on the beach below the cottage [fig 5/8]. Miss Johnes came from Croft Castle in Herefordshire, so had perhaps migrated to Torquay for its more benign climate; if so, it worked, since when she died

in 1847 she was said be ninety-seven years old.[35] Perhaps her longevity was connected with regular invigorating use of the bathing machine.

The arrival of the railways in the region, vastly reducing the journey time from major urban centres and opening up the resorts to a very different class of visitor, was of course bound to disrupt the quiet gentility that many had prized. For that reason Sidmouth, not accessible by train until as late as 1874, retained its quiet Regency character to an almost unequalled degree. In the pre-railway age anywhere much further west than Teignmouth was simply too far to attract all but the very keen or the very retiring. Salcombe, near the mouth of the Kingsbridge estuary, was occupied mainly in fishing and smuggling until it developed as a busy trading port and shipbuilding centre in the nineteenth century. The turnpike road did not arrive until 1824, and its development as a holiday centre had to wait until between the two world wars. It nevertheless acquired 'the first gentleman's seaside residence in the area'[36] in the

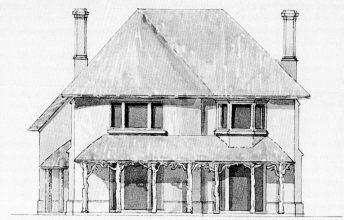

Elevation of the Lawn Front.

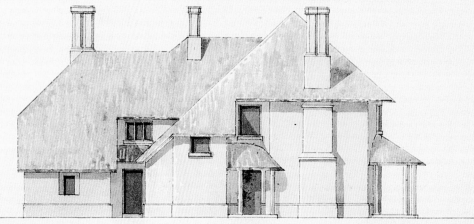

Elevation of the Entrance side.

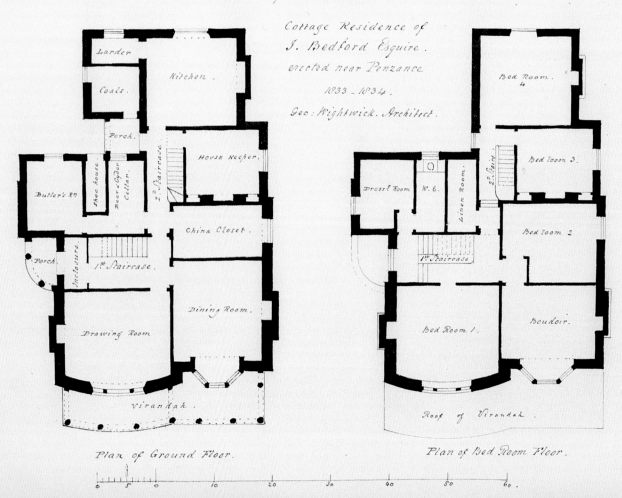

Cottage Residence of
J. Bedford Esquire.
erected near Penzance
1833 – 1834.
Geo: Wightwick. Architect.

Larder

Coals.

Kitchen.

Porch.

Shoe House

Beer & Cyder Cellar.

Butler's Rm

House Keeper.

2d Staircase

China Closet.

Porch.

Enclosure.

1st Staircase.

Dining Room.

Drawing Room

Virandah.

Plan of Ground Floor.

Bed Room 4

Dress.t Room

W.C.

Linen Room.

2d Stair

Bed Room 3

Bed Room 2

1st Staircase.

Bed Room 1.

Boudoir.

Roof of Virandah.

Plan of Bed Room Floor.

0   5   10   20   30   40   50   60.

shape of The Moult (originally Moult or Molt Cottage). Built in 1764 by John Hawkins 'as a mere pleasure box', according to his son Abraham (d. 1819), it stands on a steep wooded slope with superb views of the estuary. Although remodelled by Henry Whorewood, who acquired it in 1780, it was the next owner (from 1785), Samuel Strode who first gave it its Gothic cottage orné appearance. In 1794 the Reverend John Swete described it as

> a summer villa of Mr Strode of Peamore . . . the front of it was singular in appearance, having about one third from its roof, a projection supported by slender pillars assuming the form of a piazza or (as they have frequent in the East Indies), a Veranda. . . . Windows both below and above are of a gothic cast, pointed; and the frame-work with the mouldings, cornice and pillars of the Veranda, being painted green, an effect is produced uncommonly light and elegant.[37]

Some time after 1808 William Jackson of the Excise Office substantially extended it. The present gabled front to the estuary is asymmetrical, with wavy eaves boards and windows with Tudor dripmoulds – actually looking early Victorian rather than Georgian.[38]

In the Georgian period, as now, Penzance was the furthest west an Englishman could go, so its chances of developing as a resort must have seemed very slim. However, in 1797 W. G. Maton, physician to Queen Charlotte, wrote that 'The mildness of the air, the agreeableness of the situation and the respectability of its inhabitants render Penzance particularly inviting to residence, and, with regard to invalids, it may justly be considered as the Montpelier of England.'[39] Such an endorsement did a certain amount to draw visitors and new residents, but the early nineteenth-century housing was mainly of stucco or granite terraces. Further out were individual villas, but only Rosemorran near Madron seems to survive as an example of a cottage orné.[40] The architect George Wightwick (who moved to Plymouth in 1829 and took over John Foulston's practice) recorded his restrained design for Pendrea, a middle-class cottage orné at Gulval near Penzance, constructed in 1833–4 for John Bedford [fig 5/9]. Asymmetrically grouped and with thatch to the roof and twiggy verandah, the cottage came with four bedrooms as well as rooms for a housekeeper and butler.[41]

THE ISLE OF WIGHT

The scenic charms of the Isle of Wight were quite equal to those of the South Devon coast, and had the advantage of being closer not only to London but also to such well-frequented naval towns as Portsmouth and Southampton, from which the crossing of the Solent was neither particularly long nor – at least in reasonable weather – difficult.

From the late eighteenth century onwards, the Island (as it has always been known locally) was increasingly discovered by wealthy visitors, who either rented accommodation or built their own for summer occupation. Initially these tended to be along the north-east coast, from Cowes to Ryde (the points of arrival from Southampton and Portsmouth respectively). From here, if the location was carefully chosen, there were views over the Solent and its constant panorama of ships large and small – something of particular interest in an age when Britain's naval power was at its height and Portsmouth was its most important naval base. The first cottage residence in fact seems to have been Steephill on the south-east coast, which has been claimed as 'probably the key seaside cottage orné'.[42]

The viability of the claim depends partly on its date of construction and partly on how a cottage orné is defined, and certainly Steephill was an early example of a cottage built for permanent occupation by someone from an upper social echelon. According to Sir Richard Worsley, writing in his *History of the Isle of Wight* in 1781,[43] it was built by Hans Stanley, diplomat and MP for Southampton,[44] 'soon after he became Governor of the Isle of Wight' in 1764. The fact that Stanley committed suicide by cutting his own throat in 1784 suggests a personality disorder, which may be reflected in the fact that for the location of his cottage Stanley chose a cliff (the so-called Undercliff) overlooking the sea on a then remote and unregarded part of the Island. Worsley described the building as 'admirably contrived and most elegantly laid out', though the rather crude and uninformative engraving accompanying his description seems to show a small house distinguished only by a verandah with a rather Chinesey tented roof.

A more detailed description is given by John Hassell's *Tour of the Isle of Wight* (1790).

It is in the true cottage stile. The roof consists, cottage like, of humble thatch; and the outside of the walls are covered with neat composition: forming together a rural and pleasing appearance. But its inside for neatness and elegance beggars description. It is at once so plain, so truly elegant, and, though small, so convenient, and so pleasant, that I think I may venture to say I never met with its equal.[45]

It contained, according to William Cooke in 1808, 'some comfortable apartments, well furnished and adorned with several good pictures', including seascapes by Vandevelde. Cooke noted a singular quasi-nautical feature that was evidently a response to the diminutive size of the cottage, namely attic bedrooms 'containing fixed bed places arranged round the skylight in the roof similarly to a ship's cabin'.[46] H. P. Wyndham in 1794 (by which time Stanley's sisters had sold it to Wilbraham Tollemache from Cheshire) dismissed it as 'small and of little consequence', but noted a particular feature which was also commented upon by other writers: 'Just before the windows of the west front, a beautiful spring of the most transparent water keeps a large stone bason, in the form of a scallop shell, perpetually full.'[47] The Reverend William Gilpin, one of the most influential writers on the Picturesque, was even less impressed.

Though the situation . . . is pleasing, we could not say much for what is called the cottage. It is covered indeed with thatch; but that makes it no more a *cottage*, than ruffles would make a clown a gentleman. . . . We see everywhere the appendage of junket and good living. Who would expect to find a fountain bubbling up under the window of a cottage, into an elegant carved shell to cool wine? The thing is beautiful, but out of place.[48]

Gilpin's indignation at Steephill in fact prompted him to continue with an extended consideration of the comparative characteristics of what he called the 'natural' (i.e. vernacular) cottage and its 'artificial' counterpart.[49]

Notwithstanding Gilpin's dislike of Steephill, it became a much-visited attraction. Indeed, the Island as a whole offered all that appealed to the late Georgian tourist and seeker after the Picturesque: scenery that was by turns lush

and smiling and sublimely dramatic; and a wide range of both 'natural' and 'artificial' cottages. At Newtown, a medieval port town that had shrunk to no more than a village, Hassell remarked on

one of those subjects so often touched by the pencil of Mr Gainsborough; a cottage overshadowed by trees; while a glimmering light, just breaking through the branches, caught one side of the stone and flint fabric, and forcibly expressed the conception of that great master.[50]

Others admired the parsonage at Binsted, 'a small, thatched, hermitage-like cottage, placed in a most retired situation',[51] while feeling that 'the harmony of this delightful spot is perhaps injured by the many white benches and tables which crowd the little plat: this destroys its true character of privacy and simplicity'.[52] Sir Henry Englefield in 1816 regretted the loss of architectural innocence that tourism visited on vernacular cottages. Of Shanklin, a village of scattered thatched cottages which after 1800 began to be augmented with cottages ornés, he commented,

Nearly every cottage, however mean, being in the habit of letting lodgings in the summer season, is surrounded by a neat garden full of flowering shrubs, and is itself adorned, perhaps too much for real beauty, with whitewash and green paint.[53]

Vernon Cottage [fig 5/10], built 1817 (and later extended in keeping), is the best of the surviving orné holiday houses, with thatched roof extending over its many gables and variously cusped and fretted bargeboards.[54] Other thatched cottages ornés – some clearly created out of existing vernacular buildings – cluster tightly along a bend in the village street, creating a unique orné set-piece, albeit one now compromised by a proliferation of commercial signage [fig 5/11]. The longevity of the idiom on the Island is borne out by a component of this particular ensemble, Glenbrook, which though apparently built in about 1860 is more or less indistinguishable from its predecessors.[55] Sandown, now an urban northern extension of Shanklin, was likewise a scattered hamlet that developed into a resort. Here was

one of the Island's main cottage attractions, Sandown Cottage, to which the notorious radical politician John Wilkes retired in 1788, 'in the evening of his life'.[56] Wilkes, who called the house 'Villakin', laid out the gardens and refused admission to no one. 'The taste shown by him in ornamenting his rooms and grounds', noted John Buller severely in his guide book, 'bore a great affinity to that displayed in his person. Everything was overdone and gaudy, the very reverse of chaste simplicity.'[57]

To the other side of Shanklin the dramatic scenery of the Undercliff stretches for six miles to the southern tip of the Island [fig 5/12]. As residents and tourists became more adventurous, this landscape created by many centuries of landslips became especially admired, and is where the majority of the Island's cottages ornés were and are to be found.[58] First comes Bonchurch, where the main development was after 1830, but already in 1816 Sir Henry

Englefield noted that

> two or three small seats of gentlemen (by the courtesy of the country called cottages) give a dressed and cheerful appearance to the spot. Of these, the house built by Colonel Hill is the most beautiful, uniting in an uncommon degree the comfort of sheltered retirement, and the magnificence of a sea prospect.[59]

Bonchurch gives way in turn to Ventnor and St Lawrence, both popular with the cottage-builders. Lisle Combe (originally called Southwold), lying between the two villages, was built in 1839 for a younger son of the local magnate, the Earl of Yarborough. It was progressively enlarged in the next decade or so, but the original section has a veritable explosion of gables, large and small and variously cusped.[60]

Finally, on the southern tip, Niton is the site of Puckaster Cottage [fig 5/13], built between around 1815 for James Vine to designs by Robert Lugar, who illustrated it in his *Villa Architecture* of 1828.[61] Lugar in fact clarifies that Vine had selected a previously published design of his (he refers to Rose Hill Cottage near Henley-on-Thames, illustrated in his *Plans and Views* of 1811),[62] and that he was then brought in to supply the necessary working drawings.

> During our fireside discourses upon it, many essential improvements were suggested by Mrs Vine; and to her judgement I am desirous of paying this tribute of respect. The interior has been fitted up entirely under the guidance of Mr and Mrs Vine; and those who are permitted to see this cottage, feel their surprise and admiration equally excited.

Lugar goes on to explain that the exterior was an improved and enlarged version of a fisherman's hut, evidently in deference to the genius loci; and that the interior was fitted up with 'elegant simplicity', furnished with appropriate pieces in oak. George Brannon, a great popularizer of the Island through his publications and engravings, had already recorded that

> the sea-front is an elegant semi-circle with an overhanging thatched roof, supported by the trunks of trees entwined with flowering plants – which also climb sufficiently about the walls to add a richness and variety of effect, without concealing too much of the ornamental minutiae, which are particularly neat.[63]

The building that survives is still just recognizable as the one in Lugar's beguiling plate, which has a rounded end towards the sea with an inset tree-trunk verandah. The

thatch that added greatly to its charm had already been replaced with tiles by 1849, and in the 1860s the landward end was considerably enlarged.[64]

If the coast was unequivocally the Island's favoured location, cottages ornés also began to appear inland, particularly as lodges to estates. In 1805 Lugar dedicated his first book, *Architectural Sketches,* to George Ward Esq. Ward was 'an upstart financier of immense wealth'[65] who had in 1793 bought an estate in West Cowes, in the process becoming a neighbour and close friend of John Nash. Associated with the park of Ward's Northwood House, a building on which Nash was consulted late in his career, is Debourne Lodge. The elevation towards the former carriage drive, with a recessed verandah fronted by rough tree trunks with small curved braces, is closely related to a drawing by George Repton, made when he was Nash's chief assistant. Across the road junction from it is the Round House [fig 5/14], in the same idiom but built as a

toll house. It is circular, again with an inset rustic veran-dah, with wavy-edged bargeboards and a conical fish-scale-tiled roof rising to a patterned cylindrical chim-ney. Nash's own country residence was across the Medina river at East Cowes Castle, so it is not surprising to find him working in the cottage genre on the Island. Other presumed Nash (or G. S. Repton) lodges are in the centre of the Island at Westover, Calbourne, where he remodelled an existing house in 1813–15. The main one, in Calbourne village, is of knapped flint with slate roof, and not orné, but Sweetwater Lodge [fig 5/15], at the wooded entrance to

the long west drive, is a perfect specimen, with a roof of umbrella-like thatch and windows with the distinctive shouldered heads common to both lodges.[66]

Either Nash or G. S. Repton was also responsible for a now vanished pair of little thatched lodges that framed the entrance to St John's, an estate on the outskirts of Ryde that was landscaped by Humphry Repton after its purchase in 1797 by Edward Simeon. They were helpfully described in 1812 by William Cooke, who makes clear that, small as they were, only one was for occupation by the employee, the other being reserved for the occasional use of the owner:

Within a handsome railing and gateway the avenue commences, between two charming cottages of stone; whose thatch is disposed in a pleasing manner, and in front thrown forward over a rustic porch, formed by natural trunks of trees. The jessamine and rose entwine around the windows, intermixed with the clematis or virgin's bower, a species of creeper, that rises round the rustic pillars of the porch and is disposed beautifully above. . . . The interior of these cottages is not unworthy of remark. They are so disposed as to contain, in the small space of about 18 feet square, a sitting room and bedroom, with a pantry; the one affording a comfortable residence for the cottager who attends the gate; the other an occasional retreat for company, where a few books, some neat suitable furniture, and the pleasing novelty of the situation, must give a charm that a fastidious taste can hardly fail to allow. The porch contains rustic seats, and may be said to afford an additional and agreeable apartment.[67]

THE SOUTH COAST

Elsewhere on the south coast, the nucleus of Bournemouth was developed in the early nineteenth century by Lewis Tregonwell of Cranborne Lodge, Dorset, who had married into the county's wealthy Portman family. The nucleus, with a dotting of thatched cottages in a sylvan setting, contained Tregonwell's own rather plain cottage orné (later known as Portman Lodge and demolished circa 1925), designed in 1810 by the Wimborne architect and surveyor William Evans to whom is attributed the much more striking cottage orné lodge at Gaunt's House, Hinton Martell.[68] The grouping also included Cliff Cottage (originally Gypsey Cottage), built around 1815 for the most considerable landowners of south-east Dorset, the Drax family of Charborough Park. A photograph of 1863 shows this to have been a classic if low-key cottage orné, with thatched roof and undulating thatched verandah, and French windows.[69] The two cottages built just west of Bournemouth at Canford Cliffs[70] have been demolished, but on the other side of Poole Harbour a fine specimen of a seaside cottage survives overlooking the sea at Studland. Originally known as Studland Manor (Fig 5/16), it was built not as a manor house but as a marine villa, by the Rt Hon. George Bankes MP (1787–1856), younger brother of the principal local landowner, William Bankes of Kingston Lacy. Begun in 1825, it seems to have been designed by Bankes himself and is highly picturesque, rambling and multi-gabled in the manner of P. F. Robinson, whose pattern books Bankes might well have owned. According to John Pouncy (a Dorchester photographer and author–publisher of *Dorsetshire Photographically Illustrated*, 1857),

it was enlarged [by Bankes] from time to time, without any great regularity of plan or design, and apparently with the view of gaining an interesting relaxation during his retirement, by supplying deficiencies as they gradually presented themselves, and inventing improvements when there were no more deficiencies to supply.[71]

The structure is of rendered brick under a roof of massive Purbeck stone tiles, and the interior is embellished with a good deal of recycled woodwork, including an eighteenth-century staircase and Jacobean panelling supposedly from the old Palace of Westminster. Further additions took place in the early twentieth century, and for once the building's conversion to hotel use after World War II has ensured its survival in good order.[72]

Perhaps surprisingly, the great Regency developments at Brighton and Hove were not in practice accompanied by

even a modest dotting of cottages ornés, although Decimus Burton prepared an attractive but abortive scheme to develop the Furze Hill (fig 5/17) area north-west of the centre of Brighton for the financier Isaac Goldsmid in about 1834. This would have been a garden suburb along the lines of Nash's Park Village East, with villas in a mixture of neoclassical, Italianate, castellated and cottage-Gothic on an elevated site commanding a superb panorama of the coast westwards from Brighton.[73] Further east along the Sussex coast St Leonards was the creation of the London builder James Burton, who in 1828 bought farmland west of Hastings specifically to lay out a watering place (inspired, of course, by recent developments at Brighton). Work proceeded incredibly quickly: by 1830 the new settlement was already able to receive visitors, and in 1832 the St

Leonards Improvement Act established it as a town rather than just a private building venture. A ten-week visit by Princess Victoria and her mother in 1834 set the seal on its immediate future. Behind the grand seafront terraces is an oval subscription garden in the bottom of the valley, with villas in different styles round the perimeter. The development came hard on the heels of Calverley Park at Tunbridge Wells, laid out in 1828 by Burton's son Decimus.[74] As James by this stage was in his late sixties, and Decimus had been in practice since 1823, it is likely that the latter was involved in detailed design work at St Leonards – indeed, Robson's *Commercial Directory* of 1838 says that it was built 'upon the plan of Decimus Burton, the Architect'. A bird's eye view of 1837 shows some though not all the villas in place round the park.

Several are what the *Buildings of England* volume for East Sussex accurately calls 'weak cottage orné'. Of these the best is probably Winterbourne (originally North Villa) at the top end of the garden, of 1830, difficult to see behind its tall hedge, but with an array of barge-boarded gables of different size.[75]

THE LAKE DISTRICT

For those in search of picturesque and sublime scenery, no region in England could equal the Lake District. Distaste for its savage wildness (Daniel Defoe in 1724 had referred to the landscape as 'the wildest, most barren and frightful of any that I have passed over in England')[76] began to give way in the 1750s to an appreciation of its potential for serious visual stimulation, of a kind for which the English had been travelling with considerably more difficulty and expense to Switzerland. The more artistic started to head north with their easels and sketchbooks, spurred by the publication in 1778 of Thomas West's *Guide to the Lakes*, which directed them to particular viewpoints and encouraged them to see the prospects through the eyes of appropriate artists.[77] In the same year the *Monthly Magazine* commented that '*To make the Tour* of the Lakes, to speak in fashionable terms, is the *ton* of the present hour.'[78] William Gilpin, a native of Cumbria and one of the earliest protagonists of the Picturesque movement, published a succession of books aimed at opening the eyes of British readers, including in 1786 his *Observations . . .on . . . the mountains and*

lakes of Cumberland and Westmoreland. The poet William Wordsworth's *Guide to the Lakes*, which was published in 1810 and reached its fifth edition in 1835, was particularly influential in the process of popularization.

Architectural consequences inevitably followed. Already in 1785 John Plaw had published one of the earliest of the new generation of architectural pattern books featuring cottage designs, *Rural Architecture*, whose frontispiece [fig 5/18] very tellingly features two young ladies, representing Taste and Rural Simplicity. They are admiring a panorama of Lake Windermere, described by Plaw as 'one of the most beautiful scenes this Island can boast of'. On an island in the lake rises the distinctive profile of Belle Isle, a house designed by Plaw himself in 1774 – his first known commission, in fact. However, far from being a cottage, Belle Isle is a Pantheon-like structure, circular and domed like a giant garden temple, and the earlier gentry houses and villas that resulted from the new popularity of the Lakes were likewise classical. Plaw's client Thomas English was quickly followed by Joseph Pocklington, a Nottinghamshire gentleman-architect who first visited the area in 1776 and was to build three classical villas on and around Derwentwater.[79]

Some saw the dotting of the Lakeland landscape with such houses as a way to create a Claudeian idyll, and the practice was encouraged by William Cockin of Kendal in publishing the second edition (1780) of West's *Guide*. Others thought that, on the contrary, they ruined the views, and criticisms increasingly appeared in print. The introduction to P. F. Robinson's *Rural Architecture* of 1823 is typical:

> In the most beautiful parts of the country, the
> scenery is disfigured by the impotent attempts of
> the Workman, unaided by the pencil of the Artist,
> and even among the English and Scotch Lakes, the
> square, spruce brick house, and tiled roof, obtrudes
> itself at every turn, and carries back the ideas of the
> wanderer to the Metropolis and its environs.

J. B. Papworth in 1818 published a cottage orné alternative approach, specifically 'designed for the neighbourhood of the Lakes'. His attractive coloured plate [Chapter Four, fig 4/4] shows a typical Papworth design, single-storeyed and thatched, with French windows to maximize

appreciation of the views. In the background steep wooded hills rise up on the far side of a lake, on which a boat is sailing. The precise location is not given, but the text makes it clear that the cottage had already been built. The clients were two spinsters, who lived there with three female servants plus (in a separate building) a gardener.

> Its situation combines the romantic with the rural, and as it affords the view of a beautiful piece of water, bounded by luxuriant overhanging woods, and a country rich in cultivated scenery, the existing deficiency of ground belonging to it is the less to be regretted; because these supply the effect of an extensive and well-arranged domain.[80]

Given what sounds like a prime lake-view location, and the fact that thatch would not last long in the wet Lakeland climate, it seems probable that the cottage has long since disappeared.[81] The leading local architect of the first half of the nineteenth century, George Webster (1797–1864), knew rather better than the Londoner Papworth how to build robustly for the particular climatic circumstances, especially when designing for himself. His father Francis, likewise a Kendal-based architect, had bought and enlarged an existing vernacular cottage at Eller How, near Lindale on the southern flank of the Lakes, to which he retired in 1826. Soon after his death the following year, George Webster began to enlarge the cottage further, continuing to do so until about 1850, and indeed moving there himself in 1830. A fine watercolour [fig 5/19] by the Kendal artist Richard Stirzaker (1797–1833) shows the house and its Reptonian setting in their early phase, with a lake spanned by a bridge in the foreground and a steep wooded hill rising up behind, crowned by a folly castle. The house itself, which still exists, has an array of tall chimneys, Tudor windows and many and varied gables, with bargeboards identically edged rather like a paper doily.[82] The interior is quite modest, in a mixture of Jacobean and classical, but an inventory taken at Webster's death shows it to have been stuffed with paintings, 'articles of Vertu', mounted animal heads, pieces of armour, and drawers full of shells and geological specimens, and a sizeable library. Altogether it sounds rather like Sir Walter Scott's Abbotsford.[83]

Despite the popularity of the cottage genre in the south coast resorts, it seems to have had less appeal at what might be called inland resorts – the spas where the well-to-do flocked to socialize and (they hoped) recover their health. Bath, much the most important and frequented, was already well established by the time the cottage entered the architectural lists, and though it continued to expand relentlessly in the Regency period, classicism always reigned, whether in terraces, squares or villas. The same is true of Clifton. There was, however, more architectural variety at the celebrated spa of Tunbridge Wells, the nearest to London. This developed slowly during the eighteenth century, but the main development was after 1800, as members of the leisured classes began to settle there. On the west side of the centre, the area known as Mount Ephraim began to develop as early as the seventeenth century, with individual houses dotted randomly around on common land – for instance, dating from the early nineteenth century, Gibraltar Cottage, St Helena and Belleville [fig 5/20], the latter a Gothic cottage with cusped bargeboards, made eminently picturesque by virtue of being deliberately

Burton's own house was Baston Cottage, which stood on a prominent site adjoining the intersection of Calverley Road and Calverley Plain. Picturesquely composed in the Tudor idiom, with cusped eaves boards, finialed gables and clustered gables, it was demolished about 1900. Britton's *Descriptive Sketches of Tunbridge Wells*, published in 1832 when it was very new, noted that Calverley Park was

> laid out for the erection of villas; and connected with it is a beautiful pleasure-garden, adorned with various evergreens, flowers &c. At one extremity of this ground Mr Decimus Burton has built a rustic cottage for himself. . . . Near it is a rustic lodge, connected with a private gate entrance to Calverley Plain.[85]

nestled alongside a massive outcrop of rock.[84] More co-ordinated was the development after 1828 of Calverley Park to the east of the centre. This was promoted by John Ward, who chose the young Decimus Burton as his architect. As at Furze Hill, Brighton, Burton's model was Nash's Park Village East, with detached villas in different styles, at least one in Tudor Gothic with eaves boards.

The best cottage orné in the Tunbridge orbit is in fact Rust Hall [fig 5/21], a mile or two to the west of the spa. Very little seems to be known about it, but it occupies a

site commanding panoramic views southwards, and before extension in the same idiom in the 1960s seems to have presented a symmetrical entrance façade of narrow projecting porch sandwiched between wider bays with tripartite Gothic windows, each preceded by a single-storey projecting bay with castellations and ogee-domed turrets. Each bay has frilled eaves, and the whole stuccoed composition is attractively relaxed.

Like Tunbridge Wells, 'Royal' Leamington Spa was developed in the early nineteenth century, especially between 1820 and 1840; Queen Victoria authorized the addition of the 'Royal' prefix in 1838. Its buildings from this period are mostly classical, but Clarendon Square, of the 1820s and otherwise classical, has on its west side the former Binswood Cottage, now 'Magnolia'. This is a documented work by P. F. Robinson, who illustrated it in 1838 in his *New Series of Designs*.[86] There he describes it as 'a Villa upon a small scale in the cottage style' and states that it was erected in 1824 for Edward Willes, 'from the Author's Designs and under his superintendence'. 'It is well known to the visitors of that place, but has now lost much of its attraction in consequence of the increased number of new buildings surrounding it.' Lansdowne Circus has the same stylistic mix.

Other, more isolated examples exist of places of popular resort where the cottage orné idiom was deployed for buildings created specifically to service tourists. High up on the Cotswolds at Cranham in Gloucestershire, Todd's Cottages and Pleasure Gardens [fig 5/22] were built by William Todd in about 1821. They became a popular but short-lived excursion for residents of fashionable Cheltenham, as well as for local tradesmen and their families, until Todd went bankrupt in 1825. He was basically a timber merchant who took a lease on Cranham Woods and quickly saw an opportunity to develop them more profitably. The complex comprised a cluster of rustic buildings, single-storeyed with Gothic dormers in the thatched roofs, one of which provided accommodation for Todd and his wife. The sale particulars drawn up in 1832 following Todd's bankruptcy provide detailed information about their usage and appearance. They were, it was said, 'erected regardless of Expense and with great taste'. One contained a paved entrance hall, breakfast room and drawing room with painted glass windows, and a staircase with mahogany rail led up to three 'neat sleeping rooms'. The adjoining cottage contained service rooms – kitchen, servants' rooms, wine cellars, coach house, harness room and stabling for three horses. Beyond stood a pavilion containing a dairy with marble shelves, and a brewhouse. Other buildings included a circular 'archery room', a billiard room with 'handsome coved ceiling', and an open-fronted, moss-lined ballroom that commanded a beautiful vista through the woods. Although the buildings were sometimes known as the Swiss Cottages, there was – as so often – nothing remotely Swiss about their design. In general layout and concept they were somewhat reminiscent of the Hameau at the Chateau de Chantilly,[87] while the design of the pair of cottages with rounded ends recalls the Steward's Cottage published by J. B. Papworth in 1818 [fig 4/2].[88]

Todd's departure in 1828 did not mean the end of his cottages, which provided a desirable residence in an idyllic (if rather isolated) sylvan spot. Between 1833 and

LEFT 5/23 Bishop of Bath and Wells's cottage, Banwell,Somerset, engraving from Rutter's *Delineations of Somerset*

OPPOSITE, ABOVE 5/24 Spring Cottage, Cliveden, Buckinghamshire

OPPOSITE, BELOW 5/25 Spring Cottage, Cliveden, section and plan of tea room, from Peter Nicholson, *Architectural Dictionary*, 1819

1838 the owner was the Reverend E. Reed, of St John's Church in Cheltenham. Subsequent sale particulars extolled not only the beauty of the location and its 'pure mountain air' but also its suitability as a gentleman's shooting lodge and proximity to nearby hunts. However, following Reed's departure for Cheltenham in 1839 the cottages were tenanted, and over the course of the next two decades became very dilapidated. They experienced a very chequered existence thereafter, being completely remodelled for William Hicks Beach in the 1880s, used as a sanatorium from 1899, and finally disappearing in the 1980s, when the site reverted to woodland.[89]

Another short-lived entertainment complex with orné buildings was Beulah Spa at Upper Norwood, on the outer Surrey fringes of the metropolis. Some 25 acres, including gardens, lawns, woods and a lake, were laid out to Decimus Burton's designs in 1828 to capitalize on a mineral spring. The waters for this were contained in a stone reservoir sheltered beneath a tent-shaped thatched roof, and other buildings included an octagonal thatched reading room in the form of a cottage orné, and a concert hall – altogether amounting to more of a pleasure garden than a spa proper. The *Mirror* of 1832 described it as being 'in the best taste of ornate rusticity', but its popularity was short-lived, partly thanks to competition from the nearby Crystal Palace after 1854, and nothing now remains of it.[90]

An interesting and possibly unique example of episcopal entrepreneurship was the Bishop of Bath and Wells's cottage at Banwell in Somerset. The estate sits at the western, seaward end of the limestone Mendip Hills, well known for their water-worn caves (notably Wookey Hole), and at Banwell the Stalactite Cave was first discovered by miners in 1757 and then forgotten. Its rediscovery in 1824 coincided with the appointment as bishop of Dr George Law, whose decision to have it developed as a tourist attraction was reinforced by the discovery the following year of the Bone Cave. The local vicar had hoped that the visitor income would pay for a new school, but Dr Law's motive was theological, since he believed that

the numerous prehistoric animal bones – among them, bison, wolves, reindeer and bears – were the proof of Noah's Flood. In 1826 a small cottage was built for the use of the bishop's guests, enlarged in 1833 to provide accommodation for visiting antiquarians.[91] When senility forced Law to give up his duties he moved into the cottage himself, and died there in 1845.[92]

An early engraving [fig 5/23] shows the original cottage as a one-storeyed building, with thatched gambrel roof supported on a tree-trunk verandah. It stood at the centre of a layout of winding paths and rustic structures, on a steeply sloping hillside commanding a vast panorama over the Bristol Channel to Wales. The rustic structures included a sham prehistoric trilathon, a Druid's Temple and a Gothic pavilion called the Osteoicon or Bone House, where the prehistoric bones were displayed; there were also a Pebble Summerhouse and an octagonal Gothic prospect tower. The enlargement of the three-room cottage in 1833 turned it into a proper house, two-storeyed, thatched and asymmetrical, with a long rustic verandah that incorporated little gables with cross finials.[93] Law appointed a local farmer, William Beard, to run the attraction, and he continued to show the caves to visitors after the bishop's death, taking his last party round in 1865 when he was ninety-three. Later generations treated the place less sympathetically, the cottage orné being engulfed and transformed by additions of about 1870 (although some good marble chimneypieces remain), and the rustic structures fell into decay. More recently, a concerted effort has been made to restore remaining rustic structures such as the Pebble Summerhouse and to make the caves accessible again; the cottage orné, however, has lost its character for good.

Other cottages ornés erected to cater for tourists range from the small but pretty cottage (formerly Wrekin Cottage, now Halfway House) which traditionally provided refreshments for people climbing the Wrekin in Shropshire,[94] to the much smarter, architect-designed Spring Cottage on the banks of the Thames below Cliveden House. Spring Cottage was commissioned in 1813 by the Countess of Orkney, owner of Cliveden, from Peter Nicholson, and seems to have been prompted by a visit in the summer of 1809 by Queen Charlotte and her daughters. It existed to provide refreshments for river-borne pleasure-seekers, including royal parties

from Windsor. Pleasure boats were already mooring and picnicking at a spot where springs emerged from the steep wooded slope below the baroque mansion – indeed a previous royal party had been entertained in marquees here in 1794 – and the arrangement was formalized by the building of Spring Cottage, with its elegant umbrella-vaulted Gothic tea room [fig 5/25]. Nicholson, a Scot who began his career as a cabinetmaker and progressed to become a pioneer of technical education for workmen, provided a pavilion whose interior is reminiscent of a small chapter house.[95] This seems in its early years to have been attached to a house occupied by the keeper of the springs, which included a large room for storing fishing tackle. Nothing appears to be known of the external appearance of the tea room, but by 1852 it had become part of an unfinished fishing villa, intended to contain drawing and dining rooms, library, bedrooms and domestic offices. However, in 1849 the Cliveden estate had been bought by the 2nd Duke of Sutherland, whose wife, Mistress of the Robes to Queen Victoria, in 1857 commissioned George Devey to absorb the Regency tea room into a new and enlarged picturesque cottage [fig 5/24]. Devey's cottage, with its half-timbering, studied asymmetry and massive brick chimneys, is certainly picturesque, but it shows the cottage idiom moving unmistakably into a new Victorian phase.[96]

1 Emily J. Climenson, ed., *Passages from the Diaries of Mrs Philip Lybbe Powys* (London, 1899).

2 The first guidebook to Stowe being published as early as 1744.

3 For instance, in his *Observations on the River Wye and several parts of South Wales* (1782), volumes of *Observations* on the Lake District (1786), the Scottish Highlands (1789), the West Country and Isle of Wight (1798), and *Remarks on Forest Scenery* (1791).

4 For example, James Clarke in his 1789 *Survey of the Lakes of Cumberland, Westmorland and Lancashire*, p. 9, wrote that 'The contemplation of barren heaths, bleak, rocky mountains, and almost impassable swamps and mosses, will naturally fill the mind with gloomy and uncomfortable ideas.'

5 J. F. Travis, *The Rise of the Devon Seaside Resorts 1750–1900* (Exeter, 1993), p. 64.

6 Ibid., Chapter One.

7 A. Oliver, ed., *The Journal of Samuel Curwen, Loyalist* (Cambridge, MA, 1972), quoted in Travis, *The Rise of the Devon Seaside Resorts*, pp. 15–16.

8 Cited in Travis, *The Rise of the Devon Seaside Resorts*, p. 17.

9 Park Honan, *Jane Austen, Her Life* (London, 1997), pp. 185–6, 200–203.

10 Peter Borsay, 'The Landed Elite and Provincial Towns in Britain 1660–1800', *Georgian Group Journal*, XIII (2003), p. 290.

11 Oliver, ed., *The Journal of Samuel Curwen*.

12 Quoted in Peter Hunt ed., *Devon's Age of Elegance* (Exeter, 1984), p. 46.

13 Geoffrey Holmes, ed., *Sidmouth, A History* (Sidmouth, 1987/2000).

14 John Wallis, *Sidmouth Scenery, or Views of the principal Cottages and Residences of the Nobility and Gentry at that Admired Watering Place* (?1816–19). The plates are variously dated 1816, 1817, 1819.

15 Theodore H. Mogridge, *Descriptive Sketch of Sidmouth* (1836), p. 12. 'The air of Sidmouth', the book noted, 'may be considered pure, soft and mild, yet somewhat moist, and consequently rather relaxing', p. 24.

16 Ibid., p. 38.

17 Ibid., pp. 45–6.

18 Ibid.

19 The dining room has a coved ceiling but is not otherwise elaborate.

20 Sir Peter Burrell, 1st Baron Gwydir, 1754–1820.

21 The house was saved from demolition in 1966 and bought for hotel conversion by the Pinney family, who added extension and developed the grounds. Much of this information comes from an undated leaflet produced by John Pinney.

22 RIBA Drawings Collection 36176, 36177.

23 The building was much extended late in the nineteenth century and has functioned as a Methodist holiday home since 1931.

24 At which point, according to an engraving published earlier in the year by Wallis, it was 'the Seat of Major Gen. Baynes'.

25 The drawing room had a marble Gothic chimneypiece, shown in a 1906 photo but no longer there.

26 Mogridge, *Descriptive Sketch*, p. 56. From the east, they are now Rock Cottage; the Beacon (with triangle-headed windows); and at the top, Clifton Cottage, irregular and difficult to see from either beach or road (Bridget Cherry and Nikolaus Pevsner, *Buildings of England: Devon*, 2nd edn (Harmondsworth, 1989), p. 738) says 'very pretty, clustered chimneys, original glazing'). An engraving entitled 'West View of Sidmouth', published in Sidmouth in 1819 (in *Scenery on the Southern Coast of Devonshire*), shows the cottages climbing the hill, and none are as yet orné. It appears (according to a plaque on the building) that Rock Cottage in fact remained plain until thatched and ornamented by the Arts & Crafts architect R. W. Sampson after a fire in 1908, retaining the verandah from its predecessor.

27 This refers to the Pinney estate to the west of town, popular for its cliff walks.

28 See Chapter Four, p. 100.

29 Tim Connor, 'Too Late for the Dictionary?', *Georgian Group Journal*, XVII (2009).

30 See Chapter Nine.

31 A Wallis engraving of Cumberland Cottage in the Elysian Fields at Sidmouth, dated 1826, shows the same combination of Gothick windows and mandorla, though with the addition of an encircling verandah.

32 *Gentleman's Magazine*, lxiii, part 1 (1793), p. 593.

33 Ness Cottage at Shaldon is a modest thatched cottage with simple Gothic windows, including a dormer in the centre of the roof slope, and very simple wavy eaves. An old photograph shows a recessed centre filled with a pretty fretted screen, eminently Regency – a feature now gone.

34 According to Arthur Charles Ellis, *An Historical Survey of Torquay* (Torquay, 1930), pp. 355–6, the colonnade was constructed of pollards, although the description also refers to creepers being trained over 'eight arches springing from the capitals of a double row of cast iron columns'. The floors were inlaid with Devonshire marbles. Information from John Tucker, Torquay Library.

35 Although she is recorded in the 1841 census as being only eighty. The building survived until 1857, when its spacious grounds attracted the developers. It was auctioned in March 1857, after which the contents, 'comprising an assemblage of excellent furniture', was also put up for sale, according to the *Torquay Directory*. Information from John Tucker and Julie Connor at Torquay Library.

36 Pevsner, *Buildings of England: Devon*, p. 709.

37 Todd Gray, ed., *Travels in Georgian Devon: The Illustrated Journals of the Reverend John Swete, 1789–1800* (Exeter, 1997), pp. 199–200.

38 Michael Hunter, 'The First Seaside House?', *Georgian Group Journal*, VIII (1998), pp. 138–9. A photograph in recent sales particulars (Savills Exeter, March 2013) shows the sequence from entrance hall via dining room to inner hall through four-centred arches, but otherwise very little original detail.

39 *Observations relative chiefly to the Natural History, picturesque Scenery and Antiquities of the Western Counties of England*, quoted in Peter Beacham ad Nikolaus Pevsner, *Buildings of England: Cornwall*, 2nd edn (New Haven and London, 2014), p. 425.

40 For Rosemorran see Chapter Three, p. 84.

41 RIBA Drawings Collection VOS/204 fol. 28. Colvin, *B.D.*, p. 1117. The 1838–42 tithe map lists the occupier as John S. Bedford Esq., and the owner of the land as Mrs Sophia Praed. The house apparently still exists, much altered. Information from Claire Morgan, Cornish Studies Library. Wightwick's designs for a cottage for Thomas Robins at Windsworth near Looe, Cornwall, and another for M. S. Grigg at Tamerton Foliat in Devon, are in the RIBADC (VOS/204 fols 27 and 29).

42 Giles Worsley, 'Rustic Idylls', *Country Life* (31 August 1989), p. 77.

43 Sir Richard Worsley, *History of the Isle of Wight* (1781), p. 221.

44 His family estate was at Paultons on the Hampshire mainland.

45 John Hassell, *Tour of the Isle of Wight* (1790), vol. 1, pp.212–3.

46 William Cooke, *A New Picture of the Isle of Wight* (London, 1808), p. 99.

47 H. P. Wyndham, *A Picture of the Isle of Wight* (London, 1794), p. 74.

48 William Gilpin, *Observations on the Western Parts of England . . . to which are added a Few Remarks on the Picturesque Beauties of the Isle of Wight* (London, 1798), pp. 308–9.

49 Ibid., pp. 309–11. The cottage was bought by John Hambrough in about 1828 and demolished to make way for Steephill Castle, which in turn gave way in the 1960s to bungalows. Robin McInnes, *A Picturesque Tour of the Isle of Wight* (Newport, Isle of Wight, 1993), p. 116. I am grateful to Sue Oatley of Isle of Wight County Record Office for her assistance.

50 Hassell, op. cit., vol. 1, p. 137.

51 Wyndham, *A Picture of the Isle of Wight*, p. 39.

52 Ibid.

53 Sir Henry Englefield, *A Description of the Principal Picturesque Beauties . . . of the Isle of Wight* (London, 1816), p. 70.

54 According to Lindsay Boynton (*Georgian and Victorian Shanklin* (Shanklin, 1973), p. 17), the cottage was built by George Vernon Utterson, a clerk in Chancery, and initially suffered from the disadvantage of being approached only through a muddy farmyard.

55 Boynton, *Georgian and Victorian Shanklin*, p. 19.

56 John Buller, *A Historical and Picturesque Guide to the Isle of Wight*, 6th edn (Southampton, 1825), p. 99.

57 Ibid. According to Johanna Jones, *Castles to Cottages: The Story of Isle of Wight Houses* (Wimborne, 2000), p. 44, the building 'may have been called a cottage, but within it Wilkes had one room decorated in the fashionable Tuscan style, complete with a Latin dedication to himself'.

58 John Nash's diaries record that in September 1832 he 'went to the back of the Island', calling on the owners of two cottages at Niton, Sir William Gordon and Mrs Vine, then taking tea at the Sandrock Hotel nearby. Quoted in Nigel Temple, *George Repton's Pavilion Notebook* (Aldershot, 1993), p. 80.

59 Englefield, *A Description of the Principal Picturesque Beauties*, p. 73. The term 'cottage' was in fact rather promiscuously applied to classical villas with no vernacular features whatever.

60 David W. Lloyd and Nikolaus Pevsner, *The Buildings of England: Isle of Wight* (New Haven and London, 2006), p. 250.

61 Robert Lugar, *Villa Architecture* (1828), pls 11–12.

62 See above, Chapter Three, pp. 64–5.

63 George Brannon, *Views of the Isle of Wight* (1824), p. 38.

64 Clearly influenced by the design of Lugar's Puckaster is a cottage at Ryde known as The Swan's Nest, now closely embedded in a grid of Victorian streets but then standing in open countryside.

65 J. Summerson, *The Life and Work of John Nash Architect* (London, 1980), p. 150.

66 Similar windows appear in G. S. Repton's design for a substantial thatched house for Charles Taylor at Liphook in Hampshire (RIBADC G. S. Repton notebook, 246/4, fols 58 and 59). Sweetwater Lodge can also be compared with the lodge to Gaunt's House, Hinton Martell, Dorset (see Chapter Two, pp. 38–9).

67 William Cooke, *A New Picture of the Isle of Wight* (Southampton, 1812), pp. 77–9. For the nearby estate and cottage of the architect Lewis Wyatt, see Chapter Three, p. 84.

68 Colvin, *B.D.*, p. 369. For the Gaunt's House lodge see above, note 66.

69 Information from Peter Kazmierczak, Bournemouth Library. Cliff Cottage was demolished as early as the 1870s, its site now occupied by a conference centre.

70 Flaghead Cottage and Flaghead Lodge. John Newman and Nikolaus Pevsner, *The Buildings of England: Dorset* (Harmondsworth, 1972), p. 332.

71 Pouncey, vol. I, cited in Michael Hill, *East Dorset Country Houses* (Reading, 2013), p. 408.

72 Hill, *East Dorset Country Houses*, p. 408. See Chapter Ten for the recently added mini-cottages.

73 The design was exhibited at the Royal Academy in 1833. The development began but quickly ground to a halt, partly because of the resort's sluggish economic conditions. Information from Sue Berry.

74 See below, p. 136.

75 R. Morrice, 'Palestrina in Hastings', *Georgian Group Journal*, XI (2009). Winterbourne appears on an early engraving, on otherwise virgin hillside, sandwiched between the battlemented Gothic villa and the Tudor lodge at the northern entrance to the site.

76 Daniel Defoe, *A Tour Thro' the Whole Island of Great Britain* (1724).

77 West's *Guide* was designed to lead the tourist 'from the delicate touches of Claude, verified on Coniston Lake, to the noble scenes of Poussin, exhibited on Windermere-water, and from there to the stupendous romantic ideas of Salvator Rosa, realized in the Lake of Derwent'. Quoted in Christopher Hussey, *The Picturesque*, 3rd impression (London, 1983), p. 126. West's *Guide* had reached its seventh edition by 1799.

78 Hussey, *The Picturesque*, p.126.

79 Colvin, *B.D.*, p. 818.

80 For Papworth's description of the interior, see Chapter Four, pp. 97–8.

81 Kate Holliday of Kendal Archive Centre suggests as a possible location the St Catherine's estate just to the north of Windermere, for which sale particulars of 1857 exist that mention a cottage orné. The estate was bought by the Parker family in 1788, and by 1804 was in the sole ownership of Ann Parker, who seems to have built the cottage orné around 1810. This took place concurrent with work to establish gardens and the development of a parkland landscape fronting onto the road that runs along the west side of the estate. In 1831 the property was sold to the 2nd Earl of Bradford, who used it as an occasional holiday residence. However, Papworth's engraving does not correspond with an 1850s watercolour of St Catherine's as it was before a complete transformation in the 1890s. This shows a two-storeyed building with a verandah supported on posts running round the exterior.

82 Angus Taylor, *The Websters of Kendal*, ed. Janet Martin (Kendal, 2004). Taylor suggests that the porch, with its Venetian openings and rough columns, may have been inspired by plate X of Papworth's *Rural Residences*. The verandah at the south-western corner postdates 1847, when the house was illustrated in E. Twycross's *Mansions of England and Wales: County Palatine of Lancaster* (London, 1847), 3 vols.

83 Other houses in a cottage idiom attributed by Angus Taylor to George Webster are: Wansfell, near the head of Lake Windermere at Ambleside, built for Thomas Wrigley, papermaker, in 1840–1; this has variegated gables with wavy (and varied) eaves boards, tall, asymmetrically placed chimneys, and Tudor dripmoulds.

The slate roof and rubblestone walling make it look less charming than it otherwise might. Dykelands at Ulverston, probably of about 1840, is asymmetrical, with wavy eaves boards and variegated Gothic windows. At Conishead Priory Webster completed the mansion for Colonel Thomas Richmond Gale Braddyll, who in addition commissioned buildings for the gardens, including a cottage orné and a 'ladies cottage'. It is not clear if these survive. Howard Colvin (*B.D.*, p. 391) suggests that Webster may have assisted the amateur architect Richard Fothergill design Lowbridge House, the cottage orné that he built for himself in 1837 at Selside near Kendal. This has picturesquely grouped gables of different sizes, each with different eaves boards.

84 Ephraim Villa likewise has a bargeboarded gable and tall central chimneystack.

85 John Britton, *Descriptive Sketches of Tunbridge Wells*, 1832, p. 55. Farnborough Lodge at the southern entrance to the development survives, a minor specimen with pierced eaves boards.

86 P. F. Robinson, *A New Series of Designs . . .* (London, 1838), part 2, pl. 1.

87 See below, Chapter Eight.

88 Papworth, *Rural Residences*, pl. IV. This suggestion was first made by the late Nigel Temple.

89 J. K. Whitton, *The History of Todd's Cottages & Cranham Lodge 1821–1899*, MS research 2000, kindly supplied by Gloucestershire Record Office.

90 J. S. Curl, *Georgian Architecture in the British Isles 1714–1830*, 2nd edn (London, 2011), pp. 312–13.

91 The *Bristol Times and Mirror* of 5 August 1826 refers to the building as 'tastefully fitted out for the reception of visitors'.

92 The most complete account of the history of the site is given by John Chapman, *The Story of Banwell Caves* (Banwell Caves Heritage Group, 2013).

93 The main room of the 1826 cottage became the hall. The enlarged building appears in a drawing of 1836, an engraving in the *Gentleman's Magazine* of 1839, and a print of 1840 entitled 'Ornamental Cottage on Banwell Hill'.

94 RIBA Drawings Collection, Shropshire Box SC187.

95 Nicholson illustrated the tea room with a section and plan in his *Architectural Dictionary*, vol. II (1819), 102–3.

96 Wendy Hitchmough, *Spring Cottage Historical Documentation* report, 1996, kindly supplied by Julian Harrap Architects. Wendy Hitchmough, 'Tales from the Riverbank', *Country Life* (10 February 2000). For Devey's cottage designs more generally, see Chapter Ten.

CHAPTER SIX

THE COTTAGE ON THE CELTIC FRINGES

For the well-to-do and visually aware English tourist, appreciation of Wales followed much the same pattern as for the Peak and Lake Districts. Interest in the antiquities – the ruined castles and abbeys in which the Principality is so rich – preceded a growing awareness of the picturesque potential of the landscape. The first of William Gilpin's books on the 'picturesque beauties' of different parts of the kingdom was his *Observations on the River Wye and several Parts of South Wales*, published in 1782, and the last in the sequence, published posthumously in 1809, covered North Wales. The Wye Valley, being easily accessible from Bristol and Bath, and having the great bonus of the ruins of Tintern Abbey, was particularly popular. Valentine Morris (1727–1789) was one of the first to appreciate the tourist potential of the Wye, and already in the early 1770s was laying out the grounds of his Piercefield estate near Chepstow to capitalize on the dramatic situation above the river. With advice from Richard Owen Cambridge he laid out walks through the woodland and developed viewpoints along the clifftop, which he then opened to visitors. In 1785 bankruptcy forced him to sell the estate to George Smith, who employed John Soane to rebuild the house and continued to open the walks to the public. Morris's architectural embellishments had included a grotto, druid's temple and bathing house, but it was development for a subsequent owner, the 6th Duke of Beaufort, that resulted in the addition of a cottage orné. In 1828, shortly after the first turnpike road had been built through this part of the Wye Valley, the duke's agent Osmond Wyatt constructed a flight of 365 steps from the road up to a new viewpoint on the Wyndcliffe at the northern end of Valentine Morris's walks, dubbed the Eagle's Nest. To fortify visitors before the climb, or alternatively to revive them afterwards, Wyatt installed a tea room called Moss Cottage [fig 6/1]. This fell into ruin in the twentieth century and was demolished, but it is recorded in an attractive contemporary engraving as having been a single-storey building of rubblestone, the overhang of its thatched roof supported on exaggeratedly

rustic posts.[1] Further upstream, Captain George Rooke created a middle-class cottage orné called Pilstone on the Welsh side of the Wye at Llandogo, shortly after 1830. It incorporated part of a seventeenth-century house and was given many gables with cusped bargeboards.[2] Having built it, Rooke apparently preferred to look at it from his principal residence, Bigsweir, on the opposite, English, bank of the river.

An Englishman with a serious interest in both Welsh history and Welsh scenery was the antiquarian, archaeologist, artist and traveller Sir Richard Colt Hoare (1758–1838). In 1785 he inherited the family estate at Stourhead in Wiltshire (where he added a splendid library to the existing house), which gave him the liberty to pursue his intellectual preoccupations. His travels both on the Continent and in the British Isles were meticulously recorded and led to scholarly publications. His journey through Wales was followed in 1804 by the publication of his annotated translation of Gerald of Wales's *Descriptio Cambriae* (written in the early 1190s). He had already discovered the scenic qualities of Lake Bala in North Wales in 1796, and in about 1801 he created a cottage orné on its banks for his own use, calling it Vachdeiliog and spending several weeks fishing there every year. The building survives as a motel, much altered, but its original appearance is recorded by three pen and wash drawings by Hoare himself, two of 1810 and one of 1813.[3] These show a single-storey structure with surrounding verandah, almost colonial in its simplicity, with an elongated octagonal room at the centre of the elevation towards the lake. It was in fact tacked on to the front of an older, two-storeyed house that provided kitchen and servants' accommodation.[4]

Another pioneer of the Picturesque appreciation of Wales was William Madocks MP (1773–1828), who was also the founder of the model town of Tremadog. He came to Dolmelynllyn, in the valley of the Mawddach, in 1796, attracted by the spectacular waterfall nearby. Like Colt Hoare he too created a modest cottage-style house for himself. With just three rooms on each floor, and possibly adapted from an existing house, it survives much enlarged in the 1860s and 1870s and now minus its pretty verandahs.[5] His niece Mary Madocks, an amateur watercolourist, painted Dolmelynllyn and also an unidentified cottage – presumably in Wales – with a vast thatched roof descending onto a rustic verandah heavily enveloped in creepers [fig 6/2].[6]

OPPOSITE **6/1** Moss Cottage, Piercefield, Monmouthshire

In the same category as the tea house at Piercefield, built to service Georgian tourists, comes the tea house built for visitors to the celebrated waterfall of Pistyll Rhaeadr in the Berwyn mountains of mid-Wales. The waterfall was first appreciated by Dr William Worthington, the local vicar between 1747 and 1778, who built a cottage that Lord Torrington said was 'for tea drinking'. This was replaced with the present building by Sir Watkin Williams-Wynn (1789–1840).[7] As befits its sublime setting, the tea house (known as Tan-y-pistyll) eschews the cosy rusticity of lowland Britain and opts instead for a self-consciously, indeed aggressively rocky wall surface, combined with a tree-trunk portico – definitely not a utilitarian structure, though in a sense the reverse of ornamental. Perhaps this was a specifically Welsh approach, since it also appears in the so-called 'Ugly House' (Ty-hyll) at Capel Curig in Caernarfonshire, and in the cottage built next to a bridge over the river Ceiriog at Brynkinallt in Denbighshire.[8]

Whereas the Ugly House, built of un-mortared boulders, stands on a public road laid out by Thomas Telford (in fact the present A5 leading from England to the port of Holyhead) around 1820,[9] the Brynkinallt cottage of river boulders under doily-like eaves was built as an ornament to a secluded corner of an aristocratic estate [fig 6/3]. The chatelaine in the Regency period was Charlotte, Lady Dungannon, a social intimate of the Ladies of Llangollen. She was responsible for work carried out to the main house circa 1808 (Gothick outside, classical inside), supposedly to her own design, and she also is said to have embellished the grounds. A china room and dairy (now demolished) dated from 1813–14.

The builders of cottages ornés in Wales were often able to take advantage of natural settings enhanced by lakes or rushing waters in a way that their English counterparts rarely were. At Rheola, an estate near Neath in Glamorgan, John Nash designed the main house built for John Edwards

in 1814–18, and drawings in G. S. Repton's Pavilion Notebook relate to a simple lodge and much-altered steward's house. Also at Rheola are the ruins of Bachelor's Hall, a cottage orné with canted bay and wrap-around tree-trunk verandah, recorded in an 1817 watercolour by Thomas Hornor[10] and corresponding with the plan and elevation of a cottage not in G. S. Repton's hand.[11] It stood against a wooded slope looking down to a rustic bridge over the river. Hornor described it as 'a little ornamented building delightfully secluded in the Cwm or Dingle a short distance from the house and containing a few snug rooms which render it much too good for an anchorite; and indeed rather more comfortable than most bachelors deserve'.[12]

If the Welsh cottages so far mentioned were built inland to take advantage of dramatic natural scenery, Wales also saw the same phenomenon of coastal tourism as England, though to a less developed degree. In the early nineteenth century Swansea had pretensions to become the Brighton of Wales, although industrial growth quickly put paid to that. In 1817 Marino, an existing octagonal, tower-like villa in spacious grounds south-west of the centre, was bought by John Henry Vivian, manager of a copper-smelting works, who in 1827 employed P. F. Robinson to transform and enlarge it in Tudor idiom as a mansion renamed Singleton Abbey. Robinson also supplied cottage orné lodges, two of which survive.[13] Probably at the same time, Robinson was also employed further round the bay towards Oystermouth, where the owner of Clyne Castle, George

Warde (a mining entrepreneur) built several picturesque cottages for tenants, with ornamental tiled roofs. One is a lodge with fancy bargeboards, apparently built in reverse to a published design by Robinson.[14]

Further west, Tenby was an ancient port, which started to be developed as a resort from the 1780s.[15] This mainly resulted in classical terraces within the town itself, but Heywood Lane to the west of the centre was a fashionable little nineteenth-century suburb with villas of mixed styles, mostly built in the 1840s for a local speculator, Richard Rice Nash. If, as has been suggested, 'the seaside cottage orné style of genteel places like Sidmouth was obviously the inspiration', the results are less markedly orné and more reminiscent of Decimus Burton's diluted orné idiom, as seen at St Leonards and elsewhere.[16] The village of Penally was an outlier of Tenby two miles to the west, nestled under a wooded hillside and looking across a wide sandy bay; like Tenby it is said to have been popular with English visitors escaping their creditors. Penally Abbey [fig 6/4] was probably developed out of an earlier building that had been the vicar's residence, after a new vicarage was built 1822–4.[17] Very little is known about it but in the 1830s it may have been occupied by John Tuder and family (a local Tenby family). After 1841 the occupants were

Mrs Mary Robson, a widow from Doncaster, and her unmarried daughters.[18] The south front towards the sea is deliberately and attractively asymmetrical, the windows all incorporating ogee lights in their tracery, beneath varying patterns of frilly eaves boards. Ogee arches with sharp points are also in evidence inside, though otherwise much of the décor seems Edwardian. On the hillside immediately above, Penally Manor is said to be of 1839, and designed by James Harrison for Captain Wells. Asymmetrical on the west (entrance) and south fronts, the style is Seaside Gothic with clustered chimneys, corner polygonal shafts, frilly bargeboards, and a cusped ogee-arched doorway.[19]

Wales has a dotting of cottage orné lodges[20] but generally speaking it is not particularly rewarding territory for that aspect of the genre, and overall few examples of the cottage orné, whether extant or demolished, can be attached to a nationally known architect. An exception is the principality's best surviving cottage orné, Lancych in Pembrokeshire [fig 6/5]. This can be firmly assigned to P. F. Robinson, and strongly resembles Millfield Cottage at Bookham in Surrey, of 1814, published in Robinson's *Rural Architecture* of 1823.[21] The date 1820 is said to have been found under the library floor, although Thomas Lloyd[22] suggests that it was probably built *c*. 1831–4, after

Dr Walter Jones inherited. A substantial middle-class cottage, it is very attractively composed, with three quite different fronts. There are many and varied gables, the big ones with Robinson's characteristic exaggerated cuspings to the eaves. Robinson's contribution appears to have been added onto an existing vernacular house, which became the service wing; this is concealed on the entrance front by shrubbery, and on the other side sinks down the hillside towards the river. The plan revolves around a low Gothic plaster-vaulted hall, with the staircase to one side, lit from a stained glass rose with brightly coloured armorial glass. The ground-floor interiors (drawing room, dining room, library) are otherwise quite simply fitted out and not specifically Gothic. Lancych was designed for permanent occupation, rather than as a villa outside a town or a holiday residence. Thomas Lloyd has suggested that Dr Lloyd, who hailed from old but minor gentry and had improved his social standing by leaving West Wales to train as a doctor, building up a very successful practice outside the region, wished to create the impression of an old family home that had grown gradually through successive generations.[23] If true, this would certainly differentiate Lancych from the great majority of cottages ornés, whether in Wales or beyond.

SCOTLAND

For some reason, perhaps connected with the prevailing puritanism of Scottish religion and the no-nonsense Scottish character, Scotland is arguably the least rewarding part of the British Isles (with the possible exception of the north-east of England) to search for examples of the genre. In the half-century from the 1770s onwards, as part of the campaign whereby small upland tenant farmers were evicted from their holdings and their land consolidated into fewer but much larger farms, over 300 new farmhouses were built in the Highlands. However, these were without exception of harled rubble and very plain, and – as was generally the case in England[24] – there was no display either within or without.[25] Tourism began to flourish in Scotland at much the same time that it did in England and Wales, but seemingly without a concomitant proliferation of cottages ornés. An early example of a structure intended to cater for visitors to a particular site was the Hermitage near Dunkeld in Perthshire, erected adjacent to a path laid out alongside the turbulent River Braan for John Murray of Strowan in 1757. Externally it resembles a large bow-fronted classical gazebo, not at all rustic, but internally Bishop Forbes in 1771 noted that

> the walls of the Hermitage are decorated with some very pretty prints . . . framed in Shell Work and with pieces of Roots of Trees having the natural Moss upon them, which greatly resemble different species of Rocks. There was one Frame of Shell Work peculiarly Curious, being the several kinds of butterflies pasted on Paper by the Belly with the Wings expanded.[26]

Unfortunately the decoration was lost when the pavilion was blown up by vandals in 1869.

Rustic garden buildings always seem to have been more popular in Scotland than the cottages ornés into which such structures developed in England. In the early decades of the nineteenth century some Scottish lairds embraced the twiggy rusticity of earlier English garden buildings for use on bothies and cottages for estate workers, as well as garden summerhouses. Visiting Bonnington Lin on the Clyde in 1803, Dorothy Wordsworth was shown 'a pleasure house called the Fog House, because it was lined with fog (moss). On the outside it resembled some of the huts in the prints belonging to Captain Cook's voyages, and within was like a haystack scooped out.' Everything, including the seats and table, was covered with moss, 'snug as a bird's nest'. 'We afterwards found that huts of the same kind were common in the pleasure grounds of Scotland.'[27] The Duke of Buccleuch and Queensberry's vast estate at Drumlanrig Castle in Dumfriesshire still has a number of quite elaborate rustic summerhouses of 1844, in which materials such as heather, moss and pebbles are pressed into decorative service and incorporate the Douglas heart and ducal coronet. These may be the work of the head gardener Charles McIntosh. He was a very superior kind of head gardener, insofar as he published his own *Book of the Garden* (1853), in which he recommended that the arboretum attached to a grand house might incorporate such structures 'as woodhouses, moss houses, root houses, rock houses, or cyclopean cottages, Swiss cottages' and many more.[28] However, the most elaborate surviving specimen is probably the Bavarian Summer House built in the woodland garden of Brodick Castle, on the island of Arran, in 1845. This was a plaything intended to make Princess Marie of Baden feel at home after her marriage in 1843 to the Marquis of Douglas and Clydesdale, and is ornately patterned within and without with larch twigs and cones. Some way to the south of the castle at Drumlanrig, and adjoining the kitchen garden, is Low Gardens House [fig 6/6], built in 1831 to designs by William Burn. It is quite a sizeable building, with red-painted bargeboarded gables of different sizes that group picturesquely with the trio of tall chimneys. The use of the dark local sandstone for the structure and of slate for the roof produces overall a slightly dour effect. The results of the rustic style as deployed in Scotland were indeed usually fairly staid, although the unknown architect of the lodges on the Taymouth Castle estate in Perthshire demonstrated the wild extremes of which the idiom was capable.[29]

Although Robert Adam designed numerous buildings in variants of the rustic idiom, some of which must undoubtedly be accounted cottages ornés, very few of them were ever built, or if they were, have not survived to be judged.[30] One building in which he is traditionally said to have had an input is Barony House [fig 6/7] (originally

6/6 Low Gardens House,
Drumlanrig Castle,
Dumfries and Galloway,
by William Burn, 1831

6/7 Barony House,
Lasswade, Lothian: Walter
Scott's original cottage to
the right

known as Lasswade Cottage), at Lasswade in Lothian. This was built about 1775 as a long gabled stone building with slate roof, but a rustic thatched wing with rounded bow at one end was added by Walter Scott, who rented the cottage in 1798–1804 and brought his bride there for their honeymoon (they had married at the end of 1797). The Scott wing contains the main room of the house on the ground floor with his bedroom above; but since Adam died in 1792 it is difficult to see what his input might have been. The rustic wing, with its complete absence of frills, is in any case an example of the severity with which the Scots could approach the genre, reinforced by the gloomy grey rubblestone of which it is constructed.[31] None of the Adam rustic designs surviving in the Soane Museum is identified

as being for the 10th Earl of Cassillis, for whom he designed his finest Scottish mansion at Culzean Castle in Ayrshire. That estate does nevertheless have Swan Pond Cottage, which forms the centrepiece of an octagonal pheasantry complex designed by Robert Lugar for the 12th Earl. The dating is uncertain; the design was published in the first edition (1811) of Lugar's *Plans and Views of Buildings executed in England and Scotland in the Castellated and Other Styles*,[32] but it has been said that this is based in turn on a design for a lodge for the earl's house at St Margaret's, Twickenham, published by Lugar in 1828 in his Villa Architecture.[33] If built as depicted by Lugar in 1811, thatched, and with trellis arches connecting the verandah posts, it would have resembled a cottage orné more than

it currently does, slated, minus the treillage, and with an extra floor.[34] Lugar also published his design for a thatched Gothic gardener's cottage at Tullichewan Castle, a large castellated mansion erected to his plans on the west side of Loch Lomond; it was to be placed in a wood near the entrance to the estate, and would have been seen only when passing en route to the mansion.[35] The Old Cottage at Mellerstain – another of Adam's Scottish castle-style mansions – comprises a cylinder with conical thatched roof, immediately juxtaposed with a lower thatched square building. It has no 'orné' features as such (though it does have its own small fenced-in knot garden), and is said to have been converted by Robert Smirke from a doocot (dovecote) in 1825, at a time when such buildings were going out of fashion.[36]

Peterhead, Aberdeenshire, in the rather bleak and unpromising north-east of Scotland, is the slightly surprising location for Dales, a three-bay Gothick cottage of decided charm dating from about 1800. The windows have intersecting Gothick tracery, and there is a prominent central ogee-gabled dormer, also with Gothick glazing. The roof curves down at each end, suggesting that perhaps it was originally thatched, although it is now tiled. There is also a single-storey lodge with tree-trunk porch and decorative bargeboards.[37] Mention should also be made of Stuckgowan, Dunbartonshire, an attractive slate-roofed Gothick bungalow overlooking Loch Lomond, about which little seems to be known. However, in an admittedly not very competitive field, Scotland's prettiest example of the cottage orné must be Easter Cottage, at Charlestown on the Fife shore of the Firth of Forth [fig 6/8]. The village in which it stands was founded in the 1770s on the Broomhall estate of Charles, 5th Earl of Elgin, in order to house the labourers at his limeworks. The date of Easter Cottage is probably rather later, early nineteenth century, and the building is very modest, just a single storey plus dormers in roof. What makes the design distinctive, however, is the recessed centre over which the roof rises in a curve, supported on rustic posts that intersect to form Gothic arches; within the recess is a trio of pointed windows lighting the room in the roof. The shape of the slated roof suggests that it was originally thatched, and although the architect is inevitably unknown he may have taken his cue from plate 22 of John Plaw's *Ferme Ornée* (1795), a three-room thatched keeper's lodge with a centrepiece distinctly reminiscent of Easter Cottage. Just five miles away as the crow flies is Woodhead, Valleyfield, a late eighteenth- or early nineteenth-century farmhouse with Gothick trimmings, which could conceivably be by the same designer. Of 1-3-1 bays in two floors, it has a little portico in antis (with primitive Tuscan columns) to the ground floor centre, within which are pointed windows as at Easter Cottage; above is a single quatrefoil with elegant Gothic glazing. All the trimmings, including the window surrounds and a cusped cornice, are of knobbly flint. Like Easter Cottage, it is possible that it was originally thatched.

IRELAND

It has been suggested that cottages ornés are more common in Ireland than in England.[38] This is not in fact true, although the genre was certainly embraced more whole-heartedly and inventively than in Wales and Scotland. As in England, the idiom made its first appearance in the form of rustic garden buildings. The damp Irish climate has ensured that almost none of these survive, but examples are well recorded. Those designed by Thomas Wright have already been discussed, as has Lady Orrery's hermitage at Caledon,[39] but there were many others. Some were clearly for purely private enjoyment by the owner and his guests, while others seem to have been a spin-off of tourism. Among the assorted ornamental buildings on the Earl of Charlemont's celebrated estate at Marino outside Dublin – of which the still-surviving Casino by Sir William Chambers was always the finest – was a thatched root house, its Gothic door and windows framed by particularly twisty branches and roots, and a tiny cupola on top. The result was very similar to such Thomas Wright structures as the Root House at Badminton.[40] It is not clear whether this is the hermitage described by a visitor in 1816:

> This building is most ingeniously created with small bits of stems & roots of trees laid horizontally with the ends outward so as to form the face of the building, each bit being cut thro' smooth, and the different woods showing different colours. They are laid according to the taste of the architect and resemble something like mosaic work.[41]

However, Charlemont bought the estate in 1756, and by the early 1770s was getting short of money, so the root house must presumably have gone up before building activity ceased after 1772.

Charlemont's status, and the fame of his estate, may have helped to make such garden ornaments popular around the Irish capital. Viscount Fitzwilliam's estate at Mount Merrion in Co. Dublin had a pretty thatched summerhouse called the Wood House, with tree branches made to form cusped arches in front. It stood on the north avenue and was painted by William Ashford in 1805.[42] Another estate in the Dublin hinterland, Luttrellstown, was visited in 1831 by Prince Pückler-Muskau, who noted a 'pavillon rustique' in the pleasure ground:

> hexagonal, three sides solid, and fashioned of pieces of rough branches of trees very prettily arranged in various patterns; the other three consist of two windows and a door. The floor is covered with a mosaic of little pebbles from the brook, the ceiling with shells, and the roof is thatched with wheat straw on which the full ears are left.[43]

Bellevue, at Delgany on the coast south of Dublin, was an elysium created by the banker David La Touche between 1753 and his death in 1785. The architectural embellishments included a rustic temple entirely of wood, with Gothic arches and rustic seats overlooking a fine prospect, and a root house with roof of purple heather.[44]

In Ireland, as in England and Wales but seemingly not Scotland, the growth of tourism in the second half of the eighteenth century seems to have gone hand in hand with

the provision of rustic cottages and other ornamental structures to cater for visitors, whether on private estates for the select guests of the owner or at more generally accessible sites. Although so far from Dublin, which then as now was easily Ireland's largest centre of population, by the 1770s Killarney and its lakes had become a real visitor attraction (Louisa Conolly, chatelaine of Castletown House near Dublin, wrote ecstatically about it).[45] Much of the land was owned by Lord Kenmare, whom in 1758 Bishop Pococke recorded as having built a house for dining in on the Isle of Innisphalen.[46] The following year Edward Willes noted that

> the hermitage did not admit room for more than one servant to wait inside, so the side board was out of Doers and the wine served to us through the windows. . . . The Hermitage cover'd with ivy as old as the Reformation.[47]

This was the 4th Lord Kenmare, who died in 1795; his son lived in London and cut down all the trees. Elsewhere on Kenmare's estate was Ronayne Island, in the Upper Lake, which had the little thatched cottage shown in an aquatint by T. Medland, complete with the trumpeter laid on by Kenmare to demonstrate the remarkable echoes to his guests (a feature which inspired Tennyson's 'splendour falls on castle walls'). Another local landowner, Edward Herbert of Muckross Abbey, was reported to have built a 'simple and pleasing' cottage orné 'after the antient English style . . . entered by a porch with a flat pointed arch'.[48]

Visiting Killarney had to be done as a planned expedition of at least a week.[49] Nearer to Dublin and more easily accessible was the so-called Wicklow Tour, taking in the Wicklow mountains and the lovely valleys that run down towards the sea. The Dargle valley ten miles out of the city largely belonged to Lord Powerscourt, and included the famous cascade at Powerscourt House as well as other scenic attractions – notably Lover's Leap, drawn in 1765 by Mrs Mary Delany and painted by George Barrett around 1762. One of the most popular viewpoints was provided by Lord Powerscourt with an open thatched shelter known as the Moss House; a successor structure became a notorious 'trysting place' for amorous visitors and was not replaced once it decayed. The Powerscourt family also developed the nearby town of Enniskerry as a tourist and convalescent centre in the early nineteenth century; in

1837 it was described as being composed of about seventy houses, 'most of which are tastefully built in the cottage style and inhabited by families of respectability'.[50] By this time it had two comfortable hotels for the use of tourists.

Further into the Wicklow mountains, Avondale at Rathdrum had a 'pretty cottage', noted by William Smith in 1815 and illustrated in Samuel Hayes's *A Practical Treatise on Planting*, published in Dublin in 1794.[51] Hayes, a Dublin barrister, was also the owner of the estate from 1777 and a great forester. He built a thatched cottage orné, called the Woodhouse, which his engraving shows to have been single-storeyed with one little roof dormer. Its rustic verandah had bold Gothic cuspings formed of curved branches, and the structure as a whole appears to have been of horizontally laid pieces of wood. The inscription on the engraving says it was 'designed by S.H.', that is, Hayes himself. It shows the cottage placed alongside a stream, and although its precise location is not known, it may have been at the beauty spot known as the Meeting of the Waters, which occurs where the Avonmore and Avonbeg rivers unite to form the Avoca river at the south-ern tip of the Avondale estate. In that case, if it didn't just moulder away it may well have been swept away in a flood. It is said to have incorporated tea rooms for those passing through the estate on the picturesque carriage drives laid out by Hayes.[52] William Smith also visited Ballyarthur, at Woodenbridge in the Vale of Arklow, where he saw a

> moss house built of birch and fir handsomely
> interspersed; sides and seats which are inlaid with
> moss; it has a tessellated pavement of sea pebbles
> and the roof is formed of the cones of Fir and Larch
> in a most fanciful and elegant manner.[53]

Rushy glens and the shores of lakes – indeed the proximity of water in general – were a particularly favoured location for rustic cottages, especially ones not intended for permanent occupation. Woodstock, an estate on the banks of the river Nore at Inistioge, Co. Kilkenny, was owned by the Tighe family and featured a deep wooded glen.[54] Perched on the precipitous rim was a cottage 'a la Suisse', supposedly designed by Mrs Tighe [fig 6/9]. This

was part of an elaborate layout with bridges, seats and rustic pavilions, all of which have disappeared although the basic layout of paths and steps survived without Victorian alterations. A volume of miscellaneous topographical watercolours sheds valuable light on this and other rustic cottages of the Kilkenny region.[55] It was formed by the Kilkenny-based English architect and artist William Robertson (1770–1850), best known for his drastic restoration of Kilkenny Castle, and it has been suggested that he was also responsible for designing these structures.[56] The watercolours in the volume illustrating Woodstock[57] are by George Miller (fl. 1815–19), who shows the Swiss Cottage as thatched and single-storeyed, with rustic verandahs and latticed windows.[58] Unusually it was asymmetrical and had two non-matching façades at right angles to each other to take advantage

of the views up and down the gorge; the verandahs sheltered benches made from branches. Within were three tiny rooms, the hinge on the angle being a room with French windows opening into a projecting bow on one side and a canted bay on the other.

In the same volume are Miller watercolours of two other cottages ornés in the vicinity of Kilkenny, Dangan Cottage [fig 6/10] at Thomastown, and Kilfane. Dangan[59] is shown as a single-storey thatched building with treillage verandah, within which are large latticed French windows with what appear to be frames glazed with roundels of red and blue glass. In its grounds was a hermitage, shown in another watercolour as a stone structure with ogee-headed Gothick windows and conical thatched roof supported on tree trunks.[60] Miller's watercolours of Kilfane Cottage[61] were to prove invaluable when it was recreated in the

1990s. It had formed a key element in a romantic garden laid out in the late 1790s by Sir John and Lady Power, who were at the forefront of intellectual and artistic society in south-east Ireland, founding the Kilkenny Theatre and amassing an important library. The garden was well away from their main house, which was a normal Georgian classical box, and comprised ten acres on either side of a rocky ravine. It was described by A. Atkinson in 1815 as

> a seat of rural felicity . . . surrounded by perpendicular rocks and elevated grounds, thickly planted with ornamental timber. The plateau on which it stands is beautified by tall spruce trees, laurels, laburnums and other ornamental shrubs, but with adequate space for the observation of romantic objects which surround it, of which the river, murmuring to its rocky bed, is not the least interesting.[62]

He noted that the cottage drawing room was used for 'teas and cold dinners' and was capable of taking thirty people – though that would certainly have been a crush.

The site is shown on an estate map of 1795 before the transformation began. This entailed diverting water from the rushing river into a mile-long leat, in order to feed a 30-foot-high artificial waterfall down the cliff opposite the rustic cottage that was built in the bottom of the valley. A path winds down the cliff and originally passed through an artificial grotto. There are clear parallels with the Rousseau-inspired cascade and grotto created at Ermenonville by the Marquis René Louis de Girardin, and described by him in *Promenade ou itineraire des jardins d'Ermenonville* of 1788. The cottage is shown in Miller's watercolours of 1805, and was described by Louisa Beaufort after a visit in 1819. By this time the new planting had grown up well but it seems the cottage was already past its best.

> . . . went to Kilfayne, Mr Powers's, a very pretty place . . . we were to walk to a cottage on the mountain side. . . . All the beginning of the walk very ugly, latter part very pretty by a stream . . . rushing over large beds of rocks, the beeches high and well planted and the ground blue with harebells the cottage is prettyish, somewhat of a has-been but stands in a tiny lawn near the stream and opposite to a cataract which rushes down the opposite rock. . . . Mr Butler and I scrambled up and down every rock and bank and had much amusement.[63]

Evidently the normal effects of the Irish climate were exacerbated by the dampness of the valley bottom and no doubt heightened by the spray from the waterfall, so that what was in any case a structure of ephemeral materials decayed and disappeared faster than usual. The Kilfane landscape was progressively abandoned, the waterfall dried up and the cottage faded completely from memory. It was not until the early 1990s, when the historian Jeremy Williams mentioned the George Miller views to the new owners of the demesne, Nicholas and Susan Mosse, that they realized there had ever been a cottage there. They discovered, buried under two feet of soil, the footings of part of its walls, along with traces of a cobbled floor. Encouraged by one of Ireland's leading gardeners, Jim Reynolds, they bravely embarked on the recreation of the Georgian landscape in 1992.[64] On the basis of the surviving physical evidence and the Miller views, the architect David Sheehan brilliantly recreated the cottage [fig 6/11], and the restoration of the clogged leat reinstated the dramatic waterfall that is the main *point de vue* from its windows. Externally the cottage is again exactly as Miller depicted it: L-shaped, its thatched roof supported on tree trunks, and with latticed French windows looking straight at the waterfall from within a projecting bow. The

cobbled pavement surrounding the building has either been restored or recreated, and the alcoves given new twiggy furniture made from forest trimmings. Internally the restoration has inevitably had to be more of an informed guess, but the results are completely convincing, with appropriate furnishings and wall coverings, and a twiggy surround to the fireplace. The result is certainly one of the best places to get an accurate idea of how such superior cottage interiors must have looked.[65]

Like the Woodstock cottage, Kilfane has three rooms, which seems to have been a characteristic size for cottages built as non-residential playthings. Cane Cottage, at Florence Court, near Enniskillen, Co. Fermanagh, had a dining room, bedroom (the walls of which were lined with split cane, hence the name) and kitchen. It was built in the 1790s by John Cole, later 2nd Earl of Enniskillen, after his return from the Grand Tour, and was rectangular with a canted bay projecting from the north side. The latticed windows were Gothic, the walls a combination of brick and wood, while the steeply pitched thatched roof overhung the walls with wide eaves. Lord Enniskillen made the drinking vessels and plates for the cottage himself, turning them on a lathe.[66] A kitchen, where either

the proprietor or (more likely) a servant could prepare refreshments, was evidently an important element. Jonathan Fisher, in his *Scenery of Ireland* (1795) mentions a handsome cottage at Belleisle, also in Co. Fermanagh, 'with a little kitchen and other conveniences, in a sweet retired part, secluded from the powerful influence of the sun'[67] – the latter certainly not usually an important consideration in Ireland.

One thing that emerges from a study of cottages ornés in Ireland is that, although plentiful relative to Wales or Scotland, their social range was more restricted, being largely limited to the two extremes of the spectrum: gate lodges at one end and structures for the upper echelons of Anglo-Irish society at the other. As in England the most numerous category was probably that of the gate lodge. Irish estates (or 'demesnes') were certainly provided with such lodges, likewise designed to guard the entrances and keep out the riff-raff, but only rarely were they in the cottage style.[68] Castle Coole, the Earl of Belmore's great neoclassical mansion in Co. Fermanagh, has a lodge in the form of a picturesque thatched cottage, with deeply projecting eaves supported on rustic tree-trunk columns to create a simple loggia.[69] At Fenaghy, Co. Antrim, a lodge from as late as about 1855 was a fairly straight copy of Oak Cottage at Blaise Hamlet; the connection here is the likely local architect, Thomas Jackson, who until 1828 was articled to George Dymond in Bristol. More often the lodges related to the style of the main house, whether classical or Gothic or castellated, although interestingly those to the vast and gloomy neo-Norman pile of Gosford Castle, Co. Armagh, were designed as thatched log cabins, with tiny Gothic windows and verandahs.[70] The lack of home-grown pattern books meant that there was a reliance on ideas from across the Irish Channel. Details such as decorative eaves boards might be culled from A. C. Pugin's *Decorative Gables*, of 1831,[71] and as in England and Wales the pervasive influence of P. F. Robinson's books is also felt. The great estate of Baronscourt, Co. Tyrone, had had lodges since the mid-eighteenth century, but in the 1830s these were replaced in the latest English Picturesque style. They are technically by the leading Irish architect William Vitruvius Morrison, but in fact their designs were cribbed from Robinson's *Designs for Lodges and Park Entrances*, hot off the press in 1833.[72]

It was also rare for Irish landlords to re-house their tenants in an enhanced cottage idiom in the way that is described in England in Chapter Two. A few of the more enlightened built small model towns, in which the accommodation, however simple, would certainly have been an improvement on the small thatched hovels (or 'cabins') that were the Irish norm; but on the whole the logic advanced by English pattern book writers such as P. F. Robinson and Charles Waistell was lost on the Protestant Anglo-Irish landlord. However many centuries his forebears might have been in Ireland, he was still likely to be regarded by the Catholic peasant population at large as an alien, and the inclination was to live in his own closed environment, sequestered behind the enveloping walls of the demesne and socializing exclusively with others of his class. One exception is Adare, Co. Limerick, where from about 1810 the Earl of Dunraven replaced the collection of squalid hovels at his gates with a picturesque village complete with thatched eaves, rustic verandahs and ornamental elements straight from English pattern books.[73] At Castle Bellingham, Co. Louth [fig 6/12] the Widows' Houses of 1826–30 were built to house the widows of estate workers, and in the Blaise Hamlet tradition of varied designs in an informal group-

ing.[74] Santry, Co. Dublin, was an attractive model village which has now virtually disappeared under the site of Dublin airport. Photographs exist in the Irish Architectural Archive, one of which, of a group of cottages circa 1946, is inscribed 'demolished'. The village, completed in 1840, was an informal grouping of whitewashed houses with cusped eaves, while the post office was a version of a Swiss Cottage design, simplified. Santry was built at the behest of Lady Helena Domvile, and interestingly it seems likely that she supplied the designs since several of the houses correspond to designs apparently published by her in London around 1840 as *Eighteen Designs for Glebe Houses and Rural Cottages*.[75] In fact, though Lady Domvile was a talented amateur artist, her originality as an architect was evidently limited since several of the houses are a straight crib from published designs by P. F. Robinson.

Women appear to feature quite prominently in the Irish cottage world. Mrs Tighe may or may not have designed her cottage at Woodstock, but it is documented that Anna Maria Dawson designed and built an ornamental cottage for herself at Fairy Hill, Rostrevor, on the east shore of Carlingford Lough in Co. Down, a place beginning to establish itself as a fashionable retreat for gentry. In 1836 it was described as 'a handsome ornamented house built by Mrs Dawson, widow of the Reverend Vesey Dawson, in 1814', and to judge from her surviving drawings all its details were clearly carefully considered.[76] Farnham, Co. Cavan, has a lodge said to have been designed by one of the eighteenth-century Lady Farnhams,[77] with rustic tree-trunk columns supporting set-back corners to one side, and a recessed entrance loggia on the other. Now heavily restored, with painted windows and tiled roof, it has lost much of its original character, though traces of pebbled decoration remain. However, the setting, on the tree-lined edge of a lake, is much more beautiful than that of the Castle Coole gate lodge, and still resembles that shown in an early nineteenth-century watercolour. At Burrenwood, Castlewellan, Co. Down, an ornamental demesne with cottage was conceived by Theodora Magill, Countess of Clanwilliam (1743–1817), who inherited her father's estates when she was only four.[78] What started as a small cottage on the road south from Gill Hall, where the countess normally stayed, was expanded by her son General Robert Meade after he left the army in 1817; he lived mainly in London and used it solely as a summer cottage.[79]

Perhaps it is an index of how insulated such grand ladies were from the realities of rural life in Ireland that some at least indulged in Marie-Antoinette-like fantasies of bucolic simplicity without any evident sense of irony. In her *Recollections of a Beloved Mother*, published in Belfast in 1824,[80] Lady Dufferin described how in about 1780 her father, John Foster (the last Speaker of the Irish House of Commons, created 1st Lord Oriel), enlarged a garden house – the drawing room being in the form of a Doric temple – for summer occupation by the family. Known as Oriel Temple, this in due course became the permanent family residence, visitors being expected to stay in the mid-Georgian Collon House in nearby Collon village, Co. Louth. Foster then indulged his beloved wife Margaret by building a cottage, where she, her daughters and cousins wore 'stuff gowns'[81] and played at being simple cottagers (Lady Oriel called herself 'Madge of the Cottage'). Lady Oriel apparently wanted it to be built of mud in order to be truly authentic, but her husband 'persuaded her to let him build it of stone and mortar, with a strong projecting thatched roof.' The cottage, said Lady Dufferin,

> proved such a source of amusement to her for many years, and remains such a beautiful monument of the elegance and simplicity of her taste. . . . Whilst the building was going on she directed the furnishing of the walls, the recesses all to suit the plans she made from the first in her own mind, of what she wished it should be when finished. The very model of what a real cottage should be – in the furniture the same plan was pursued. All was useful, simple and well-adapted. . . . The prints with which the walls were hung she had been for some time collecting – and many friends, when they knew what she was about, contributed little decorations that they thought would gratify her. In this dear Cottage many happy hours were spent. We used often to drink tea there from the Temple and have dances in the evening, or stroll about the grounds surrounding it, till the close of evening sent us home. . . . In due course, to keep herself amused, Mother created a grotto in an old quarry near the Cottage, pressing into service all sorts of materials – sealing wax, broken china, beads, lobster shells, coloured parchment, plus spars, shells, stones, coloured glass, mirror, pebbles, even fish bones.[82]

Unfortunately the appearance of the building seems not to have been recorded and it has now largely disappeared, but the *Buildings of Ireland* records the remains of a small rubble and brick structure at the south end of the lake which, 'looking more like the stump of some tower house, now sprouts bushes and trees from its roof'.[83] It contained two rooms, one square and the other apse-ended, with pointed windows, roughly formed niches, a fireplace in the first room and a corbelled vault. 'Cows have taken up residence today.'[84] The remains of Lady Oriel's grotto or shell house, now minus its shells, are in a dell in woodlands to the west of the house.[85]

If Lady Oriel's cottage was an escape from a really quite modest main residence, the same cannot be said of the

very early cottage that was created as an appendage to Ireland's grandest Georgian mansion, Castletown House at Celbridge, west of Dublin. In 1761 the chatelaine Lady Louisa Conolly wrote to her sister Lady Sarah Bunbury that she was building a little lodge of her own design, which was a 'prodigious entertainment' to her.[86] In 1764, back from visiting London, she wrote that she was sitting in an alcove in her 'Cottage' with a porch before it, in a wood three quarters of a mile from the main house. The grass was very green, honeysuckle and roses were in abundance, mignonette was coming up, and the seringa was in bloom. Her sister-in-law Mrs Staples was playing her guitar in the porch while she worked and read – 'my work and my book by me, inkstand as you may perceive and a little comfortable table and chairs, two stands with China bowls filled with immense nosegays'. As the much later Thornery at Woburn Abbey was provided with custom-made Wedgwood crockery, so Louisa's cottage was 'neatly fitted up with Tunbridge Ware', from which she drank tea in the

summer.[87] Not far away from Castletown at Lucan, Louisa's friend Mrs Vesey also had a cottage, referred to in 1773 by the English tourist the Reverend J. Burrowes as 'a place for the owners of a grand house actually to retire to (as in fact they live there all the harvest months)'. Lucan House itself was a handsome classical villa with interiors by James Wyatt, whereas the cottage, according to Burrowes, was located 'in the most rural situation . . . in a grass farm on the banks of the [River] Liffey'. It is recorded in an amateur pencil sketch,[88] which seems to show a building with a rounded end, thatched roof and trellis applied to the exterior walls – as Burrowes put it, 'none but rural ornaments'.[89] The fact that apparently the Veseys actually took up extended residence rather than just visiting for occasional amusement is perhaps the most surprising aspect of the Lucan cottage.

Of all the aristocratic Anglo-Irish ladies who indulged in the charms of the simple life, the grandest was undoubtedly Louisa Conolly's sister Emily, who as a daughter of the English 2nd Duke of Richmond and wife of the Duke of Leinster, Ireland's premier peer, was doubly grand. At Carton, west of Dublin near Maynooth, she created the Shell Cottage [figs 6/13, 14, 15], which happily still survives. In 1776 Arthur Young noted, on the banks of the little river Rye, 'a large shrubbery, very elegantly laid out, and dressed in the highest order, with a cottage, the scenery about which is uncommonly pleasing'.[90] In fact Emily had probably begun her plaything in the late 1740s when she was still Countess of Kildare, and the shell room for which it quickly became famous was apparently created within an existing thatched cottage. It may be more than pure coincidence that this was shortly after her mother, the Duchess of Richmond, had begun work on a very formal shell house, essentially Palladian in form, at Goodwood in Sussex. The Carton cottage is invisible from the main house and is reached either through a little wood or by a rustic bridge across a cascade on the river. Less architecturally conceived than the Goodwood interior, the main room combines shells of many different shapes, sizes and colours with glass, mirrors, lumps of rough tufa, bark, branches and fir cones.[91] These are mainly organized into geometric patterns, with light and dark materials juxtaposed to provide a loose overall structure; indeed, in general views of the room the dark can seem to predominate over the light, despite the shell-lined domed skylight.

Even on a bright day it can seem gloomy, not helped by the tall trees that shade the cottage on its south side. Jonathan Fisher's description of the cottage at Belleisle, 'in a sweet retired part, secluded from the powerful influence of the sun', could equally apply at Carton. Nor are light levels improved by the painted glass in the bow window at one end, featuring chivalric scenes that are pure Eglinton Tournament.[92] These are dated 1834, and were added by the 3rd duchess, Charlotte Augusta Stanhope, along with the bay window in which they sit.[93]

The shell room remains largely unspoilt, but a visit by Queen Victoria prompted the transformation of the exterior. A large extension at right angles to the original cottage doubled its size without necessarily doubling its charm, and most of what is now visible must date from this phase – tiled roofs instead of the presumed thatch, Blaise Hamlet-type Tudoresque chimneys, half-timbering in the gable ends. The oddest feature on the Victorian wing is the use of cast-iron tree-trunk columns for the verandahs and to support the overhanging gable end. The pebble floor of the verandah confirms the date and occasion for the extension, since it incorporates the date 1849, the letters V & A, and the queen's monogram.

Whereas in England the cottage orné genre became increasingly popular with the 'middling' ranks of society, both for permanent homes in urban hinterlands and for residences on or near the coast, in Ireland the middling ranks were less developed and in any case showed little interest in living in a cottage, however superior; perhaps they were put off by the knowledge that the vast majority of the population lived in cottages that were far from charming or romantic. As a generalization, the cottage in Ireland was very largely the preserve of the Anglo-Irish Ascendancy, who had large demesnes on which they could play at the simple life, and for the most part they had no intention of spending more than the occasional night there. An exception was Derrymore House, Co. Armagh [fig 6/16]. Isaac Corry, who otherwise had a townhouse in Merrion Square, Dublin, became MP for Newry in 1776 and may have built his cottage soon afterwards as a necessary base for visits to his constituency. Certainly it was in existence by 1787. The building is single-storeyed on a U-plan (like Burrenwood, not far away), thatched, harled and very straightforward, indeed unromantic – what the current owners, the National Trust, call 'gentleman's vernacular'. It has a central saloon

lit by a full-height bay window, and flanking wings with eight bedrooms (potentially for use by the five children he had by his mistress, although it is unclear how much time they spent there). The only name known in connection with Derrymore is John Sutherland, a landscape designer, although he may just have done the planting.

Mistresses also enter the picture at Shane's Castle, Co. Antrim. The 2nd Viscount O'Neill built a series of rustic seats and thatched cottages over the demesne, in which he apparently housed his mistresses. All their residences are now gone, but the plan and elevation of one of them, Raymond Cottage, survives.[94] Interestingly it too shares the U-plan, which was perhaps a northern Irish vernacular speciality. It was again single-storeyed and heather-thatched, but made much more individual than Derrymore by its tripartite front elevation. This had a large bow flanked by two small ones, and there were striking oval windows, elaborately glazed. The plan shows it to have been a proper dwelling, with oval entrance hall, spacious parlour, one main and three smaller bedrooms, housekeeper's room and so on, and wings enclosing a rear courtyard. When the estate was inherited in 1855 by the Rev. William Chichester, he ordered 'all such dens of iniquity to be razed to the ground'.[95]

Although Ireland was clearly once quite rich in examples of the rustic and cottage genres, the Irish climate and Irish history have ensured that very few actually survive. Of those that do, easily the finest and, nowadays, best known is the Swiss Cottage at Cahir, Co. Tipperary, built around 1810 for the 12th Lord Cahir, later created 1st Earl of Glengall [figs 6/17–20]. It was always exceptional in itself and indeed can now fairly stake a claim to be one of the finest cottages ornés to survive anywhere. Equally remarkable are the background to its creation and the story of its modern survival.

The Cahir branch of the Ormonde Butlers were created Barons Cahir in 1543 and, despite remaining Catholic, managed to hold on to their estates until the death of the 11th baron in 1788. The death of closer relatives in quick succession meant that at that point the title went to Richard Butler, a boy of thirteen who was then living in poverty in Cahir with his mother and sister, his father having abandoned the family. Knowing nothing of his rights and entitlements, he and his sister were kidnapped by rival claimants and packed off to France to conceal

OPPOSITE 6/18 Swiss Cottage, Cahir: Music Room

OPPOSITE, BELOW 6/19 Swiss Cottage, Cahir: 'Dufours Room'

6/20 Swiss Cottage, Cahir: entrance hall

their existence. The Irish Lord Chancellor, Lord Fitzgibbon, discovered the situation and sent his sister Mrs Jeffereys, of Blarney Castle, to France to find them. She discovered them 'in a miserable garret, all over grown with hair',[96] took charge of them and brought them up. In due course she managed to marry the young 12th baron to her daughter Emily – this was in 1793, when he was just seventeen and she sixteen. With access to the income from considerable estates they became a fashionable couple, mainly dividing their time between London and Paris and coming to Ireland only for short periods.

The ancestral seat of Cahir Castle had been in ruins since a visit from Oliver Cromwell in 1650, and its successor Cahir House was an unremarkable building on the town square. From about 1802 Lord and Lady Cahir started to create a park along the River Suir immediately south of the town, clearing away existing cottages and planting extensively. Beginning in about 1810 they had a small cot-

tage on a knoll above the west bank of the river transformed into a cottage orné, almost certainly to designs by John Nash, who was then in Ireland and was in cottage orné mode, sending back to England the designs for Blaise Hamlet. The attribution is strengthened by the fact that in 1816–17 Cahir Protestant church was rebuilt to Nash's designs and at Lord Cahir's expense. The work on the church, and that on the cottage, was probably supervised by James and Richard Pain, two brothers sent over to Ireland to superintend Nash's other Irish projects. The Swiss Cottage (not so called until later in the century) was certainly complete by 1814, when it was drawn by a local artist, J. S. Alpenny.[97]

In Nash's cottage output the Swiss Cottage is midway in scale between those at Blaise Hamlet and the gigantic specimen he was to begin for the Prince Regent at Windsor in 1813. It is not large, even by the standards of English cottages such as Houghton Lodge or Mr Fish's cottage at Sidmouth, but it does have two reasonably spacious reception rooms, and bedrooms of the same dimensions above them, separated by a stairhall. The building is free-standing, with verandahs on all four sides, and the problem of what to do about services without spoiling the look of the place was solved by placing them within the hillock on which the cottage stands. Thus, the cottage itself was approached by a drive that curves up to the south front, while servants came and went at a lower level on the north, the two different worlds being connected by a discreet internal staircase. The bedrooms meant that it was perfectly possible for Lord and Lady Cahir to stay overnight if they wished, but they would probably have felt the accommodation was too restricted for longer stays. Privacy was ensured by the planting, which screened the cottage from a public lane to the east and from the town to the north, while permitting a panoramic view of the Galtee Mountains to the west.[98]

However, though the Cahirs could come here to relax and lead the simple life away from prying eyes if they wished, part of the purpose of the cottage must have been to provide a setting for entertaining. Their first appearance in local society was in the year of their marriage, 1793, when Dorothea Herbert (daughter of a clergyman from the local town of Carrick-on-Suir, later to be a noted diarist and poetess) attended a fête champêtre at Cahir House that presumably provided a template for later events once the cottage was built.

> We dined under marquees in the lawn and danced all evening – Lady Caher [sic] danced an Irish jig for us in her stockings to the music of an old blind piper. All was conducted in the old Irish Stile. Lord Caher and she did everything to make it agreeable to each individual guest, and though the throng of fine folks was immense his Lordship did me the honour to dance with me.[99]

The Cahirs evidently took seriously their social responsibilities in the area, for instance hosting the annual horse races in the grounds. A local newspaper report in 1816 – the year Lord Cahir was created Earl of Glengall – referred to 'the tout ensemble of the Cottage affording a display of rural decoration not easy to be equalled in this country for chasteness of character and richness of fancy'.[100]

Both in overall design and in its details the exterior of the Cottage is very deliberately asymmetrical, with each façade differently designed. On the main, south, elevation, which is basically three bays wide, the right-hand third is made wider and higher than the rest. Each of the three windows lighting the first-floor rooms is different from the others, and the two dormers are also non-matching. On the east side the thatch is tweaked into a far-projecting peak, while the opposite elevation towards the Galtee Mountains is given a two-tier twiggy verandah. On the north side a bowed verandah offers views down the slope to the River Suir. The verandah that wraps around most of the ground floor is now roofed in wooden shingles but was for its first few years thatched like the main roof; this no doubt looked charming but quickly proved to be completely impractical, since rain poured off the roof thatch onto the lower tier of thatch and rotted it.

Inside the keynote is sophisticated simplicity. The spiral staircase is by no means showy but nevertheless elegantly designed, and it rises from a wooden hall floor very skilfully constructed on a spider's web pattern; in what might be considered a rather perverse form of sophistication the floor is actually walnut, painted and grained to look like cheap pine, while the mahogany of the staircase is also painted over. To maximize the amount of light available underneath the verandah, the windows are generously large, and designed as French windows; indeed the whole south side of the hall is a curved wall of latticed glazing. The most memorable feature is not in fact due to Nash, though he very possibly sanctioned it. This is the scenic wallpaper, produced in Paris by the Dufours firm from 1812, which lines the main reception room. The theme is 'Rives du Bosphore' (Banks of the Bosphorus), depicting very largely imaginary Turkish scenes well stocked with minarets, domes and a cast of turbaned figures. Such papers were immensely expensive, and to the local visitors allowed to see them must have seemed extraordinarily exotic and chic.[101]

The 1st Earl of Glengall died in 1819 aged only forty-three but his widow lived on, continuing to entertain at the Cottage with help from the military band from the local barracks. The 2nd earl married an exceptionally rich heiress and poured her money into well-intended improvements in the town and locality. Notwithstanding her resources, his extravagance and the effects of the

Famine led to him being declared bankrupt in 1849. Their only surviving child, Margaret, married into the Scottish Charteris family, earls of Wemyss and March, and it was her son Lieutenant Colonel Richard Charteris who owned and maintained the Cottage until his death in 1961 at the age of ninety-four. By that stage the tenant had for some years been John Heavey, who looked after the fishing on the river. After the colonel died he bought the freehold and lived in the gradually deteriorating Cottage until his death in 1980. In the years immediately following, physical decay was exacerbated by shocking vandalism, and it very quickly seemed inevitable that the building would either fall down or be pulled down. Its rescue and restoration in 1985–9, which had widely been thought impossible, was one of the more heartening episodes in the Republic of Ireland's changing attitude to its Anglo-Irish architectural heritage.[102]

Arguably even finer than the Swiss Cottage, or at least larger and more ambitious, was Bantry Lodge [fig 6/21] at Glengariff, Co. Cork, which alas has disappeared completely. An undated photograph, perhaps of about 1860,[103] shows a large, roughly square building set against a hillside, of two storeys and surrounded by a two-tier verandah reminiscent of that on the Swiss Cottage at Endsleigh, Devon.[104] Irregularly undulating thatch wraps around the clusters of Tudoresque chimneys. At the centre of the main front a very elaborately cusped gable shelters a concatenation of traceried Gothick windows at first-floor level, which presumably lit the main reception room and no doubt commanded a fine view. Very little seems to be known about the building, except that it functioned as a hunting lodge on a two-acre island that the Earl of Bantry created by diverting the Glengarriff river, some ten miles from his main seat at Bantry. Sporting lodges were quite common in Ireland, particularly on big estates in remote areas where game was plentiful, but most were quite simple, even basic, built to accommodate parties of friends of the owner. They tended to be male preserves, something reflected in the plain decoration and sturdy furnishings, without frills and furbelows though usually equipped with a billiard table and volumes of game or fishing records. From an architectural point of view Bantry Lodge was always exceptional.[105] It is likely to have been the creation of Richard White, who was made Baron Bantry for his role in repelling a French invasion via Bantry Bay in 1796, was upgraded to earl in 1816 and died in 1851. Confusingly, there exist amateurish pencil sketches on paper watermarked 1816 which are clearly for the Glengariff lodge but differ in significant details, such as the fact that the thatch overhang is supported on giant rustic posts but there is no gallery.[106] The likelihood is that they are the owner's idea of what he had in mind, which was then worked up by the anonymous architect, although they have also been attributed to the first earl's eldest son, Viscount Berehaven (born 1800), who would still have been a teenager in 1817.

The earldom of Bantry became extinct in 1891, but the lodge remained in the possession of the family until the 1940s. It survived until effectively destroyed by fire in the 1960s, after which it was rebuilt to a completely unrelated design.

The largest of the recorded Irish cottages ornés is, appropriately, Martinstown House, Co. Kildare [fig 6/22], apparently built for Ireland's premier peer, Augustus, 3rd Duke of Leinster, who was born in 1791 and reigned from 1804 to his death in 1874. Martinstown is by the standards of the residential cottage orné relatively large, though by no means extravagant in its design. The style is basically Tudor Gothic, with a succession of gracefully bargeboarded and pinnacled gables on the long south elevation, and a spot of half-timbering (very un-Irish) on the entrance porch on the short west elevation. The building is long and low, so that both the ground-floor rooms and the bedrooms are generally low-ceilinged, with the exception of a double-height reception room which may have been added to the north side a little later, albeit in matching style; the internal detailing is simple throughout.[107] The likelihood is that the architect was English, and indeed it has traditionally been attributed to Decimus Burton, though documentary evidence seems to be lacking. There are sufficient similarities to Burton's own Baston Cottage at Tunbridge Wells, or North Villa at St Leonard's[108] for the attribution to be acceptable, although comparison can also be made with some of P. F. Robinson's larger cottage designs.

The precise history of the cottage's creation is confusing, since the land actually belonged to Robert Borrowes of Barretstown Castle, who from 1818 planted up 130 acres of it. An estate map dated February 1833 gives the estate name as Martinstown and Borrowes as its owner, but a vignette at the top shows only a tiny cottage that bears no relation to the present house. That was clearly finished by 1840, and is accurately depicted in a pen and

wash drawing of that year, with what is obviously a newly established garden in front, the lawn dotted with fashionable little circular flower beds. According to tradition Borrowes was leaned on by the duke to allow him to build a house which, though nominally a hunting lodge, he could use as a love nest for his mistress Miss Martin, well away from the family seat at Carton – hence, supposedly, the name, although that was already current in 1833. The duke had married Lady Charlotte Augusta Stanhope in 1818, so in 1834 he would have been forty-three and married for sixteen years, with four children – time perhaps for his thoughts to be straying to a younger woman. It was his wife who made alterations to the shell cottage at Carton in 1834, and one can perhaps speculate that this was to occupy her while her errant husband was away philandering.[109]

1 'Drawn from nature by J Steeple, Sherbourne Road, Birmingham' and published by Robert Taylor, Chepstow. I am grateful to Elizabeth Whittle, Thomas Lloyd and Stephen Astley for information relating to Moss Cottage. Pre-World War I postcards show it in good condition, so probably it disappeared after the war.

2 The bargeboards have disappeared. John Newman, *Buildings of Wales: Gwent/ Monmouthshire* (London, 2000), p. 275.

3 National Library of Wales, Drawings Volume 9, fols 55, 56 and 74.

4 Hoare had apparently been taken with 'the little retired villa' of Lord William Gordon on Derwentwater in the Lake District, also single-storeyed. Richard Haslam and Julian Orbach, *Buildings of Wales: Gwynedd* (New Haven and London, 2009), p. 664. I am grateful to Thomas Lloyd for drawing my attention to Vachdeiliog.

5 Haslam and Orbach, *Gwynedd*, p. 602.

6 Dated 25 May 1801. Private collection.

7 Edward Hubbard, *Buildings of Wales: Clwyd* (Harmondsworth, 1986), p. 229.

8 The lodge to Pontypool Park, discussed in Chapter Two, is another such.

9 It is not clear whether it dates from the Telford period or was built for Lord Willoughby d'Eresby on his Gwydir estate around 1840. Haslam and Orbach, *Gwynedd*, p. 313.

10 National Library of Wales, Hornor Album no. 13.

11 National Library of Wales.

12 Nigel Temple, *George Repton's Pavilion Notebook* (Aldershot, 1993), pp. 151–5.

13 Bernard Morris, 'William Booth's Watercolours of "Marino" in 1804', *Journal of the Gower Society*, vol. XLIV (1993), pp. 14–20. The lodges are Thatched Lodge, for which Robinson supplied the design in 1833, and another, somewhat enlarged, at the south-west corner of the park. In 1923 the estate became the administrative headquarters of University College, which in time filled the grounds with buildings. John Newman, *Buildings of Wales: Glamorgan* (London, 1995), p. 600.

14 According to Nigel Temple, cited in ibid., p. 487.

15 Jane Austen's family talked of visiting Tenby and Barmouth from their base in Bath in the summer of 1802, but it is unclear whether they actually did so.

16 Thomas Lloyd, Julian Orbach and Robert Scourfield, *The Buildings of Wales: Pembrokeshire* (New Haven and London, 2004), p. 483. Nevertheless, the houses include The Gables, of about 1850, with decorative bargeboards and marginally glazed casements with Tudor hoodmoulds; Heywood Lodge with a pretty stone front of 1844, the gable with curly bargeboards; and Heywood Mount, of 1847, with a bargeboarded centre gable.

17 The plan is not coherent and some walls are much thicker than others.

18 'A Murder of Crows – the Story of Penally' (Penally History Society pamphlet).

19 'Almost Moorish in effect,' according to Thomas Lloyd, *Pembrokeshire*, p. 354.

20 For instance, Plas Boduan, at Boduan on the Lleyn peninsula, with Tudor windows and a verandah on tree-trunk posts (Haslam and Orbach, *Gwynedd*, p. 271); a lodge to the dower house of Stackpole Court, Pembrokeshire, with a verandah of tree-trunk columns that formerly supported a thatched roof; the lodge to the Bishop's Palace at Abergwili, Carmarthen, built by John Foster c.1825–30, probably originally thatched; and the octagonal lodge with thatched roof, tree-trunk columns and Gothic windows to Gelli, at Trefilan, Ceredigion, a house on which Nash may have worked c.1800 (Thomas Lloyd, Julian Orbach and Robert Scourfield, *Buildings of Wales: Carmarthenshire & Ceredigion* (New Haven and London, 2006), p. 581). A good many other lodges are picturesque to some degree. According to Robert Scourfield (Robert Scourfield and Richard Haslam, *The Buildings of Wales: Powys* (New Haven and London, 2013), p. 562), a roadside cottage at Penpont, Breconshire, linked with the estate smithy on the opposite side of road, could have been designed by Robert Lugar, another leading pattern-book architect. Dated 1846, it has a stone-tiled roof, windows with latticed leading, Tudor dripmoulds, and frilly eaves.

21 P. F. Robinson, *Rural Architecture* (1823), Design No. XX, pls 89–96. See Chapter Four, p. 106.

22 Lloyd et al., *Pembrokeshire*, p. 119.

23 A small castellated folly tower on the hill behind the house was meant to represent the home of Lloyd's medieval ancestors. Personal communication from Thomas Lloyd, who notes that most minor Welsh gentry had little ambition beyond staying on their ancestral acres and hoping to marry a little money.

24 But see Chapter Three, p. 85.

25 Daniel Maudlin, 'Modern Houses for Modern People: Identifying and Interpreting the Highland Building Boom, 1775–1825', *Vernacular Architecture*, vol. XXXIX (2008), pp. 1–8.

26 Rev. J. B. Craven, ed., *Journals of the Episcopal Visitations of the Right Rev. Robert Forbes* (London, 1886), p. 239, quoted in Tim Buxbaum, *Scottish Garden Buildings* (Edinburgh, 1989), p. 151.

27 Dorothy Wordsworth, *Recollections of a Tour made in Scotland* (1803), quoted by Buxbaum, *Scottish Garden Buildings*, p. 152.

28 Buxbaum, *Scottish Garden Buildings*, p. 22.

29 See Chapter Two, pp. 41–3.

30 See Chapter One. Also, Roger White, 'Robert Adam's Rustic Designs', *Georgian Group Journal* (2015), pp. 167–78.

31 The house was much extended in the nineteenth century and again in 1914.

32 Robert Lugar, *Plans and Views of Buildings executed in England and Scotland in the Castellated and Other Styles* (1811), pl. 31, 'Pheasantry at Cullean [sic]'; Colvin, *B.D.*, p. 662.

33 Robert Lugar, *Villa Architecture* (1828), pl. 3; Rob Close and Anne Riches, *The Buildings of Scotland: Ayrshire and Arran* (New Haven and London, 2012), p. 257; Colvin, *B.D.*, p. 663.

34 It housed the member of staff whose job it was to look after the ornamental pheasants.

35 Robert Lugar, *Plans and Views of Buildings* (London, 1811), pl. VI. The castle (which Lugar calls 'Tillicheun') was built for John Stirling in 1808 and demolished in 1954. Colvin, *B.D.*, p. 663.

36 Buxbaum, *Scottish Garden Buildings*, p. 184. However, no evidence is cited and *The Buildings of Scotland* volume for the Borders (Kitty Cruft, John Dunbar and Richard Fawcett, New Haven and London, 2006, p. 532) calls it mid-to late nineteenth century, the same period as a rustic summerhouse with walls of vertical split logs and ceiling of pine cones. The Mellerstain guidebook says late nineteenth century.

37 David Walker and Matthew Woodworth, *The Buildings of Scotland: Aberdeenshire North and Moray* (New Haven and London, 2015), p. 354. The same volume 9p. 712) mentions St Mary's Cottage in the vicinity of Orton House near Rothes, 'a charming Gothic cottage orné by Matthews & Mackenzie, 1851–4'.

38 Edward Malins and the Knight of Glin, *Lost Demesnes (Irish Landscape Gardening 1660–1845)* (London 1976), p. 120.

39 See Chapter One.

40 A drawing by Thomas Santelle Roberts is in the Charlemont Album in the Irish Architectural Archive (2003/044). It is illustrated in Malins and Glin, *Lost Demesnes*, pl. 159.

41 Anon., *Diary of a Tour in Ireland*, National Library, Dublin MS 194, quoted by Malins and Glin, *Lost Demesnes*, p. 140.

42 Ashford's watercolour is in the Fitzwilliam Museum, Cambridge and is illustrated in Malins and Glin, *Lost Demesnes*, pl. 17.

43 Prince Pückler-Muskau, *A Tour in England, Ireland and France* (London 1832), quoted in Malins and Glin, *Lost Demesnes*, p. 76.

44 Malins and Glin, *Lost Demesnes*, p. 168. La Touche's son Peter continued his work, adding enormous glasshouses. The house was demolished in the 1950s.

45 Irish Architectural Archive, Conolly MSS f.1777 – Louisa Conolly writing to her sister Sarah Bunbury on 8 October 1777. Quoted in Finola O'Kane, *Ireland and the Picturesque: Design, Landscape Painting and Tourism 1700–1840* (New Haven and London, 2013), p. 84.

46 Nowadays known as Inisfallen.

47 Malins and Glin, *Lost Demesnes*, p. 160.

48 O'Kane, *Ireland and the Picturesque*, p. 100.

49 The Dublin painter Jonathan Fisher was the first to exploit Killarney's specific potential by painting and publishing views of it in 1770, then in 1789 producing a volume of twenty views with descriptions (*A Picturesque Tour of Killarney*), formed into a three-day itinerary. O'Kane, *Ireland and the Picturesque*, p. 86.

50 Samuel Lewis, *A Topographical Tour of Ireland* (London, 1837), vol. I, pp. 604–5. Quoted in O'Kane, *Ireland and the Picturesque*, p. 122.

51 Samuel Hayes, *A Practical Treatise on Planting* (Dublin, 1794), p. 67.

52 Paddy Bowe, 'Samuel Hayes' Avondale', *Irish Arts Review*, XXVI/2 (Summer 2009), pp. 96–101.

53 William Smith, *Journal of an Excursion to the County of Wicklow* (1815), National Library, Dublin, MS 678, quoted by Malins and Glin, *Lost Demesnes*, p. 174.

54 Woodstock had been the home of Sarah Ponsonby from 1773 until she eloped with Lady Eleanor Butler in 1778 to become one of the Ladies

of Llangollen (see Chapter Three). The house was burnt in about 1920 during 'The Troubles'.

55 Now in the Royal Society of Antiquaries in Dublin but formerly owned by Kilkenny Archaeological Society.

56 Jeremy Williams, 'The Lost Swiss Cottage of Woodstock: Its Architect and its Illustrator', Old Kilkenny Review, vol. LI (1999), pp. 103–11; Terence Reeves-Smith, 'Arcadia Regained: The Park and Gardens at Woodstock, Co. Kilkenny', Irish Arts Review, XIX/2 (2002), pp. 104–11.

57 Fols 79 and 89.

58 Anne Crookshank & the Knight of Glin, The Watercolours of Ireland, 1994.

59 Royal Society of Antiquaries volume, fol. 65.

60 Ibid., fol. 67. See illustration on p. 272.

61 Ibid., fols 51. and 55.

62 A. Atkinson, The Irish Tourist (Dublin, 1815), p. 409.

63 Louisa Beaufort writing to Sophy Edgeworth. Information from Mrs Susan Mosse, from a source apparently in the collection of the late Hubert Butler.

64 The re-creation of the cottage was completed in 1994.

65 See Chapter Ten for a recent cottage directly inspired by Kilfane.

66 Cane Cottage remained intact until a gale in 1961 caused the roof to collapse, and the rest was demolished by the Forestry Service in the 1970s. Information from Heather Hamilton, National Trust, Florence Court.

67 Cited in Malins and Glin, Lost Demesnes, p. 78.

68 The only study of this category in Ireland is J.A.K. Dean's The Gate Lodges of Ulster (Ulster Architectural Heritage Society, 1994), which estimates that Ulster alone once had as many as 2,000 lodges.

69 James Howley, The Follies and Garden Buildings of Ireland (New Haven and London, 1993), p. 81. The remarkable Laugier-inspired 'primitive hut' lodge at Belline, Co. Kilkenny is discussed in Chapter Two.

70 Dean, The Gate Lodges of Ulster, suggests a date around 1840, with Thomas Hopper (d. 1856), architect of the Castle, as designer. One lodge survives, the other has gone.

71 In this context Dean, The Gate Lodges of Ulster, mentions the lodges to Shane's Castle. Co. Antrim, probably built around 1850 to designs by the local architect James Sands.

72 Rock Cottage is a variant of Robinson's Design No. 2, built of boulders, and the Newtownstewart Gate is adapted from Design No. 4. Dean, The Gate Lodges of Ulster, pp. 134–5. The client would have been the 2nd Marquess of Abercorn, created 1st Duke of Abercorn in 1868.

73 When Detmar Blow added to the Adare housing stock in the early twentieth century he also adopted verandahs with rustic posts. Gillian Darley, Villages of Vision (London, 1975), p. 203.

74 Alistair Rowan and Christine Casey, Buildings of Ireland: North Leinster (London, 1993), p. 221, attribute them to William Vitruvius Morrison on the basis of their similarity to picturesque gabled cottages by him at Lough Bray, Co. Wicklow and Carpenham, Rostrevor, Co. Down.

75 Irish Architectural Archive, D611. The book is undated but has been placed at 1840 by the watermark. Ruth Thorpe, Women, Architecture and Building in the East of Ireland, c.1790–1840 (Maynooth, 2013), pp. 36–49.

76 Ibid., pp. 28–35.

77 James Howley, The Follies and Garden Buildings of Ireland, p. 81. This may have been the wife of the 3rd Lord Farnham, 1st Earl of the 2nd creation, who employed James Wyatt to add a library to the main house c. 1780, and then had the house rebuilt by Francis Johnston from 1802.

78 P. J. Rankin, Historic Buildings . . . in the Mourne Area of South Down (Ulster Architectural Heritage Society, 1975), pp. 40–41. The Castlewellan estate is near the Mountains of Mourne and not too far from Lady Clanwilliam's mother's residence at Castle Ward (she had married Bernard Ward as her second husband).

79 The cottage is single-storeyed with a U-plan (central block with two non-matching wings). Originally, log columns supported the overhanging thatched roof, but the structure is now much degraded, minus its columns and with the thatch replaced by corrugated iron.

80 Lady Dufferin, Recollections of a Beloved Mother (Belfast, 1824), National Library of Ireland, MS 5643.

81 'Stuff' was an ordinary woollen clothing material, not the silks and brocades normally worn by grand ladies.

82 Malins and Glin, Lost Demesnes, p. 108.

83 Rowan and Casey, North Leinster, p. 221.

84 Ibid., p. 221.

85 The estate, including the much-enlarged main house, Oriel Temple, now belongs to monks from Mellifont Abbey.

86 Lady Louisa Lennox, one of the four surviving daughters of the 2nd Duke of Richmond and sister to Emily, Countess of Kildare/Duchess of Leinster, married Thomas Conolly of Castleton in 1758, aged fifteen.

87 Louisa Conolly to Sarah Bunbury, 29 June 1764, Irish Architectural Archive CL, 94.136. Malins and Glin, Lost Demesnes, p. 58; Thorpe, Women, Architecture and Building in the East of Ireland, p. 28. This was presumably the cottage on the river, with a pretty shrubbery, that Arthur Young noted at Castletown in 1776 in A Tour in Ireland (London, 1780), p. 31. Photographs of the ruins, taken in 1998, are in the Irish Architectural Archive.

88 Formerly in the collection of the late Knight of Glin.

89 Rev. J. Burrowes, 'Diary of a Journey through England and Wales to Ireland', Public Record office of Northern Ireland, T.3551, quoted in O'Kane, Ireland and the Picturesque, p. 180. The pencil sketch of the Lucan cottage is reproduced as fig. 165 in O'Kane.

90 Young, A Tour in Ireland, p. 32.

91 Barbara Jones, Follies and Grottoes, 2nd edn (London, 1974), p. 155, felt that some of the decoration 'is notably like that of Goodwood, though all is less crisp and much more amateur and much more lovable'.

92 The tournament took place in 1839 at Eglinton Castle in Ayrshire.

93 Jones, Follies and Grottoes, p. 156.

94 Reproduced by Malins and Glin, Lost Demesnes, p. 82, pl. 87; the current whereabouts of the drawing is unclear. The cottage was in place by 1787, when it was described in print by a Dutch visitor: J. Meerman, Eenige berichten omtrent Groot-Britannien en Ierland ('s Gravenhage, 1987) p. 439, cited by Rolf Loeber in Art and Architecture in Ireland, vol. 4, Royal Irish Academy, Dublin, 2015, p. 359. Raymond's Cottage has been described by Patrick O'Neill, a present-day member of the family, as being 'more a cottage débauché than a cottage orné' (personal communication).

95 Information from Patrick O'Neill. Chichester was created Baron O'Neill in 1868, the viscountcy having died out with the death of the 3rd viscount in 1855.

96 Retrospections of Dorothea Herbert (Dublin, 2004), p. 308.

97 The drawing is recorded but has not been seen since about 1984 when it was sold and left Ireland for Canada. Information from Joe Walsh.

98 Unfortunately the Irish Office of Public Works, which owns and opens the building, has allowed the latter view to be blocked by a recent growth of trees.

99 Retrospections of Dorothea Herbert, p. 325. Herbert records that in 1791 her family embarked on the construction of what she calls a cottage at Bonmahon on the coast of Co. Waterford, where they liked to go for summer bathing, but it is not clear whether this was in any way orné. In her journal for 1793 she says that 'We were quite enchanted with our Cottage which was built quite to our Satisfaction on our own Plan', pp. 301, 310.

100 Quoted in the official Office of Public Works guidebook, published in 1993.

101 Roughly one-third of the present wallpaper is original, the rest having been copied at the restoration from a complete set identified in Houston, Texas.

102 Mark Girouard, 'The Swiss Cottage, Cahir, Co. Tipperary', Country Life (26 October 1989), pp. 72–7. Robert McCarthy, 'The Cahir Estate in the 19th & 20th Centuries', Tipperary Historical Journal (2011), pp. 68–76. The redecoration and furnishing of the interior was directed by Sybil Conolly. Contributions to the cost of the project came from the Irish government, Irish Georgian Society and the American Port Royal Foundation.

103 Irish Architectural Archive Acc 85/155 (neg C6/691).

104 See Chapter Seven.

105 Patrick Bowe, 'Irish Sporting Lodges', Irish Architectural and Decorative Studies vol. VII (2004), pp. 107–39.

106 These are in an album previously at Bantry House and now at University College, Cork, ref. BL/EP/B/3302; photographs of the drawings are in the Irish Architectural Archive, 20/19/P3 and P4.

107 The tail end of the house is probably an existing farmhouse converted to the service wing; the original kitchen was at the furthest possible remove from the dining room.

108 See Chapter Five.

109 I am grateful to the present owner Edward Booth for his help.

THE SOCIAL APOTHEOSIS

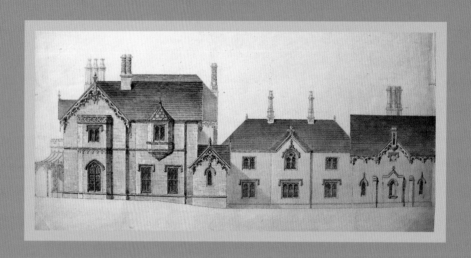

'It is one of the enjoyments of those habituated to live in a style of high art and refinement to take occasional refuge in the contrast produced by comparative artlessness and simplicity', noted John Claudius Loudon in 1836.[1] He was certainly talking of the cottage orné genre and what had been the underlying rationale of many of its adherents since the mid-eighteenth century; but he may have been thinking specifically of what was always one of the most ambitious examples, the 6th Duke of Bedford's Endsleigh Cottage in Devon. Endsleigh had been created in 1810–15 as the fruit of a collaboration between the architect Jeffry Wyatt, who designed the house, and Humphry Repton, who transformed the surrounding landscape from which it is inseparable [fig 7/2]. Endsleigh at last provided the Russell family with a tolerable residence on their extensive Devon estates around Tavistock,[2] a town largely remodelled by the 6th duke and from which the family's subsidiary title, Marquess of Tavistock, derives.

The duke succeeded his bachelor brother – a leading agricultural improver – in 1802 when the latter succumbed to a strangulated hernia while playing tennis. The 5th duke had been engaged to Georgina, daughter of the Scottish Duke of Gordon, and when the new duke (whose first wife had died young in 1801) visited her in Paris to deliver a keepsake lock of her dead fiancé's hair, romance followed. The 6th duke was not universally liked – Charles Greville called him good-natured and plausible, but also uninteresting, weak-minded and selfish[3] – whereas his bride was lively, lovely and very romantic in her outlook on life. Passionate about the wild beauties of the

Scottish Highlands[4] and attuned to the informality of sporting lodges, she came to long for a release from the starched formality of Woburn Abbey. An inscription still at Endsleigh records that

> Endsleigh Cottage was built and a residence created in this sequestered valley by John, Duke of Bedford, the spot having been previously chosen for the natural and picturesque beauties which surround it by Georgiana, Duchess of Bedford. The first stone of the building was laid by her four eldest sons . . . September 7 1810.[5]

Repton had already in 1809, with assistance from his sons, produced a proposal for a cottage residence at Endsleigh, architecturally a somewhat humdrum huddle of thatched structures that from a distance would have resembled a typical Devon farmstead. Moreover, the suggested setting was in a visually enclosed tributary valley of the River Tamar, immediately adjoining a series of cascades.[6] By contrast, the site selected by the duchess, though only a few hundred yards away, commands glorious views west across the main valley of the Tamar from Devon into Cornwall. At the same time the Bedfords decided to turn to Wyatt for the architecture.

This may be the moment to introduce a fascinating group of drawings [figs 7/1, 3], attributable on stylistic grounds to Jeffry Wyatt (or Wyatville as he became in 1824), for a cottage orné that would have been one of the most ambitious of the entire genre had it been built. The group comprises six elevations,[7] all intricately designed with many projections and recessions, and with much ornamental detail in the way of varied cuspings and finials to the gables, sections of tented verandah that extend across the south elevation and around the angle onto the west, and assorted bay windows, oriels and niches. Although there is no plan, it is clear that the family side lay across the south end, with windows also facing west and east, while the service side was on the north; there would almost certainly have been at least

OPPOSITE 7/1 Jeffry Wyatt (later Sir Jeffry Wyattville), attrib., possible preliminary design for Endsleigh House

LEFT 7/2 Endsleigh House, Devon: general view from Swiss Cottage

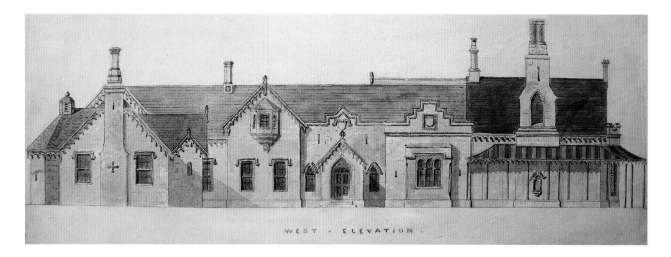

WEST · ELEVATION ·

one internal courtyard. A sizeable wing projecting at the north-west angle probably contained the kitchen, and projecting from that in turn is a canted structure with fish-scale tiled roof and crowning louvred vent. The drawings are colour-washed, indicating that the building was to be of golden ashlar stone with slated roof, and at various points on the north, west and east elevations there are ornamental shields, mostly set into square panels or under Tudor hoodmoulds. All this suggests a very expensive project for a very high-status client. Many of the motifs (shields, chimneys, oriel windows, cusped and finialed gables) also appear on Wyatt's perspective of Endsleigh,[8] and there is a further overlap in motifs with his work at Royal Lodge[9] and Adelaide Cottage,[10] Windsor. The armorial embellishments, and the possibility that the canted projection from the kitchen might have been intended as a salmon larder,[11] allow a very tentative link with the Bedfords and Endsleigh – perhaps, since the paper used is watermarked 1802, a project dating from shortly after the duke married his second wife in 1803.

For whatever reason the Endsleigh project did not get under way until 1810, and then in a quite different overall form.[12] The unseen nucleus of the present house is a pre-existing farmhouse, and if the resulting cottage seems, despite the lushness of the setting, to be somewhat less orné than a good many examples of the genre, it is because there was a conscious espousal of local vernacular materials – granite and slate – on what are after all the fringes of Dartmoor. According to Repton,

an irregular farmhouse little better than a cottage, backed by a hill and beautiful group of trees, presented an object so picturesque that it was impossible to wish it removed or replaced in any other style of building that architecture has invented, viz., a castle or an abbey or a palace, not one of which could have been convenient and so applicable to the scenery, as this cottage, or rather, group of rural buildings.[13]

In a remarkable response to the setting above a bend in the river, the plan of the house is made to follow the convex curve of the valley side, cranking round by degrees so that all the finest views are commanded by one room or another.[14] The entrance side on the north is decidedly austere, and indeed seems to prefigure many informally grouped Arts & Crafts houses of a century or so later.[15] The façades to the valley [fig 7/4] are experienced as a progression of seemingly unrelated shapes and angles, the transitions and outlines softened by a variety of gables, windows, fretted eaves and twiggy verandahs. Consciously or otherwise, it is in fact the realization of Uvedale Price's recommendation in 1798 that houses should be planned in response to aspect, rather than always striving for symmetry.

If the owner of such a spot, instead of making a regular front and sides were to insist on having the windows turned towards the points where objects were most happily arranged, the architect would be

forced into inventing a number of picturesque forms and combinations which otherwise might never have occurred to him, and obliged to do what has so seldom been done – accommodate his building to the scenery, not make that give way to the building. . . . Then the blank spaces where the aspect suddenly changed – which by admirers of strict regularity would be thought incurable blemishes – might by means of shrubs or climbing plants be transformed into beauties.[16]

A century later, Edwin Lutyens (employed elsewhere on the estate)[17] was to dismiss the results as 'a conglomeration in the style of Mary Anne',[18] and yet it is difficult not to feel a strong kinship between Endsleigh and his own accomplished exercises in Arts & Crafts vernacular.

Work on the house proceeded at quite a leisurely pace, and meanwhile the clients were becoming dissatisfied with Wyatt's proposals for the gardens and wider landscape. They therefore turned back to Repton, who by this stage was a sick man and reluctant to make the long journey from Essex down to the far west of Devon. Repton nevertheless produced a Red Book – his last – for the landscape in 1814 and met Wyatt on site in August that

year.[19] It was another decade before George IV was to authorize Wyatt to call himself 'Wyatville', and fourteen years before he was knighted for his transformation of Windsor Castle, but already he was very full of himself – as Repton put it to the duke's lawyer, 'grown out of all due proportion for a bodkin as either yourself or me'.[20] Nevertheless, Wyatt succeeded in tailoring the house closely to his clients' needs. It has the three main rooms that were usual in superior cottages, namely drawing room, dining room and library, lined with grained panelling and originally equipped with furniture that 'corresponds in all respects with the exquisite simplicity' [fig 7/5].[21] The duke's interest in heraldry and his hereditary rights is reflected in the coats of arms that appear in stained glass and in shields applied to the panelling. However, the house also responded to the fact that the duchess was a fond mother (just as well, since she bore ten offspring), and instead of being banished to the attics her children were provided with their own little cottage [fig 7/6], linked by a corridor and trellised verandah to the main building. This had a schoolroom, playroom and governess's room on the ground floor, with bedrooms above. Immediately in front is the children's garden, a formal parterre enclosed with a low wall along the top of

which runs a water channel in which they could sail their toy boats.[22] At the other end of the south elevation, the drawing room is fronted by a rustic verandah of knobbly, branching tree trunks, with flooring of pebbles and sheep's knucklebones, and suitably rustic furniture [fig 7/7]. In 1818 the verandahs were described as containing 'odoriferous plants', while vines formed 'natural festoons above the windows in which birds build their nest and cheer the scene with their notes'.[23]

The true glory of Endsleigh is not so much the architecture of the cottage – though the planning of that was truly prophetic – but the fact that it forms an integrated whole with the Repton setting, to an extent almost unequalled in its period. The main rooms look south down a wide grassy terrace, bounded on the left by an arcaded retaining wall and above that a deep herbaceous border and an exceptionally long rose pergola. To the right, beyond a low, rose-clad trellis fence, the grassy slopes fall away towards the river. The far, Cornish side of the river is a well-wooded hillside, nestling within which is a very modest vernacular cottage. Repton famously decreed that a servant should light a fire in the cottage every day, whether it was actually inhabited or not, so that the smoke from the chimney would introduce an additional element of interest in the view from the main house. Other parts of the setting are enlivened with more consciously architectural features supplied by Wyatt. At the

OPPOSITE 7/8 Endsleigh House: Shell House interior
BELOW 7/9 Endsleigh House: Shell House exterior
BOTTOM 7/10 Endsleigh House: the Swiss Cottage

far end of the grass terrace, in a belvedere position look-ing down on the glittering river, is an octagonal shell house [7/8, 9], its walls encrusted with a mixture of shells, minerals, fossils and corals, and with triangular cobwebs of amber glass in its gables. A little spring-fed pool sits in the centre of the patterned pebble floor. Much further down this side of the valley a thatched Swiss Cottage [fig 7/10] – one of the earliest such examples in England, and more convincingly Swiss than most – com-mands a distant view back towards the house.[24] Its walls are of split logs, it has a double-height gallery around the exterior, and patterned pebble pavements. The interiors were always quite simple; the lower storey was occupied by a labourer, but the upper floor was 'furnished *à la Suisse*, with wooden chairs and platters, horn-spoons etc.'[25] A quite different kind of landscape is found behind the house, where a narrow valley is lushly planted and haunted by the sounds of water tumbling over rocks.[26] Perched on a bastion overlooking the lower end is an octag-onal ornamental dairy (also referred to as a salmon larder). The thatched exterior is austere, but the cool, dim interior is full of restrained Regency charm. Its walls are lined in white tiles edged with green ivy-trails, and it is lit from sim-ple Gothic windows with borders of characteristically vivid stained glass – amethyst, amber, crimson and royal blue.[27]

When Repton paid his site visit and produced his Red Book in 1814 he was already in serious physical decline, thanks to angina – indeed the Red Book records that 'I could only become acquainted with [Endsleigh's] recon-dite beauties, by being carried to places otherwise inaccessible to a cripple' – and he was to die just four years later. This did not prevent him producing one of his finest achievements, responding with great brilliance to the natural potential of the landscape and meshing his work perfectly with that of the tiresome Wyatt. As he told the duke's lawyer, 'I will confess I never [was] so well pleased with myself – but we are apt to make a favorite of the youngest child'.[28] The Bedfords evidently agreed, pre-ferring Endsleigh to Woburn and going there every year until the duke's death in 1839. There were pheasants for the duke and his guests to shoot in season, but the place performed primarily as a fishing lodge; there were also boat trips on the river, downstream towards Plymouth. Endsleigh continued to serve its intended function as a holiday residence for the Dukes of Bedford, and indeed the lighting of the fire in the cottage across the river was maintained as recommended by Repton, at least when the family were in residence, right up to the death of the 11th duke in 1940. The death of the next duke while shooting in the Endsleigh woods in 1953 brought an end to its family phase, and from then until 2002 the house found a highly suitable use as a select private fishing hotel.[29] Although there may be architecturally finer examples of the genre, none achieved more completely the blissful, escapist idyll that was the ultimate aim of the cottage orné concept, and that remains the case today.

By the time Endsleigh was created, the rustic cottage had long been a feature of aristocratic life in England (and indeed Ireland), particularly that of aristocratic ladies. From the 1760s such buildings as the Lady's Cottage at Blickling, Louisa Conolly's at Castletown, or the Countess of Kildare's at Carton, supplied a way in which time could be agreeably passed in the pretence of rural simplicity, though this rarely extended to spending a night there. It was the middling classes who first warmed to the possibility of actually living in such cottages, and Endsleigh marks the point at which that idea reached the highest levels of aristocratic society. One of the more remarkable aspects of the history of the cottage orné is that its social trajectory continued upwards into royalty.

In fact the very first self-consciously rustic structure in England may have been a royal one: Merlin's Cave, the thatched garden pavilion designed in 1735 by William Kent for Queen Caroline's garden at Richmond [fig 1/1].[30] Some if not all of the rustic designs of Thomas Sandby are likely to have been intended for royal implementation in Windsor Great Park, of which his patron the Duke of Cumberland, favourite son of George II, had appointed him deputy ranger in 1746. The duke died in 1765 but the patronage continued under his successor Henry Frederick, Duke of Cumberland and indeed under George III, who retained Sandby as deputy ranger after the death of Prince Frederick in 1790. Given the long time-span of his association with Windsor Great Park, these designs could be from any time in the 1750s, 1760s, 1770s or 1780s. Apart from the hermitage-like structures, quite possibly intended for Cumberland's park around Virginia Water, other Sandby designs are clearly intended for less fleeting occupation, although since they are not in the Royal

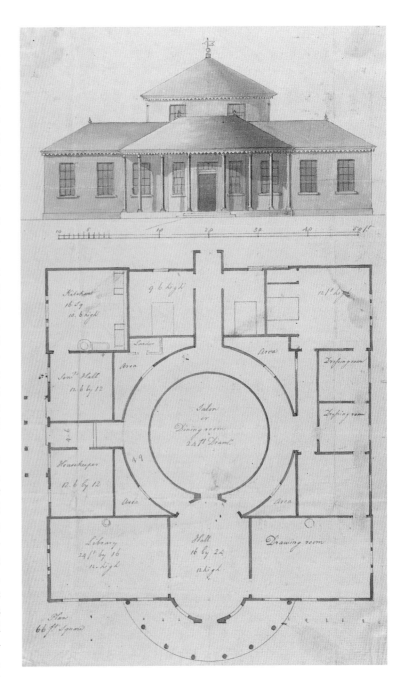

Collection it cannot be proved that they were made for royal clients. The Soane Museum has a plan and elevation for what must certainly be accounted a proper cottage orné [fig 7/11]. It would have been quite an ambitious building, 66 feet square, with rooms of varying sizes – drawing room, library, one main bedroom and two smaller, dressing rooms, kitchen, housekeeper's room and servants' hall – arranged around a central 'salon or dining room', circular and top-lit. Apart from the conically roofed lantern to this space, the building is single-storey, with a verandah (with slim astylar columns rather than rustic tree trunks) wrapping around the bow of a projecting entrance hall. The eaves throughout are scalloped, but judging from the colour-washed elevation the roofs were to be slated rather than thatched.[31] Evidently it was for a client with serious resources, with all the facilities necessary for both entertaining and for prolonged occupation. One Sandby item that is in the Royal Collection is a design for a simple thatched cottage with projecting semicircular tree-trunk porch. This has been described as a farmhouse, but the porch perhaps suggests otherwise, since such a refinement might have been considered unnecessary for a farmer unless the building doubled as a park ornament.[32]

THE QUEEN'S COTTAGE, KEW

It has often been maintained that the whole fashion for the cottage orné was inaugurated by the Petit Hameau at Versailles, built for Queen Marie Antoinette from 1783.[33] This is not even true in the French context, where the Petit Hameau was preceded by that at Chantilly of 1774–5, and certainly not in relation to England, where the genre can be traced back at least to the 1750s, and Straw Hall at Hardwick. Nor is it true of royal cottages, of which the earliest was almost certainly the cottage created for Queen Charlotte at Kew, apparently by 1771 [fig 7/12]. It was built in what was then the menagerie of Richmond Gardens (and consequently was sometimes referred to as Richmond Cottage), and there seems to be a difference of opinion as to whether it was built from scratch for Charlotte or adapted from an existing building.[34] It was probably paid for out of the queen's Privy Purse, and unfortunately the relevant royal accounts for 1771 are missing. That however seems the most likely approximate moment for its erection, since a building is shown on the site in Thomas Richardson's 1771 survey map, and late that year or early the next Charlotte was writing to her brother Prince Ernst of Mecklenburg suggesting he too should build a 'cottage

QUEEN'S COTTAGE . RICHMOND GARDENS.

comme la nôtre à Richmond' on his own estate in Germany.[35] In August 1774 the *London Magazine* described it as 'a pretty retreat'. The queen and family could take tea there and observe the exotic animals, which at one time or another included wallabies (the first to arrive in England), zebra and buffalo.

As first built, or adapted, the cottage appears to have been single-storeyed, although there seem to be no illustrations of it in this form. At an unknown date, perhaps in 1804–5 but conceivably in 1788 (the building was re-thatched in that year and a window cleaner's account for 1788 cites twelve windows, the same number as now),[36] an upper floor was added which gave it approximately its present appearance, first recorded in a print by George Ernest Papendiek of about 1820 [fig 7/13].[37] Unlike most English cottages ornés – but like the fractionally later Sealwood Cottage at Linton in Derbyshire[38]

– the Queen's Cottage is of workmanlike brick and half-timbering. In this it resembles early examples of the genre in France, which externally have little or nothing that could be called orné and look passably like genuine vernacular cottages in Normandy.[39] One aspect of the construction that points to two building phases is that the ground floor is of poor-quality brick laid in random bonds, apparently deliberately 'distressed' to create a rustic effect (perhaps suggesting a building cheaply run up for the menagerie keeper and then pressed into a more ornamental function), whereas the first floor uses better-quality brick laid in regular bonds, in combination with half-timbering. The large room at the centre of the ground floor, framed on both fronts by lower porches, was from the start decorated as a print room [fig 7/14].[40] as confirmed by an entry in the *London Magazine* for August 1774:[41] 'The queen's cottage in the shade of the

garden is a pretty retreat: the furniture is all English prints of elegance and humour. The design is said to be her majesty's.' The presence of prints and the possibility that the cottage was designed by the queen herself is reinforced by the account of her 'from authentic documents' published in 1819 by John Watkins. Here he describes the gardens 'where Her Majesty has erected a cottage after a design of her own, in a chaste style, and ornamented it with a large collection of the best English prints'.[42] Charlotte was certainly a keen collector of prints, and from physical evidence it is clear that soon after its erection her cottage was decorated with prints by Hogarth and others,[43] pasted onto a verditer green background. The woodwork was olive-brown. As to whether she was her own architect, this is impossible to prove one way or the other, although like her husband she had taken drawing lessons from Joshua Kirby (1716–1774), who at the time of the cottage's construction was joint clerk of works (with his son William) at Richmond and Kew and therefore probably superintended the work.[44] Certainly there is no hard evidence for the involvement of a professional architect, such as William Chambers, who designed other ornamental structures for Kew for the Dowager Princess of Wales, or Lancelot 'Capability' Brown, who also worked on the gardens. However, despite its small size the building is quite a complex piece of spatial geometry, and this may point to the involvement of someone like Chambers.[45]

From the beginning there was a programme of regular maintenance at the cottage and its setting. However, in 1804–5 there were much more extensive works, coinciding with the royal family's increased use of Kew during the illness of Charlotte's husband George III. The *Morning Chronicle* of 5 November 1805 recorded:

Kew Cottage in Kew Gardens has undergone considerable alterations and improvements under the direction of the tasteful genius of the Princess Elizabeth. . . . Several of the rooms have been hung with the principal originals of Hogarth, and a number of valuable paintings. . . . The Cottage has likewise been new furnished. The outside of the buildings stands in great need of being made to correspond with the inside. . . . The cottage is intended for the Royal Family to breakfast and drink tea in, when they are at Kew, and occasionally to dine in it.

At this stage the menagerie was replaced by a flower garden. The overhaul referred to may have entailed the addition of the extra floor and the half-timbered staircase compartments that project at each end. Also as part of the improvements, the prints were removed from their original positions and combined with additional ones in a new decorative scheme, applied to canvas on stretchers. One staircase, leading out of the entrance hall, was for royal use. The other, a relatively spacious spiral stair, was for servants only, connecting the ground-floor kitchen with the big first-floor room.[46] The latter, known as the Picnic Room [fig 7/15], was probably painted by the queen's daughter, the artistic Princess Elizabeth, as a floral arbour with convolvulus and nasturtiums growing up the walls and faux-bamboo frames to the doors, in much the same manner as her work at Frogmore House, the queen's private retreat at Windsor.[47] On either side of the fireplace a door leads to a landing from which there is discreet access, via doors lined with sound-proofing felt, to a tiny room within the eaves containing the queen's close stool.[48]

Despite the money and effort lavished on the Queen's Cottage, it seems to have been one of many victims of the vagaries of royal taste, apparently being little used from as early as 1806. An exception occurred in 1818 when, following the joint wedding of the Duke of Clarence (later William IV) to Princess Adelaide, and the Duke of Kent to Princess Victoire, the wedding party repaired to the cottage to take tea. Unlike so many other expensive royal buildings, however, it did at least survive, and when a grant of public access to Kew Gardens was made in 1898 Queen Victoria expressed a specific wish that the cottage should be preserved.

PRINCESS ELIZABETH'S COTTAGE

Born in 1770, the third of George III's six daughters, Princess Elizabeth had her artistic potential nurtured by Mary Moser, England's leading flower painter. Like many other high-born young ladies of her day, she craved informality; in 1796 she wrote from Kew to her friends Lord and Lady Harcourt, 'At this place my great hoop [skirt] is dropped and my plumes are lowered, so that the Princess is left in town and the humble miss steps forward.'[49] She also apparently longed to be a farmer's wife, though the nearest she could have got to that ambition would have

been to marry a princeling with the same agricultural interests as her own father. However, rather like Queen Victoria, Queen Charlotte preferred to keep her daughters selfishly close to her, and in 1808 effectively vetoed a prospective alliance with Louis Philippe, Duc d'Orleans, who was then living in exile at Twickenham. That year Elizabeth wrote resentfully from Windsor, 'We go on vegetating as we have done for the last twenty years of our lives.' The answer, in default of a husband and motherhood, was to create a cottage orné to keep herself amused. In fact, she had already in 1807 or 1808 taken a lease on a cottage at Old Windsor, on the banks of the Thames outside the boundaries of Windsor Great Park.[50] This she completely transformed, the results being illustrated by an engraving published in 1812 [fig 7/16].[51] It is inscribed, 'To Her Royal Highness the Princess Elizabeth, This View of Her Royal Highness's Cottage at Old Windsor is by permission dedicated.' It shows a rather plain specimen of the genre, its roof tiled or slated rather than thatched, and with its overhang supported on simple posts swathed in ivy. Inset is a small monochrome view of 'The Moss House', a simple thatched rustic cottage,[52] framed by stanzas of syrupy doggerel verse:

> Shepherds now is the month of the May,
> In a band let our village unite.
> To yon Cottage with flowers let us stray,
> The Mansion of rural delight.
>
> What a beauteous Elysium around,
> Here peace and simplicity reign,
> Here the birds and asylum have found,
> And with carols enliven the scene.
>
> O may verdure for ever appear
> Unfading, the verdure of spring,
> No tempests be heard through the year,
> But zephyr with health in his wing.
>
> Sweet Cottage our chaplets receive,
> Who, with envy e'en cities must see.
> When Eliza can Palaces leave
> For the charms of retirement in thee.

The cottage and its garden were very much Elizabeth's independent little domain. In 1808 she wrote to Lady Harcourt, 'I have spent my whole morning at the cottage walking about and determining what shall be done – for I must plan a great deal, and the flower garden shall be as pretty as I can make it.'[53] The planting shown in the engraving was suitably informal, with clumps of trees and serpentining flower beds. Fields of corn advanced quite close to the perimeter of the garden, and agricultural aspirations were reflected in the raising of cattle and Chinese pigs. Inside the cottage the princess kept her collection of teapots of all shapes and sizes, and other ceramics that she had been collecting for the past decade. Several times a year she invited her relatives to visit her there, usually in celebration of a family birthday, and on such occasions she would decorate the cottage with garlands of artificial roses. A particularly elaborate festivity took place in 1816 in honour of the marriage of the Duke and Duchess of Gloucester.[54] The decoration included rustic emblems, trophies of plenty and fruitfulness, and pan pipes with tassels. The guests danced in a tent and tucked into a sandwich supper.[55]

An engraving published in 1824[56] seems to indicate that the cottage had in the meantime been further transformed, since although the basic shape remains the same as in 1812, the windows have intricate leading in hexagons and diamonds, and the plain posts of the verandah have been replaced by arcaded treillage. The planting has also changed, with trees pressing closer round the cottage and hollyhocks growing out of the grass instead of constrained in beds. In fact by 1824 Elizabeth had already flown the stifling parental nest, since in April 1818, at the age of forty-eight, she had married Prince Frederick of Hesse-Homburg and moved to his little principality.[57] Queen Charlotte had finally relented – too late for Elizabeth's aspirations to motherhood – and in November that year Charlotte died. After her husband's death in 1829 Elizabeth built herself another cottage in the gardens at Hesse-Homburg. In 1833 she wrote to a friend,

> My house in the garden I am making very nice and comfortable, the prints are hung and I am now finishing the last touches to my room at the cottage, placing brackets for china which dresses it, and making it look gayer.

The princess made occasional return visits to England, but the inevitable consequence of her residence in Hesse-Homburg was that in time the Old Windsor cottage disappeared from consciousness, finally being demolished in 1873.[58]

ROYAL LODGE, WINDSOR GREAT PARK

Given that by the early years of the nineteenth century the cottage orné had become a deeply fashionable genre, and given that both his mother and sister Elizabeth had their own specimens, it was almost inevitable that the Prince Regent should want one too, and moreover that this should end up as the largest cottage of all. The prince, who became Regent, with greatly increased access to public funds, in 1811, was himself the epitome of all that was fashionable. He was an avowed admirer of the novels of Jane Austen, and had undoubtedly read *Sense and Sensibility*, with its references to the cottage phenomenon, when it was published in 1811.[59] He had already ploughed huge sums into the endless remodelling of both his London residence Carlton House and his seaside pied-à-terre in Brighton, and he loved to have a building project of some kind always on the boil – though usually, when they finally came to fruition he then lost interest in them. His elevation to Regent meant that he needed a house from which he could easily reach both London and Windsor. Windsor Castle itself was ruled out as being the asylum of the mad King and the main residence of his mother and sisters, and after some debate he decided that he would have the then vacant Cumberland Lodge in the Great Park extensively overhauled. In the meantime, however, a nearby cottage would be adapted as a temporary bolt hole. Perhaps aptly, it had been the residence of Thomas Sandy in his capacity as Deputy Ranger of the park; Sandby's own watercolours shows it to have been a perfectly normal Georgian box with sash windows, more of a house than a cottage.[60] The necessary work was authorized in November 1812, and so began the evolution of Royal Lodge.[61]

Predictably, the architect tasked with these modest alterations (then estimated to cost just £2,750) was John Nash, whose Blaise Hamlet was recently completed and who was in any case busy on the Regent's behalf in central London.[62] His first step was to replace the cottage's tiled roof with thatch. Within the year his client had apparently lost interest in Cumberland Lodge and had decided that the cottage was to be much more than a temporary expedient. Nash was accordingly required to come up with more ambitious proposals [fig 7/17], estimated to cost £13,250.[63] This was to cover the addition of a new 'imperial' main staircase in Portland stone, and an entrance hall and spinal corridor-cum-gallery likewise paved in Portland. What had been Sandby's dining room at the south-east angle of the house was to be made to open via a succession of folding doors into a new dining room, roughly circular in shape. Above all this were to be additional bedrooms, and the whole enlarged building was to be rendered in creamy stucco to disguise the joins. The existing verandah on the short east elevation was to be extended round the corner and along the entire length of the south front.

As the Regent's architectural doings were always news, it may not be coincidental that in the same year, 1813, John Smith in his *Metrical Remarks on Modern Castles and Cottages*, wrote, apropos cottage architecture,

> no style requires a tighter reign on the fancy, and in
> no style is it so apt to indulge itself in all its gambols.
> . . . If the Castle has been contracted into a dwarf
> deformed with unnatural excrescences, the Cottage
> has been expanded into the gigantic dimensions of
> a Palace.[64]

This was far from being an end to the additions, however, for in April 1814 Nash's earlier proposal for the building of an enormous conservatory beyond the new dining room was revived, taking the total length of the cottage to 170 feet. The new structure, of cast iron, had a dual purpose in that it was also to screen the enlarged service wing – containing such non-standard features as a game larder and confectionery storeroom – of the cottage from view. In August the works were sufficiently advanced for the prince to show them off to his mother and his sisters Elizabeth and Mary.

Royal Lodge was first used during Ascot Week 1815, when the prince entertained a select party to dinner. By that stage a total of £39,000 had been expended and there were mutterings of criticism. In a Commons debate on the Regent's finances in May that year Lord Castlereagh,[65]

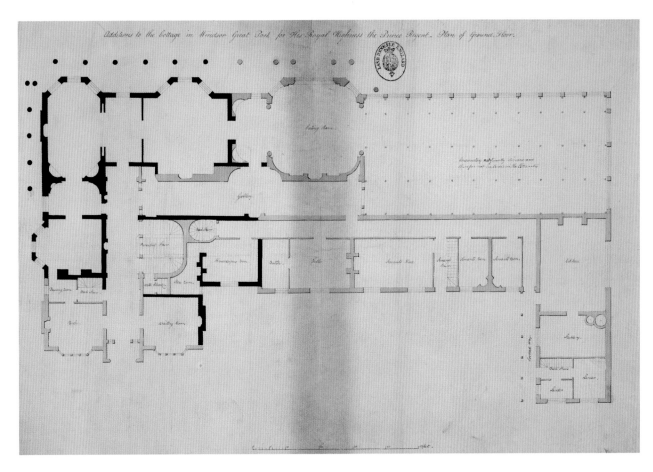

noting that £17,000 had been spent on the furnishings alone, defended him by saying, 'Though called a Cottage . . . because it happened to be thatched, it was still a very comfortable residence for a family, and the only one the Prince could make use of when he went to Windsor.'[66] A subsequent debate in February 1816 drew the acid comment that 'The Prince Regent expends as great a sum for a thatched cottage as another monarch would on a palace; he cannot endure to see the same furniture . . . for two successive years . . . he pays 6000£ for a Chinese Cabinet.'[67]

For the next few years matters rested at Royal Lodge, but the Regent's accession as George IV in January 1820 set him thinking of further works. The *Reading Mercury* of 2 April that year revealed:

Most extensive alterations and additions are now making to this Cottage by command of his Majesty and under the superintendence of Mr Nash.

A new suite of apartments are building for the accommodation of Sir Benjamin Bloomfield [the king's private secretary], and a large dining room and billiard room for the King himself. Carpenters, gardeners and bricklayers are ordered to work double tides to complete the whole before Ascot Heath Races. A covered walk, in a serpentine form, leading from the Conservatory into the grounds for the convenience of his Majesty and his visitors during wet weather is intended to contain all the rare shrubs, flowers and creeping plants that can be collected. A new lodge is likewise building at the entrance to the grounds, and the most strict orders are given not to admit strangers without especial permission.[68]

The appearance of Royal Lodge in its final Nash form is recorded in two views published in 1823 [figs 7/18, 19].[69]

ENTRANCE FRONT OF HIS MAJESTY'S COTTAGE,
Windsor Great Park.

These show the extreme length of the building when seen from the garden (as against the entrance front on the north, of a mere three bays, which looked genuinely cottagey), with acres of thatch and a forest of chimneys.

Mention of the new lodge to enforce the king's privacy is a reminder that in his last decade George IV became increasingly reclusive, reluctant to go to London to discharge his regal duties and show himself in public. Aware that he was unpopular with ordinary people (who sympathized with his estranged wife, Caroline), he preferred to avoid contact with them, to the extent that servants caught watching him in any of his residences were liable to dismissal. There was further expenditure in laying out new rides through the Great Park – over

twenty miles of them – that were not accessible to the public, and where these crossed public routes servants were stationed to make sure that no one watched the king passing in his carriage. The author William Cobbett recorded how in the summer of 1826 he attempted to visit Royal Lodge in the hope of petitioning the king in connection with the Corn Laws controversy. The cottage, he said, stood in the middle of a wood, which in turn was surrounded by inner and outer rings of fences, the gates through them guarded against unauthorized visitors; he got no further than the inner ring.[70] It is not surprising that public dissatisfaction found its way into print. In February 1826 the *World of Fashion* magazine commented:

Plate 2. Vol. I.

HIS MAJESTY'S COTTAGE.
as seen from the Lawn

No.1 of R. ACKERMANN'S REPOSITORY of ARTS &c. Pub. Jany 1 1824.

His Majesty is passing so very retired a life at Windsor that the inhabitants of every other part of the United Kingdom seldom hear or know of our beloved King being in existence. To speak plainly, we do not approve of such retirement; we think so great a Monarch, and one so universally cherished, should be more frequently in his capital.[71]

George habitually spent the winter in Brighton, but the beginning in 1824 of the building campaign to transform Windsor Castle meant that he was otherwise more and more at the cottage, from which he made frequent visits to inspect progress. This in turn meant yet more works at the cottage itself in preparation. Nash had now left the scene, at least at

Windsor, and from now on projects were in the hands of Jeffry Wyatt. Perhaps more practical, certainly less imaginative, than Nash, Wyatt ordered the replacement of the decaying thatch with slate, thereby removing an important element in the building's charm – and indeed it ended up looking more like Endsleigh, as can be seen from a later perspective [fig 7/20] made prior to demolition in 1831.[72] The rustic verandah was also replaced, with one that was flat-roofed and admitted more light to the ground-floor reception rooms. As usual, the changes had to be made against a tight deadline, so that the king could take up residence as soon as he made way for the builders at the castle in June 1824.

George IV may have wanted to avoid public appearances and undue contact with the man in the street (or the park), but he was by no means unsocial on his own terms. As a description of Royal Lodge put it in December 1823:

> The charms of rural retirement are naturally no less inviting to the highest than to the middle classes; and to them indeed its enjoyment must be infinitely augmented by the effect of its unrestrained contrast with the stateliness of elevated life. For the purposes of devoting hours of contemplative leisure to such repose of the mind; to participate in the healthfulness afforded by pure air, and something of the advantages of a country life, this cottage was erected by his present Majesty.[73]

The king was prepared to endure the necessary meetings with his ministers to discuss the business of government, but by and large he restricted his socializing to his chosen friends – the 'Cottage Coterie' made up of his mistress Lady Conyngham and her family, along with figures like Princess Lieven and Princess Esterhazy. Close friends such as these stayed in the cottage, but other visitors were put up at Cumberland Lodge. The ménage was entertainingly satirized in a print of 1824 entitled 'Brobdignag Cottage: Rusticating' [fig 7/21], which shows the king doing a little light gardening with a silver-gilt spade, accompanied by a very overweight Lady Conyngham pushing a mobile watering device, while an effete-looking footman trundles plants around in a wheelbarrow. In the background the cottage in its thatched Nash incarnation extends across the horizon.

It is through the recollections of visitors that a good deal is known about life at the cottage. Charles Greville, a guest during Ascot Week 1827, recorded that

> about thirty people sat down to dinner, and the company was changed nearly every day. It is a delightful place to live in, but the rooms are too low and small for very large parties. Nothing can exceed the luxury of the internal arrangements. . . .
> Though [the] evening went off well enough, it is clear that nothing would be more insupportable than to live at this Court; the dullness must be excessive, and the people who compose his habitual society are the most insipid and uninteresting that can be found. As for Lady Conyngham, she looks

bored to death, and she never speaks, never appears to have one word to say to the King, who, however, talks himself without ceasing.[74]

Princess Lieven, a frequent overnight guest, later described how

> it was a dwelling place at once royal and rustic, on the outside the simplicity of a cottage, within the rarest union of comfort, elegance and magnificence. . . . The site is pretty, fine, superb trees, very picturesque glimpses of landscape, a charming place. We led a lazy and very agreeable life there, always in the King's society. Many promenades in the forest, on the lake, sometimes dinners under tents, always music in the evening, and in everything a habit of unspoiled magnificence, which left behind the sentiment of *une charmante béatitude*.

However, she continued, 'I will not say that this state of bliss was not sometimes exchanged for great boredom.'[75] The Duke of Wellington, a favourite of the king who was always welcome, confirmed the restricted make-up of the company combined with a 'constant state of junketing'. A visitor in 1825 noted that during parties the king's private band played in the conservatory that led off the dining room. On such occasions, according to a local guidebook in 1828, the enfilade of ground-floor rooms would be thrown together by opening the folding doors between them, and all would be brilliantly illuminated. 'The furniture and decorations are plain but elegant, the hangings being principally silk.'[76] Over the silk hangings (pink, according to Lady Granville in 1828) were arranged the king's favourite English paintings, moved from Carlton House.

As at Endsleigh, the cottage and its setting were inseparable, and in fine weather the gardens were an important adjunct for entertaining. The layout was probably devised by Nash and W. T. Aiton, and the intention was not just to create the impression of a cottage garden, with serpentine paths, shrubberies and irregular flower beds, but also to disguise the enormous, un-cottagey length of the building. *The Mirror of Literature, Amusement and Instruction* praised Nash's skill in combining 'the most interesting features of cottage

South East View of King George the 4th Cottage in Windsor Great Park razed to the Ground by Order of King William the 4th

architecture' in such a way as to conceal the actual magnitude of the building. 'The arrangement of the plantations in the immediate vicinity of the building has been successfully made to produce this diminishing result.'[77] Sir Walter Scott called it 'a kind of cottage, too large perhaps for the style, but yet so managed that in the walks you only see parts of it at once, and these well composed, and grouping with the immense trees.'[78] In 1814 there were plans for a number of subsidiary rustic structures in the garden, including a thatched ice house, a thatched dairy 'with rustic columns of rough trees' and a circular rustic temple, likewise to be built with rough trees. According to the specification the latter was

to have a coved ceiling lined with the rough bark of trees.[79] That was in the Nash phase. The rustic entrance lodge at which William Cobbett's way was barred in 1826 would have been the one built the previous year to Wyatt's designs, though still in the Nash idiom.[80]

Notwithstanding all the money that had already been laid out on Royal Lodge, each year brought new schemes, new requirements, new demands on the public purse – all in tandem with the even more astronomical expenditure on the Castle and on Buckingham Palace. Late in 1828 the king drove over to view the completed work on the private apartments at the castle, on which occasion Jeffry Wyattville knelt to offer him the keys in a

Brobdignag Cottage.

RUSTICATING

London Pub march 29ʰ 1824 by SW Fores 41 Piccadilly

29 March 1824.

crimson bag and arose as Sir Jeffry. Hardly had George moved into the castle than yet another campaign of works to Royal Lodge was announced, once again to be completed in time for Ascot Week. These were mostly in the nature of essential repairs (including dealing with the noxious smells which rose from the drains into the royal apartment). When an ailing George returned to the castle in time for Christmas 1829, work began on one final addition to Royal Lodge, a large Gothic dining room at the west end of the cottage. 'Extraordinary exertions' were made in order to have it ready for the king's return in summer 1830,[81] but in the event he never saw it, for he died at the castle on 26 June.

ADELAIDE COTTAGE, WINDSOR HOME PARK

With the death of the sophisticated and luxury-loving George IV, and the accession of his unsophisticated and plain-living brother as William IV, there was an abrupt change in everything to do with the new king's modus vivendi. All the restrictions that had kept everyone except close friends and government ministers at arm's length from George were removed, and within a month the private drives through Windsor Great Park were thrown open to pedestrians of all social ranks. There was inevitable speculation as to what would become of George's private elysium at Royal Lodge. By the end of August

William had taken a decision that not only would he not use it but that he would have most of the cottage demolished. Thus, like a soap bubble bursting, this most costly and extravagant creation of the whole cottage orné genre vanished as if it had never been after less than two decades. The new Wyatville dining room, just completed, was allowed to remain, along with an adjoining octagonal room, which William's wife Adelaide had fitted up as a tent room. Thereafter the royal couple occasionally visited the remains for picnics, but spent no further money on maintenance. The building rapidly deteriorated, and might well have been pulled down too if Prince Albert had not intervened in 1840.

At this point the rump of Royal Lodge was patched up and used to accommodate a succession of occupants, mostly members of the royal household and none of them royal until 1931.[82] In that year the Duke and Duchess of York were allocated the property as a home for them and the two young princesses, Elizabeth and Margaret Rose. Acting as his own architect, the duke adapted the Wyatville dining room as the main living room; the surviving verandah in front of it was removed, and a family wing added in place of the conservatory. On his accession as George VI in 1937 he and his family inevitably moved to the Castle, but in her widowhood Queen Elizabeth the Queen Mother returned to it for another half-century, dying there in 2002.

George IV was the only British monarch to live, or want to live, in a cottage, as opposed to using such a building as a place to while away a few agreeable hours. When William IV demolished much of Royal Lodge and cannibalized the materials to create a new cottage, it was for somewhere that would be used much as Queen Charlotte had used hers at Kew. What became Adelaide Cottage was located much closer to Windsor Castle – on the south side of a hill at the south-east end of the North Slopes – and was always intended for limited summer use by William's consort Adelaide. It in fact seems to have been developed from a modest keeper's cottage where Queen Charlotte, her daughters and ladies-in-waiting repaired of a morning to consume 'new milk, an egg, a rasher of home-cured bacon' and a cup of coffee.[83] Once the queen acquired Frogmore House and developed its gardens such visits probably ceased, and it was not until the end of 1830 that the decision was made to transform the little building into another royal cottage orné. This was reported in a local newspaper in December that year, which said it was 'intended as a summer box for Her Majesty, where the visitors from the Castle will occasionally take refreshment' – in other words, it would function as it had half a century previously, only this time the cottage would be purpose-built.

As with George IV's projects, the time-scale was remarkably short, since the deadline was Adelaide's birthday on 13 August 1831. It was achieved – just – with the workmen still busy in the morning and William IV hosting a 'petit déjeuner' in the afternoon. The operation was superintended by Wyatville, who in 1834 told the Office of Works that Adelaide Cottage 'was well finished under my direction about three years ago, and the materials were from Royal Lodge when pulled down'. The materials in question were used to create two large additional rooms, tacked onto the old cottage, which then supplied the domestic accommodation. Described as 'Her Majesty's Tea and Sitting Rooms', the new rooms were apparently furnished with items likewise brought from Royal Lodge rather than newly ordered. In contrast to the previous reign, economy was now the watchword. The finished results can be seen in a watercolour of 1839 by Caleb Robert Stanley [fig 7/22] and in two sepia watercolours by Wyatville himself, pleasant enough though (like much of this architect's oeuvre) lacking too much distinction or charm.[84] Certainly more truly cottagey in scale than Royal Lodge, the building has mullioned Tudor windows, a short section of verandah, and frilly eaves. Although enclosed by high iron railings, the surrounding picturesque garden was meant to appear part of the North Slopes plantation, whose winding paths led up to the Castle.

The cottage was never intended for permanent occupation, at least by a member of the royal family, and Queen Adelaide used it for its intended purpose only for the six years until William IV died in 1837, after which she left Windsor and moved to Bushey Park. Queen Victoria seems to have visited it a good deal with her children, but since 1941 it has served as a residence for members of the royal household.

With the creation of cottages for dukes and royalty, the orné genre now spanned the entire British social spectrum. It might be thought that it could ascend no higher, but developments on the Continent were to demonstrate that in fact it could.

1 John Claudius Loudon in *Magazine of Gardening* (1836), quoted by Christopher Hussey, 'Endsleigh, Devon – II', *Country Life* (10 August 1961), p. 296.

2 Amounting to 15,000 acres.

3 Hussey, 'Endsleigh, Devon – II'.

4 To which she was later to introduce her lover Edwin Landseer. Clive Aslet, 'Endsleigh Cottage', *Country Life* (9 February 2006), p. 43.

5 Hussey, 'Endsleigh, Devon – II', p. 297. The duchess seems to have been known as both Georgiana and Georgina.

6 Bedford Estate, reproduced in Stephen Daniels, *Humphry Repton* (New Haven and London, 1999), fig. 182.

7 Four were sold at auction in November 1999, and the remaining two are in a private collection. Four are for the north, south, east and west elevations, and two are variants of the east and west elevations. The entrance porch was on the west.

8 Reproduced in Hussey, 'Endsleigh, Devon – II'.

9 See below, fig. 7/20.

10 See below, fig. 7/22. The lettering on the drawings is also found on other Wyatt drawings.

11 The current house at Endsleigh has a canted projection from the service wing that is marked 'larder' on Wyatt's plan (RIBADC 37251). The other possibility is a game

larder, but these, being inherently smelly, were usually free-standing and placed away from the house.

12 For one thing, a cottage on the lines of the putative first design would have been much more expensive, being larger and involving stone – perhaps Bath stone – being imported from outside the region. The Woburn estate office has a bound volume of designs for the present house and its furnishings.

13 Quoted in J. C. Loudon, ed., *The Landscape Gardening and Landscape Architecture of the Late Humphry Repton* (1840), p. 99.

14 Wyatt's plan of the ground floor of the main house is RIBADC 37248.

15 See Chapter Ten.

16 Uvedale Price *Essay on Architecture* (1798), cited in C. Hussey, *The Picturesque* (London, 1983), p. 211

17 See Chapter Ten.

18 Quoted by Hussey, 'Endsleigh, Devon – II', p. 297.

19 Repton declined to share a carriage down with Wyatt, fearing that in the confined space he would be squashed by the architect's corpulence. The duke and duchess were then away on an extended European tour, following what was thought to be the end of the Napoleonic wars. Repton made a

final visit a year later in order to meet the duke on site, managing to combine the expedition with a holiday in Sidmouth. Daniels, *Humphry Repton*, p. 189.

20 Cited in Aslet, 'Endsleigh Cottage'.

21 *Neale's Seats*, quoted by Hussey, 'Endsleigh, Devon – II', p. 299. The furniture remained in the cottage until 2004, when it was sold. Hussey described the chairs as 'a characteristically hideous cross between Regency with some vaguely Jacobean pattern'.

22 The Red Book, which is in the possession of the Bedford Estate, contains a charming vignette of two of the boys doing just that.

23 *Neale's Seats*, quoted by Hussey, 'Endsleigh, Devon – II', p. 298. The children's wing is balanced at the other end of the house by a substantial service wing, which in the usual way is screened so as not to form part of the main composition.

24 Wyatt's perspective is RIBADC 29775. Wyatt probably designed the very similar Swiss cottage for the 5th Earl of Essex on his Cassiobury estate in Hertfordshire, recorded by J. Britton (*Cassiobury Park*) in 1837. D. Linstrum, *Sir Jeffry Wyatville* (Oxford, 1972), p234.

25 Linstrum, *Sir Jeffry Wyatville*, p. 95.

26 The location proposed by Repton for the main house in 1809.

27 The estate is entered from the public road by a thatched rustic lodge, again on the austere side, with simple latticed windows and a verandah of massy, knobbly tree trunks.

28 Cited in Aslet, 'Endsleigh Cottage'.

29 The building was restored for further hotel use and reopened in 2005.

30 See Chapter One.

31 Soane Museum, vol. 35/63.

32 Jane Roberts, *Royal Landscape: The Gardens and Parks of Windsor* (New Haven and London, 1997), pp. 58–9.

33 See Chapter Eight.

34 Kate Heard, 'The Print Room at Queen Charlotte's Cottage', *British Art Journal*, XIII/3, pp. 53–60.

35 Olwen Headley, *Queen Charlotte* (London, 1975), p. 308. Ernst, who was born in 1742, had followed his sister to England in 1761 and was well acquainted with the country. It is interesting that Charlotte, although writing in the court language of French, uses the term 'cottage' rather than 'chaumière'.

36 Information from Mary Gillespie, Historic Royal Palaces.

37 Yale Center for British Art. Papendiek shows the roof thatch shaped into points at the ends of the main gables, a feature that has been blunted in later re-thatching.

38 See Chapter Three, p.60.

39 See Chapter Eight.

40 Print rooms, and the creation of them by ladies of leisure, had become increasingly fashionable from the 1750s.

41 *London Magazine* (August 1774), p. 361.

42 John Watkins, *Memoirs of Her Most Excellent Majesty Sophia-Charlotte, Queen of Great Britain, from authentic documents* (London, 1819), p. 253.

43 Lord Ailesbury, visiting the menagerie in 1786, noted that 'there are neat rooms in house here [*sic*] with Hogarth's prints'. Heard, 'The Print Room at Queen Charlotte's Cottage', p. 54.

44 This was pointed out to me by Clarissa Orr, who thinks there is a strong case for the queen's direct involvement.

45 Polly Putnam of Historic Royal Palaces suggests that the cottage may have been conceived by Chambers as part of a kind of architectural world tour, which also included the pagoda, mosque and Alhambra designed by him in this part of the gardens.

46 The kitchen contains a chimneypiece and storage cupboards, but no oven, suggesting that only cold collations were served to visitors.

47 The room painted by her at Frogmore was noted by a visitor in 1797. Roberts, *Royal Landscape*, p. 219.

48 Headley, *Queen Charlotte*.

49 Flora Fraser, *Princesses: The Six Daughters of George III* (London, 2004), p. 170.

50 Ibid., p. 221. According to T. E. Harwood, *Windsor Old and New* (privately printed, 1929), pp. 315 and 333, the building was known as the Garden House and had been converted from a cow shed by the Hon. Richard Bateman, a member of Horace Walpole's Committee of Taste, some time between 1730 and 1741. Bateman, himself an amateur architect mainly in the Gothick vein, lived at the adjoining property later known as The Priory. Information from Pamela Clark, senior archivist, Royal Archives. Somewhat mysteriously, in his pattern book *Sketches in Architecture* published in 1807, Thomas Dearn noted that 'under the sanction of

fashion, we have seen royalty itself become the inmate and inhabitant of a cottage'. Since Royal Lodge at Windsor was not begun until 1812 and Queen Charlotte never lived in her cottage at Kew, this can only be a very prompt reference to Princess Elizabeth's cottage.

51 By S. & J. Fuller. Royal Library, Windsor Castle I.1/58.

52 No doubt designed by Elizabeth, who had designed similar structures at Kew. In 1793 a circular thatched hermitage was built to her designs in the gardens of Frogmore, shown in Samuel Howitt's view of 1802 (Royal Library 17753). The text accompanying the view of this in *Ackermann's Repository* for March 1823 describes both the exterior and interior as covered in moss. 'It is furnished with such accommodations as a recluse may be supposed to want – wooden utensils, rude seats, and a rough table, covered with excellent imitations of fruit, while a picture of a venerable hermit graces one corner.' Roberts, *Royal Landscape*, p. 225.

53 Fraser, *Princesses: The Six Daughters of George III*, p. 225.

54 The duchess was Elizabeth's youngest sister Mary.

55 Fraser, *Princesses: The Six Daughters of George III*, p. 294.

56 *Ackermann's Repository of Arts* (January 1824), Royal Library I.1/60.

57 They spent their honeymoon at the Prince Regent's Royal Lodge, a much larger specimen of the cottage orné.

58 According to T. E. Harwood, *Windsor Old and New*, it was pulled down to make way for the present house on the site, known as The Friary.

59 The Regent kept a set of Miss Austen's novels in each of his residences. She was to dedicate *Emma* to him in 1816. Roger Fulford, *George the Fourth* (London,1935), p. 183, quoted by Sir Owen Morshead, *George IV and Royal Lodge* (Brighton, 1965), p. 10.

60 E.g. Royal Collection RL 14634.

61 The most detailed account of the evolution of Royal Lodge is found in Roberts, *Royal Landscape*, pp. 311–30.

62 The great project for Regent Street and Regent's Park began in 1809. From 1815 Nash was also engaged in transforming the Royal Pavilion at Brighton.

63 Nash's plan is in the Public Record Office, MPE 1594/109.

64 John Smith, *Metrical Remarks on Modern Castles and Cottages* (1813), Preface, p. 6.

65 Presumably in his role as Leader of the House of Commons.

66 Roberts, *Royal Landscape*, p. 315.

67 Ibid., p. 574, note 40.

68 Quoted in Morshead, *George IV and Royal Lodge*, p. 15.

69 *Ackermann's Repository* (January 1823), RCIN 700918 and 700920.

70 *Reading Mercury* (7 August 1826), quoted in Morshead, *George IV and Royal Lodge*, p. 27.

71 Morshead, *George IV and Royal Lodge*, p. 26. This opinion was echoed later the same year by Sir Walter Scott, who dined and stayed overnight.

72 Royal Collection RL 32768.

73 *The Mirror of Literature, Amusement and Instruction* (6 December 1823). Royal Library 700923.

74 *Greville Memoirs* I, p. 177, quoted by Roberts, *Royal Landscape*, p. 317.

75 Morshead, *George IV and Royal Lodge*, pp. 30–31.

76 *The Visitants' Guide to Windsor Castle* (1828), p. 66, quoted by Roberts, *Royal Landscape*, p. 318.

77 *The Mirror of Literature, Amusement and Instruction* (6 December 1823).

78 Morshead, *George IV and Royal Lodge*, p. 30.

79 PRO WORK 19/44.15, cited in Roberts, *Royal Landscape*, p. 324.

80 Recorded in a watercolour of 1838 by T. F. Wainwright, Royal Library 17588. Roberts, *Royal Landscape*, p. 327.

81 *Windsor & Eton Express* (19 June 1830), quoted in Morshead, *George IV and Royal Lodge*, p. 39.

82 In 1865 Queen Victoria failed to persuade the Prince of Wales and his bride to use the place as a country retreat; the prince preferred Sandringham, well away from his mother's disapproving surveillance. Morshead, *George IV and Royal Lodge*, p. 46.

83 *Papendiek Journals* II, pp. 200–202, cited by Roberts, *Royal Landscape*, p. 193.

84 Potsdam, Acquarellsammlung, reproduced in Roberts, *Royal Landscape*, pls 192, 193. Neither original plans nor accounts for the building survive.

THE CONTINENTAL COTTAGE ORNÉ

Whereas in the British Isles the cottage orné was a genre that in one way or another encompassed all social classes, on the Continent it was very much the preserve of the aristocracy and royalty. One consequence of this is that there seem to have been very few examples that were intended for residence, as opposed to a few fleeting hours of charming make-believe. The exceptions were those that aristocrats erected on their estates as genuine cottages for peasant occupation, forming part of the general *mise en scène* but having no ornamental features either within or without. The contrast between the relative profusion of architect-designed cottages in Britain and the paucity of such structures abroad was not lost on British visitors to the Continent.[1]

In the second half of the eighteenth century Continental tourists visiting England made a point of including the latest gardens, all of which were likely to be 'natural' or 'picturesque'. The tourists might be aristocrats such as the Prince de Ligne, whose book on European gardens entitled *Coup d'Oeil sur Beloeil*, first published in 1781, drew on his travels around England and Europe, as well as his own park at Beloeil in present-day Belgium; but they might also be artists, architects or garden designers. Those from the latter categories included F. M. Piper from Sweden and F.-J. Belanger from France, both of whom returned home with numerous sketches that could inform their own garden designs. In addition relevant English garden-related books were translated into French and other European languages – the views on gardening of Alexander Pope and Joseph Addison, for instance, were available in French translations from the early 1720s. Opinions differ as to the extent to which Continental gardens in an informal manner were dependent on, or inspired by, English examples, although Horace Walpole famously remarked that because of the old cross-Channel rivalries the French preferred to give half the credit to the Chinese by calling them *jardins anglo-chinois*.

French visitors to England began to publish their views in the 1740s. Abbé Le Blanc, for instance, visited Merlin's Cave at Richmond and remarked that 'it is impossible to

conceive of anything of worse taste', although he praised English agriculture and marvelled at the well-kept and well-furnished farmhouses and cottages. Jean-Jacques Rousseau, visiting in 1766–7, was quoted as saying that he wished that the numerous temples in the English gardens he saw 'were changed into cottages, and other dwellings, which (under the tenure of keeping up the picturesque circumstances required by the owner) might be made the reward of industry and the consolation of distress' – a very prescient remark in the light of how the cottage orné genre was to develop in the British Isles.[2] Visitors to England from elsewhere on the Continent were less sniffy and superior than the French. Eighteenth-century England had led the way in what might be called the rationalization of the countryside, with large landowners absorbing the smaller holdings of the yeoman farmer that had existed since time immemorial, at the same time introducing the latest farming methods. Agricultural output soared, but simultaneously there was a growing class of labourers dependent on the goodwill of the landowners. News of these developments spread quickly on the Continent, and aristocratic foreigners came to see for themselves, admiring English farming methods at the same time as they absorbed the new English fashion for the landscape garden.[3] Some Anglophile French aristocrats were sufficiently inspired to follow English practice on their own farming estates, notably the Duc de Chartres at Monceau and the Duc d'Orleans at Le Raincy.[4]

FRANCE

It was probably from Dutch and Flemish artists that the French first developed a taste for picturesque rustic scenes incorporating cottages and barns, and in the later eighteenth century actual working farms would be incorporated into idealized landscape parks, as at Ermenonville, or built as romantic stage sets at the Petit Trianon. Practising artists indeed had more active involvement in the designing of picturesque gardens in France than ever their counterparts did in England. Working for himself with advice from his artist friends François Boucher and Hubert Robert, in the 1760s the writer and amateur artist Claude-Henri Watelet remodelled an existing farmhouse at Moulin Joli, on the Seine at Colombes near Paris, turning it into a picturesque

OPPOSITE **Chateau de Chantilly, the Hameau, detail from the Album du Comte du Nord**

HAMEAU

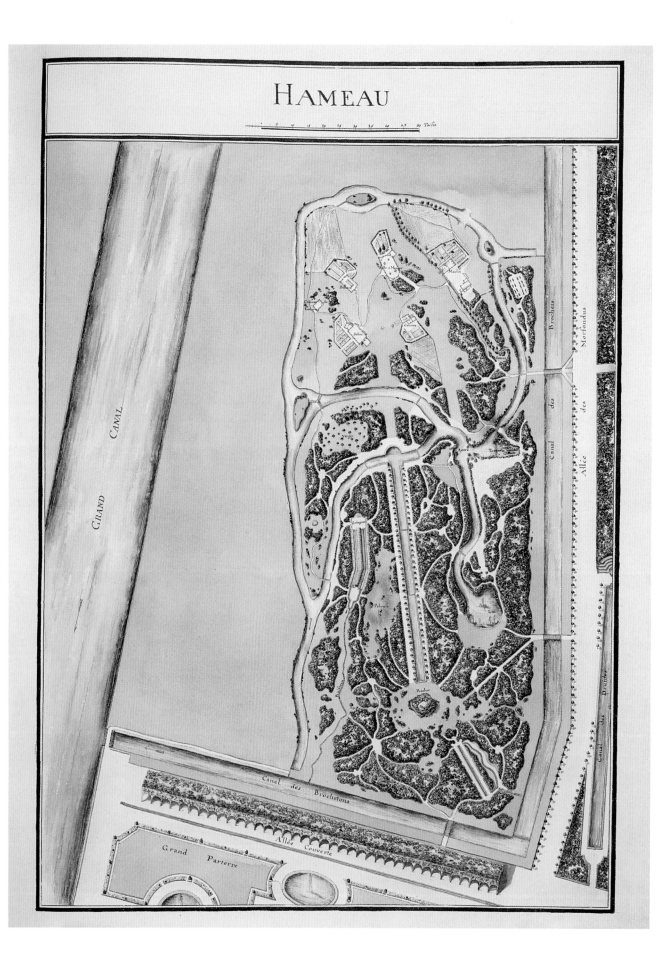

maison bourgeoise while maintaining the utmost simplicity.[5] Both Boucher and Robert were to be actively involved in the creation of other, more important gardens, such as that of the Petit Trianon at Versailles. At the same time there was a long-established French fashion for pastoral romances, depicting a bucolic, moralizing and sentimental life. Horace Walpole drew attention to the paintings of Watteau, which he said 'described a kind of impossible pastoral, a rural life led by those opposites of rural simplicity, people of fashion and rank'.[6] If civilization with its suavity – and corruption – were too much, the sensitive aristocrat could always find the opposite in rusticity, with its simplicity and virtue. This radical change in point of view encouraged the development of farms and villages where those eager to return to nature could follow their preferences for milk over champagne.[7] The introduction of rustic structures also related to contemporary curiosity about the primitive origins of architecture, most famously in the writings of the Abbé Laugier.[8]

In France, the gardens containing self-consciously rustic elements were an aristocratic and royal preoccupation, created in the period before the Revolution. As a result, most were destroyed or allowed to fall into ruin after 1789, and the documentation for them is extremely patchy. One element that was popular in France but not in Britain was the inclusion in gardens of artificial rustic villages or 'hameaux', most famously Marie Antoinette's Petit Hameau in the grounds of the Petit Trianon at Versailles. An early precursor of this phenomenon was found in the garden created in 1737–47 by Louis XV's father-in-law, the exiled Polish King Stanislaus, at his chateau of Lunéville, which included a small village of guest cottages. However, these were identical square pavilions lined up along a straight canal and had nothing cottagey or rustic about them, so they were hardly a prototype for the later hamlets of the 'jardin anglo-chinois'. A real oddity at Lunéville was a model village with an automaton population, created on the canal bank right next to the chateau. An English critic, James Stuart, called it 'one of the most flagrant perversions of taste that was ever exhibited to public view', where 'real pastoral objects and rustick images' are degraded by 'sticking-up clockwork hills, wooden cows and canvas milk maids'.[9]

By the 1770s the idea of the garden *hameau* was being developed more picturesquely. An anonymous satirical letter published in 1775 has a steward offering his employer a scheme for remodelling his Le Nôtre-style garden, to include a hamlet of twenty thatched guest houses, each with its own potager and orchard, and all serviced from a Temple of Comus where a kitchen, dining room and withdrawing room, plus gaming cabinets, would be installed.[10] One would think that if the idea was already being satirized it must already have been current, but in fact the letter seems to coincide almost exactly with the creation of the first fully fledged *hameau*, that at the Chateau of Chantilly. This forms part of a garden said to have been conceived one afternoon in the winter of 1772–3, when Prince Louis-Joseph de Condé was walking with his architect Jean-François Leroy. He decided that an open area beyond the eastern boundary of the rigidly formal Le Nôtre layout around the chateau was the perfect place to create a *jardin anglais*, enhanced by the natural abundance of water. Though predominantly and self-consciously irregular and informal, the spine of the garden is an entirely formal canal (parallel with Le Nôtre's dead straight Canal des Brochets), which bisects the bosquet with its informal meandering paths [fig 8/1]. The bosquet is threaded by equally meandering little streams, crossed by rocky bridges; this area was referred to as the *Jardin Anglo-Chinois*, and its creators must have thought the rockwork supplied the Chinese element. Visitors could traverse the bosquet on foot or travel through by thoughtfully provided canoes. Work was carried out rapidly in the spring of 1773, when the prince surprised his family and entourage by leading them into this new Arcadia. Supposedly on 12 June 1773 the Duc de Chartres visited the site and waded through the water 'from the Grotto up to the Rock where he had water up to his waist'. The day after, the Condés and their guests did the same: 'they got into the water where they started dancing'.[11]

The following year, 1774, the prince had the idea of adding a new attraction, the Hameau, in the more open area at the east end of the bosquet.[12] Arthur Young visited Chantilly in 1787 and recorded rather dismissively that 'the *hameau* contains an imitation of the English garden; the taste is but first introduced in France, so that it will not stand a critical examination'.[13] Leroy designed seven small buildings, distributed in a seemingly random way, on the model of agricultural buildings in Normandy, with half-timbered walls, thatched roofs, little lean-to annexes and

BELOW 8/2 Chateau de Chantilly, the Hameau: the Salon

OPPOSITE 8/3 Chateau de Chantilly, the Hameau, sections through the Salon and dining room, from the Album du Comte du Nord

a small garden planted with vegetables and fruit trees [fig 8/2]. The appearance of each reflected its supposed function, as water mill, dairy, cow-shed, barn and farmers' houses. In fact they contained all that was necessary to entertain the visitors who came for meals, conversation and music: kitchen, dining room, salon, billiard room and library. They were grouped round a little green, a predecessor of Nash's Blaise Hamlet though with far fewer components and certainly no humble residents.

Two of the buildings, the Salon, or *grange*, and the dining room [fig 8/3], were large, half-timbered cottages; a little building called the Caserne was used for storing items used in the rooms of entertainment. The dining room was decorated as if it were a leafy wood: the seats were imitations of tree trunks, the walls were lined with flowery banks and trees, the branches spreading over the ceiling. An oval within a rectangle, the leftover spaces were used for service areas. The *grange* contained a 'large and superb salon' ornamented with Corinthian pilasters alternating with mirrors, richly decorated frieze, painted ceiling and drapes of rose-coloured taffeta.[14] A very recent precursor and inspiration may have been the *jardin anglais* begun by the Duc de Chartres at Parc Monceau on the outskirts of

Paris in about 1772. Among its many embellishments was the *Jardin d'hiver*, which combined a simple rustic exterior with an interior that had trees painted and sculpted along the walls, their branches extending over the painted ceiling.[15] This extreme contrast between a convincingly rustic exterior and lavish, sophisticated interior, is a Continental as opposed to a British approach. It was commented on by contemporaries such as the Prince de Ligne, who wrote:

> Huts and cottages should have much red or black lacquer, with mirrors, paintings on glass, little gilded pilasters and so forth – in a word magnificence – because of the contrast and surprise. This need not be terribly expensive, since neither of these two types of folly is very large.[16]

In June 1782 the Grand Duke Paul (later Tsar) and his wife Maria Feodorovna visited Chantilly under the pseudonyms the Comte and Comtesse du Nord. This fooled no one, but allowed them to escape the usual rigid protocol; many other European royals adopted the same transparent subterfuge, including Christian VII of Denmark, the future Gustav III of Sweden and Joseph II

VUE D'UN CHALET SUISSE, CONSTRUIT DANS LA MONTAGNE DE FRANCONVILLE, APPARTENANT A MADAME LA COMTESSE D'ALBON.

of Austria. Nearly all foreign royalty visited Chantilly, and it is the illustrated album produced for the Russian couple in 1784 that memorializes the vanished interiors.[17] The artist appears to have been a certain Chambé, who also produced similar illustrations of the component buildings of the later Hameau at Versailles. Describing the reception of the Russian court, Baronne d'Oberkirch noted that the supper was served in the Hameau.

> The largest of the huts is decorated inside with leafy greenery, and the outside is surrounded by all that a good workman requires. It is in this cottage, which comprises a single oval room, that one sups at a dozen small tables, each with ten or twelve places. It is spacious, gay, informal, and perfectly contrived.[18]

Inaugurated by the prince at Easter 1775, the Chantilly Hameau was visited by Joseph II of Austria and the daughters of Louis XV, and it inspired a number of imitations amongst the upper echelons of French pre-Revolutionary society. As remodelled in 1786–93 by the Duc d'Orleans, Philippe-Egalité, the *jardin anglais* on his estate at Le Raincy in the environs of Paris had a farm and hamlet. All the structures were for practical use, though not exclusively agricultural, since one of them seems to have been let as a Russian coffee house, according to the inscription on a late eighteenth-century engraving.[19] At much the same date the Duchesse de Bourbon, inspired by Chantilly (her main residence), built her own hamlet in the grounds of the Elysée Palace, her residence close to the centre of Paris. She left in

more extensive than at Chantilly, as befitted the status of the client – was begun in 1783 to designs by Richard Mique, with advice from the Prince de Ligne, Hubert Robert and others, and the component buildings were first mocked up to allow the queen and Mique to assess the effect.[21] They included a farmhouse (intended to produce milk and eggs for the queen), mill, barn, the queen's own house and boudoir, cottages for the gardener and the guards, a tower, dairy, dovecot and hen house.[22] As at Chantilly, some of the buildings had very sophisticated interiors, none of which survives: the barn, for instance, contained a ballroom,[23] while the queen's house incorporated a dining room, gaming room, billiard room, library, antechamber (this in the form of a Chinese cabinet) and private apartment, the furniture being supplied by Jacob and Riesener.[24] The ultimate inspiration, as with so much of the French interest in the rustic, probably came from Dutch and Flemish genre paintings, combined with influence from Rousseau, Watelet and the philosophers who advocated the virtues of simple rural life.[25] Famously, the queen and her friends liked to play at being simple milkmaids, using porcelain milk pails specially made at Sèvres – not the only grand ladies in Europe to indulge in such comic fantasy but certainly the most notorious. Being the creation of a terminally frivolous and doomed queen, the Versailles Hameau has not only tended to eclipse Chantilly but also to be awarded a primacy in the whole cottage orné field that it does not warrant.

Other French aristocrats who did not want a whole hameau might nevertheless create a single cottage that followed the formula of deceptively humdrum exterior and ultra-chic interior. The garden of the Comte d'Harcourt at Chaillot, Paris had such a cottage or *chaumière*, recorded by Le Rouge [figs 8/6, 7]. His engravings show on the one hand the rustic exterior (and – an unusual designated feature – adjoining barn for romantic romping in the hay) and on the other the richly appointed interior, decked out like a campaign tent adorned with banners and armour, in a manner that anticipates the tented military dining room added to the Rosendal Palace outside Stockholm in the 1820s by Carl XIV Johann (born Jean-Baptiste Bernadotte).[26] However, much the finest surviving example is the Chaumière aux Coquillages [figs 8/8, 9] at Rambouillet. The estate belonged to the Duc de Penthièvre, son of the Comte de Toulouse and grandson of Louis XIV, supposedly

1797, and in 1801 a short-lived drinking, eating and dancing establishment was opened by Velloni, son of a Neapolitan-born café proprietor in Paris. At Betz and Beloeil the cottages were inhabited by workers. For the owners themselves to occupy such buildings for more than a few hours at a time was very exceptional, though at Franconville the 'Swiss Village' [fig 8/4] with chalets and cows seems to have been inhabited by the Comte d'Albion and his wife.[20] At Ermenonville north of Paris, where the picturesque park very much in the Capability Brown manner was created from about 1764 by Rousseau's friend the Marquis de Girardin, the embellishments included a Philosopher's Hut with rough rocky walls and thatched roof. A half-timbered cottage was built for Rousseau's use, though it was still unfinished at his death in 1778, and near the Wilderness was a picturesque hamlet remodelled from one of the old mills.

By far the most celebrated example of the artificial hamlet in France was of course the Petit Hameau [fig 8/5] at Versailles, another creation directly inspired by Chantilly. Louis XVI gave Marie Antoinette the area round the Petit Trianon in June 1774. Here she and her innumerable advisers and professionals contrived an informal layout of meadowland interspersed with lakes and meandering streams. As a final scenographic elaboration, the various buildings of the Hameau were created in a rustic or vernacular style in imitation of a Normandy farm, placed around an irregular artificial pond fed by a stream that turned the mill wheel. The ensemble – considerably

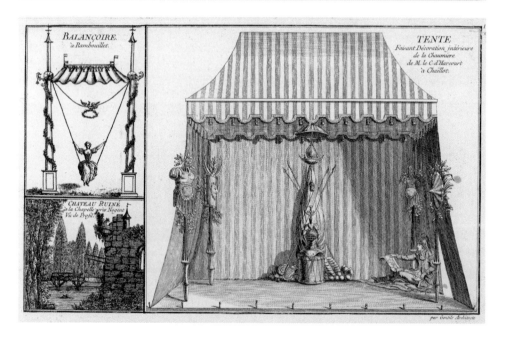

the wealthiest man in France. His debauched son married Marie-Louise, princesse de Lamballe (1749–1792), abandoning her and then leaving her a widow at nineteen. Her father-in-law doted on her, and built her a little cottage on an artificial island, connected to the banks by rustic wooden bridges and set in a 'jardin anglais' designed by Jean-Baptiste Paindebled in collaboration with the architect Claude-Martin Goupy. The cottage is around a half-mile walk across a level meadow from the more celebrated royal dairy, with its spectacular and equally artificial neoclassical interior. It was built in 1779–81 and formed part of a garden that also included a thatched hermitage and Chinese pavilion. The contrast between exterior and interior is extreme. The exterior is Brittany vernacular, with ox-thigh bones embedded in the plaster (these apparently

help to dehumidify the interior and also provided support for climbing plants like honeysuckle). Inside are just two rooms, one quite large, the other tiny. The larger is a shell-encrusted domed rotunda, very architectural, with the walls divided up by fluted Ionic pilasters that frame shallow niches. The shells were sourced from, amongst other places, the Seine, Dieppe and the West Indies. Pieces of glass and metal are also incorporated into the scheme. The small room is a boudoir or ladies' powder room (there was a close stool in it), its panelling palest green and painted with exquisite arabesques, floral bouquets and birds. In one corner a narrow panel opens to disclose the ultra-refinement of two niches from which cosmetics and perfumes could be dispensed by automata. Furniture was specially commissioned from the cabinetmaker François Folliot,

incorporating naturalistic motifs within the usual French neoclassical formula. In the shell room the sofas were curved to match the shape of the niches in front of which they stood. Originally there were curtains with fringeing of glass beads and tassels.[27]

As with the Chantilly cottages, the exterior has no orné features and looks convincingly vernacular, so at both places the aim must have been to deceive visitors until they actually set foot inside. This element of surprise was obviously important, though of course it could not be sustained for more than the first visit. The contrast between simple exterior and lavish interior was in both places more extreme than in almost all British examples, including the Queen's Cottage at Kew, perhaps because the British wanted to maintain the fiction of experiencing the (relatively) simple life. Tragically for the Princesse de Lamballe, the idyll had not long to run. In 1791 she left for the safety of England, in the hope of enlisting practical help for her beloved friend Marie Antoinette, whose chief lady-in-waiting she was. The following year she ill-advisedly returned to Paris, and after a summary trial was hideously murdered by the mob, her severed head paraded on a pike before the window of the imprisoned queen. It was very emphatically the end of the era of aristocratic *douceur de vivre*.[28]

THE COTTAGE OUTSIDE FRANCE

Examples of the rustic cottage seem never to have been particularly numerous in France, and thanks to their more or less exclusive association with the royal family and aristocracy fewer still have survived. The same appears to be even truer elsewhere in Europe, where a scattering of such buildings is recorded but almost none is now extant.

The Prince de Ligne, who showed so much interest in other people's gardens, might be expected to have followed the rustic fashion on his own estate at Beloeil, near Mons in present-day Belgium; and indeed, in his book *Coup d'Oeil sur Beloeil*[29] he recorded that he had created a 'Tartar village', with huts for shepherds and sheep 'in outlandish style', and 'with projections of tree trunks forming verandahs'. 'There is also a dairy in the form of a mosque', he noted. He referred to the village as 'just finished' – that is, in the early 1790s – but if so he did not enjoy it for long, as he was forced into exile in Austria in 1794, and nothing

survives. The Beloeil archives do contain several designs for rustic structures, the most fascinating being a two-storeyed circular or octagonal thatched pavilion apparently to be constructed around a living tree; the lower floor was to open out via arches with louvred doors, while the upper floor, reached by a staircase spiralling around the tree trunk, would have had Chinoiserie glazing to the windows and twiggy seating round the perimeter.[30]

Exile at least allowed de Ligne the opportunity to visit a new range of estates, and at Marshal Lascy's Neuwaldegg, on the edge of Wienerwald, some five miles north-west of Vienna, he admired 'a hamlet with two little houses, a saloon furnished to perfection', not to mention a Chinese pavilion, artificial ruin, and a 'Scotch bath'.[31] Even in exile the creative urge stayed with him, and on the Kahlenburg mountain north of Vienna he and a group of five others purchased and developed the remains of a Carthusian monastery. Unlike most monastic orders, the Carthusians lived in collections of tiny individual houses or cells, each with its own little garden, and these were taken over by the consortium and their servants – a unique aristocratic version, perhaps, of the artificial villages he observed on French estate, though hardly rustic or picturesque.[32]

The rustic and the picturesque fashions were nevertheless reflected on a number of estates in other parts of the Austrian monarchy's territories and the German-speaking world more generally. English-style gardens were popular, and sometimes these layouts incorporated rustic elements. The fashion started to arrive in Hungary in the 1780s, and by the early nineteenth century it was a positive mania (an English visitor in 1829 said that 'there is scarcely a European country in which the Anglomania rages more fiercely'), but although this resulted in plenty of informal gardens dotted with the usual range of ornamental structures, cottages ornés barely seem to feature. Interestingly, the archives of the Festetics estate do contain two designs for small orné cottages or lodges dated 1855, but they are by the Scottish architect William Burn, similar to ones he designed for British sites, with Tudor chimneys and frilly eaves boards.[33] There is also a lithograph recording a sizeable cottage at Kistapolcsany, seemingly constructed of logs in the 1840s, with a massive thatched roof, arcaded gable with a balcony supported on rough posts, and a chimney with smoke issuing as if it were a cottage in a Repton Red Book.[34] At Kremsier (modern-day Kroměříž)

in Bohemia, Prince-Archbishop Colloredo between 1790 and 1802 created a garden whose range of embellishments, much like an English garden such as Hawkstone, included the obligatory hermitage. More unusually, it also had a private study for the archbishop disguised as a carefully stacked pile of logs.[35] Vignettes of the garden created from the mid-1780s at Freundenhain, the summer residence of the Archbishop of Passau, show a rustic cottage-like thatched hermitage – in fact a Janus-faced structure, since the other façade was classical and fronted a rose garden.[36] Cerveny Dvur, the Schwarzenberg family's summer retreat near Cesky Krumlov, still has a modest cottage called Mauricovna, probably associated with the Anglicization of the formal park. The cottage is said to date from 1790; however, one of the young Schwarzenberg princes and his wife apparently got the English bug when representing Emperor Ferdinand at Queen Victoria's wedding in 1840, and this may tie in with the Tudor Gothic look of the cottage.[37]

English influence was felt much earlier than this in the German world, both through the dissemination of engravings and publications and through the observations that princelings and their architects or garden designers made while visiting England. When the gardens at Rheinsberg were remodelled after 1764 for Prince Heinrich of Prussia, the picturesque embellishments were generally English in feel, although they did include a 'Rousseau cottage'.[38] Wörlitz, probably the most important German garden in the English style, was created from 1764 for Prince Leopold Friedrich Franz of Anhalt-Dessau, who had himself travelled in England, and it drew on identifiable sources such as Stowe and Kew. In 1799 a different English source provided the model for the Gardener's House there, albeit indirectly [fig 4/14]. This was a design by John Plaw 'intended to be built by a Gentleman in Wales'.[39] Published in England in *Ferme Ornée* in 1795 [fig 4/13], it was plagiarized within two years of publication, appearing verbatim (with German labels) in Grohmann's *Gartenmagazin für Liebhaber Englischer Garten*, published in Leipzig in 1797.[40] Prince Hermann von Pückler-Muskau, an Anglophile German aristocrat whose accounts of his travels in the British Isles provide much useful information about the picturesque landscapes and buildings he saw there, created his own English-inspired landscape garden on his vast estate of

Muskau south-east of Berlin, beginning in 1815. This too he recorded in published form,[41] from which we learn that it included what he called 'a spacious *cottage ornée* known as "the English House", which serves as a place for Sunday outings for the town and surrounding area'.[42] Plate XXVI of his book *Hints on Landscape Gardening* shows this to have been a substantial thatched building, though hardly *orné* in the accepted English sense. The estate also included 'colonies of rustic houses' around the village of Kobeln (also known as Gobelin) [fig 8/10], each meant to provide free accommodation for garden workers, miners and 'the needy'.[43] Plate XXXIX, entitled 'Cottages of the Gobelin Colony', illustrates half a dozen cottages set behind wicket fences, widely spaced in an open arable landscape, and with a definite feel of Blaise Hamlet about them.

The most delightful ensemble of its kind in western Continental Europe must surely be found on the Danish island of Møn. A small estate there was purchased in 1783 by Antoine de la Calmette, a Gentleman of the Royal Bedchamber, whose father, the Dutch ambassador to Denmark,[44] had already bought the manor of Marienborg on the island in 1777. Calmette changed the name of the estate to Liselund, after his wife Lisa. The couple's interests included the new Romantic movement, the writings of Rousseau promoting the virtues of Nature and the simple life, and the English approach to landscape and garden design, all of which are enchantingly reflected at their summer retreat. At Marienborg they laid out the grounds in the English style, with winding canals, rare trees and garden buildings in varied styles. But the ground there was flat, whereas Liselund had much greater potential, more undulating and with dramatic chalk cliffs falling abruptly into the sea. Calmette began by transforming a marshy valley overgrown with alders, creating an artificial river that widened into a lake with little islands, and felling or planting trees to form a picturesque frame. Only after nine years did he move on to building a new house, employing the architect Andreas Kirkerup to create a thatched T-plan cottage that was very grandly dubbed 'the Palace' [fig 8/11].[45]

Kirkerup's instincts were classical, but his client insisted that he make it rustic, at least on the exterior, which unites French-style fenestration with a deep thatched roof that descends over verandahs made up of pillars halfway between Doric columns and logs. The combination of whitewashed walls and pale blue paintwork is very Danish. So too are the interiors, which could be seen as a bucolic version of the latest international neoclassical styles. Thus, the panelling of the entrance hall was painted with arabesques (now largely destroyed), while the adjoining Cabinet or 'Monkey Room' [fig 8/13] has a dado with Chinoiserie trellis in the William Chambers manner, and painted wall decoration incorporating Wedgwood-style blue and white medallions. The mirrored rear wall is divided into three by carved palm trees, the glass overpainted with foliage seen through bamboo treillage, and with the

little monkey that gives the room its name.[46] The largest room is the dining hall [fig 8/12] at the rear of the building, which looks out through tall French windows on three sides into the verandah. The walls here are said to have been painted initially with trees, possibly inspired by the dining hall at the Chantilly hamlet; quite early on, perhaps as the newly planted trees outside grew to maturity, these gave way to the present, more architectural, scheme. The Danish-made furnishings, which largely survive, are an eclectic mixture, some following French models and others clearly indebted to English designers such as Adam, Sheraton and Hepplewhite. Some appear to have been designed by the Court decorator Joseph Christian Lillie, who often worked with Kirkerup and may have masterminded the whole interior.

The Calmettes intended the Cottage Palace only for

OPPOSITE, ABOVE 8/14 Liselund, Denmark: Norwegian House interior, view from the Chinoiserie Room to the Pompeian/ Etruscan Room

OPPOSITE, BELOW 8/15 Liselund, Denmark: Norwegian House

8/16 Alte Turm, Hohenheim, Germany

short summer stays of a few days. Husband and wife had their own adjoining rooms on the ground floor, separated by a tiny room with a close stool, and low-ceilinged bedrooms in the roof. There are other small rooms in the roof, but any guests staying in them would have had to avail themselves of the outside privy designed as a pile of logs. Others would have been accommodated in the so-called Swiss House, another building with a big thatched roof supported on posts, where they would have been looked after by the wife of the resident gardener.

The house has no views of the sea but is protected by wooded slopes from the cold Baltic winds from the east. In addition to the Swiss House the grounds were further embellished with a red and yellow Chinese House (added in 1800, and also designed by Kirkerup, with Chinoiserie furniture made in Copenhagen after published designs by Sir William Chambers), and a Norwegian House [figs 8/14, 15]. This last is in effect another cottage orné, very much Scandinavian vernacular without, but containing a Chinoiserie Room, a Pompeian/Etruscan Room, and a bedroom known as the Moon Room on account of the moon-shaped aperture in the shutter, glazed with amber glass.

Calmette died in 1803, Lisa in 1805, leaving an only son, Charles (1781–1820), who was dissipated and financially incompetent. After his death Marienborg was sold, but his widow lived on at Liselund for fifty-seven years, always dressed in white and surrounded by albino peacocks and albino pet deer.

Liselund is not quite unique in Denmark, as it was preceded by the more modest cottage built in 1786 for General Johann Fredrik Claussen (1725–1792) at his estate at Corselitze, on the neighbouring island of Falster. It sits right on the Baltic shore and was used for bathing and tea parties. As at Liselund, the architect was Andreas Kirkerup (who remodelled the main mansion in austere neoclassical vein in 1774–7), and once again the simple exterior, with thatch and verandah, belies a more sophisticated interior – in this case a single room whose deep ceiling cove is rather oddly ornamented with painted sepia grisaille roundels of negroid heads by Johannes Wiedewelt,[47] linked by leafy swags. The room retains its simple but elegant seat furniture, and there is said to be an inscription declaring, 'Wer Ruhe hat, der findet Sie Hier' (If you are looking for peace, you will find it here).[48]

Scandinavia as a whole seems to lack other examples of

the cottage orné, although a claim might possibly be made for the villa built on the Norwegian island of Lysoen as late as 1872–3. Designed by Conrad Frederik von der Lippe for the violin virtuoso Ole Bull and his new American wife, it is an extraordinary confection. Built of wood on a stone ground floor, it combines a Russian-looking onion-domed tower at one end, Moorish-looking two-tier entrance portico in the middle, and at the other end cottagey features like fancy eaves and Gothic windows.

A German princely estate provides the link between Western European and Russian rusticity. Hohenheim, near Stuttgart, was a property of Carl Eugen, the ruling Duke of Württemberg, who lived there with his mistress. He created a so-called English village of buildings in assorted styles, much influenced by Kew, which he visited in 1776 before starting work. This included a dairy[49] and the Alte Turm [fig 8/16], a single-storey building with thatched roof, belfry and outside stairs leading to a loft. The models for the latter were French rather than English, and as with French royal models, the interior was elegant and comfortable. Carl Eugen's younger brother Friedrich Eugen was father to Sophia Dorothea, the future Tsarina Maria Feodorovna. A third brother, Ludwig Eugen, was a friend and disciple of Rousseau, and seems to have been a considerable influence on Sophia Dorothea. The latter's first childhood home was Treptow (now Poland), where her parents added a dairy that they frequently visited. After Friedrich Eugen's retirement from the army in 1769 the family went to live at Montbéliard in eastern France, where their summer residence was given a *jardin anglo-chinois* with grottoes, hermit's cell and a dairy with handsome interior. So it was almost inevitable that when Sophia Dorothea married the heir to the Russian throne she would transmit such Western fashions to her adoptive country.

RUSSIA

In 1776 Catherine the Great's son and heir Paul (born 1754) married the sixteen-year-old Sophie-Dorothea of Württemberg as his second wife (a marriage promoted by Frederick the Great). She adopted the name Maria Feodorovna and gave him four sons, two of whom became tsar in turn as Alexander I and Nicholas I. In 1782 the couple, thinly disguised as the Comte and Comtesse du Nord, embarked on a fourteen-month European tour that included Germany (where they visited her family's parks), and France, where – as has been seen – they were particularly taken with the Hameau at Chantilly.

In 1777, on the occasion of the birth of her first grandson, the empress gave Paul a large estate near Tsarskoye Selo, which was renamed Pavlovsk. Here Maria Feodorovna aimed to recreate the relatively simple, natural life she had enjoyed as a girl on her family's estates, and in 1778 she had two small rustic pavilions built, conforming to current German taste. One, intended for Paul, was called 'Mariental' (Maria's valley), while the other for herself was called 'Paullust' (Paul's consolation). They each had a little garden in the English taste, with miscellaneous ornamental buildings including a Chinese summerhouse, ruin and mill. The hermitage was inspired by one in the grounds of Maria's childhood home in eastern France, Etupes near Montbéliard. There was also a building called the Old Chalet [fig 8/17], loosely copied from the Alte Turm at Hohenheim. It was here that her children were given lessons in gardening. An adjacent kitchen supplied lunches, to which the children were summoned by the bell in the turret on the thatched roof.[50] The Prince de Ligne visited Pavlovsk and recorded that 'a chalet that appears to be a cottage from the outside contains, within, a salon in the most decorative and exquisite fashion of private homes in Paris',[51]

thus following the example of the Hameau cottages at Chantilly. This was probably about as close to the simple life as was ever likely to be achieved on an imperial Russian estate.

The two pavilions quickly became inadequate, so in 1782 the couple commissioned a proper palace, designed by the English architect Charles Cameron, who had been invited to Russia by the empress in 1779. They were kept informed of progress on it as they travelled around Europe. For the English-style park at Pavlovsk, in addition to numerous more conventional classical ornaments, Cameron reluctantly designed three rustic buildings: a thatched stone dairy, a hermit's cell and charcoal-burner's hut. Of these only the dairy survives. Cameron was clearly more interested in the classical language of architecture than the rustic, and his slowness to come up with designs irritated Maria Feodorovna, far away in Rome. Her secretary wrote from there in March 1782 to Karl Kuchelbecker, the estate manager at Pavlovsk, with clear instructions that the dairy [fig 8/19] was to be based on that at Hohenheim, of which plans were supplied along with directions for its location.

> Her Highness thinks that the best situation for this building would be on the high ground on the edge [of the park] so that the cows can walk straight out of the stalls into the wood. It's also essential that the building should be hidden so that people don't suspect it's there until they draw near to it.[52]

Its walls of rough stone boulders[53] and thatched roof supported on tree trunks concealed a lavish interior: 'a refined

hall with a dome and this held white and gold stools with down cushions and covers . . . made of East Indian material with flowers on . . . the windows [had] matching curtains with fringes, scallops and tassels'.[54] The hermitage, with thatched roof and bark-covered walls, was relatively basic inside, but the charcoal-burner's hut was sufficiently elegant to contain a harpsichord.[55] Cameron also designed an endearingly tottery-looking rustic kitchen [fig 8/18] to accompany the magnificent domed rotunda of the Temple of Friendship.[56]

Although Maria Feodorovna always loved Pavlovsk best of all her residences, Paul came to prefer the estate at Gatchina, which his mother bought for him in 1783 from the executors of her late favourite Prince Grigory Orlov. The palace was ugly, but John Bush and his Scottish gardeners Charles and John Sparrow had already created an outstandingly fine English park threaded by lakes, pools and streams. Most of the architectural embellishments were classical, and others inspired by Chantilly were added for Paul. The most unusual and fascinating addition, however, was commissioned by Maria as a surprise for her husband. This is the Little Birch House [fig 8/20], made to

look externally like a giant, neatly stacked pile of birch logs, but inside the walls are covered with mirrors painted with treillage, there is a marquetry floor, and the ceiling was frescoed with Zephyr and garlands of flowers – a far cry from the log-pile privy at Liselund, though perhaps more akin to the archbishop's log-pile study at Kremsier. The architect is unknown.[57] The ubiquitous Prince de Ligne, visiting the imperial estate at Peterhof, recorded something along similar lines:

> in the new garden there is a hideaway in the form of a hayrick. A few bundles of hay, which must be removed to enter, block the door and windows and fool the visitor, who easily forgives such trickery on entering a room decorated in the latest Parisian taste.[58]

Catherine the Great may not have been tempted to emulate the democratic arrangements of English eighteenth-century politics, but in cultural matters she was very much an Anglophile, and never more so than in the subject of gardening. In 1772 she wrote to Voltaire, 'I adore English gardens, with their curved lines . . . and I deeply despise

straight lines and identical allées.' Neither she nor her son Paul actually visited England, but four of Paul's children did. These included the Grand Duke Michael, who between June and October 1818 toured English country seats, cities, towns and even seaside resorts like Brighton and Sidmouth. The fact that the rustic fashion had been introduced to Russia at the highest level encouraged many of the aristocracy to remodel their estates in the English style. As early as 1770 Count Czernichen, Russian ambassador to London, solicited plans via Lord Lyttelton from Sanderson Miller for a new house, having admired what he saw at Hagley Hall in Warwickshire.[59] Princess Catherine Dashkova, both of whose brothers served as ambassador, visited gardens such as Painshill and Claremont during her visit to England in 1770 and reflected what she had seen in her park at Troitskoe. At Otrada, south of Moscow, Vladimir Orlov was inspired by his visit in 1772 to lay out a park that included a picturesque farm in addition to the usual pavilions and summerhouses. At a slightly less socially elevated level, Lev Naryshkin's dacha on the road from St Petersburg to Peterhof included in its gardens stretching down to the sea buildings such as a Russian peasant's house, Dutch peasant's house, hermitage and shepherd's hut. The empress was charmed and took two visiting monarchs to see it – Gustav III of Sweden in 1777, and Joseph II of Austria in 1780.[60]

Like their French counterparts, neither Catherine nor Paul ever wanted to spend more than a few hours at a time in anything resembling a cottage, however sumptuously appointed inside. However, it was under Paul's son Nicholas that the cottage orné as somewhere to live may be said to have reached its ultimate social apogee. Tsar Alexander I, eldest son of Paul and Maria Feodorovna, gave his younger brother Grand Duke Nicholas an estate adjoining the imperial one at Peterhof in 1825, shortly before he died. On his accession as tsar,[61] Nicholas I issued orders for the building of 'a country house or cottage, with all auxiliary services and with a park'.[62] Nicholas has come down through history as a military martinet, a political conservative whose reign was characterized by repression of dissent, economic stagnation, corrupt bureaucracy and frequent wars, but he was nevertheless a loving husband and an indulgent father. Like Maria Feodorovna before her, his wife Alexandra was a German princess, born Charlotte, daughter of King Frederick William III of Prussia. In common with many Germans (and other Europeans) of her generation, she was a convinced Anglophile with a hankering for what might be thought frankly bourgeois taste. Neither she nor her husband relished the idea of living out their daily lives in the vast baroque goldfish bowls at Tsarskoe Seloe or Peterhof, and they therefore commissioned a house in what they fondly imagined was the English cottage style, located in what was then renamed the Alexandria Park and oxymoronically known as the Cottage Palace [fig 8/21]. It sits on the crest of a ridge commanding views north to the sea, and south over English-inspired parkland.

The Cottage Palace was built in 1826–9 to designs by Adam Menelaws, who if not actually an English architect did come from the British Isles, having been born around 1749, possibly in Greenock. He was one of several Scots who responded to an advertisement placed by Charles Cameron in the *Edinburgh Evening News* in January 1784, encouraging artisans to come to Russia to work in the service of Catherine the Great. As an experienced mason he started work on Cameron's new buildings at Tsarskoe Seloe, but in time he began to receive independent architectural commissions. The results at Alexandria were not exactly like any existing British cottage orné, but nor were they like anything seen hitherto in Russia. The building's three main fronts are different from each other but each is divided into three symmetrical parts. There are two main floors, the windows are Tudor Gothic, and the gables are mainly sharply pointed, with cusped eaves. So far, so English. What gives the exterior a distinctly un-English appearance is the centre section of the west front, which is deeply recessed into the body of the building beneath an extraordinary gable shaped rather like a bonnet, which comes right forward to the main building line. Each of these façades incorporates elaborately frilled cast-iron verandahs, Tudor in detail but nevertheless managing to seem somewhat exotic and oriental.

The interiors are sometimes said to have been designed by Andrej Stackenschneider, an architect of German extraction, but he did not start working for Nicholas until 1838, by which time the Cottage was finished both inside and out. Enough of the detail is clearly of English Gothick inspiration to make it highly likely that Menelaws had a considerable input. The main drawing room or Green Salon, for instance [fig 8/23], which has a bow with plate-glass windows commanding the view to the sea, has a cusped Gothick frieze and a plaster ceiling close-patterned with Gothick rose windows and fans. It is conventionally

said that the latter were inspired by the rose windows in Chartres Cathedral,[63] but they are much more reminiscent of the papery Georgian Gothick ceilings of English buildings such as Strawberry Hill or Alscot Park. The library, large reception room and small study on the ground floor likewise have patterned ceilings of obviously English Tudor derivation, while the tsar's main study on the first floor has a frieze of fan pendants for which there are a number of English eighteenth- and early nineteenth-century precedents. The principal staircase in the centre of the building [fig 8/22] is entirely frescoed in pale blue and stoney-grey architectural *trompe l'oeil*, executed by the Italian Giovanni Scotti, which is said to have been inspired by the cathedrals of Chartres and Rheims.[64] The *trompe l'oeil* architecture of the walls in reality has very little to do with genuine medieval French cathedrals and everything to do with the Romantic Gothic or 'Troubador' style then starting to make its appearance on mainland Europe, including Italy.

Generally speaking, both the interior design and the furnishings of the Cottage Palace are predominantly Gothic-inspired – Gothic chairs,[65] Gothic screens, Gothic clocks, Gothic knick-knacks, Gothic lanterns and chandeliers. By the standards of imperial palaces the rooms are small and cluttered, achieving the kind of expensive but middle-brow bourgeois domesticity that the empress in particular craved. The partial stylistic exception is the tsar's 'Maritime Study' on the top floor [fig 8/24], from whose balcony he liked to issue orders by megaphone to a signal tower on the seashore, which were then transmitted to the Kronstadt naval base. The shallow vaulted ceiling is again exquisitely painted in Gothick *trompe l'oeil*, but elaborately swagged drapes (again *trompe l'oeil*) hang down the walls and the furniture could be called Russian Biedermeier.

Throughout the nineteenth century the Cottage Palace was carefully preserved, and it continued to be used by the imperial family for summer holidays until the Revolution. Like the other imperial residences, it was maintained more or less in aspic by the Soviet authorities (who renamed the Aleksandrinsky Park 'Proletarsky Park'), and escaped the devastations of the World War Two relatively unscathed, most of its contents evacuated and then meticulously reinstated. It remains comparatively unknown, a uniquely complete example of the cottage orné genre at the very top end of its social range.[66]

1 The fact was regretted by Samuel H. Brookes in his book *Designs of Villa and Cottage Architecture* of 1839.

2 Dora Wiebenson, *The Picturesque Garden in France* (Princeton, 1978), p. 30, citing R. L. Girardin, *Essay on Landscape* (London, 1783), pp. liii–liv.

3 For instance, the La Rochefoucauld brothers, who toured England in 1785. Norman Scarfe, *Innocent Espionage: The La Rochefoucauld Brothers' Tour of England in 1785* (Woodbridge, 1995).

4 J. M. Robinson, *Georgian Model Farms* (Oxford, 1983), p. 12.

5 William Howard Adams, *The French Garden 1500–1800* (New York, 1979), p. 109.

6 Horace Walpole, *Anecdotes of Painting* (1762–71), IV, pp. 35–6, quoted by Wiebenson, *The Picturesque Garden in France*, p. 4.

7 Basil Guy, introduction to Prince Charles-Joseph de Ligne, *Coup d'Oeil sur Beloeil*, 1795 edn (Berkeley, 1991).

8 Abbé Laugier, *Essai sur l'Architecture* (1753). See Chapter One.

9 James Stuart, *Critical Observations* (1771), pp. 10–12, quoted in Wiebenson *The Picturesque Garden in France*, p. 12, n. 69.

10 Cited, without source, by John Dixon Hunt, *The Picturesque Garden in Europe* (London, 2003), p. 110.

11 Diary of Toudouze, Hunting Captain of the Prince de Condé, quoted on site.

12 There is some dispute about the precise dating of the Chantilly *hameau*. The Prince de Ligne (*Coup d'Oeil sur Beloeil*) in 1782 said it was begun eight years previously, i.e. 1774; Thiéry, in his *Guide aux environs de Paris* (1788), says it was constructed in less than three months in 1780; and G. Macon, *Les arts dans la Maison de Condé* (1903), says it was begun in 1774 and inaugurated in April 1775.

13 Arthur Young, *Travels in France* (1787), p. 11.

14 J. A. Dulaure, *Nouvelle Description des environs de Paris* (1786), I, p. 66.

15 Illustrated by G.L. Le Rouge, *Détails des Nouveaux jardins à la mode* (Paris, 1783), cahier x. The other embellishments included a 'rustic farm' and a dairy.

16 De Ligne, *Coup d'Oeil sur Beloeil*, Book III.32.

17 It was sent to Paul and kept at Gatchina, outside St Petersburg, till sold by the Soviets in 1930, when it was bought back by the Institut de France. Jean-Pierre Babelon, *Album du Comte du Nord: Recueil des Plans des Chateaux, Parcs et Jardins de Chantilly*, republished 2000. The album was also published at the time in Paris,

seemingly in very small numbers, and was probably not available in booksellers, so had very little circulation or influence. The exteriors of the surviving Hameau cottages were restored authentically 2007–8, but the original interiors disappeared in the nineteenth century.

18 Framed up in a corridor in the Grandes Apartements of the chateau at Chantilly is a series of pen and watercolour vignettes, c. 1770–80, of episodes in the gardens (called 'jeu de Cavagnole') including the Hameau (no. 8), Le Rocher (no. 10 – this is in the centre of the circular pool at the chateau end of the bosquet, and taller than at present), and others of the Hameau and its environs (118, 119, 120 etc.). There is also a separate framed watercolour of the Hameau ('Vue prise dans le hameau'), complete with cows, a group of visitors, and a woman who is perhaps the dairy maid or cow-herd.

19 Wiebenson, *The Picturesque Garden in France*, fig. 109.

20 Ibid., p. 100 and fig. 108, from J. C. Le Prieur, *Description d'une partie de la vallée de Montmorency* (Paris, 1784).

21 David Watkin, *The English Vision* (London, 1982), p. 168.

22 Marie-France Boyer, *The Private Realm of Marie Antoinette* (London and Paris, 1995), p. 62.

23 This was badly damaged during the Revolution and finally destroyed under the First Empire.

24 Pierre Arizzoli-Clémentel, *Vues et plans du Petit Trianon à Versailles* (Paris, 1998), p. 98.

25 Adams, *The French Garden 1500–1800*, p. 121.

26 G. L. le Rouge, *Cahiers des jardins anglo-chinois* (Paris, 1776–85), illustrated in Adams, *The French Garden 1500–1800*, pls 145, 146. Ernest de Ganay, in his edition of *Coup d'Oeil a Beloeil*, (Paris, 1922) mentions a cottage with luxurious interior on the estate of Marechal de Noailles at Saint-Germain, now destroyed.

27 Marie-France Boyer, 'The Princess' Folly', *World of Interiors* (March 2008).

28 Louis XVI was very fond of Rambouillet and in 1783 pressured a reluctant Penthièvre to sell the estate to him. He immediately employed Hubert Robert to create a new *jardin anglais*, with the Laiterie de la Reine, or Queen's Dairy, as its centrepiece, hoping this would make his wife like the place better (she found it boring). The building was designed by Jean-Jacques Thévenin and presented to Marie Antoinette in 1787, and was very much in the latest neoclassical idiom – unlike the thatched ornamental dairy at Versailles, built

in 1782–4 to Richard Mique's design – with circular domed vestibule leading to an inner chamber with a spectacular rocky cascade at the far end. Beyond, out of sight, Louis had a proper experimental sheep farm constructed with the aim of improving the quality of French wool.

29 De Ligne, *Coup d'Oeil sur Beloeil*, 1795 edn, Book I.

30 I am grateful to the present Prince de Ligne and his archivist Quentin Wicquart for information about Beloeil. M. Wicquart suggests that the design may have been offered to the Prince by his favoured architect, the Frenchman François-Joseph Bélanger.

31 De Ligne, *Coup d'Oeil sur Beloeil*, Book III.57. The estate is now within the city boundaries and much reduced in size.

32 De Ligne was buried there in 1814.

33 J. Sisa, 'Landscape Gardening in Hungary and its English Connections', *Acta Hist.Art.Hung.*Tomus 35, 1990–92.

34 Hungarian National Museum, Historical Picture Gallery; information from Dr Jozsef Sisa.

35 Hunt, *The Picturesque Garden in Europe*, p. 170.

36 Ibid., pp. 168–9.

37 The original architect's elevation is in the estate archives (information kindly supplied by James Robertson).

38 Hunt, *The Picturesque Garden in Europe*, p. 166.

39 John Plaw, *Ferme Ornée* (London, 1795). See Chapter Four, pp. 102–3.

40 Grohmann, *Gartenmagazin für Liebhaber englischer Garten* (Leipzig, 1797), vol. 1, pl. 10.

41 Published as *Andeutungen uber Landshaftsgartnerei* in Stuttgart in 1834, translated into English as *Hints on Landscape Gardening* in 1917, and the English version reprinted in Basel 2014.

42 Prince Hermann von Pückler-Muskau, *Hints on Landscape Gardening*, p. 89.

43 Ibid.

44 Originally French, he had left France because he was Protestant.

45 Sven-Ingvar Andersson and Inge Mejer Antonsen, *Liselund on Møn* (National Museum of Denmark, 2005).

46 The monkey commemorates a family pet that by tradition saved the Calmette family from the 1755 Lisbon earthquake. There was a monument to the same event in the Marienborg garden, so the story is very likely true.

47 Denmark's leading neoclassical sculptor of the generation preceding Thorvaldsen.

48 Classen bought the estate in1768 and laid out a small English-style

park behind the house. This contains a thatched ice house of 1779. Steen Estvad Petersen, *Den Denske Herregård* (Copenhagen, 1999), also illustrates a little thatched Gothic cottage at Lovenborg, Zealand, and a thatched, half-timbered summerhouse-cum-gazebo with verandah at Sanderumgård, Fyn.

49 Illustrated in C. Hirschfeld, *Théorie de l'art des jardins* (1779 etc.), vol. V, p. 413.

50 Peter Hayden, *Russian Parks and Gardens* (London, 2005), p. 118.

51 De Ligne, *Coup d'Oeil sur Beloeil*, Book IV.31.

52 Cited by Hayden, *Russian Parks and Gardens*, p. 117.

53 Reminiscent of later Welsh examples such as Brynkinallt; see Chapter Six. pp. 144–5.

54 Dimitri Schvidkovsky, *The Empress and the Architect* (New Haven and London, 1996), pp. 135–6. The interior has been lost and the building now serves as a tea room. Information from Lisa Renne.

55 Hayden, *Russian Parks and Gardens*, p. 118.

56 Schvidkovsky, *The Empress and the Architect*, p. 153.

57 Hayden, *Russian Parks and Gardens*, pp. 132–4. Elisabeth Selse, 'Gatchina's Birch Pavilion', *World of Interiors* (November 1994). There was a minute kitchen from which a servant could serve refreshments. The building was destroyed in World War II and recreated as accurately as possible in 1976.

58 De Ligne, *Coup d'Oeil sur Beloeil*, Book IV.30.

59 Hayden, *Russian Parks and Gardens*, pp. 166–7.

60 Ibid., p. 148.

61 Paul's second son Constantine had renounced his claim to the throne in 1823.

62 Yelena Boitsova et al., *Alexandria* (St Petersburg, 2000), p. 1.

63 Henry Ledoux, 'A Cottage for a King', *House and Garden*, January 1993, pp. 78–83.

64 Ibid.

65 The Gothic furniture is said to have been designed by Menelaws and made at the Gambs furniture factory in St Petersburg. Schvidkovsky, *The Empress and the Architect*, p. 236.

66 To the south of the cottage the Aleksandrinsky Park was informally landscaped by Menelaws. The artificial lake had three islands, one with a Swiss cottage by I. I. Charlemagne. Also close by was Stakenschneider's Farm Palace of 1838 onwards. Hayden, *Russian Parks and Gardens*, p. 161.

CHAPTER NINE

DISTANT SHORES

CAPE COLONY

It was to be expected that as the British Empire expanded it would export British (or rather English) architectural styles to its new colonies, at least to the limited extent of providing accommodation for homesick British officials, expatriates and their wives. Although the psychological need may have been greater in somewhere like India, with its overpoweringly strong local culture and architectural traditions,[1] the process was actually easier in a colony where the indigenous culture was less dominant or where the scenery and/or weather could be considered to approximate to something back home. In the American colonies, of course, the introduction of English architectural styles had been going on since the seventeenth century, but, as will be discussed, the debut of the cottage idiom had to wait until well after independence was achieved in 1776. On the other side of the Atlantic, but in the southern hemisphere, Britain had acquired the southern tip of Africa from the Dutch following the Battle of Muizenberg in 1795. Returned temporarily to Holland by the 1802 Peace of Amiens, it was reoccupied by the British after the Battle of Blaauwberg in 1806, and British possession was confirmed by the Anglo-Dutch Treaty in 1814. The colony had been established in 1652 by the Dutch East India Company as a staging post en route to India and the Far East, and it was even more valuable for this purpose as the British hold on India gathered pace in the early nineteenth century.

For the British the Cape of Good Hope, or Cape Colony as it became known, offered a beautiful and richly varied landscape that at times reminded them of Scotland, together with a climate far more temperate and agreeable than that of India. The architecture bequeathed by the Dutch was characteristically simple, whitewashed and thatched, and even those buildings ornamented with curvaceous baroque gables were visibly part of a comfortingly European culture. For the British officers and administrators who began to arrive, often with their wives, from the 1790s onwards, it was not particularly difficult either to adapt the simple Cape Dutch vernacular buildings they took over, enhancing them with dormers, verandahs and French windows, or to build new ones reminding them still more piquantly of home.[2] Since this was now the heyday of the cottage orné in England, it was almost inevitable that the idiom would soon be reflected in Cape Colony. The first such reflection was a house called The Vineyard [fig 9/1], built as early as 1798 as a retreat for Lady Anne Barnard, wife of the Colonial Secretary. This went up on the banks of the Liesbeek river, overlooked by the towering flanks of Table Mountain. By Cape standards it was quite a large house, but its simple cottagey exterior, with French windows within a rustic verandah supporting a sweeping

OPPOSITE **Rotch House, New Bedford, Massachusetts, A. J. Davies, watercolour**

LEFT **9/1 The Vineyard, Cape Colony**

thatched roof, belied its size, not to mention the fashionable accoutrements of the interior. Lady Anne imported her English wallpapers and knick-knacks and designed the elegant chaises longues, made up for her by Malay carpenters and upholstered by regimental tailors. The cottage prompted General Dundas to exclaim, ''Pon my word, this is a dashing thing to build a house such as this at the Cape of Good Hope, Lady Anne!'[3]

A generation later a further architectural lead from the colony's social apex was provided in about 1825 when the Governor, Lord Charles Somerset,[4] and his wife converted existing Dutch buildings into their Marine Villa [fig 9/2]. The proximity of the sea provided an opportunity for the bathing then becoming medically fashionable back home. Like many English cottages ornés, it was of one main storey, with the thatched roof descending onto a verandah; in this case the verandah posts alternated with pendant swags, perhaps of fabric, perhaps of wood, and all painted

bright green.[5] Not surprisingly, where governors and their wives led, those further down the social pecking order followed. The garrison village of Wynberg was a favourite place for houses with cottage overtones. A charmingly naive drawing of the 1830s records Mr Carey's Cottage, with its sash windows, thatched roof and treillage porch, and similar features were found on Major Rogers's villa there. Houses with names like Rose Cottage, Ashdene and Belmont, accompanied by gardens with honeysuckle, hollyhocks and rustic summerhouses, sprang up in the colony's main residential areas, somewhat to the bemusement of intrepid travellers who arrived in expectation of something more savage.[6]

This Regency Picturesque idyll was to prove sadly transient, especially once the British left in 1910, and now none of the Cape cottages survives, although they provided the prototype for many thousands of houses built in South Africa later in the nineteenth century.

THE AMERICAN COTTAGE

The newly independent United States of America might have been expected to strike out in a fresh architectural direction influenced by France rather than by its old colonial power, but in fact British influence continued to be paramount. Robert Adam's idiom was the key factor in the development of the so-called Federal style, while immigrant architects from the old country were to play a powerful role in cities and towns along the eastern seaboard – Benjamin Latrobe in Washington, Baltimore and Philadelphia, George Hadfield in Washington, William Jay in Savannah, and Richard Upjohn in New York and New England, to name just four. There was also the enduring influence of English pattern books, both for classical idioms and for the Gothic.

In eighteenth- and early nineteenth-century America, the Gothic idiom was known via English pattern books but only very occasionally used. Batty Langley's *Gothic Architecture Improved* (1747) crossed the Atlantic and was plundered (as it was in the British Isles) for details such as doorcases and windows. An early instance was the porch of Gunston Hall, Virginia (by the English joiner and architect William Buckland, 1756), a rather later one the portal of Old St Patrick's Cathedral in Lower Manhattan (by Joseph-François Mangin, 1809–15). Gothic then began to be used more widely for churches, especially Episcopalian and Catholic ones. In 1805 Latrobe proposed a Gothic design for Baltimore's Catholic cathedral, soon abandoned in favour of the neoclassical one that was built. Nevertheless, he was the author of the earliest complete Gothic house to be built in America, the Sedgeley Villa on the outskirts of Philadelphia, for which he supplied a local merchant called William Cramond with designs in about 1799. Despite being picturesquely sited on a steep ridge above the Schuylkill River, the house itself was an entirely unpicturesque, symmetrical Gothic villa, with colonnades of vaguely Gothic columns running between low pyramid-roofed towers at the angles of the building. The accompanying tenant's lodge was America's first Gothic cottage. As designed by Latrobe it was a three-bay, single-storey building, the wider centre bay having a deep four-centred Tudor arch that sheltered a Gothic door, flanking lancets and Gothic fanlight. Although in that state there was nothing orné about the design, late nine-

teenth-century alterations did give the building more the character of a cottage orné, with fretted eaves, tall moulded terracotta chimneys and projecting 'Stick Style' wooden porches [fig 9/3]. Whereas the main villa disappeared in 1855, the tenant's lodge survives as the headquarters of the Fairmount Park Preservation Trust.[7]

Such Gothic church schemes as were produced were initially more often than not by immigrant English architects, notably Richard Upjohn's Trinity Church, Wall Street, New York, of 1841–6.[8] Already in the 1810s English publications such as *Ackermann's Repository* were on sale in the United States, and J. B. Papworth's *Rural Residences* of 1818 (many of whose plates had already been published in the *Repository*) subsequently achieved popularity, not least through its visually attractive format. Another English pattern book, Thomas Dearn's *Sketches in Architecture*, was in the library of the Boston Athenaeum by 1827.[9] Accordingly, in the second quarter of the century the influence of the English Picturesque began to make itself felt, with formal classical villas giving way to informal, asymmetrical houses, some of them Gothic. This was considered to accord better with rural settings, and it is no accident that Gothic flourished first in America in the Hudson Valley, a centre of landscape painting and poetic literature.

Sedgeley Villa apart, America's earliest substantial Gothic house may have been Glen Ellen near Baltimore, built in 1832–3 by Robert Gilmor and inspired by his visit to Sir Walter Scott's Abbotsford; the architects were Ithiel Town and Alexander Jackson Davis from New York. Bristling as it was with castellations, pinnacles and turrets, however, Glen Ellen was definitely not a cottage. One of the earliest and best-known Gothic houses to qualify for the appellation 'cottage' was designed by Richard Upjohn,

who had arrived in America in 1829. This was Kingscote, at Newport, Rhode Island, completed in 1839. Built for George Noble Jones, a Savannah plantation owner, it was one of the first summer 'cottages' in Newport, and a very modest precursor of the sumptuously immodest mansions that were erected along the waterfront from the 1850s. Upjohn's design [fig 9/4] is picturesquely irregular and very much in the Tudor cottage vein, with Tudor dripmoulds to the windows, numerous gables and dormers with frilly eaves boards, clustered chimneys and sections of verandah.[10] The Tudor Gothic detail continues inside, with a screen of three four-centred arches separating the front door from the staircase hall, Gothic dado and Tudor dripmoulds to the doors.[11]

Upjohn failed to follow up on this innovative project and the remainder of his career was devoted overwhelmingly to the design of churches – to the extent that he is honoured with a feast day in the calendar of the Episcopal Church. Instead, the pioneer of the American cottage was to be the New York City architect Alexander Jackson Davis (1803–1892). Davis was enormously prolific, and like an English Regency architect could design in any style, including Greek Revival, Italianate, Tudor Gothic, neo-Norman, Swiss and even Egyptian; he could indeed be seen as America's answer to John Nash or Thomas Hopper. He

began his architectural career in the New York office of Ithiel Town, one of America's leading Greek Revival architects, and remained in partnership with Town until the latter's death in 1844. In the years before the Civil War his commissions came from as far afield as Kentucky, Michigan, Virginia, Indiana, North Carolina and even New Orleans. With his own pattern book *Rural Residences*, published in 1837, he announced his interest in the English Gothic and cottage styles.[12] The introductory Advertisement states:

The bald and uninteresting aspect of our houses must be obvious to every traveller; and to those who are familiar with the picturesque Cottages and Villas of England, it is positively painful to witness here the wasteful and tasteless expenditure of money on building. . . . The Greek Temple form, perfect in itself, and well adapted as it is to public edifices, and even to town mansions, is inappropriate for country residences, and yet it is the only style ever attempted in our more costly habitations. The English collegiate style is for many reasons to be preferred. It admits of greater variety both of plan and outline; – is susceptible of additions from time to time, while its bay windows, oriels, turrets and chimney shafts, give a pictorial effect to the elevation.[13]

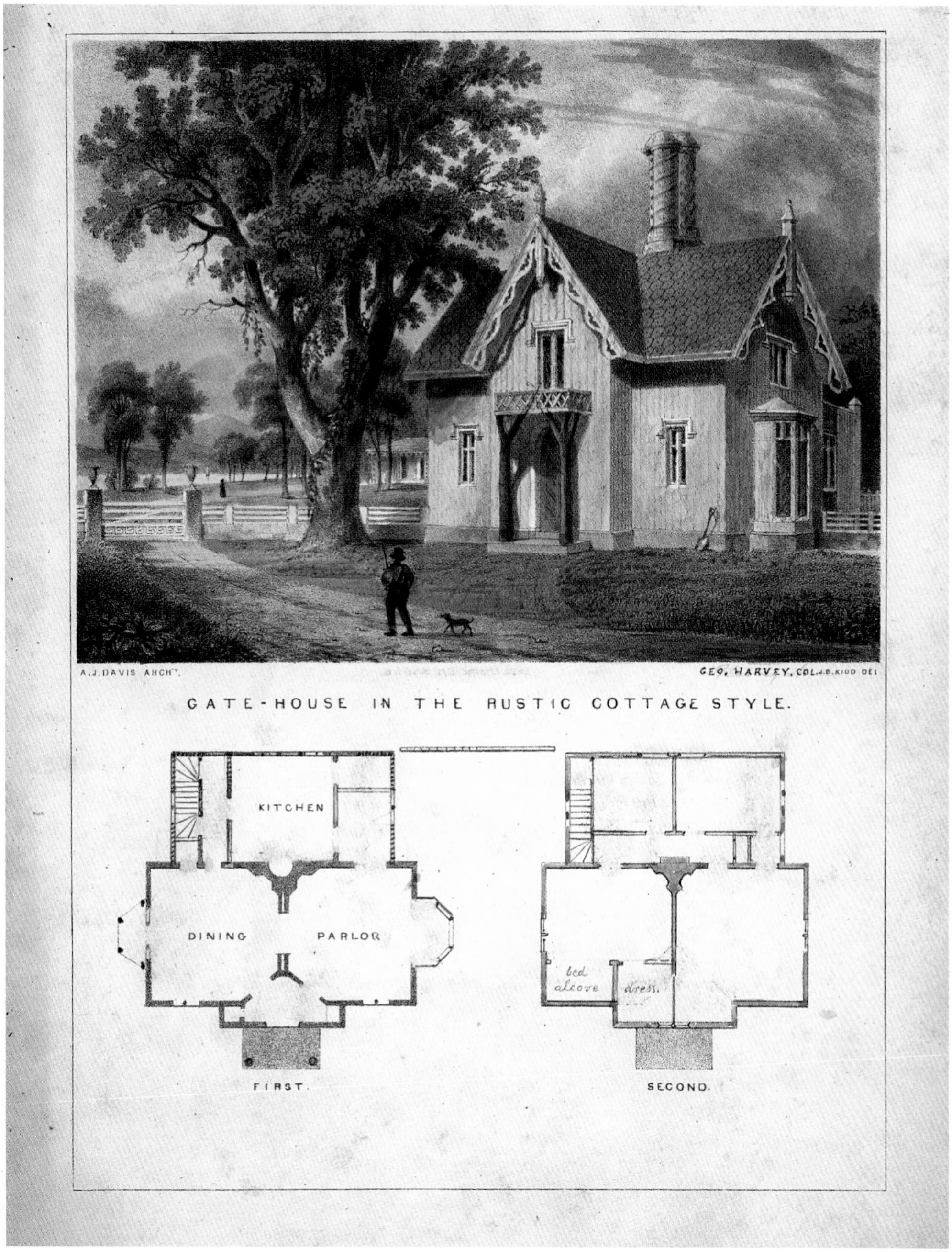

9/5 Lodge to Blithewood, Barrytown, New York: perspective and plans by A. J. Davis

A.J. DAVIS ARCH.T.   GEO. HARVEY, COL. &.B.KIDD DEL

GATE-HOUSE IN THE RUSTIC COTTAGE STYLE.

KITCHEN

DINING   PARLOR

bed alcove   dress.

FIRST.   SECOND.

Rural Residences contains just eight designs: 1 Cottage Orné; 2 Farmer's House; 3 Villa in the English Collegiate Style; 4 Village Church; 5 Gate-House in the Rustic Cottage Style; 6 Villa in the Oriental Style; 7 American House; 8 Village School-House. Of these, No. 1 is not a cottage orné in the sense adopted by this book, and No. 5 is the relevant design for the cottage theme. The text explains that it had already been erected as the lodge (or 'gate-house') to Blithewood [fig 9/5], near Barrytown on the Hudson River, for R. Donaldson Esq.[14] The construction comprised a foundation and basement of stone, supporting a wood-framed superstructure, boarded vertically – that is, the board-and-batten facing that was to become standard in American cottages, here making possibly its first appearance. The porch was of cedar boles, with a rustic trellis balcony. Bargeboards (called 'vergeboards') with pendants to the gables reinforced the orné element, and the roof covering was of shingles cut to hexagonal shape. 'The whole exterior', noted Davis, 'is painted and grained in imitation of oak'. The accompanying plan showed that the ground floor consisted of an interconnecting parlour and dining room, with kitchen behind. Looking ahead to the possibility of commissions for larger cottages, Davis added that, 'If this design should be adopted for a summer retreat, it may be much improved by enlarging the porch and windows.'[15]

Sure enough, in 1838 Davis designed a larger version of the Blithewood lodge for Henry Sheldon at Millbrook [fig 9/6], Tarrytown, also on the Hudson River. Thanks to its prompt publication in Andrew Jackson Downing's *Theory and Practice of Landscape Gardening* of 1841,[16] Millbrook's prominent bargeboarded main gable with pinnacled finial became almost a *sine qua non* of American Gothic cottages. Also to become standard issue were the projecting ground-floor bay window with Gothic window above, the flanking sections of treillage verandah and the tall clustered chimneys. Verandahs in particular, used as outdoor living spaces, became henceforth an important element in American country houses, whether cottages or not.[17] From here onwards Davis was to design one or two cottages most years until around 1850, when the commissions seem to have slackened. The tally includes two in Rhinebeck, in the Hudson Valley, one in 1841 for Dr Federal Vanderburgh, the other in 1844 for Henry Delamater, a banker. The Vanderburgh house had what became the usual format for such a cottage, with a central steep-sided gable with cusped eaves boards and finial, a Tudor Gothic verandah wrapped around, and lofty clustered chimneys. The house does not survive but its plan and elevation are known from Davis's drawing.[18] The Delamater house, which still exists, is a variant on the same formula.[19]

One of Davis's most attractive cottage designs is the Rotch House [fig 9/7], in the whaling port of New Bedford, Massachusetts, built in 1845–6 for William J. Rotch, a member of one of the town's leading whaling families. He was given the land, on a rural part of the family's New Bedford estate, by his grandfather, but the house was moved from its original location in 1908 and has lost its rural setting. Like so many American cottages, the building is of timber, with a roof of wood shingles laid diamond-wise as specified by Davis. In this case the big central gable, with its elaborately cusped and sub-cusped eaves, is pierced by a Tudor arch to form a porch, above which is an oriel window and above that, tight into the gable, a tiny Gothic window with traceried balcony.[20] The plan has a central hall flanked by two main rooms each side on both floors; on the ground floor an octagonal entrance hall leads to the stairhall at the rear. To the left are the living room and library, to the right the dining room and kitchen, separated by a pantry. The Tudor Gothic detail of the exterior carries through into the interior, with panelled doors and crenellated cornices, and marble chimneypieces. The house achieved early fame by being published in A. J. Downing's *The Architecture of Country Houses* in 1850, where Downing wrote of it, 'The character expressed by the exterior of this design is that of a man or family of domestic tastes, but with strong aspirations after something higher than social pleasures.' Prior to 1832 Rotch had been a devout Quaker, but his 'aspirations' led to business and political interests. In 1842 he and his brother founded the New Bedford Cordage Company, and from 1842 he served two terms in the Massachusetts legislature. In 1872 he moved his family into a Federal period mansion that had belonged to an uncle, thereby confirming his pre-eminence in New Bedford society. For some reason Rotch's Quaker father considered the 'rural' cottage 'disgusting';[21] what he thought about a Quaker living in a Federal mansion is not recorded.

For some at least, the Gothic cottage, as the potential architectural symbol of a wholesome rural life, had clear associations of social reform and Christian benevolence attached to it – in 1869 it was put forward as the very embodiment of the 'Christian Home' in the *American Woman's Home* by Catherine E. Beecher and her sister Harriet Beecher Stowe.[22] Davis's Cottage Lawn, Oneida, New York, fits this pattern, being built in 1849–50 for a devout and upright Presbyterian banker Niles Higinbotham at the time of his marriage (his father had effectively founded the town).[23] Equally, however, the idiom seems to have appealed

9/7 Rotch House, New Bedford,
Massachusetts, A. J. Davis, watercolour

to clients whose background and aspirations were anything but rural. An example is the Henry G. Thompson House at Thompsonville, Connecticut. The client here was a factory owner – indeed the town itself had grown up around the carpet mill established by his father in 1829 – who had previously lived in a Greek Revival house. In 1848 Davis designed him a board-and-batten cottage with Tudoresque porch and verandah, Tudor trim to the windows, and sinuous eaves.

Though Davis culled ideas from English pattern books, he argued (in the draft for an introduction to a proposed later edition of *Rural Residences*) that just copying English designs would not do as they 'are on a scale far more extended and expensive than we can accomplish with our limited means'. Interestingly, he placed far more emphasis on the inclusion of mod cons than would be true of his English models, since (as his friend Andrew Jackson Downing wrote in his book *Cottage Residences* of 1842) he acknowledged that in the democratic United States it was difficult to find good domestic servants who would stay for any length of time (this was presumably more of a problem in the northern than the southern states). Labour-saving devices were therefore strongly advised – he particularly recommended 'for cottages . . . the rising cupboard or dumb waiter, the speaking tube, and the rotary pump'.[24]

Notwithstanding Davis's longevity and prolific output, it was his friend Downing who in the course of his short career (he died aged only thirty-six) proved by far the most influential popularizer of 'Romantic' domestic architecture in America, particularly by publishing designs by Davis and others. He published just three books: *A Treatise on the Theory and Practice of Landscape Gardening, Adapted to North America* (1841); *Cottage Residences* (1842, in collaboration with Davis); and *The Architecture of Country Houses* (1850). In addition, however, he directed his American readers to English pattern books, including Robert Lugar's *Villa Architecture* of 1828 and publications by J. C. Loudon, J. B. Papworth, P. F. Robinson and the little-known Thomas Frederick Hunt.[25] Downing's own *Cottage Residences* was actually reviewed by Loudon, who wrote that 'it cannot fail to be a great service in adding to the comforts and improving the taste of the citizens of the United States'.[26] Downing himself commented in the 1849 edition of his *Treatise* on the rapid spread of the English cottage style (what he preferred to call 'Rural Gothic'):

It is gratifying to see the progressive improvement in Rural Architecture, which within a few years past has evinced itself in various parts of the country, and particularly on the banks of the Hudson and Connecticut Rivers, as well as the suburbs of our largest cities.[27]

When Downing died in 1852, in a steamboat explosion on the Hudson, the *South-Western Monthly* of Nashville, Tennessee, proclaimed: 'he still lives! Is not his monument already on every hilltop and in every valley, in every town and every village where Gothic art expresses its vertical lines, lofty towers and pointed arches?'[28] Davis and Downing were also to inspire other, more home-grown pattern books, for instance William Ranlett's *The Architect* (published 1847–9). The latter provided the model[29] for Tudor Hall, Bel Air, Maryland, a modest cottage built in the 1850s for the English-born actor Junius Brutus Booth (father of the infamous John Wilkes Booth, assassin of Abraham Lincoln).

Davis's last recorded cottage seems to have been the John G. Baker House in South Orange, New Jersey,[30] whose construction in 1861–5 coincided exactly with the duration of the Civil War. The war inevitably resulted in his commissions diminishing, and after its conclusion tastes and circumstances had changed. The great majority of Davis's cottage commissions were in New York and adjoining states – Connecticut, Massachusetts, New Jersey – with one in Virginia[31] and one in Ohio.[32] However, his influence, and that of Downing, was strongly felt much further afield, at least until the outbreak of war put an end to house building in the southern states, especially ones designed or influenced by northern architects. Davis's published cottage designs were simple enough to be readily copied by local carpenters and builders – indeed the style became widely known as 'Carpenter Gothic' – and thereby provided the basis for a simplified version that could be adapted for farmhouses, homes for farm workers, and indeed rural churches.

The Davis/Downing influence is certainly clear with Roseland Cottage [figs 9/8, 9] at Woodstock, Connecticut. It was built for Henry Chandler Bowen, the son of a local storekeeper who moved to New York at the age of twenty and developed a hugely successful dry goods emporium specializing in silks. He married in 1844 and in 1846

commissioned a summerhouse back in Woodstock from the English architect Joseph Wells, who was already known for his Gothic churches. The construction is of the board-and-batten technique recommended by Davis, in whose style it very much is. It also seems to relate closely to plate XXIV in Downing's *Architecture of Country Houses*, 'Cottage Villa in the Rural Gothic Style', in this case retaining the projecting oriel window in the central gable, the arch below being filled with a large Perpendicular Gothic traceried window. The gable itself is steeply pitched, with boldly cusped eaves boards and prominent central finial. The flanking verandahs combine Tudor arches, panels of quatrefoiled trellis and a cusped cresting. The paired chimneys are patterned as they would be on an English cottage orné. The present strong pink colour of the exterior is not what is shown on the watercolour attributed to Wells, which has it an ochre-stone colour. Much of the furniture ordered for the house is still in place, and a good deal is likewise Gothic in style, as is much of the internal detailing, though overlaid with more Victorian decoration installed in the 1880s when the house was updated.[33] In this case the cottage idiom was probably chosen by Bowen for its supposed Christian associations, since he was a pillar of the New England community and founded a newspaper that specialized in publishing sermons and religious tracts – though in the years preceding the Civil War he avoided nailing his colours explicitly to the abolitionist cause, which he thought might be bad for business with the southern states.

The Morrill Homestead [fig 9/10] at Strafford, Vermont demonstrates what the American and English pattern books made possible, since it was designed by Justin Smith Morrill (1810–1898) for himself and built in 1848–51. Morrill married in the year of its completion and used it as a summer home, since as a politician he spent most of his time in Washington DC. Having left school at fifteen because his family could not afford to send him to college, he became self-educated in business, architecture, horticulture and politics, serving in the House of Representatives and Senate for over forty years (his main legacy was legislation to make possible the establishment of state-funded universities). Like all these American cottages, his house is built of wood (in this case with slate roof). The two main gables have particularly elaborate eaves, and projecting bay windows with a first-floor window over with a little canopy.

The interior detail is mostly Gothic, though the main parlour is more Greek Revival.

A good example of the cottage in the southern states is Rosehill Cottage [fig 9/11] near Beaufort, South Carolina.[34] The land on which it was eventually built was acquired by James Kirk in 1828, and probably given by him to his daughter on her marriage to her first cousin, John Kirk. He had received his MD from the University of Pennsylvania in 1834, and he contrived to combine his medical practice with a successful career as a planter. Construction of Rosehill began shortly before the outbreak of the Civil War in 1861. The likely architect was E. B. White of Charleston, who probably designed the Gothic church in nearby Bluffton. The cottage is of the usual board-and-batten construction, with high, steeply pitched roofs punctuated by sharply pointed dormers (the eaves in this case are all plain). The main gable projects over a Gothic loggia which contains the front door, with a section of frilly cast-iron verandah asymmetrically to one side. In characteristic Southern fashion, the front door leads into a spacious hall with sweeping staircase. The arrival of Yankee troops was so sudden that the Kirks are said to have been caught in the middle of a meal, and construction was inevitably interrupted. Mrs Kirk died in 1864, and her widower apparently failed to complete the house, so that after the war it was nicknamed Kirk's Folly. It was tenanted until sold by the family in 1928, and it seems the interior was finally completed after its purchase by John and Betsy Sturgeon in 1946.[35] Other examples of the influence of Downing's publications in South Carolina

include an undocumented cottage at Barnwell, built about 1848 (board-and-batten, with Tudor Gothic windows and steeply pitched gables with decorative eaves boards).[36] A Gothic cottage called Sunnyside at Greenwood, built by a local farmer around 1851, seems to have been inspired by Washington Irving's home of the same name in the Hudson Valley.[37]

In the same state, the town of Graniteville was founded in 1846 by William Gregg, who started life as a Pennsylvania orphan and became a prosperous South Carolina merchant. It was intended as a model industrial and social community and included forty 'cottages of the Gothic order of architecture . . . after handsome Architectural plans', for which he sought advice at the outset from Richard Upjohn of New York. Upjohn certainly designed the Baptist church and the local architect E. B. White the Methodist church, but it is not known who designed the cottagey houses, which were all board-and-batten with decorative eaves boards.[38]

Georgia's first Gothic building was the State House at Milledgeville, as remodelled in 1827 by an English engineer called Hamilton Fulton. Gothic cottages had to wait another two decades, and as elsewhere the published works of Davis and Downing provided the sources. Woodlands at Clarkesville, a summer resort in the mountains of north Georgia, was built in 1848 as a derivative of Design II in Downing's Cottage Residences (1842).[39] The architect was Jarvis Van Buren, a carpenter from New York State. Two years later he designed another Gothic cottage, Blythewood, just across the road, which (appropriately for a carpenter) is notable for its particularly intricate and varied eaves boards.[40]

The earliest documented Gothic house in Louisiana was Orange Grove, built in 1847–9 near Braithwaite, on the east bank of the Mississippi. The client was Thomas Asheton Morgan, an absentee cotton planter from Philadelphia; the architect, William L. Johnston (1811–1849) also came from Philadelphia. His design, showing steep gables with deeply cusped eaves boards, Tudor dripmoulds to the windows and a Tudor verandah in wrought iron, and clustered chimneys, survives in Louisiana State Museum, although the house itself burned in 1982.[41] A yet more striking Louisiana cottage was Afton Villa [fig 9/12], near St Francisville. Here a small four-room cottage of 1790 was transformed in 1849

by the wealthy planter David Barrow for his young Kentucky bride.[42] Thirty-six rooms were added and encased in a memorable Gothic exterior, with a double-height verandah that was a Gothic equivalent to the classical ones so popular on the plantation houses of the Deep South. The architect is unknown but Mills Lane speculates that Barrow might have got the design from James Dakin, architect of the Gothic State Capitol at Baton Rouge, via his friend Maunsell White, for whom Dakin had designed a Gothic villa.[43] Timber construction inevitably increased combustibility and Afton Villa was unfortunately destroyed by fire in 1963.[44]

The Briggs-Staub House [fig 9/13] in the Garden District of New Orleans was built in 1849 for Cuthbert Bullit, a gambler who refused to pay for it, whereupon it was bought by an English insurance executive, Charles Briggs. The architect was the Irish-born Protestant architect James Gallier senior (1798–1866). Gallier, who emigrated to the United States in 1832 when he became bankrupt in England, was born 'Gallagher', changing his name to the more French-sounding Gallier when he moved to New Orleans in 1834; he and his wife drowned when the paddle steamer in which they were sailing from New York to New Orleans sank in a hurricane. In the 1840s the Garden District was being developed for English-speaking Protestant northerners. Their houses were almost entirely in variations of classicism, and they seem to have associated Gothic with Catholicism, so this house was an isolated exception. The windows are mostly pointed, and the front door sits within a verandah of depressed Tudor arches topped by a cast-iron Gothic balustrade. It leads into a central hall, and the Gothic idiom is continued in the ground-floor rooms. The exterior eschews the usual frilly eaves. There are corresponding Gothic servants' quarters adjoining.

Suburban New Orleans has two other examples of the cottage genre: the Nathaniel Newton Wilkinson House on South Carrollton Avenue of 1850, built, unusually, on a cruciform plan, and in Tudor Gothic, with a verandah in one of the angles and eaves boards fretted to different patterns; and the 'Swiss Villa' [fig 9/14] (as it was called in a local paper on its completion in 1868) at 3627 Carondelet Street. This was another Cuthbert Bullit commission, this time from German-born architect Edward Gottheil, and was built originally on St Charles Avenue. The plan has the

conventional centre hall, but the exterior is striking, with its far-projecting gable edged with a fretted fringe reminiscent of a Victorian railway station.[45]

Andrew Jackson Downing's influence extended into Mississippi in the shape of Manship House, Jackson [fig 9/15]. This was built in 1857 for Charles Manship, one of the town's leading businessmen, who served as mayor in 1862–3 and surrendered Jackson to the Yankee General Sherman on 16 July 1863.[46] Manship (born in 1812) came from Maryland and trained in Baltimore as a maker of painted furniture. In 1835 he travelled to New Orleans and then up the Mississippi, settling in Jackson in 1836. He flourished as a decorator, marrying and eventually doing well enough to build his own house. He died in 1895 and

the house remained in his family until 1975. Like Roseland Cottage in faraway Connecticut, it is modelled on plate XXIV in Downing's *Architecture of Country Houses*, adapted to the southern climate by eliminating the upper floor, raising the house on a high, open plinth, extending the central hall and lengthening the windows to the floor, all with a view to maximizing ventilation. The simple trellised panels of Downing's verandah are here replaced by elaborately frilly cast ironwork. As a demonstration of his own decorative skills Manship himself grained and marbled the interior surfaces – pine and cypress doors in imitation of mahogany, the papered walls of the dining room to look like oak panelling, the wooden chimneypieces marbled.

The outbreak of the Civil War brought an abrupt end

to the influence of northern designers in the South, but once the bitterness and disruption had started to fade there were some southern signs of revived interest in the cottage idiom. Rugby, Tennessee was an utopian community founded in 1880 by the English author Thomas Hughes, and one or two of the houses have cottagey features – for instance the one called Kingston Lisle, built in 1884 for Hughes himself, who actually came from the tiny village of Kingston Lisle in Berkshire. The St Francisville Inn [fig 9/16], in the Louisiana town of the same name, is one of numerous examples where, as in England, the cottage orné vocabulary was the starting point for an evolution into something more distinctively late nineteenth century or 'Victorian'. The sharply pointed gables that rise above its front verandah still frame Gothic windows, but the apexes are filled with elaborate fretwork panels instead of the cusped eaves that would have been expected in earlier decades. Perhaps the most extravagant and striking of all these late cottages is Ardoyne Plantation [fig 9/17] near Houma, Louisiana. Built as late as 1894 by Louisiana state senator John D. Shaffer for his wife, who asked for a cottage to be erected while she travelled abroad for her health, it was constructed by the estate carpenters and labourers during breaks from the sugar cane harvest. The architects were the New Orleans firm of W. C. Williams, and the cypress and pine of which it is built were sourced on the plantation. Although said to have been copied from a castle in Scotland, the exterior has nothing whatever Scottish about it, being an extreme example of the cottage orné, with Tudor Gothic verandah, Gothic windows and frilly edgings to every gable. At one corner the gables rise with exaggerated steepness to form a steeple-like tower. In broad daylight it is extraordinary enough; at night it must appear to some as a suitable setting to Hitchcock's *Psycho*.[47]

While the story of the cottage orné in the United States is inevitably largely one of individual examples, one extraordinary exception is the so-called 'Cottage City' at Oak Bluffs [fig 9/18], on the island of Martha's Vineyard, Massachusetts. This originated with the Methodist summer camp meeting at Wesleyan Grove, which began as a tented encampment in 1835. By the late 1850s this had grown enormously, and in 1859 the first of the cottages appeared that were gradually to supersede the tents. This was the Mason and Lawton Cottage, prefabricated and shipped out from Rhode Island. In 1864 four more cottages

went up among the 500 tents; four years later there were no fewer than 203, and by the end of the decade 250. They were built by carpenters (the majority from Edgartown and New Bedford), in a tongue-and-groove version of Carpenter's Gothic. Typically they were two-storeyed and one room wide, two up and two down. The gingerbread trim that gave them their individuality was added last, and some of the resulting cottages were considerably fancier than might have been expected of Methodists. Today some 200 survive, making this easily the largest concentration of cottage orné derivatives anywhere.[48]

AUSTRALIA AND NEW ZEALAND

If Britain's Antipodean colonies were slower to evince an interest in the cottage idiom than the Cape, it was due not just to the sheer distance from the mother country but also to the circumstances prevailing there. Australia was of course initially treated as a penal colony, in which the refinements of the cottage orné must have seemed superfluous even for the small governing and administrative class. Nor, unlike the Cape, was there an indigenous culture in any way related to what the colonists were familiar with back home. Neither was there the money available to spend on architectural niceties since, unlike the Cape and still more so India, conquest was not primarily related to commerce and trade, and the priority was to establish a toe-hold in a completely unfamiliar and hostile environment. In the case of Australia it was really General Lachlan Macquarie (1762–1824), fifth and last autocratic governor of New South Wales in the years 1810–21, who oversaw the transition from penal colony to free settlement, and in the process strongly influenced Australia's social, economic and architectural development. He established the plan of central Sydney and other towns while his wife Elizabeth, who had a keen interest in building, brought English pattern books out with her that were utilized by her husband's chosen architect Francis Greenway, a Bristol-born architect who had been transported to the colony for forgery. Many of Greenway's projects (and surprisingly he was allowed to begin private practice almost as soon as he arrived in 1814) were for public buildings, but he also designed private houses.

In fact few if any of the early colonial houses in Australia

could realistically be described as 'cottages' in the English Georgian sense. Experiment Farm Cottage, one of Australia's oldest surviving houses, was built in 1793 on an experimental farm set up at the behest of Governor Philip in 1789. It is, however, an archetypal colonial bungalow,[49] single storeyed with very simple verandah, such as the British in India had learnt were suitable for savagely hot climates.[50] So too is Elizabeth Farm, Parrammatta, Sydney. This is a very early house of the 1790s, remodelled in the 1820s, and once again a typical colonial bungalow with verandah, but absolutely no features that could justify calling it a cottage, still less a cottage orné.

It seems to have taken several decades more before Australian settlers felt confident enough to risk a significant degree of architectural embellishment. A particularly elaborate example is Corio Villa [fig 9/19] at Geelong, Victoria. This was Australia's first prefabricated cast-iron house, made in 1855 in Scotland by Edinburgh iron founders Charles D. Young & Co. (to the design of the firm of Bell & Miller) and shipped out in 1856. Shortly afterwards fire destroyed the Edinburgh foundry, along with the moulds. The very intricate detail, including the fretted piers and arches of the verandahs (incorporating roses and thistles) and the cusped eaves and finials, makes it much more reminiscent of a cottage orné in the conventional sense. Later cottages seem in practice to have looked not to the home country but to the United States for inspiration. Meroogal, at Nowra, New South Wales is a late example, begun in 1885 for the Thorburn family. It is basically a weatherboarded cottage with decorative details: boldly curvaceous eaves to the gables, fancy ironwork panels to the verandahs. The main influence behind the design is the pattern books of A. J. Davis and A. J. Downing, published between 1837 and 1850.

Much the same architectural progression can be observed in New Zealand. Although its coastline was mapped by Captain James Cook in 1769, the islands did not formally become a British colony until 1841, when they were separated off from New South Wales. Between those dates British involvement was largely a matter of low-level trade and the activities of missionaries, so any resultant buildings were very basic.[51] As a colony New Zealand required a governor, and to accommodate him the first Government House, in Auckland, was sent out as a kit from London in 1842. It was in fact one of 'Manning's

Portable Colonial Cottages', which had been advertised in the very first *New Zealand Gazette* in 1839. Single-storeyed with verandahs, like the usual colonial bungalow, everything was constructed of wood except the floors, and perhaps not surprisingly it burnt down in 1848, though not before it had been recorded in a watercolour. Hulme Court, now the second-oldest house to survive in Auckland, was built the year after Government House for Colonel Hulme, commander of British troops in New Zealand, and is a smaller version of its predecessor, except that its main structure is of stone. Single-storeyed, with trellis verandahs on three sides, it again conforms to the standard colonial bungalow model.

As in Australia, it took several decades for a more orné idiom to appear, and in both countries (as in the United States) the idiom was generally referred to as 'Carpenter Gothic'. Highwic [fig 9/20] in Auckland is perhaps the best surviving example of a cottage in the manner already popularized by Davis and Downing in America, and indeed it is interesting that both in New Zealand and Australia the influence was directly from America and only indirectly from the mother country. Highwic was begun in 1862 for Alfred Buckland and his first wife and is based on a plan for 'A Symmetrical Cottage . . . designed in the rural Gothic or English manner' in Downing's *The Architecture of Country Houses*, 1850. Buckland (1825–1903) had in fact originated in Newton Abbot, Devon – indeed his New Zealand house was named after Highweek, the original settlement at Newton Abbot – so he may well have had the opportunity to see some of that county's many cottages ornés before he and his wife emigrated to New Zealand in 1850. There he settled in the Auckland suburb of Newmarket, which had been named after its livestock market, and flourished sufficiently as a horse-breeder, auctioneer, farmer and businessman to be able to afford a smart new house on a ridge overlooking the town. Built of board-and-batten, with Tudor verandah and scalloped eaves, it was extended in the same vein in 1873 (not surprisingly, as Buckland's second marriage added a further eleven children to the ten from his first marriage). Given that by this time Buckland was the largest private landowner in Auckland province, the relative modesty of his house by European or even American standards is an index of the extent to which showy private residences were frowned on in New Zealand.

Another well-preserved cottage with American origins to the design is Oneida Homestead, at Fordell near Whanganui, which was begun in 1870 for Joseph and Mary Burnett to designs by the Whanganui architect and surveyor George Frederic Allen. The Burnetts came to New Zealand from Oneida County in the United States, so it is perhaps to be expected that the board-and-batten construction, steep-pitched gables and dormers, and Tudor trim are all reminiscent of the designs of Davis and Downing.[52]

Both Highwic and Oneida are certainly larger and more elaborate than the New Zealand norm, which might be characterized as modest simplicity. Even Bishopscourt, Auckland, which was built in 1863–6 as the episcopal residence of Bishop Selwyn, could hardly have been called ornate. As a member of the Cambridge Camden Society, Selwyn tried to introduce English fourteenth-cen-

tury Gothic to New Zealand, but the lack of suitable stone around Auckland meant that his churches had to be of wood, which severely limited his options in a style otherwise known as 'Decorated'. Bishopscourt, which was designed by Selwyn's favoured ecclesiastical architect the Reverend Frederick Thatcher,[53] was likewise built mainly of wood, in board-and-batten. It is mainly single-storeyed,[54] with latticed windows and a high cat-slide roof punctuated by chimneys; with the addition of a thatched roof and cusped eaves it would certainly begin to evoke a British cottage orné, but in fact there are no such features.[55] One unusual feature that certainly makes the composition more picturesque but would probably not have been found even on a British episcopal cottage is the octagonal steeple. The complex also incorporated the bishop's private chapel, later moved to another site but shown in early photographs.[56]

1 The homesickness of the British in India resulted in the importation of not only minor items like cucumber slicers but also a herd of English cows, installed in the grounds of the Residence at Lucknow in 1827 in an attempt to recreate an English pastoral idyll. Rosie Llewellyn-Jones, *A Fatal Friendship: The Nawabs, the British, and the City of Lucknow* (Oxford, 1985), p. 56. I owe this reference to John Goodall.

2 Graham Viney and P. Brooke Simons, *The Cape of Good Hope 1806 to 1872* (Houghton, South Africa, 1994), Chapter Eight. I am grateful to Graham Viney for this reference.

3 Quoted by Graham Viney in 'Cape of Good Taste', *World of Interiors* (January 1996), pp. 86–91.

4 Governor 1814–26.

5 The paintwork was originally the dark green available in the colony's naval dockyards, which then bleached in the bright sun. The governor and his wife also transformed the old Government House – which when he first saw it he described as 'a dog kennel' – by adding a bow-ended ballroom, Chinoiserie drawing room and tented verandahs.

6 Viney and Simons, *The Cape of Good Hope*.

7 Michael Fazio and Patrick Snadon, *The Domestic Architecture of Benjamin Henry Latrobe* (Baltimore, 2006), pp. 267–82.

8 The finest Gothic church in the southern states, St Patrick's in New Orleans (begun 1838), was initially designed by the New York architects Charles and James Dakin, taking York Minster as the model for the exterior and Exeter Cathedral for the interior.

9 Information from Sarah E. Mitchell.

10 Upjohn's original watercolour perspective is in the Avery Library, NYDA 1000.011.00761. The Library also has two elevations and two floor plans.

11 At the outbreak of the Civil War in 1861 the Jones family left Newport and in 1864 the house was sold to the King family, who twice remodelled and extended it – the second time (1880) using Stanford White to add a dining room with Tiffany glass – though retaining the original Gothic character. The house was renamed Kingscote in 1880. In 1974 the last of the King family gave it, with its furnishings, to the Preservation Society of Newport County.

12 In the winters of 1827 and 1828 Davis was in Boston and spent time reading in the library of the Athenaeum, where he could have consulted Thomas Dearn's *Sketches in Architecture*, containing at least one design for a cottage orné. Information from Sarah E. Mitchell.

13 In 1854 Benjamin Silliman, a professor at Yale, enunciated a feeling, already well established, that classicism was apt to be 'ponderous and frigid', and said that 'the solemn affectation of Greek and Roman forms was so ridiculous'. Quoted in Marshall B. Davidson, *History of Notable American Houses* (New York, 1971), p. 191.

14 Davis's first important Gothic villa, Knoll at Tarrytown on the Hudson of 1838–42, incorporated a cottage element into a structure that was not otherwise so. He returned in the 1860s to expand it for a new owner, at which point the cottage element disappeared and the much enlarged house was renamed Lyndhurst – still today America's best-known and best-preserved Gothic house.

15 Davis's perspective and plans are in the Avery Library, Columbia University (1940.001.00093R). The lodge no longer exists. Interestingly, Davis's design has much in common with the lodge to Hooke, Chailey, East Sussex, which could be by Decimus Burton but is likely to be slightly later, *c.*1838.

16 Andrew Jackson Downing, *Theory and Practice of Landscape Gardening* (1841), fig. 38.

17 The house has been demolished. Davis also remodelled an existing mill building for Sheldon, turning it into a billiard room with a touch of the Swiss cottage about it.

18 Avery Library (1955.001.00303).

19 For a complete list of Davis's oeuvre, including his cottages, see Amelia Peck ed., *Alexander Jackson Davis, American Architect 1803–1892* (Metropolitan Museum of Art, 1992), pp. 105–19.

20 Davis's watercolour elevation is in the Metropolitan Museum (Harris Brisbane Dick Fund 1924, Acc.no. 24.66.20). The Gothic dormers now flanking the main gable were added *c.*1870 by the Rotches to improve the lighting of the bedrooms.

21 Kingston William Heath, *The Patina of Place* (Knoxville, 2001), p. 32.

22 Ibid., p. 31.

23 The house now belongs to Madison County Historical Society. It is of brick and stucco, the latter painted earth colour and scored to imitate ashlar masonry, but with the usual components.

24 Andrew Jackson Downing, *Cottage Residences* (1842), 1873 edn, cited by Susan Brendel Pandich, 'From Cottages to Castles: The Country House Designs of Alexander Jackson Davis', in Peck, ed., *Alexander Jackson Davis*, p. 61.

25 A. J. Downing, *Treatise on the Theory and Practice of Landscape Gardening* (1841), p. 417.

26 Gillian Darley, *Villages of Vision* (London, 1975), p. 91, footnote 5.

27 Downing, *Treatise on the Theory and Practice of Landscape Gardening*, p.408.

28 Quoted in Mills Lane, *Architecture of the Old South* (New York, 1993), p. 302.

29 William Ranlett, *The Architect* (1847–9), Design XVII, a Gothic parsonage.

30 Demolished.

31 Charles E. Miller House, Chalk Level, Pittsylvania County, 1848.

32 George Washington Penney House, Oakwood, Newport, 1849–51.

33 Historic New England guidebook.

34 Now known as Rose Hill Mansion.

35 William P. Baldwin, *Plantations of the Low Country: South Carolina, 1697–1865* (Greensboro, 1985), pp. 141–3.

36 Mills Lane, *Architecture of the Old South: South Carolina* (Savannah, 1984), pp. 224–5.

37 Ibid., p. 224.

38 Ibid., p. 229.

39 Mills Lane, *Architecture of the Old South: Georgia* (Savannah, 1996), p. 191.

40 Ibid., p. 197.

41 Lane, *Architecture of the Old South*, (New York, 1993), p. 287.

42 Family tradition suggests that she acquired her fondness for Gothic from reading Walter Scott's Waverley novels. Calder Loth and Julius Tronsdale Sadler, *The Only Proper Style: Gothic Architecture in America* (Boston, 1975), pp. 79–80.

43 Ibid., p. 289. Dakin's drawings for Maunsell White's villa do not survive, nor is it known to have been built.

44 David King Gleason, *Plantation Houses of Louisiana and the Natchez Area* (Baton Rouge, 1982), p. 94.

45 Roulhac Toledano, *The National Trust Guide to New Orleans* (New York, 1996), pp. 163–6.

46 Helen Kerr Kempe, *Old Homes of Mississippi: Natchez and the South*, 2nd edn (Gretna, Louisiana, 1989), pp. 114–15.

47 Anne Butler, ed., *Plantation Homes of Louisiana*, Gretna, LA, 2009), p. 62. The interior has a 60-foot entrance hall, from which the carved staircase rises.

48 Peter A. Jones, *Oak Bluffs: The Cottage City Years on Martha's Vineyard* (Charleston, SC, 2007). I am grateful to Calder Loth for drawing my attention to Wesleyan Grove.

49 The term 'bungalow', first found in English in 1696, derives from a Gujarati word meaning 'in the Bengal style', and always applied to a single-storey building with wide verandah. What were originally quite small and humble dwellings expanded under the Raj to become the sizeable homes of British colonial officials.

50 Interestingly, the English architect John Plaw, in his *Sketches for Country Houses, Villas and Rural Dwellings* of 1800, had published a design for two cottages under a single steep pyramidal roof 'with a viranda in the manner of an Indian Bungalow' (pl. VII), so the model was consciously acknowledged. See Chapter Four, fig. 4/10

51 Examples of early mission houses, all predictably very simple, include Kemp House (1820–21), Waimate North (1830) and The Elms (1838), all in the Bay of Islands area. Information from Paul Waite.

52 An 1870s photograph is in the Alexander Turnbull Library, National Library of New Zealand. Another cottagey building showing the Davis influence is the Russell Police Station on the Bay of Islands, from as late as the 1870s.

53 Thatcher (1814–1890) was born in Hastings, on the south coast of England, and emigrated to New Zealand where he was ordained. Having designed many churches for Selwyn he returned to England in 1868.

54 The fall in ground level allows for a stone-built basement originally containing the private rooms. The reception rooms were on the main level, entered from the courtyard.

55 Indeed, thatched roofs were sensibly outlawed in New Zealand from the later nineteenth century.

56 R. H. Thomas, 'Saint Barnabas, the History of Bishop Selwyn's Private Chapel', *Art New Zealand*, 14 (Summer 1979–80). Auckland Public Library has several early photographs of Bishopscourt. The remaining structure is now the residence of the Dean of the Auckland diocese. Information from Paul Waite and Alison Dangerfield.

CHAPTER TEN

POSTLUDE
The ornamental cottage in the Victorian era and after

The cottage orné proper could be said to have peaked in popularity in the British Isles in the last decades of the Georgian era, and the continued publication of quantities of pattern books, whether in first or subsequent editions, was testament to the fact that it was still going strong in the 1830s. However, from the 1840s pattern books increasingly gave way to illustrated periodicals such as *The Builder*, launched in 1843,[1] and the nature of the genre began slowly but surely to evolve away from its original Georgian character.

The legacy of Nash and the Reptons lingered far longer than might have been expected, partly because of the esteem in which Humphry continued to be held (particularly by the influential writer J. C. Loudon) and partly through the enduring popularity of Blaise Hamlet as a model for individual small cottages and for village builders and remodellers. Eastern Lodge [fig 10/1], on the Baring family's Membland estate at Newton Ferrers in Devon, was built as late as 1883, and yet is clearly still closely modelled on Nash's Circular Cottage at Blaise Hamlet of 1810–11.[2] As late as 1898 'grossly debased' versions of Blaise's Oak

Cottage and Vine Cottage were still being published by C. J. Richardson in *The Englishman's House*.[3]

The Duke of Devonshire and his architect Joseph Paxton visited Blaise Hamlet in 1835, and the duke noted in his diary, 'the most perfect cottages . . . I ever saw'.[4] From 1838 they built a new estate village at Edensor near Chatsworth, although this bears no resemblance to Blaise – even though the variety of styles and shapes adopted was undoubtedly meant to be picturesque.[5] At Harlaxton, Lincolnshire, Anthony Salvin remodelled the existing village in the 1830s at the same time as he was building the enormous mansion. Loudon admired and described it at length,[6] although the results are not picturesque in the usual orné sense of Blaise or Old Warden. The village of Ilam, Staffordshire, commissioned in 1854 by Jesse Watts Russell,[7] was Sir George Gilbert Scott's attempt in the Blaise vein, though the cottages are decorated with Home Counties-inspired tile-hanging and with characteristically Victorian polychrome tiling, and are arranged back-to-back with their gardens round them, rather than around a green. The underlying social motivation for Blaise was reflected at Talbot Village, Bournemouth, which was created in the

OPPOSITE Thomas Ricauti, design for forester's cottage

LEFT **10/1** Eastern Lodge, Membland, Newton Ferrers, Devon

1860s at the instigation of the wealthy Talbot sisters for poor families dispossessed by early nineteenth-century land enclosures. The picturesque houses have verandahs and tall chimneys, and are hidden behind pine trees. The residents had to be teetotal, and the social programme was underlined by the provision of an acre of land for each family.[8] Holly Village [fig 10/2], on what was then the northern edge of London at Highgate, was designed by H. A. Darbyshire in 1865 for Baroness Burdett-Coutts, said to have been the wealthiest woman in England in her day, and a leading philanthropist.[9] It is a Victorian version of Blaise, likewise for elderly servants and arranged around a green, but the vocabulary has a spikiness unmistakably of its time (even though Darbyshire frankly admitted to not knowing much about Gothic architecture).[10]

Generally speaking, the Victorians took the housing of rural workers more seriously than the Georgians, but the results were usually plainer.[11] The villages of Westonbirt and Beverston, on R. S. Holford's extensive estates outside Tetbury in the Cotswolds, are examples of estate housing designed to be slightly but not overtly picturesque, with orné twiddles kept to a minimum. Designed by Lewis Vulliamy in the 1840s and 1850s,[12] they are in a simple Tudor style, with occasional finials and bargeboards to relieve the plainness – a far cry from (or at any rate a foil to) the extravagant Jacobethan idiom of

Westonbirt House, begun to Vulliamy's designs in 1864. At Hursley in Hampshire the village street is dotted with elaborate Tudorish estate cottages, with tile-hanging, latticed glazing and particularly prominent clustered chimneys. These may have been erected by Sir William Heathcote, 5th baronet, who inherited the Hursley estate in 1825, but perhaps under the influence of his second wife Selina, whom he married in 1841.[13] In some cases at least the motifs seem to have been applied to existing cottages, both in the village and elsewhere on the extensive estate. Although G. S. Repton designed a new Doric porch for the mansion in about 1834,[14] there is no evidence that he was involved in the cottages, and in any case the picture is confused by the fact that the motifs seem to have continued to be used much later, including on two lodges designed in the 1860s by the High Victorian William Butterfield and even later on cottages dated to the 1880s and 1890s.[15]

On the Albury Park estate in Surrey, as at Hursley, cottages were made to look more picturesque by the addition of eaves boards and elaborate chimneys. This can be observed along the village street, but perhaps the best example is Gardener's Cottage [fig 10/3], which stands at one end of the remarkable seventeenth-century terraced garden attached to the main mansion. Here an existing modest cottage was doubled in size and made to straddle the garden wall, with simply cusped eaves and a row of six enormous variously patterned brick chimneys. Although E. W. Pugin had remodelled the mansion in 1847–52 and carried out further work on the estate in the 1850s, the recasting of the cottage (and indeed those elsewhere in the village) is likely to date from as late as the 1870s, when the 6th Duke of Northumberland carried out alterations to the gardens. The size and elaboration of the cottage would have been considered commensurate with the status of the head gardener who was to occupy it.[16]

A characteristic of such later cottages is often an increase in scale over that of the Georgian working-class norm. This is true of Seacox Cottages [fig 10/4] at Flimwell in East Sussex. These comprise two sets of cottages (units of two and three) as estate housing for Seacox Heath, a house built 1868–72 by the firm of Slater & Carpenter for George (later Viscount) Goschen MP. Assuming that they are of the same date, they show how the vocabulary of the cottage orné had been taken up and modified by the mid-Victorian period. There are clustered chimneys, the upper floor is tile-hung, with a pair of steep-sided half-timbered gables at the centre of the elevation, and with cusping to the eaves and to the two porches and dormer windows. The chimneys and cuspings still recall the cottage orné idiom, but the ground floor is of stone with unmistakable Victorian Gothic windows edged in brick, and the overall scale is quite un-Georgian.

The progression from Georgian to Victorian is neatly demonstrated by comparing two ornamental cottages on the Orwell Park estate in Suffolk, where Yachtsman's Cottage is small and thatched and has an encircling tree-trunk verandah.[17] Decoy Cottage [fig 10/6], by contrast, is markedly larger in scale, with cast-iron latticed glazing, slightly overhanging upper floor and a tiled roof with two groups of chimneys, variously patterned.[18] The building was originally two cottages, and on the plainer north side there are indeed two doors. However, on the more elaborate south side it is designed to look like a single dwelling, with central jettied porch on rustic supports, and the gable above has exaggeratedly cusped eaves with acorn drop finials. The reason for all this is that the south side could be seen by the estate owner as he used the drive

between the villages of Nacton and Levington. Decoy Cottage was no doubt built for Colonel George Tomline (1813–1889), at the same time as he built a duck decoy (apparently to annoy the owner of the neighbouring estate).[19] Tomline employed William Burn to enlarge the Georgian mansion enormously in 1851–3, so it is conceivable that Burn also designed Decoy Cottage. Another possibility, however, might be Thomas Ricauti (or Rickard), a pupil of John Foulston. At the end of his short life – he died in 1842 aged only about twenty-four – Ricauti published two of the later cottage pattern books, *Rustic Architecture* of 1840 and *Sketches for Rustic Work* of 1842. The latter is dedicated to the then owner of Orwell Park, Sir Robert Harland, 2nd baronet (died 1848), and acknowledges him as his first patron. However, the similarities between Decoy Cottage and Ricauti's published designs are perhaps less

marked than those for a gamekeeper's house published by T. F. Hunt in 1825 [fig 10/5].[20]

If Ricauti's influence is to be found anywhere, it may be elsewhere in Suffolk, a few miles from Orwell Park at Sudbourne. Here Sir Richard Wallace (of the Wallace Collection) remodelled the late eighteenth-century Hall in 1872–3, Thomas Ambler assisting as architect. Ambler and, after his death in 1875, F. Barnes seem to have designed numerous estate buildings, including the Head Gardener's House and possibly the undated Rustic Lodge and Smoky House.[21] The Head Gardener's House, with half-timbered first floor over a hard red brick ground floor, looks like any number of rather charmless Victorian villas, whereas the aptly named Rustic Lodge [fig 10/7] is a cottage orné on steroids. The massive thatched roof, punctuated by an equally massive clustered chimney-stack, is brought down low over a half-timbered ground

floor, and a projecting bow with thatched half-dome is immediately juxtaposed with a frantically rustic porch. The similarities to Ricauti's published design for a forester's cottage [fig 10/8][22] are quite marked, so it is not impossible that this was referred to by whoever actually designed Rustic Lodge. Smoky House too is characteristic of the way the cottage orné tradition became subtly (and not so subtly) transmuted in the Victorian period, for although it retains the classic thatched roof and its eaves have drooping pendants, the brickwork is plainer and the overall scale larger than it would have been fifty years earlier. Chillesford Lodge, the model farm for the estate, which dates from 1875–6, has an ornamental dairy with two-storeyed half-timbered porch, open below and continued as a verandah, along with polychromatic brickwork, decorative roof tiling and Tudoresque chimneys. The dairy bears the monogram of Arthur Wood, owner from 1898 to 1904, so that alto-

gether, the Sudbourne buildings indicate that motifs that originated in the orné idiom lingered for a very long time.

One way in which the frivolity inherent in much of the Georgian phase of the cottage orné was progressively snuffed out was the gradual spread of a more archaeological attitude to the Gothic vocabulary. This had famously been pioneered by Horace Walpole at Strawberry Hill, with its chimneypieces, bookcases and other interior features derived (however loosely) from engravings of genuine medieval tombs. However, it was arguably Humphry Repton who could be said to have set the ornamental cottage on its road from orné to authentic, frivolous to deadly serious, with the Henry VII Lodge on the Woburn estate [fig 10/9]. This was designed in 1810 at the request of the 6th Duke of Bedford who – despite simultaneously commissioning Endsleigh Cottage on his Devon estate – did not like fanciful cottages ornés and wanted something in an authentic pre-Henry VIII style. With the aid of his

son John Adey, who was knowledgeable in antiquarian matters, Repton put together a series of quotations from geographically scattered late medieval and Tudor buildings.[23] The predictably earnest result was published in *Hints* in 1816, identifying the sources, and was noted by P. F. Robinson (possibly damning with faint praise?) as 'a good example of a modern building in this style'.[24]

The widespread influence of P. F. Robinson's many published designs – though they were mostly far from spreading any gospel of authenticity – was also significant in steering the cottage genre into new and potentially regrettable directions. This was particularly true when his imitators were tackling commissions for large cottages for the nouveaux riches. Bentham Hill [fig 10/10], at Southborough near Tunbridge Wells, was built in 1832–3 by Decimus Burton for Arthur Pott, an upwardly mobile vinegar manufacturer.[25] Influenced by P. F. Robinson designs such as that for Millfield Cottage at Bookham in

Surrey,[26] it shows the cottage orné becoming oversized, ungainly and rather charmless in a way that George IV's Royal Lodge, for all its preposterously inflated extent, had not been. It retains the self-consciously informal grouping of Millfield Cottage, with roofs and gables going in all directions, but for the most part the trimmings that produce the necessary light-heartedness have been pruned away: just two main gables have cuspings, and the windows are austere Elizabethan grids without dripmoulds. Overall there is a heaviness, and the form has become rather meaningless in its studied informality. Philip Miller notes that 'Some elements of the house . . . are so reminiscent of the work of the 1850s that only the existence of Burton's preliminary sketches for the house [in Hastings Museum] make it possible to believe the date.'[27]

Bentham Hill was a portent of things to come. It was also a relatively early example of how the Home Counties, especially Kent and Surrey, were to be increasingly colonized

by people – particularly artistic types, though this seems not to apply to Arthur Pott – who wanted a rural life while taking advantage of new rail links with London. Interestingly, in an age where traditionalists all around the countryside were profoundly alarmed at the potential disruption to their ordered way of life posed by the arrival of the railways – one has only to think of Elizabeth Gaskell's novel *Cranford*, serialized between 1851 and 1853 – the reassuring cottage idiom was even adopted for rural railway stations. The architectural achievements most associated with the age of steam may be the great iron and glass sheds of King's Cross, St Pancras, York and Newcastle, but at Fenny Stratford [fig 10/11] in Buckinghamshire in 1846 the major local landowner, the 7th Duke of Bedford (who was also patron of the Bedford Railway Company, and clearly not as averse to a proper

cottage orné as his predecessor the 6th duke), insisted that the station should come with half-timbering and gables with cusps and pendants.[28]

The railway arrived at Tunbridge Wells in 1845, at Godalming in the Surrey hills in 1859, making it possible for middle-class people to experience the rural idyll while still being able to pop up to town to make money or to spend it. Architects like George Devey supplied them with authentic-looking tile-hung or half-timbered cottages in villages such as Penshurst, Leigh, Benenden and Cranbrook. As a young man, Devey (1820–1886) had trained as an artist under the great watercolourist John Sell Cotman, mastering not just his technique but also his eye for picturesque composition. This is reflected in his early cottage work of the 1850s for Lord de L'Isle at Penshurst [fig 10/12], which certainly looks superficially

books. The way in which he and his sometime partner Richard Norman Shaw picked up and developed the vernacular vocabulary, in houses small and not so small, is a large subject and quite outside the scope of this study.[33] Shaw was the main creative mind behind Bedford Park, a brand new rural idyll in the London suburbs, developed from the late 1870s and satirized in 'The Ballad of Bedford Park':

> Thus was a village builded
> For all who are aesthete
> Whose precious souls it fill did
> With utter joy complete.[34]

Of course, the buildings were now roomy houses for the comfortable suburban middle class, rather than cottages for the rural working class. Yet despite the straight streets

authentic, with no orné trimmings, and indeed his style as a whole was based on a close study of the genuine vernacular of Kent, Surrey and Sussex – what Mark Girouard has called 'rural archaeology'.[29] The firm of Ernest George and Peto followed his lead some thirty years later in nearby Leigh,[30] and as a generalization it may be said that Devey and his imitators steered the new-built country cottage decisively away from the ornamental and towards authenticity, even though it is almost always possible to tell the difference between the medieval and Tudor originals and their Victorian spin-offs. The new approach was buttressed by artists such as Helen Allingham (1848–1926), whose cottage views perpetuated the supposed picturesqueness of rural life with their ubiquitous hollyhocks and rambling roses, generally in combination with what were clearly genuine half-timbered vernacular houses of Surrey and Sussex.[31] Interestingly, this whole trend seems to have been prefigured by two cottages just to the north of Penshurst at Redleaf [fig 10/13], designed by the art collector William Wells for his head gardener and under-gardener in the 1820s but remarkably prescient of what was later derided as Stockbrokers Tudor.[32]

As Devey had trained under Cotman, so William Eden Nesfield (1835–1888) had been the pupil of the topographical artist J. D. Harding, illustrator of P. F. Robinson's

and uniform façades, picturesque compositions were achieved, particularly at street junctions, and the development provided much inspiration for early twentieth-century garden suburbs.

In the decades to either side of 1900, architects such as Voysey, Lutyens, E. S. Prior and Baillie Scott once again raised the vernacular vocabulary to an art form. None of their Arts & Crafts buildings could accurately be called cottages ornés; artful simplicity was the watchword, even if discreet decorative flourishes might sometimes be permitted in the internal woodwork or metalwork. Nevertheless, it could be said that the underlying ethos of the Arts & Crafts cottage had much in common with that of the Georgian middle- and upper-class cottage orné: that is, a desire to experience the charms of the simple rural life, often at considerable expense and without the sacrifice of too many creature comforts. In leafy Surrey, where the agricultural depression of the 1870s had led to estates being broken up for spacious building plots among the pinewoods, the celebrated garden designer Gertrude Jekyll (who had spent all her life in the area)

realized that at least some of the incomers offered valuable commissions for new gardens and houses, which she and her young protégé Edwin Lutyens (1869–1944) were well placed to hoover up. Lutyens's early Surrey 'cottages' (some of which were quite sizeable houses) are among his most successful and likeable designs, and even after he moved on generally to a more classical style he continued to build cottage groups, for instance at Ashby St Ledgers (Northamptonshire),[35] Upper Slaughter (Gloucestershire)[36] and Milton Abbott (part of the Endsleigh estate in Devon).[37] Indeed, it is interesting to note that, despite having dismissed Wyatville's Endsleigh House as 'a conglomeration in the style of Mary Anne',[38] Lutyens seems to have learned lessons both from its flexible overall composition and from the relative austerity of its entrance frontage, as do architects such as Devey, Shaw, Detmar Blow and E. S. Prior.[39]

Rustic cottages continued to be built, especially on the big estates, but by now the proprietors tended to be bankers and businessmen like the Rothschilds or the Astors who, being themselves not quite English, tended to opt for a style which was considered quintessentially English, only perhaps more so. For Leopold de Rothschild at Ascott in Buckinghamshire, Devey designed a house that was described by Mary Gladstone[40] as 'a palace-like cottage', externally half-timbered and rambling but internally the height of *de luxe*.[41] On the nearby Mentmore estate in Buckinghamshire, though the vast mansion of 1850–55 was designed by Sir Joseph Paxton for Baron Mayer Amschel de Rothschild in Jacobethan idiom, rustic cottages in a post-orné style were built in the 1860s by Paxton's son-in-law G. H. Stokes and then in the 1870s by Devey – the latter's thatched and half-timbered

Cheddington Lodge [fig 10/14] is particularly appealing and might be seen as a calmer version of the Rustic Lodge at Sudbourne. The guest accommodation at Hever Castle in Kent, built *c.*1904 for the American-born businessman and newspaper proprietor William Waldorf Astor[42] to designs by F. L. Pearson, took the form of an Old English village in the manner of P. F. Robinson.

One architectural element that was seized on by the Victorians and Edwardians to an extent it had never been during the late Georgian cottage heyday[43] was that of half-timbering – very often being made considerably fancier and more dense than the authentic article, as can be seen by looking at The Rows in Chester and comparing the original sections of half-timbering with the nineteenth-century emulations. This going overboard for historicist ornament was something deplored in 1904 by the German architectural critic Hermann Muthesius, who judged it to be 'the fundamental failure' of English architects in the previous half-century.[44] Pruned of its fancy detail, however, the historicist cottage segued into compositions not so different from the designs of Malton. This in turn formed the debased basis for innumerable housing developments between the wars, including ones intended for the working class. Promoted by high-circulation magazines such as *Ideal Home*, first published in 1919, the pre-war houses individually designed by architects for upper-middle-class clients had their vocabulary bowdlerized for the mass market.[45] Just as in the first decades of the nineteenth century, when unease amongst the ruling class about the possibility of social unrest caused a certain focus on the need to keep the working class on side with improved housing conditions, so rather the same situation recurred a century later when World War I destroyed many of the underlying certainties and assumptions of the British social order, and revolutionary upheaval on the Continent threatened to infect the working class at home. This was certainly one reason why King George V refused asylum to his doomed Romanov cousins in 1917, and why in 1919 he threw his weight behind the government's programme of public housing. 'If unrest is to be converted into contentment', he noted, 'the provision of good houses may provide one of the most potent agents in that conversion.'[46]

For at least a few more years, private estates continued to take the occasional initiative in commissioning cottage developments. Immediately after World War I, Sir Ernest Debenham[47] employed Halsey Ricardo and McDonald Gill to build estate cottages on his Dorset property at Briantspuddle, together with a new hamlet at nearby Bladen Valley [fig 10/15], the latter thatched and white-washed and grouped round a war memorial. Similar and contemporary is Ardeley in Hertfordshire, by F. C. Eden, with thatched cottages arranged around a village green with spreading oak tree – an exercise described by Nikolaus Pevsner as 'a Blaise Castle Revived, though without the capriciousness of the original'.[48] On the eve of the World War Two Lord Portal had a long curving terrace of eighteen separate houses built on his family estate at Laverstoke in Hampshire. They are reminiscent of local vernacular in the use of thatch, mullioned windows, heavy chimneys and half-timbering, something which Pevsner – perhaps the leading proponent for International Modernism – writing in 1967, found 'all a little ridiculous'.[49] The development came complete with thatched wells and a thatched bus stop.

Private enterprise also made possible the escapist fantasies of Thorpeness (1910 onwards) and Portmeirion (1920s onwards), both examples of picturesque villages created for the holidaying middle classes. Thorpeness, on the sandy Suffolk coast just north of Aldeburgh, is a disarming combination of bogus half-timbering and Arts & Crafts Tudor brick and flint. It was the brainchild of the landowner G. S. Ogilvie, a friend of the author J. M. Barrie whose *Peter Pan* had first been staged in 1904, and it has aptly been remarked that 'it is as if the place were a Never Never Land, designed to suit Peter and all the other boys (and girls) who never grow up'.[50] Portmeirion, the celebrated creation of the architect and landowner Clough Williams-Ellis (1883–1978), was built over a period of

half a century, from 1925 onwards, on a site of great natural beauty overlooking an estuary on the Welsh coast. Although the earlier buildings reflected Williams-Ellis's Arts & Crafts training, later contributions were increasingly indebted to picturesque – not to say theatrical – Italianate models.[51]

Certainly neither Thorpeness nor Portmeirion showed the slightest influence of the precepts of International Modernism that started to make themselves felt in England from the early 1930s, and so were ignored or regarded with contempt by the rising generation of architects and critics. English architectural modernism gathered momentum from about 1930, when the so-called Twentieth Century Group was established with Wells Coates, Serge Chermayeff and Raymond McGrath as its leading lights. Such men approached their commissions with the proselytizing zeal of religious converts and had no time for anything that smacked of historicism, so it is not surprising that they and their followers in the ensuing decades were exasperated by the stubbornly lingering English instinct for the traditional and picturesque, whether in matters of style or materials. So too was the emigré German architectural historian Nikolaus Pevsner who, much as he came to love the culture of his adopted land and what he called 'the Englishness of English art', rarely lost an opportunity in print to lament the backwardness of the natives in such matters. In his view, while

the Arts & Crafts architects could be classed as 'pioneers' of the Modern Movement, thereafter English architects were largely guilty of failing to subscribe to the modernism that was the true and indeed only legitimate style of the twentieth century.[52]

This might be thought to be the moment in British architectural history when the cottage orné thread, which since the 1840s had been progressively changing course and changing character, finally fizzled out. It is certainly difficult to identify any convincing examples built in the second half of the twentieth century,[53] and it does indeed seem improbable that there will ever be a substantial return to the idiom that for nearly a century had been so popular and widespread – this despite the enduring popularity of other neo-Georgian variants. Yet it may be that there is still potential profit and inspiration to be gained by modern architects in looking at the late Georgian pattern books, and even implementing particular designs – for instance, the crisp rustic geometry of Thomas Dearn's cottage design [fig 10/16] in *Sketches in Architecture*,[54] or of John Plaw's circular cottage [fig 4/7];[55] the elegant simplicity of Papworth's Lake District cottage [fig 4/4];[56] or the eye-catching originality of Francis Goodwin's vanished Dunstall lodge [fig 4/23].[57] However, the fact that the cottage orné is even now not quite dead, or even terminally ill, seems to be indicated by a number of individual projects in recent years. To set against the far too numerous examples of historic cottages ornés being ruined by unsympathetic extensions (often in a 'frankly modern' idiom), there have also been instances, perhaps not so surprising, of additions that respect and imitate the character of the original building. A good example is Pembroke Cottage [fig 10/17] on the edge of Richmond Park, an early nineteenth-century cottage lodge that had previously been very inappropriately extended but in 2003 was tactfully doubled in size by the architect Roderick Maclennan, so that externally it now gives an entirely convincing impression of being an authentic middle-class cottage orné of the Regency era.[58]

Another example of how to enlarge a genuine cottage orné sympathetically is Cox's Cottage, on the northern edge of Hereford. Named after the watercolourist David Cox (1783–1859) who lived there in 1817–23 and used the sitting room as his studio, this was in origin possibly

an eighteenth-century thatched house that Cox prettified by adding Gothick glazing and a tree-trunk verandah across the front. In 1990 it was given a cottage orné extension by a local Herefordshire designer called Ted Wade, with thatched roof and decorative eaves board to the gable. Mr Wade was quoted in an article in the *Architect's Journal*[59] as saying, 'what builders may not realize is that the cottage orné style need not break budgets', estimating that his work at Cox's Cottage had cost only 5 per cent more than a conventional extension to build. If this fact were more widely known, then perhaps others would consider not only extending their cottages 'in keeping', but also creating new examples from scratch. It is perhaps an idle dream to hope that some of the uncountable thousands of dreary bungalows might be converted into something visually pleasing by the addition of the kind of embellishments promoted by the late

Georgian pattern book authors. And yet, in 1993 *Country Life* magazine published Ted Wade's transformation of just such a bungalow into a modest cottage orné. Rectory Cottage, at Croft in Herefordshire, originated as an unprepossessing 1960s bungalow that in 1986 had its blockwork walls rendered and painted ochre, its picture windows replaced with old cast-iron casements, and its concrete roof tiles with patterned slates. Its eaves were given gentle scalloping and pendants, and its roof ridges acquired terracotta crestings – all for the very modest sum of £8,000. This sort of process was dubbed 'bungalow eating' by the architect Roderick James.[60]

Since then, examples of newly built cottages have appeared that give some hope for the continuation of the idiom. In 2012 the proprietors of Studland Manor Hotel, itself a large marine cottage orné of the 1820s,[61] commissioned Ben Pentreath to design a not-quite-matching pair

of diminutive octagonal cottages ornés to provide additional guest accommodation [fig 10/18]. Attached to the perimeter wall of the kitchen garden, they were built in 2014 and make a delightful and entirely sympathetic addition to the ensemble.[62] Another recent project is Eastridge, Hampshire, designed by Nigel Anderson of the Robert Adam Architects partnership in 2000 and completed in 2002. Externally the appearance is convincingly Regency, with Gothick glazing under Tudor dripmoulds, yellow-washed walls and fretted bargeboards. The client was Lord Andrew Hay, whose wife was brought up at the former cottage orné of the Dukes of Leinster, Martinstown in Co. Kildare,[63] and the interiors too nod towards that exemplar, with an arched Gothic screen between the hall and staircase, and simple Gothic cornices and chimneypieces.[64] In 2016, for a site in rural south Somerset, the Yorkshire architect Digby Harris designed a new country house in cottage orné idiom modelled on John Nash's Hollycombe Lodge.[65] It seems appropriate, however, to conclude with Kay's Cottage [figs 10/19, 20], at Churchill in Co. Kerry, Ireland, which was designed in 1995 by the Dublin architect Angela Jupe as a secret wedding anniversary present for the Irish wife of the American owner of the estate.[66] The building, with thatched roof, tree-trunk posts, irregular plan and just one bedroom, was constructed to nestle up against a limestone outcrop and be invisible from the classical main house. The direct inspi-

ration was the recently recreated Kilfane Cottage,[67] which also gave a lead for the decoration of the interior, carried out by Imogen Taylor and Pierre Serrurier, who designed twiggy chimneypieces like that in the main room at Kilfane.[68] With Kay's Cottage, the cottage genre in a sense comes full circle, returning to the direct inspiration of a genuine late eighteenth-century example.

As was stated at the outset, there is no point in pretending that the cottage orné is a weighty manifestation of anything, and it is therefore not a serious style for serious people, but at its best it offers a great deal of lightweight charm. In its heyday in the late Georgian period it offered an alternative to the more substantial virtues of classicism, and notwithstanding the many thousands of words poured out by pattern book authors in explaining and promoting it, it was essentially a variety of escapism and make-believe. To expend too much theoretical effort in making it appear more of an intellectual exercise than it was is to miss the point of the genre. It comes with a good deal of fascinating sociological and aesthetic baggage, but at the end of the day it is perhaps best simply to surrender to its shallow but frequently seductive charms. If those charms have anything to teach a modern generation of architects, it is that it is not morally wrong for architecture sometimes to be fun.

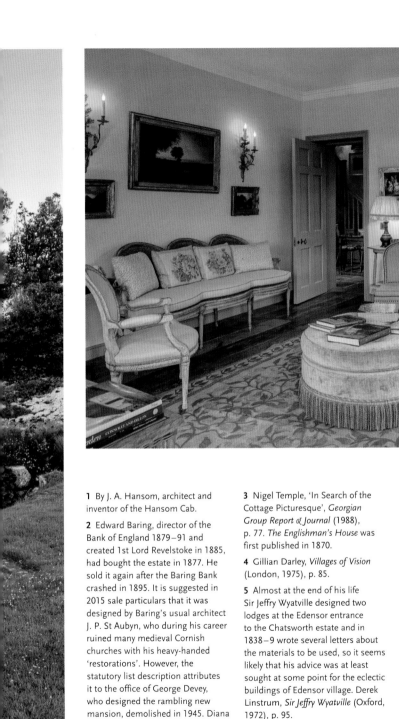

1 By J. A. Hansom, architect and inventor of the Hansom Cab.

2 Edward Baring, director of the Bank of England 1879–91 and created 1st Lord Revelstoke in 1885, had bought the estate in 1877. He sold it again after the Baring Bank crashed in 1895. It is suggested in 2015 sale particulars that it was designed by Baring's usual architect J. P. St Aubyn, who during his career ruined many medieval Cornish churches with his heavy-handed 'restorations'. However, the statutory list description attributes it to the office of George Devey, who designed the rambling new mansion, demolished in 1945. Diana Hopkinson ('A Passion for Building: the Barings at Membland', *Country Life* (29 April 1982), p. 1236) introduces the further name of J. D. Sedding, who designed a lodge for the neighbouring Baring estate at Flete in 1887.

3 Nigel Temple, 'In Search of the Cottage Picturesque', *Georgian Group Report & Journal* (1988), p. 77. *The Englishman's House* was first published in 1870.

4 Gillian Darley, *Villages of Vision* (London, 1975), p. 85.

5 Almost at the end of his life Sir Jeffry Wyatville designed two lodges at the Edensor entrance to the Chatsworth estate and in 1838–9 wrote several letters about the materials to be used, so it seems likely that his advice was at least sought at some point for the eclectic buildings of Edensor village. Derek Linstrum, *Sir Jeffry Wyatville* (Oxford, 1972), p. 95.

6 J. C. Loudon, *Encyclopaedia* (London, 1842 edn).

7 The son of an East End soap manufacturer who reinvented himself as a country gentleman.

8 Darley, *Villages of Vision*, p.103.

9 Despite the immense worthiness of her philanthropic activities, she shocked contemporary society by marrying at the age of sixty-seven her American secretary, who was considerably less than half her age.

10 Darley, *Villages of Vision*, p. 72.

11 An exception was Earl Lovelace's cottages in East Horsley and Ockham in Surrey.

12 Holford inherited the Westonbirt estate in 1839 and added Beverston by purchase in 1842.

13 After his death in 1888 his widow sold the estate to Joseph Baxendale, owner of Pickfords, who sold it on in 1902 to George (Sir George from 1905) Cooper, whose wife was an American railways heiress. She paid for extensive alterations and additions to Hursley Park itself.

14 RIBADC, SD III/10 (1–2). He also altered the church tower.

15 Information from Charles O'Brien.

16 Information from Michael Baxter, Albury Estate.

17 Previous names included Quay Cottage, Ferryman's and Boatman's Cottage, which suggests that very likely there was a ferry from here across to Pin Mill on the opposite bank of the mile-wide River Orwell.

18 The central chimney in each case is now plain but originally had a diamond diaper, according to the tenant.

19 Information from Dr James Bettley and Mrs Mark Bence-Jones.

20 T. F. Hunt, *Half-a-Dozen Hints* (1825), Design 3. See Chapter Four.

21 James Bettley and Nikolaus Pevsner, *The Buildings of England: Suffolk: East* (New Haven and London, 2015), pp. 534–5. The bailiff's cottage, across the road from Rustic Lodge, was another very good example of an exaggeratedly orné cottage, but has now been much altered.

22 Thomas Ricauti, *Rustic Architecture* (London, 1840), Design II, pl. IX. Both Ricauti's books were intended to demonstrate 'the picturesque and pleasing appearance of rough wood, thatch etc., when applied as the only decoration of rural buildings'. A design for a half-timbered cottage by Ricauti is given in Loudon's *Encyclopaedia of Rural Architecture*, Supplement 1842, 1155. The six designs in *Rustic Architecture* are all cottages ornés, starting with 'a peasant's Cottage on a Gentleman's Estate' and gradually going up the scale (forester, gamekeeper, gardener, bailiff on a gentleman's estate, steward on a nobleman's estate). He also suggests that, with the exception of the peasant's cottage, they would also do for 'genteel families'. The elaboration increases as they go up the scale.

23 He also supplied the lodge with accompanying Tudor-style knot gardens.

24 P. F. Robinson, *Village Architecture* (1830), p. 2.

25 He became High Sheriff and Deputy Lieutenant of Kent, which must have been a first for a vinegar manufacturer. *The Kent Compendium of Historic Parks and Gardens for Tunbridge Wells Borough.*

26 A project of 1814, published in P. F. Robinson, *Rural Architecture* (1823), pl. 96. See Chapter Four, p. 106–107.

27 Philip Miller, *The Long Life and Changing Times of Decimus Burton, Architect*, section 27. www.castlehillsberwick.com/burtonexhibition/index.htm

28 Similar stations are found along the same Bedford to Bletchley line at Millbrook, Ridgmont and Woburn Sands, all in Bedfordshire. Charles O'Brien and Nikolaus Pevsner, *The Buildings of England: Bedfordshire, Huntingdonshire and Peterborough* (New Haven and London, 2014), pp. 250, 120, 340.

29 Mark Girouard, 'George Devey in Kent', *Country Life* (1 April 1971), pp. 744–7. Girouard calls the Penshurst cottages a pioneer example of the revival of local vernacular traditions in building and says that they 'could easily be taken for buildings of 1650 rather than 1850. . . . This kind of rural archaeology had never been tried before.'

30 For the industrialist Samuel Morley, who began by commissioning Devey to replace a Georgian house with a neo-Elizabethan one in 1871 and followed this with estate buildings. In 1886–7 his son Samuel Hope Morley (created Lord Hollenden in 1912) commissioned George and

Peto to build Forge Square, which has been described as a 'virtuoso interplay between sandstone, red brick, half-timbering, tile- and shingle-hanging, and thatch' (John Newman, *The Buildings of England. Kent: West Kent and the Weald*, (New Haven and London, 2012), pp. 360–61).

31 The area to which she moved with her family in 1881.

32 The cottages are dated 1825 and 1826, and bear Wells's initials on their gables. Wells was a generous patron and entertainer of artists, Landseer in particular. Lilac Cottage of 1825 is without the half-timbering found on Redleaf Cottage of a year later. 'Stockbrokers Tudor' is the term invented by Osbert Lancaster (*Pillar to Post*, London, 1938) to categorize the early twentieth-century descendants of such exercises in faux half-timbering.

33 See Andrew Saint, *Richard Norman Shaw*, 2nd edn (New Haven and London, 2010).

34 Anon., *St James Gazette*, quoted in Darley, *Villages of Vision*, p. 118.

35 For Lord Wimborne, 1908–9.

36 A group of vernacular cottages known as Bagshot's Square, remodelled 1906–13.

37 Venn Hill, an irregular group of four cottages dating from 1909.

38 See Chapter Seven.

39 Examples of this influence include E. S. Prior's The Barn, Exmouth, Devon (1896), Detmar Blow's Happisburgh Manor, Norfolk (1900), and Lutyens's Greywalls, Gullane, Lothian (1900).

40 Daughter of the prime minister.

41 Andrew Ballantyne and Andrew Law, *Tudoresque, In Pursuit of the Ideal Home* (London, 2011), pp. 150–51. 'Like Endsleigh and the King's Cottage at Windsor, rather than being a "palace-like cottage", [Ascott] is really a "cottage-like palace", and in this respect it belongs firmly in the class of *cottages ornés.*'

42 Created 1st Baron Astor in 1916.

43 Although it should be noted that quite a high proportion of the largely unexecuted cottage designs in G. S. Repton's RIBA notebook (RIBADC 246/4) feature half-timbering.

44 Muthesius, *The English House* (Berlin, 1904), English translation London 2007, p. 101, cited in D. Maudlin, *The Idea of the Cottage in English Architecture 1760–1860* (London, 2015), p. 185.

45 Ballantyne and Law, *Tudoresque, In Pursuit of the Ideal Home*, p. 161.

46 Quoted in Sutherland Lyall, *Dream Cottages: From Cottage Ornée*

to Stockbroker Tudor (London, 1988), p. 114.

47 Proprietor of the eponymous stores, created a baronet in 1931.

48 Nikolaus Pevsner, revised Bridget Cherry, *The Buildings of England: Hertfordshire* (Harmondsworth, 1977), p. 73.

49 Nikolaus Pevsner and David Lloyd, *The Buildings of England: Hampshire* (Harmondsworth, 1967), p. 317.

50 Bettley and Pevsner, *Suffolk: East*, p. 549. The architects were F. Forbes Glennie, followed by W. G. Wilson. At exactly the same time that Thorpeness was being created on the Suffolk coast, two holiday settlements were being created on the Danish coast: at Tibirke on the north coast of Zealand and at Hesnaes on the Baltic coast of Falster. In both cases the houses were architect-designed and derived from the local thatched vernacular (in the case of Hesnaes, with the exterior walls rather oddly faced in panels of reed for insulation).

51 Clough Williams-Ellis, *Portmeirion, The Place and its Meaning*, rev. edn (Portmeirion, 1973).

52 One of Pevsner's Arts & Crafts heroes was Voysey, who lived on until 1941 and said he 'heartily disliked' Pevsner's modernism and did not want to be seen as a pioneer of it. Ballantyne and Law, *Tudoresque, In Pursuit of the Ideal Home*, p. 161.

53 A possible exception is The Hermitage at Crichel in Dorset, designed by Quinlan Terry in 1983–6. A single-storey T-plan house of banded flint and brick under a thatched roof, it is a somewhat self-denying design that eschews anything that might be considered orné – slightly perversely, given that it occupies the site of a Regency dairy that had Gothick windows. Clive Aslet, *Quinlan Terry, The Revival of Architecture* (Harmondsworth, 1986), pp. 73–4.

54 T.D.W. Dearn, *Sketches in Architecture; consisting of Original Designs for Cottages and Rural Dwellings, suitable to persons of moderate fortune, and for convenient retirement* (London, 1807), Pl. 16.

55 John Plaw, *Sketches for Country Houses* (1800), pl. XII. See Chapter Four, p. 99.

56 J. B. Papworth, *Rural Residences* (London, 1818), pl. XII. See Chapter Four, p. 97.

57 Francis Goodwin, *Rural Architecture* (London, 1835), Design 6. See Chapter Four, p. 109.

58 I am grateful to Daniel Hearsum for showing me Pembroke Cottage.

59 'Plotting a Picturesque Revival', *Architect's Journal* (1 August 1990), p. 13.

60 Giles Worsley, 'Cottage Cover-Up', *Country Life* (14 January 1993), pp. 30–31.

61 See Chapter Five, p. 132, fig. 5/16.

62 The proposal was developed in consultation with the landscape architect Kim Wilkie.

63 See Chapter Six, p. 153.

64 Jeremy Musson, *The Country House Ideal: Recent Work by Robert Adam Architecture* (London, 2015), pp. 120–31.

65 A substantial villa in the cottage idiom, designed for Sir Charles Taylor's Sussex estate in 1805, rebuilt in the 1890s and known from G. S. Repton's sketchbook. Michael Mansbridge, *John Nash* (London, 1991), p. 116.

66 Rather like the Chinese Palace at Drottningholm outside Stockholm, a surprise birthday present for Queen Louisa Ulrike from her husband in 1753, construction of Kay's Cottage was kept a secret until completed.

67 See Chapter Six, p. 153.

68 William Laffan, ed., *A Year at Churchill* (Churchill House Press, 2003). Information from Imogen Taylor.

ACKNOWLEDGEMENTS

This book brings to fruition an embarrassingly long period of research and the steady accumulation of material. Over the years many people have encouraged the project in different ways, but it is only right that the resulting volume should be dedicated to two particular individuals: my old friend Charles Hind, curator of the RIBA Drawings Collection, who has been endlessly helpful and supportive, feeding me ideas and reading the texts as they were written; and my partner John Boodle, who has driven me thousands of miles and accompanied me (mainly) uncomplainingly on countless site visits. Without their encouragement and companionship it is probably doubtful that the project would ever have been finished.

Special thanks are also due to my friends Peter and Ann Stephenson-Wright, for allowing me to escape the distractions of London and write in peace at their house on the Suffolk coast; and to Clarissa Orr for reading and commenting on a majority of the chapters. Others who have read particular chapters or sections are Professor Edward McParland (Ireland); Thomas Lloyd and Elizabeth Whittle (Wales); Calder Loth (America); and Paul Waite (New Zealand).

Many people, including friends and acquaintances, have fed me information and performed other kindnesses over the years, and I record them alphabetically: Stephen and Alison Alexander; Bruce Bailey (Northamptonshire); the late Mavis Batey; John Batten; Sue Berry (Brighton); Dr James Bettley (Suffolk and Essex); David and Rachel Blissett; Donald Church; Georgina Craufurd; Richard Emerson; Simon Garratt; Argus Gaythorne-Hardy; Ian Gow; Julian Harrap; Digby Harris; Dr Eileen Harris (Thomas Wright); John Harris; Jeffery Haworth; Malcolm and Jane Hemmings; Olive Herbert; Robert Jennings; Nicholas Kingsley; Andrew Martindale; Dr Robert McCarthy; Jacqueline Morley; Charles O'Brien; John Redmill; Jeremy Rye; Matthew Saunders; the late Norman Scarfe and the Scarfe Trust; Michael Snodin; Lanto Synge; Michael Tree; Sarah Tsang (Julian Harrap Architects); Graham Viney; Joe Walsh; Kim Wilkie; Professor Richard Wilson; Robin Wyatt.

I am grateful to a number of libraries and record offices for responding to my enquiries, notably the following: The Hon. Lady Roberts and Rosie Razzle, Royal Library, Windsor; Pamela Clark, Royal Archives, Windsor; Helen Dorey, Frances Sands, Stephen Astley and Sue Palmer, Sir John Soane Museum; Andrew Parry, Gloucestershire Record Office; David Ryall, Hampshire Record Office; Mary Gillespie and Polly Putnam, Historic Royal Palaces at Kew; Jonathan Makepiece, RIBA Drawings Collection; Valerie Hart, Guildhall Library; Kate Hanlon, Saffron Walden Library; Beverley Burgess and Kenneth Hicks, Isle of Wight College; Ingrid Smith, Camden Local Studies Centre; Peter Kazmierczak, Bournemouth Library; Clare Morgan, Cornish Studies Library; Sue Oatley, Isle of Wight Record Office; Kate Godfrey, Enfield Local Studies Centre; Kate Holliday, Kendal Archive Centre; Graham Davies, Lyme Regis Museum; John Tucker and Julie Connor, Torquay Library; Ann Smith, Sherborne Castle; Dr Jane Bradney, Enville Hall; Ann Lund, National Trust, Selworthy; Trevor Adams, National Trust, A La Ronde; Anna Forrest, National Trust, Ickworth; Heather Hamilton, National Trust, Florence Court; Geoffrey Kelly, Dr Clive Wilkins-Jones, re Harford Hills House; Michael Brian Redhead, re Houghton Lodge; Judith Patrick, re Bishopswood, Fareham; Michael Baxter (Albury Estate).

The following have kindly helped with queries outside the United Kingdom: Colum O'Riordan, Irish Architectural Archive; Quentin Wicquart, Archivist at Chateau de Beloeil, Belgium, on behalf of the present Prince de Ligne; Dr Marcus Köhler, Dr Jarl Kremeier (Germany); Dr Jozsef Sisa (Hungary); James Robertson (Czech Republic); Lisa Renne, Alexey Guzanov, Olga Lameko (Pavlovsk Palace); Mme Yveline Hollier-Larousse (for the Cottage Palace, Peterhof); Sarah E Mitchell and Calder Loth (USA); Linda Lott and Alyson Williams, Dumbarton Oaks Library; Marilynn Jones, Manship House Museum, Jackson, Mississippi; Ann Sumners (Rose Hill Mansion, Beaufort, South Carolina); Vici Surr (Oak Bluffs, Massachussetts); Pauline Hitchens, Heritage Council of Victoria; Elaine Marland and Alison Dangerfield, Heritage New Zealand.

A number of house owners have been generous in allowing access, and I particularly wish to thank the following: The 11th Duke of Beaufort (Badminton); the late Captain and Mrs Martin Busk (Houghton Lodge); Daniel Hearsum (Pembroke Lodge); Mrs Maldwyn Drummond (Cadland); Michael Jackson (Ham Hill, Powick); Ben and Juliet Browne (Angeston Grange); Shirley Anne Spenser (Tavy Lodge, Tavistock); Miss Anne Measures (Stonely); Polly Fry (Selwood Lodge, Frome); Stella Gibbs (Roxton Congregational Chapel); Peter Speke (Jordans); Warren Davis (Winterborne Came Old Rectory); Mr and Mrs Mark Sedgeley (Blackbrook Cottage, Fareham); Lord O'Neill, Patrick O'Neill, Anne Crutchley (Shane's Castle); Edward Booth (Martinstown); Connor Mallaghan (Carton).

Many cottages ornés, particularly lodges at the entrance to country estates, can readily be seen from the public road; however I should stress that the mention of a building in this book emphatically does not mean that it is accessible to the public. At Yale University Press, Sally Salvesen strongly supported the early stages of the project, which was then taken forward by Sophie Sheldrake, Anjali Bulley and Beth O'Rafferty, the copy editor Charley Chapman and the designer Ray Watkins. I am particularly grateful to the Annie Burr Lewis Fund and the Marc Fitch Fund.

Although the book has been so long in the making, I make no claims to it being 'definitive' or comprehensive in its coverage. There are without doubt plenty of examples still unknown to me, particularly tucked away down disused drives to English country houses, and the chapters on the cottage idiom on the Continent or far-flung parts of the former British Empire are best regarded as an introduction to a subject which could usefully be followed up by local historians. In a project that has lasted so many years it is entirely possible that I have lost track of some of those who have very kindly assisted in one way or another, and I apologise in advance if this proves to be the case: it is a sin of omission rather than commission. Needless to say, I shall be very glad to hear of such omissions, and also of course to have corrections of errors pointed out.

Roger White

133, 143
Gladstone, Mary 257
Glasse, Reverend George 68
Glendalough estate, Co. Wicklow: Oldbridge (Lough Dan) Lodge 102
Glevering Hall, Suffolk: primitive lodge 32
Goodwin, Francis
    Domestic Architecture (*Rural Architecture*) 94, 96, 98, *108–9*, 109
    Dunstall lodge design 109, *109*, 259
Gosford Castle, Co. Armagh: lodge 155
Gothic Farm, Heveningham, Suffolk 85
Gothic style and features 11, 20, 55, 56, 70
    Adam's designs and interest in 21, *23*, 24–5
    Cottage Palace at Peterhof, Russia 216, *216–18*, 218
    Houghton fishing lodge 72
    middle-class remodelling of farmhouses 84–5
    pattern book designs 100
    Scottish cottages 149
    as suitable style for clergy 68
    twenty-first-century cottage orné 261
    in United States 223, 224, 225, 232, 235, 238
        Carpenter's Gothic 228, 241
        Downing's 'Rural Gothic' 228, 231
    in Victorian era 252–3
Gottheil, Edward 235
Goupy, Claude-Martin 204
Graham, James Gillespie 41
Great Hampden, Buckinghamshire: Old Rectory 68
Great Tew, Oxfordshire: picturesque cottages 55
Greek Revival style in United States 224, 232
Greenway, Francis 241
Gregg, William 232
Gresley, Reverend Thomas 60, 68
Greville, Charles 190
Grohmann, J. G. 102, 206
The Grove, Great Glemham, Suffolk: lodge 34
guidebooks and travel books 113, 115, 133
    guide to Knowle Cottage 116, 118
Gulval, nr Penzance, Cornwall: Pendrea *124*, 125
Gurney, Joseph 63, 100
Gwydir, Lord 119
Gyfford, Edward 90

Hackwood Park, Hampshire: lodge design *28*, 29–30
Hadfield, George 223
half-timbered houses in Victorian era 257
Ham Hill, Powick, Worcestershire 60, *61–2*, 62
Hamilton, 10th Duke of 55, 98
hamlets *see* villages and hamlets
Hampstead, London
    cottages 83
    Fitzroy Farm Cottage 83
Hanbury Leigh, Capel 43
Hanbury Leigh, Molly Ann (*formerly* Mackworth) 43
Hanwell, Middlesex: Hermitage 68, *69*, 81
Harding, J. D. 255
Hardwick Court, Oxfordshire: 'Straw Hall' 18–19, *18*, 179
Harford, John Scandrett 47, 48, 49
Harford Hills House, nr Norwich 63, 100
Harlaxton, Lincolnshire 247
Harleston House, Northamptonshire:

primitive lodge 32
Harris, Digby 261
Harrison, James 146
Harvey, John 116, 118
Hassell, John 106, 125–6
Hawkins, John 125
Hawkstone, Shropshire 113
Hayes, Samuel 151
health tourism and spa resorts 113–15, 125, 135–9
Heathcote, Sir William, 5th Baronet 248
Heavey, John 165
Heely, Joseph 12
Helene, Grand Duchess of Russia 120
Henley-on-Thames, Oxfordshire: Rose Hill Cottage 64, *65*, 102, 128
Herbert, Dorothea 164
Hereford: Cox's Cottage 259–60
hermitages 12, 13–17, 81, 150
Hever Castle, Kent 257
High Legh estate, Cheshire: village and approach 45
Highgate, London
    cottages *82*, 83
    Holly Village 248, *248*
    Ivy Cottage *82*, 83
Hill, Sir Richard 113
historicist cottages in early 1900s 257
Hoare, Sir Richard Colt 20, 143
Hohenheim estate, Germany: English village and Alte Turm 211, *211*, 212
Holford, R. S. 248
holiday destinations and cottages 113–39, 258–9
Holkham Hall, Norfolk: public tours 113
Holland, Henry 8, 95, 104
    Cadland fishing lodge 71, *71*, 72
Holly Village, Highgate, London 248, *248*
Holnicote House and estate, Somerset: Selworthy hamlet 49–50, *50*
Home Counties: Victorian cottages and commuter links 253–6
Hopper, Thomas 80
Hornor, Thomas 145
Horton, Somerset, Gingerbread House *37*, 37, 39
Houghton, Norfolk: relocation of village 44, *44*
Houghton Lodge, Stockbridge, Hampshire 72–6, *73–6*
housing development in interwar years 257–8
Hughes, Thomas 238
Hulcote, Northamptonshire
    design of village 45
    Pomfret Lodge as vicarage 68–9
Hungary: imitation of English gardens 206
Hunt, T. F. (Thomas Frederick) 102, 228
    design for gamekeeper's cottage 250, *251*
hunting lodges in Ireland 165–6, *165*
Hursley, Hampshire 248

Ickworth House, Suffolk
    estate cottages 52, 55
    Round House 98, *99*
Ideal Home magazine 257
Ilam, Staffordshire 247
Ingleman, Richard 39
interiors 96–8
    Cottage Palace at Peterhof, Russia in Gothick Style 216, *216–18*, 218
    decoration of A la Ronde 78–9, *79*
    decoration of cottage, Lake District *97*, 98
    decoration of Ham Hill 60, *61–2*, 62
    Endsleigh Swiss Cottage 177
    French cottages ornés
        Chateau de Chantilly *hameau*

buildings 200, 202
    Chaumière aux Coquillages at Rambouillet 204–5, *205*
    Petit Hameau at Versailles 203
    lavish interior of Knowle Cottage 116, 118, *118*
    layout for daytime entertainment and lower-class lodgings 91, 98, 130, 131, 154
    layout of superior cottages 173–4
    'Palace' at Liselund, Denmark 208, *208–10*
    Queen's Cottage
        Picnic Room and Princess Elizabeth's decoration 182, *183*
        print room 180, *181*, 182
    Roseland Cottage, United States *230–31*, 231
    Royal Lodge at Windsor 190
    Russian Cottage Palace at Peterhof in Gothick style 216, *216–18*, 218
    seaside cottages 118, 128–9
    simplicity of 8, 66, 156, 173
    Swiss Cottage at Cahir *162–3*, 164
    twentieth-century cottages ornés 261, *263*
    see also furniture and furnishings
International Modernism 258, 259
Intwood Hall, Norfolk: lodge 34
Ireland 9, 14, 102, 108, 149–67, 178, 261
Isle of Wight 125–31
    Cliff Cottage (now Puckpool House), nr Ryde 84
    Debourne Lodge, West Cowes 129
    Elm Cottage, Cowes 100
    Nash's Calbourne cottages 130
    Puckaster Cottage, Niton 102, 128–9, *129*
    Round House, West Cowes 129–30, *130*
    Steephill, The Undercliff 125–6, *128*
    Sweetwater Lodge, Calbourne 130–31, *131*
Islington, Trowbridge, Wiltshire: toll house 35
Ixworth Abbey, Suffolk: Round House 98, 100, *100*

Jackson, Thomas 155
James, Roderick 260
Jay, William 223
Jekyll, Gertrude 256
Jenkins, Captain Thomas 115
Johnes, Anne 122–3
Johnston, William L. 232
Johnstone, Mr (Knowle Cottage) 119
Jolland, Wolley 17
Jones, Barbara 16
Jordans estate, Horton, Somerset: Gingerbread House *37*, 37, 39
Jupe, Angela 261

Kedleston Hall, Derbyshire: Adam's sketch for 20, 21, *22*
Kenmare estate, Killarney 150
    Drenagh Lodge 102
Kent, Duke and Duchess of 120
Kent, William 12–13, 44, 51
    capriccio with cottage 12, *13*
    influence on Vardy 29–30, 32
    Merlin's Cave, Richmond Gardens *10*, 11, 178, 197
Kett, George Samuel 63
Kew 211
    see also Queen's Cottage, Kew Gardens
Kildare, Countess of *see* Leinster
Kilfane Cottage, Co. Kilkenny 152–4, *153*
    restoration in 1990s 153–4, 261
Kilkenny rustic cottages 151–3
Killarney estate and lakes and tourism 150

Kingsteignton, Devon: Old Vicarage/ Vicars Hill 69, *69*
Kirby, Joshua 182
Kirkerup, Andreas 207, 208, 211
Knight, Richard Payne 59, 92, 93–4
    The Landscape (poem) 96
Kremsier, Bohemia 214
    English garden 206

Ladies of Llangollen 76–7, 144
Lake District 133–4
    Dykelands, Ulverston 141*n*.83
    Eller How 134, *135*
    Lowbridge House, Selside 141*n*.83
    Papworth's cottage design for *97*, 133–4, 259
    Wansfell, Ambleside 141*n*.83
Lamballe, Marie-Louise, princesse de 204, *205*
Lancych, Pembrokeshire 106, 146, *146*
Lane, Joseph 19
Langley, Batty: *Gothic Architecture Improved* 74, 223
Langston, John Haughton 64
Langton by Spilsby, Lincolnshire: lodge 34, *35*
Lascy, Marshal 206
Lasswade, Lothian: Barony House (Lasswade Cottage) 147–8, *148*
Latrobe, Benjamin 223
Laugier, Abbé Marc-Antoine 32, 45, 199
    Essai sur l'Architecture 21, *21*, 30
Laverstoke estate, Hampshire: housing for workers 258
Law, George, Bishop of Bath and Wells 138
Laxton estate, Northamptonshire
    design of estate cottages 45
    Woodland Cottage 45
Le Blanc, Abbé 197
Le Rouge, Georges Louis: *chaumière* at Chaillot 203, *204*
Leamington Spa, Warwickshire: Binswood Cottage (Magnolia) 137
Lees Court, Kent: lodge 34
Leigh, Capel Hanbury *see* Hanbury Leigh, Capel
Leinster, Augustus FitzGerald, 3rd Duke of 166
Leinster, Charlotte Augusta FitzGerald, Duchess of (*née* Stanhope) 167
Leinster, Emily FitzGerald, Countess of Kildare and Duchess of (*née* Lennox) 157, 178
Leinster, James FitzGerald, 1st Duke of 157
Leroy, Jean-François 199–200
Lettsom, John Coakley 81, *82*
Lieven, Princess 190
Ligne, Prince de 197, 200, 203, 205–6, 212, 214
Lillie, Joseph Christian 208
Linton, Derbyshire: Sealwood Cottage 60, 68
Lippe, Conrad Frederik von der 211
Liselund estate, Denmark
    Chinese House 211
    Norwegian House *210*, 211
    'Palace' 207–211, *208–9*
    Swiss House 211
Lisle, Mary 113
Lisle Combe, Isle of Wight 128
Little Bredy, Dorset: design of village 56
Little Milton, nr Oxford: pair of lodges 33
Llandogo, Monmouthshire: Pilstone 143
Llanfyllin, Powys: The Hall 106
Llangollen, Denbighshire: Plas Newydd 76–7
Loch Lomond 149
lodges
    criticism of lodges in cottage idiom 40
    diversity of styles 40–43
    fishing lodges 70–76, 91, 143, 177

PICTURE CREDITS

First published by Yale University Press 2017
302 Temple Street, P.O. Box 209040, New Haven CT 06520-9040
47 Bedford Square, London WC1B 3DP
yalebooks.com / yalebooks.co.uk

Published with assistance from the Annie Burr Lewis Fund

MARC FITCH FUND   Marc Fitch Fund

ISBN 978-0-300-22677-5 HB
Library of Congress Control Number: 2016055767

2021 2020 2019 2018 2017
10 9 8 7 6 5 4 3 2 1

Copyeditor: Charley Chapman
Designer: Raymonde Watkins
Printed in China

Front cover: Royal Lodge, Windsor Great Park
Back cover: Entrance hall, Houghton Lodge,
Half-title: Ceramic cottage orné of a kind produced in the early and
mid-nineteenth century by Staffordshire and other English potteries
Frontispiece: Woodlands, dormer detail, Sidmouth, Devon
Title page: Alte Turm, Hohenheim, Germany
Imprint page: The Hermitage, Dangan Cottage, Co. Kilkenny